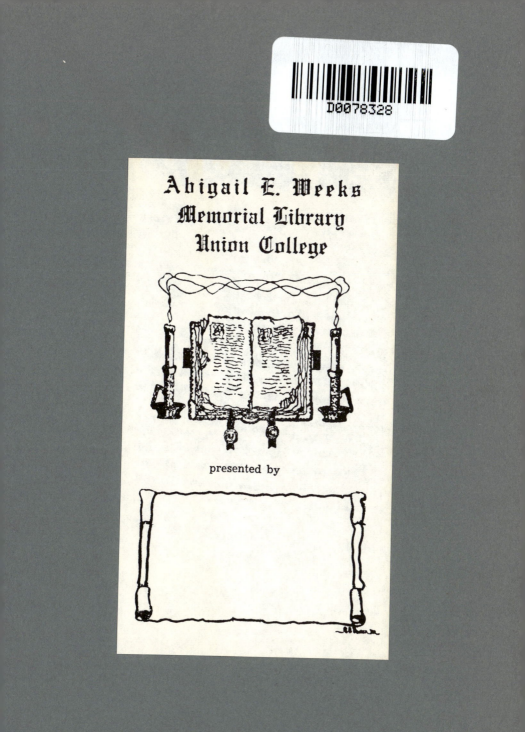

After MacIntyre

After MacIntyre

Critical Perspectives on the Work of Alasdair MacIntyre

Edited by
John Horton and Susan Mendus

University of Notre Dame Press
Notre Dame, Indiana

Copyright © this collection Polity Press 1994.
Each individual chapter © the author.

First published in 1994 by Polity Press
in association with Blackwell Publishers.

University of Notre Dame Press
edition 1994

ISBN 0 268 00642 3
ISBN 0 268 00643 1 (pbk)

Library of Congress Cataloging-in-Publication Data
A CIP catalogue record for this book is available from the Library of Congress.

Typeset in 10½ on 12 pt Garamond Stempel
by Graphicraft Typesetters Ltd., Hong Kong
Printed in Great Britain by T.J. Press, Padstow, Cornwall

This book is printed on acid-free paper.

Contents

Contributors

Janet Coleman is Reader in Ancient and Medieval Political Thought at the London School of Economics and Political Science. Her latest book is *Ancient and Medieval Memories: Studies in the Reconstruction of the Past* (1992). She has been Team Leader of the European Science Foundation international project on The Individual in Political Theory and Practice in relation to the genesis of the modern state, and has edited and contributed to the resulting volume to be published soon.

Elizabeth Frazer is Fellow and Tutor, and University Lecturer in Politics, at New College, Oxford. She is co-author (with Nicola Lacey) of *The Politics of Community* (1993), and is currently conducting research on young people's conception of citizenship.

Gordon Graham is Reader in Moral Philosophy at the University of St Andrews in Scotland, and Chairman of Department. His books include *Politics in its Place* (1986), *Contemporary Social Philosophy* (1987), *Living the Good Life* (1990) and *The Idea of Christian Charity* (1990). His next book is an essay in philosophical history entitled *The Shape of the Past*.

John Haldane is Reader in Moral Philosophy and Director of the Centre for Philosophy and Public Affairs, University of St Andrews. He has published widely in the philosophy of mind, history of philosophy and social and political philosophy. He is co-editor (with Crispin Wright) of *Reality, Representation and Projection* (1993) and is currently co-authoring (with J. J. C. Smart) a book on *Atheism and Theism*.

John Horton is Senior Lecturer in Politics and Director of the Morrell Studies in Toleration, University of York. He is most recently editor of *Liberalism, Multiculturalism and Toleration* (1993) and the author of *Political Obligation* (1992).

Peter Johnson is Lecturer in Politics at the University of Southampton. He is the author of *Politics, Innocence and the Limits of Goodness* (1988) and *Frames of Deceit: A Study of the Loss and Recovery of Public and Private Trust* (1993).

Paul Kelly is Lecturer in Politics at University College, Swansea. He is the author of *Utilitarianism and Distributive Justice: Jeremy Bentham and the Civil Law* (1990) and is co-editor (with D. Boucher) of *The Social Contract: Hobbes to Rawls* (1994). He is currently completing a book on the work of Ronald Dworkin, and editing the volume on Jeremy Bentham's writings on political economy for the new *Collected Works of Jeremy Bentham*.

Nicola Lacey is Fellow and Tutor, and University Lecturer in Law, at New College, Oxford. She is the author of *State Punishment: Political Principles and Community Values* (1988) and co-author (with Elizabeth Frazer) of *The Politics of Community* (1993). She is currently engaged in research on criminal justice.

Andrew Mason is Lecturer in Philosophy at the University of Reading. He is the author of *Explaining Political Disagreement* (1993) and is currently working on a study of the relationship between community and personal autonomy.

Susan Mendus is Senior Lecturer in Politics, and was formerly Morrell Fellow in Toleration, at the University of York. She is the author of *Toleration and the Limits of Liberalism* (1989) and is currently working on a study of conceptions of the self in political philosophy.

David Miller is Official Fellow in Social and Political Theory at Nuffield College, Oxford. His most recent books are *Market, State and Community* (1989) and (edited) *Liberty* (1991). He is currently working on a book on nationality and compiling a volume of essays on problems of social justice.

Stephen Mulhall is Reader in Philosophy at the University of Essex. He is the author of *On Being in the World: Wittgenstein and Heidegger on Seeing Aspects* (1990), *Stanley Cavell: Philosophy's Recounting of the Ordinary* (1994) and co-author (with Adam Swift) of *Liberals and Communitarians* (1992).

Philip Pettit is Professor of Social and Political Theory, Research School of Social Sciences, Australian National University. He is the author of

The Common Mind: An Essay on Psychology, Society and Politics (1993), co-author (with John Braithwaite) of *Not Just Deserts: A Republican Theory of Criminal Justice* and co-editor (with Robert E. Goodin) of *A Companion to Contemporary Political Philosophy* (1993). He was a Centennial Visiting Professor at the London School of Economics in 1992.

Robert Stern is Lecturer in Philosophy at the University of Sheffield. He is the author of *Hegel, Kant and the Structure of the Object* (1990) and editor of *G. W. F. Hegel: Critical Assessments* (1993). He is currently working on a philosophical and historical study of the links between idealism and rationalism.

Charles Taylor is Professor of Philosophy at McGill University. He is the author of *Hegel* (1975), *Philosophical Papers* (1985) and *Sources of the Self: The Making of Modern Identity* (1989). He has been interested in political theory, philosophy of social science and philosophy of language.

Robert Wokler is Reader in the History of Political Thought at the University of Manchester. He is the author of *Rousseau* (1994), and co-editor of John Plamenatz's *Man and Society* (1992), *Diderot's Political Writings* (1992), *Rousseau and the Eighteenth Century* (1992) and the *Cambridge History of Eighteenth-Century Political Thought* (1995).

Preface

Several of the contributions to this volume arose from a conference on the work of Alasdair MacIntyre held at the University of York in September 1991. The editors wish to acknowledge their gratitude to the trustees of the C. and J. B. Morrell Trust for their financial support of the conference, and also for their continuing support for our work in political theory more generally. We are also very grateful to all the participants at the conference; to Andrew Williams for his useful comments on our opening chapter; to David Held, a patient, tactful and constructive editor; to Ann Bone for her helpful and efficient work in improving the manuscript; to Jackie Morgan for her assistance in organizing the conference and preparing the typescript; and most especially to Peter Nicholson for his manifold help and particularly for preparing the bibliography. We are further very pleased to record publicly our thanks to Alasdair MacIntyre himself, not only for the stimulus of his writings, but for his willingness to contribute his reply and look over our opening chapter, and his generally most generous and encouraging response to our endeavours.

John Horton
Susan Mendus

1

Alasdair MacIntyre: *After Virtue* and After

John Horton and Susan Mendus

Since 1981 Alasdair MacIntyre has published three substantial books of moral and political philosophy: *After Virtue, Whose Justice? Which Rationality?* and *Three Rival Versions of Moral Enquiry*.[1] Taken together, and complemented by numerous articles and papers, they constitute an enormously ambitious and challenging undertaking comprising an extended and powerful critique of the perceived ills of modernity, including modern moral philosophy and political theory, and some radical and highly controversial suggestions as to how those ills might be remedied.

Before *After Virtue*

After Virtue, which was published in 1981, surprised the philosophical world by the depth of its disillusion with modern morality in general, and what MacIntyre called 'the Enlightenment project' in particular. Though deeply sceptical of some aspects of modernity, MacIntyre's earlier works had lacked the complete disenchantment which characterized *After Virtue*. Those earlier works are often fiercely critical of particular thinkers and structures of belief or ideologies, but they are also frequently marked by passionate commitment, as reflected, for example, in his enthusiasm at different times for both Christianity and Marxism. Indeed it was this very quality of commitment which led one critic to comment, not without irony, on his *Against the Self-Images of the Age* that 'what distinguishes Professor MacIntyre is not the number of beliefs he has doubted, but the number of beliefs he has embraced. His capacity for doubt we share or surpass; it is his capacity for faith which is distinctive and perhaps unrivalled.'[2] Although, as we shall later explain, *After Virtue* does contain important positive theses, it is MacIntyre's pessimism about modernity which is most striking. It might be useful to begin, however, by very briefly relating *After Virtue* to some of his preceding works, to see how some of the later books' central theses were foreshadowed in them.

Among the earlier works two books are perhaps particularly significant and revealing in relation to MacIntyre's later views. *A Short History of Ethics* was first published in 1967 and was notable primarily for its methodological approach to moral philosophy.[3] MacIntyre explicitly rejected the belief, common in philosophical circles at the time, that 'moral concepts were a timeless, limited, unchanging, determinate species of concept [that] can be examined and understood apart from their history'.[4] On the contrary, he maintained that moral concepts and beliefs have to be studied historically and contextually because 'moral concepts are embodied in and are partially constitutive of forms of social life.'[5] This approach has consistently informed his more recent work which frequently is contemptuously dismissive of much analytical moral philosophy for being unhistorical and excessively parochial. While there are both continuities and radical changes of mind about the details of the history of ethical thought and in the valuation of particular thinkers – Aquinas for example is treated as a very minor figure in *A Short History* – the importance of history and social context to moral philosophy is a persistent theme throughout MacIntyre's work.

This contention is also central to *Against the Self-Images of the Age*, published in 1971 and reprinting articles written both before and after *A Short History of Ethics*.[6] However, this book is additionally significant because it most clearly reveals the agenda informing MacIntyre's own philosophical quest. What unifies the otherwise rather diverse collection of essays is MacIntyre's passionate conviction in the need for an 'ideology' and his belief that the inherited ideologies – particularly psychoanalysis, Marxism and Christianity – have failed. MacIntyre does not deny that these ideologies have made positive contributions to our self-understanding (and as we shall see later he subsequently revises his judgement on Christianity), but the crucial point is that at this time he believed that none of them is 'able to provide the light that our individual and social lives need'.[7] In this diagnosis of the current situation we can see, at least with the benefit of hindsight, the seeds of the still more radical critique of modernity to be found in *After Virtue*.

The Project of *After Virtue*

In *After Virtue* MacIntyre reveals himself as not merely critical of some facets of modernity, but as despairing of both modern morality and post-Enlightenment moral philosophy in their entirety; and in his account these failures are intimately connected. The implications could hardly be more serious. The book ends with the claim that 'we still, in spite of the efforts of three centuries of moral philosophy and one of sociology, lack any coherent rationally defensible statement of [the] liberal individualist viewpoint' which dominates the modern age.[8] Moreover, we are doomed to remain in this parlous state unless and until we can restore rationality and intelligibility to our own moral attitudes and commitments; and this is impossible within the dominant paradigms of modern moral thought.

According to MacIntyre, the Enlightenment project which has dominated philosophy during the past three hundred years promised a conception of rationality independent of historical and social context, and independent of any specific understanding of man's nature or purpose. But not only has that promise in fact been unfulfilled, the project is itself fundamentally flawed and the promise could never be fulfilled. In consequence, modern moral and political thought are in a state of disarray from which they can be rescued only if we revert to an Aristotelian paradigm, with its essential commitment to teleology, and construct an account of practical reason premised on that commitment. Of course whether, and how, this might be possible is a large question, which *After Virtue* only begins to address. Certainly both theoretical and social changes of a fundamental nature would be necessary, and one of the deepest difficulties with the argument of *After Virtue* is that the very extent of its critique of the modern world seems to cast doubt on the possibility of any realistic revival under the conditions of modernity of the Aristotelianism which MacIntyre advocates. His references to 'the construction of local forms of community' and the need 'for another – doubtless very different – St Benedict'[9] seem little more than whistling in the dark to keep the spirits up when set against his coruscating critique of modernity.

MacIntyre was well aware that *After Virtue* left many important questions unanswered and *Whose Justice? Which Rationality?* was published in 1988 as a sequel to the earlier book. Here MacIntyre aims to make good his earlier promise to 'attempt to say both what makes it rational to act in one way rather than another and what makes it rational to advance and defend one conception of practical rationality rather than another.'[10] However, the hero of this second book is not Aristotle but Aquinas, though the significance of this shift is a matter of debate and tends to be minimized by MacIntyre himself. Its consequence is that *Whose Justice?* ends with an 'emerging conclusion' in favour of the Thomist tradition, which is preferred because *as a tradition* it possesses the intellectual and cognitive resources necessary for the rational resolution of tensions within and between earlier traditions. This is worked out in most detail through a discussion of the critical synthesis by Thomism of the preceding Aristotelian and Augustinian traditions. For MacIntyre, the important lesson is that the possibility of rational enquiry does not depend on any Enlightenment conception of 'pure' rationality, divorced from considerations of time and place. Rather, 'what the Enlightenment made us for the most part blind to [is that] standards of rational justification themselves emerge from and are part of a history in which they are vindicated by the way in which they transcend the limitations of and provide remedies for the defects of their predecessors within the history of that same tradition.'[11] The hope, therefore, of extricating modern moral philosophy from its current state of disarray is founded upon the contextualising and historicising of our moral concepts in a way which does not dispense with rational argument or deny the possibility of moral progress.

In his most recent book, *Three Rival Versions of Moral Enquiry*, published in 1990, MacIntyre expands on this theme and aims to show how the existence of 'significant incommensurability and untranslatability' between opposed systems of thought may nevertheless be compatible with rational debate, and indeed may be a prologue to 'the kind of debate from which one party can emerge as undoubtedly rationally superior'.[12] The 'rival versions' of his title are the 'Encyclopaedic', a recognizable descendant of what was earlier referred to as 'the Enlightenment Project', particularly as embodied in the ninth edition of the *Encyclopaedia Britannica*; the Genealogical, essentially post-Nietzscheanism, as embodied in his *Genealogy of Morals*; and the Thomist, distorted by Pope Leo XIII's encyclical *Aeterni Patris*, but ultimately the most satisfactory. The last can be interpreted as a *via media* between the bogus universalism of the Encyclopaedist and the radical scepticism of the Genealogist, and is vindicated by its ability to overcome the shortcomings of the other traditions. Thus MacIntyre's insistence on the tradition-dependent nature of rationality is not, he claims, a harbinger of moral relativism, nor does it issue in the conclusion that we are all uncritically sunk in the particularity of our own traditions. Rather it is the cue for a dialectical or critical enquiry which can result in genuine moral progress.

MacIntyre's recent work therefore has both a negative and a positive dimension: throughout the three books he expresses deep discontent with modernity and with the Enlightenment project which gave rise to it. This is most marked in *After Virtue*, but it survives throughout his work, even though the focus tends to shift towards his own positive conception of moral and political philosophy. However, MacIntyre's positive conception of ethical enquiry does imply that at least one tradition of rational moral enquiry has survived and that in this respect our situation is not as bleak as it sometimes appeared in the earlier book. If *After Virtue* is, as one commentator has put it, 'a sermon of despair',[13] both *Whose Justice? Which Rationality?* and *Three Rival Versions of Moral Enquiry* offer increasing hope even from the midst of despair.

We have so far very sketchily described MacIntyre's enterprise and its development. In the remainder of this chapter we seek to elaborate on a few of the most interesting and controversial themes in his work. In the next section our attention is focused on the precise reasons for MacIntyre's disenchantment with modernity and the Enlightenment project; and in the final section we explain some of the more important conceptual terms which he employs in providing his own account of how moral and political philosophy might proceed. Inevitably this approach is highly selective, and in particular we have chosen to emphasize the debate between MacIntyre and contemporary liberals. This is not false to MacIntyre's work but it is partial. MacIntyre is also very concerned to rebut the radical scepticism of post-Nietzschean thought, but this is a dimension of his work we shall largely ignore.

The Malaise of Modernity

After Virtue begins with a 'disquieting suggestion'. This is that modern morality is in a state of grave disorder, perhaps of chaos, and that we lack the resources even to recognize the full extent of the chaos, much less to extricate ourselves from it. MacIntyre says, 'the most striking feature of contemporary moral utterance is that much of it is used to express disagreements; and the most striking feature of the debates in which these disagreements are expressed is their interminable character.'[14] We argue endlessly about the justice of wars, the morality of abortion, the nature of freedom, but not only do we not in fact reach agreement about these matters, we do not even agree about what criteria a satisfactory resolution to these disagreements would need to meet.

At the same time, however, the language in which these arguments is conducted implies that disagreement *can* be rationally resolved. On the surface our moral language is the language of objectivity, rationality and truth; but that language deceives because, in the modern world, the concepts which it employs have become so etiolated that they can no longer do any serious moral work, nor are they able to provide criteria by which to decide what, in a moral context, counts as rational. Thus the condition of modernity is a condition in which we possess only 'fragments of a conceptual scheme, parts which now lack those contexts from which their significance was derived. We possess indeed the simulacra of morality, we continue to use many of the key expressions.

But we have – very largely, if not entirely – lost our comprehension, both theoretical and practical, of morality.'[15]

After Virtue is the story of how we came to be in this parlous state, how we continue to be deceived by it, and how we might escape it. The argument of the book has been described as 'profoundly pessimistic' and as 'lugubriously conservative' and 'bleakly Manichean'.[16] Whatever the justice of these judgements, the centrality of the book for modern moral and political philosophy is undeniable: for, as the above quotations indicate, MacIntyre's attack is not simply an attack on the plausibility of specific moral theories. It is not, for example, concerned with the relative merits of Kantianism and utilitarianism. Rather it is an indictment of modern moral philosophy as a whole, which MacIntyre perceives as devoid of the resources which are necessary to make coherent moral thought and argument possible.

In order to highlight the poverty of modern moral theory, MacIntyre begins by contrasting modern conceptions of morality with those which were prevalent in ancient Greek society, specifically in the work of Aristotle. For Aristotle, the good life is the life lived in accordance with virtue (*arete*), where virtue is to be understood against the background of a teleological conception of man – a conception according to which human beings have a specific nature which determines their proper aims and goals. On his account, the virtues are excellences of character which enable people to move towards their goal (*telos*), and are an essential part of the attainment of that goal.

However, in the post-Enlightenment period, this Aristotelian conception of morality has been supplanted by a rejection of teleology, and a denial that we have any specific or identifiable purpose beyond that which we choose. Where Aristotle understood man as a creature with a definite function which he might fulfil or deny, modern morality sees man simply as a rational agent who has no true or definable purpose independent of his own will. This changed understanding of morality, according to MacIntyre, has immensely important implications. By appealing to a telos, Aristotle was able to distinguish between the way we actually are and the way we should be. His conception of human beings as having a specific telos brought with it the possibility that we might fall short of the ideal – it implied the possibility of acting in ways which contradict or negate our purpose. But with the rejection of Aristotelianism came the rejection of any such distinction between what we are and what we should be. Post-Enlightenment man is seen as governed, not by a telos external to him, but simply by the dictates of his own inner reason. And the result of this move from a teleology independent of the will of the individual to an internally given rationality is that we can no longer coherently distinguish, as Aristotle did, between what we are and what we should be. In consequence, our understanding of the virtues has become deformed, and our moral language has degenerated into an incoherent set of rules or principles deprived of the teleological background which originally gave them meaning: for without this background, we find ourselves with no secure point of reference against which to adjudicate between rival moral positions. Hence the interminable and ultimately pointless character of modern moral argument.

Thus the abandonment of an Aristotelian conception of the good has not only left us without standards by which to evaluate our moral arguments, it has also cast us adrift in the moral world. For Aristotle, a conception of the good for man has an essentially societal dimension: excellence is not fixed and determined for all time, but is inextricably linked to the nature of one's society, and this in turn sets limits to the ability of individuals to 'create' their own conception of the good. Through such a conception it is possible to situate ourselves socially and to find a distinctive place within a society. But that possibility is largely lost within the anomic and alienating conditions of modernity. In the modern world we are not merely choosers but essentially isolated choosers, for we are no longer able to understand our good as at least partly determined by the society and circumstances in which we find ourselves.

These two features of MacIntyre's account – his insistence on the need for a teleology which will enable us to distinguish between what we are and what we ought to be, and his insistence on the social embeddedness of our telos – together serve to situate his thought in (or against) the wider context of contemporary moral and political philosophy. His denial of the power of 'pure' or 'abstract' rationality divorced from tradition, his insistence on the social embeddedness of conceptions of the good, sets him at odds both with moral philosophers such as Alan Gewirth or Alan Donagan, who have tried to derive morality from considerations of rational agency, and with political theorists such as John Rawls (at least the Rawls of *A Theory of Justice*) and Ronald Dworkin, who have often been interpreted as aspiring to provide an account of social justice which will appeal to all individuals independently of their specific conceptions of the good.

Against individualist liberals, MacIntyre insists that there is no rationality independent of a tradition – no 'view from nowhere', to borrow a phrase from Thomas Nagel – and no set of rules or principles which will commend themselves to all independent of their conception of the good. The liberal promise to provide a neutral framework of rational principles within which different conceptions of the good might flourish is a promise which cannot be redeemed. In *After Virtue* MacIntyre, therefore, tended to contrast sharply liberalism and the Enlightenment project on the one hand, with tradition on the other; but in *Whose Justice? Which Rationality?* this position seems to undergo some modification. There he argues that liberalism has itself been transformed into a tradition, though one which is deeply and irremediably flawed both because it denies its own status as a tradition and because it lacks the conceptual resources to resolve its own internal disagreements and tensions.

Self, Society and History

As we have seen, MacIntyre's objections to contemporary liberalism are far-reaching. He objects to the liberal conception of the self, which implies that moral value is determined by individual choice or decision; he objects to liberalism's denial of a telos for man, which results in its inability to differentiate satisfactorily between what we are and what we ought to be; and he objects to liberalism's disregard of social context, which results in its inability to acknowledge fully the role of what is 'given' in moral life. Each of these three features plays an important part in the construction of his own moral theory. Thus, in place of the merely expressive, or emotivist, self of Enlightenment thinking in general and liberal theory in particular, he proposes a narrative conception of the self; in place of the exclusively abstract and rule-governed ethic of modernity he proposes a conception of ethics which restores the centrality of the virtues; and in place of asocial individualism he appeals to traditions. These three concepts – narrative, practice and tradition – lie at the heart of the development of his moral theory, and it is to the elucidation of these that we now turn.

The narrative self

In *After Virtue* MacIntyre identifies the self of modern philosophy as a self which has been denied access to an understanding of the good independent of its own decisions and choices. It is a self which says: 'I am what I myself choose to be. I can always, if I wish to, put in question what are taken to be merely the contingent social features of my existence.' Against this understanding of the self as essentially, or ideally, a decider and chooser, MacIntyre advances what he calls a narrative conception. He says:

> man is in his actions and practice, as well as in his fictions, essentially a story-telling animal . . . the key question for men is not about their own authorship; I can only answer the question 'What am I to do?' if I can

answer the prior question 'Of what story or stories do I find myself a part?' We enter human society, that is, with one or more imputed characters – roles into which we have been drafted – and we have to learn what they are in order to be able to understand how others respond to us and how our responses to them are apt to be construed.[17]

As will be clear from this quotation, MacIntyre rejects the conception of a person as principally a chooser and decider, in favour of a conception of a person as having an identity which is at least partly given in advance of any decisions or choices the person makes. In consequence, the central question of our moral lives is not, as liberals maintain, about which choices we ought to make, but rather a question about how we are to understand who we are, independent of and antecedent to our choices. Put differently, where liberalism emphasizes our status as choosing and deciding beings, MacIntyre draws attention to the importance of the background circumstances and moral context which inform and make intelligible those choices but which are themselves unchosen. This narrative understanding of the self is so called because it implies that answers to questions about what we ought to do involve not merely (or primarily) choosing what to do as individuals, but also, and essentially, discovering who we are in relation to others.

There is, therefore, here as elsewhere in MacIntyre, both an epistemological (sometimes ontological) and a normative dimension to the argument: individuals cannot properly be understood without reference to their being at least partially socially constituted, and this fact has implications for the way in which people should live. This relationship between the epistemological and the normative is one of the most interesting and problematic aspects of MacIntyre's work, and some who have accepted many of his claims about the social constitution of the person have been less inclined to accept that this has any very interesting or important normative consequences.

To understand what it is that I ought to do, I must, according to MacIntyre, recognize that the story of my life possesses a certain narrative structure in which what I am now is continuous with what I was in the past. Thus the search for what I am, and for what I ought to do, is indeed a *search* and not simply a set of decisions. It is this search, or 'quest' as MacIntyre calls it, which is essential to the unity of a person's life. He writes:

In what does the unity of an individual life consist? The answer is that its unity is the unity of a narrative embodied in a single life. To ask 'What is the good for me?' is to ask how best I might live out that unity and bring it to completion. To ask 'What is the good for man?' is to ask what all answers to the former question must have in common. But now it is

important to emphasise that it is the systematic asking of these two questions and the attempt to answer them in deed as well as in word which
provide the moral life with its unity. The unity of a human life is the unity
of a narrative quest.[18]

However, this unity always has to be understood in a social context.
Only social context can give substance to a person's life; and social context is not something a person chooses.

Practices

MacIntyre's references to the importance of the wider social context and
to the importance of acknowledging what is 'given' are elaborated in his
discussion of practices, and here again a contrast may be drawn between
his conception of morality and that favoured by the Enlightenment
conception inherent in contemporary liberalism. According to MacIntyre
a practice is:

> any coherent and complex form of socially established co-operative human
> activity through which goods internal to that form of activity are realised
> in the course of trying to achieve those standards of excellence which are
> appropriate to, and partially definitive of, that form of activity, with the
> result that human powers to achieve excellence, and human conceptions of
> the ends and goods involved, are systematically extended.[19]

He goes on to cite chess, football, farming, architecture and the creation
of political communities as examples of practices. This definition and
MacIntyre's examples leave many important questions unanswered, but
for the purposes of moral philosophy one crucial feature of a practice is
that it implies a standard of excellence internal to that practice. For
example, in order to play chess well, a player must heed the standards
which define the playing of chess. Not just anything counts as playing
chess well, and the features which do count are ones which are defined
by the practice. They are not matters for individual preference or decision-making.

Extending this point, MacIntyre urges that we should construe morality in general, and the virtues in particular, as practice-based: acting
morally well, like playing chess well, is not a matter of individual preference or decision. Rather, the criteria for acting well are determined by
the kind of practice in which we are engaged. Moreover, this conception
of morality gives a central place to the virtues rather than to general
rules or abstract principles. MacIntyre insists that morality should be

construed primarily in terms of a life embodying the virtues; and our understanding of what the virtues are, and why they are virtues, is crucially dependent on coming to recognize their place in the practices which define them and their centrality to the narrative unity of the self.

For MacIntyre, the virtues are essential to the process by which a person relates his or her life to the various practices which constitute the context of that life. They are:

> those dispositions which will not only sustain practices and enable us to achieve the goods internal to practices, but which will also sustain us in the relevant kind of quest for the good, by enabling us to overcome the harms, dangers, temptations and distractions which we encounter, and which will furnish us with increasing self-knowledge and increasing knowledge of the good.[20]

However, practices in turn need to be situated in a wider context. Ultimately we have to locate our individual lives and existing practices within the broader social and temporal context of a tradition.

Tradition

Stephen Mulhall and Adam Swift give the following account of MacIntyre's concept of tradition:

> A tradition is constituted by a set of practices and is a mode of understanding their importance and worth; it is the medium by which such practices are shaped and transmitted across generations. Traditions may be primarily religious or moral (for example Catholicism or humanism), economic (for example a particular craft or profession, trade union or manufacturer), aesthetic (for example modes of literature or painting), or geographical (for example crystallising around the history and culture of a particular house, village or region).[21]

This understanding of traditions, taken together with the earlier points made about the self and about practices, gives a sense of the widening circles which constitute MacIntyre's moral theory. For MacIntyre, the narrative of an individual's life is to be understood against the background of the wider social context within which that individual finds himself or herself. This wider social context consists of sets of practices which serve to define the virtues, and those practices, in turn, sustain and are situated within a tradition which provides the resources with which the individual may pursue his or her quest for the good. It is traditions which are the repositories of standards of rationality and which are crucial to moral deliberation and action. And it is traditions which have increasingly become the central focus of MacIntyre's work subsequent to *After Virtue*.

However, it is important to avoid some potential misunderstandings of what is meant by tradition. In particular, MacIntyre is most concerned to emphasize, against his critics, that traditions are not static but dynamic. The quest of the individual must involve not only discovery and an acknowledgement of what is given, but also the possibility of critical reflection on the practices and traditions within which one finds oneself: 'a living tradition then is an historically extended, socially embodied argument, and an argument precisely in part about the goods which constitute that tradition.'[22] Traditions change and develop over time; some decay and fall into terminal disrepair and some emerge in response to changed circumstances. Thus MacIntyre insists that there is nothing inherently conservative about his conception of tradition. However, his emphasis on the importance of tradition does give rise to the objection that he is unavoidably committed to a form of moral relativism which construes people as trapped within their own traditions and lacking the resources to engage with and adjudicate between different traditions.

This charge against *After Virtue* is one which MacIntyre clearly takes very seriously, and it is addressed at great length in both *Whose Justice? Which Rationality?* and *Three Rival Versions of Moral Enquiry*. In both the later works he takes issue with those who accuse him of relativism, and attempts to show how the dynamic interaction of rival traditions may provide room for critical reflection on a tradition and the avoidance of relativism.

Broadly, the claim he advances and defends in these works is that although morality is itself tradition-dependent, and although traditions constitute the 'given' of life, it is nevertheless the case that rational argument is possible not only within traditions but also between them. All traditions experience from time to time their own internal contradictions and tensions. When these become serious, and when the adherents of a tradition themselves come to recognize a crisis, progress is possible through a critical engagement with other traditions. Such a confrontation may help to transcend the tensions within a tradition and also to resolve tensions between rival traditions. MacIntyre argues at length that this happened for example in thirteenth-century Paris, where the tensions within and between Aristotelianism and Augustinianism were largely resolved by the emergent Thomist tradition. While the details of this account are of considerable philosophical interest, they are largely resistant to brief summary. What they suggest, though, is that a similar process could help to resolve the confusions of modernity. For this to be possible, however, what is required is a recognition that modern liberalism is at best only one among a number of modes of enquiry, and not the most adequate; and MacIntyre argues that the most promising possibility of moral progress lies in Thomism.

However, MacIntyre's treatment of tradition in his most recent book is also marked by a certain ambiguity or unclarity. This concerns the status of Thomism, which is MacIntyre's own favoured tradition. In the subtitle of *Three Rival Versions*, and in much of the text, the three rival versions of moral enquiry are identified as encyclopaedia, genealogy and tradition. However, there is also a tendency to run together tradition with Thomism such that the two become coextensive. Yet surely Thomism is a particular tradition, and commitment to it entails much more than simply commitment to the idea of tradition? Similarly the other versions of moral enquiry are sometimes counterposed to tradition while at other times they seem to be understood as distinct alternative traditions. It is difficult to know quite what to make of this, but it appears to be an issue which needs further explanation. It is also relevant to the more institutional and political matters which are touched on at the end of the book.

In the final chapter MacIntyre briefly considers how his tradition-based conception of moral enquiry might be institutionally embodied. He sketches what he calls a postliberal university system in which different universities would be organized around distinct forms of enquiry. Members of such universities would be concerned both to advance enquiry within their tradition and to enter into controversy with rival traditions. At a political level MacIntyre's proposals are interestingly Janus-faced. On the one hand, his recognition that there is a variety of traditions in the modern world, each with legitimate claims to serious investigation, intimates a pluralism which, if not straightforwardly liberal, is at least an embodiment of mutual toleration between proponents of different traditions. On the other hand, his insistence on the role of authority within traditions and his apparent acceptance of the idea that the guardians of a tradition can, for example, legitimately exclude from their own universities those who do not share the basic assumptions of their tradition seem potentially more authoritarian and socially divisive.

These suggestions about the reform of education along lines oriented towards separate traditions also make more pressing some fundamental questions which it is not clear that MacIntyre has sufficiently resolved, such as how traditions are to be individuated and, in matters of policy, whose interpretation of what counts as a tradition is to be treated as authoritative. Moreover, given the importance which MacIntyre attaches to the social embeddedness of thought and enquiry, his largely negative view of modernity continually threatens to undermine any attempt to root his positive proposals in the contemporary world of advanced industrial societies. Thus in the end we are taken back to the beginning – to MacIntyre's uncompromising critique of modernity.

Of course many questions arise from the themes and arguments we have touched on in this introduction and many from those we have neglected. The papers which are gathered together in this volume analyse various aspects of Alasdair MacIntyre's work and do so from a variety of historical and philosophical perspectives. Any writer who places as much emphasis as MacIntyre does on the importance of history and who ranges as widely as he does is likely to be accused of misrepresenting the philosophers and traditions which he discusses. Several of the papers question MacIntyre's historical understanding of key thinkers and traditions, such as Aristotle, Aquinas, utilitarianism and the Enlightenment. Equally, any writer who is as sceptical, and at times dismissive, of modernity as MacIntyre is will inevitably be criticized by its defenders. More particularly his consistent contempt for modern liberalism, which many see as one of the most valuable achievements of modernity, is likely to be subject to especially close scrutiny. Hence several of the papers engage with aspects of MacIntyre's treatment of modernity, and some raise specific questions about whether, and to what extent, the alleged defects of liberalism are in fact defects in MacIntyre's own understanding of it.

MacIntyre speaks for himself in response to the various criticisms and objections which are raised. Our aim in this opening essay has simply been to provide a context for the subsequent papers, not to pre-empt the more detailed discussions to which they give rise. Our concern has been to indicate the scope and ambition of MacIntyre's enterprise; to show the importance of the questions which he raises; to sketch briefly some of the key concepts in his argument; and to identify in a preliminary way a few of the issues which are pursued more fully in the subsequent chapters.

NOTES

1 *After Virtue: A Study in Moral Theory* (Duckworth, London, 1981); *Whose Justice? Which Rationality?* (Duckworth, London, 1988); *Three Rival Versions of Moral Enquiry: Encyclopaedia, Genealogy, Tradition* (Duckworth, London, 1990). These titles are published in the USA by the University of Notre Dame Press.

2 Ernest Gellner, *The Devil in Modern Philosophy* (Routledge and Kegan Paul, London, 1974), p. 193.

3 Alasdair MacIntyre, *A Short History of Ethics* (Routledge and Kegan Paul, London, 1967).

4   Ibid., p. 1.
5   Ibid.
6   Alasdair MacIntyre, *Against the Self-Images of the Age* (Duckworth, London, 1971).
7   Ibid., p. viii.
8   *After Virtue*, p. 241.
9   Ibid., p. 245.
10 *Whose Justice? Which Rationality?*, p. ix.
11 Ibid., p. 7.
12 *Three Rival Versions*, p. 5.
13 Benjamin Barber, *The Conquest of Politics: Liberal Philosophy in Democratic Times* (Princeton University Press, Princeton, 1988), p. 190.
14 *After Virtue*, p. 6.
15 Ibid., p. 2.
16 J. B. Schneewind, 'Virtue, narrative and community: MacIntyre and morality', *Journal of Philosophy*, 79, 1982, p. 662; Benjamin Barber, *The Conquest of Politics* (Princeton University Press, Princeton, 1988), pp. 190, 187.
17 *After Virtue*, p. 201.
18 Ibid., p. 203.
19 Ibid., p. 175.
20 Ibid., p. 204.
21 Stephen Mulhall and Adam Swift, *Liberals and Communitarians* (Blackwell, Oxford, 1992), p. 90.
22 *After Virtue*, p. 207.

2

Justice After Virtue

Charles Taylor

In this paper I shall try to come to grips with the extraordinarily rich analysis of the modern predicament in Alasdair MacIntyre's *After Virtue*.[1] I will not even begin to do justice to the very great number of insights and telling detail with which the book abounds. What I want to do rather is to clear my own mind as to what its central theses are, and at the same time clarify my own position relative to them. In fact, this will not really be a two-stage operation, as I have made it sound. Rather, I will be throughout trying to reconstruct what I see to be the central insights of the book in my own terms, and therein also from time to time offering amendments. In doing this I shall come around to the issue of the nature and scope of theories of justice. MacIntyre himself, of course, takes a stand on it in his chapter 17.

I

A good place to start is with the thesis expounded in chapter 5 of *After Virtue*. Following Elizabeth Anscombe's path-breaking article,[2] MacIntyre shows how the growing sense among many different schools of modern philosophy that no 'ought' can be derived from an 'is' is not the slow dawning of a context-free logical truth, but rather the correlate of the decline or rejection of the conception central to much ancient philosophy that human life was defined by a telos. The sharp gap between the permissible ways to argue that something is a good watch and someone a good farmer, on the one hand, and what one needs to say to show that someone is a good human being, on the other, just does not arise, for instance, on Aristotle's theory, which was undoubtedly the most powerful and widespread of ancient traditions at the dawn of the modern world. (p. 56)

The crucial point which MacIntyre adds to this is that the decline of teleological conceptions cannot just be understood as an independent

development in science and epistemology. It also reflects a new understanding of man's moral and spiritual predicament. He points here to
the important role of Protestant and Jansenist theologies, with their
sense of the powerlessness of fallen human reason. (pp. 51–2) Because it
will play a role in my later argument, I should like to spell this connection out a little more fully.

We might think that there are sufficient grounds to reject Aristotle's
teleology once natural science has made the crucial transformation described as 'the mechanization of the world-picture', wrought by Galileo,
Descartes and their successors. This seems radically to undercut teleological accounts in general, and in particular in biology. MacIntyre
mentions the dependence of Aristotle's ethical views on his 'metaphysical biology'. But this is not so. The notion that human beings have
something like a telos *qua* human can be separated from the thesis that
everything in nature belongs to some class or other, whose behaviour is
explained by some Form or Idea. Because we no longer explain the movements of stars and stones teleologically does not mean that we cannot
explain humans in these terms. This is not to say that the demise of
explanation by the Forms did not have a traumatic effect on the teleological outlook, or to deny that other big problems still remain, notably
that of relating human to natural science once they are seen to invoke
quite different explanatory principles. But it does mean that the
mechanization of natural science by no means makes inevitable the
changes in moral outlook which have often been justified by it. (I shall
argue below that the very tendency to exalt scientific reasoning, and
depreciate practical reason in relation to it, itself springs from the moral
outlook of modernity.)

Rather, the thesis which MacIntyre puts forward here, and with which
I entirely agree, is that the change in the understanding of morality is to
be explained itself in terms of changing moral vision. Changed views
about the very nature of moral discourse and thought – like the new no
'ought' from 'is' principle – spring from substantive changes in moral
outlook. The new meta-ethics may indeed be assisted in its progress by
new scientific theories, but then there is also a notorious line of influence in the other direction. It has been well documented, for instance,
how one important motive for embracing the new mechanism in the
seventeenth century was theological in nature. One very important tradition of thought in Christendom, which stressed the sovereignty of
Good and tended to be suspicious of Greek conceptions of a fixed cosmic order, was happy to embrace mechanism in the seventeenth century,
particularly over against the more extravagant neo-pagan excesses (as
they saw them) of high Renaissance animism, as we see it in figures like
Giordano Bruno. Something like this was the motivation, for instance,

of Marin Mersenne, who played such an important role in the diffusion of the new scientific outlook.

A great deal of reciprocal action there certainly was between science and morality in these centuries, as at any time in our civilization. But it is quite wrong to fix on only one direction of causation, and propound a story in which scientific discovery simply brings changes in moral outlook in its train.

Behind the fact/value split, which one sees emerging in David Hume, and then becoming a dominant theme in our century, lies a new understanding and valuation of freedom and dignity. Let me try to gesture briefly towards this in a few sentences.

MacIntyre points out its theological origins. These must be understood, I think, in terms of the strand of Christian thought I mentioned above. In fact, the synthesis with Greek thought was always an uneasy one. For some thinkers the notion of a fixed and ordered cosmos, whose principles of justification could be found in itself, was incompatible with the sovereignty of God. Think of the nominalist rebellion against Thomism. The issue in one formulation concerned the relation in God of reason and will. Is God constrained by his own creation, so that he has to will a good which is as it were built into it? Occam and others offer a more voluntaristic view of God's power. Anything else seems to belittle God. The Reformers took this spiritual side, even where they did not always adopt the same intellectual formulations. The right of Thomas versus Occam then carries down in Christendom in ever new forms, through, for example, the battle between Jesuit and Jansenist, right up to our day.

We can see easily enough why the Occamite temper might welcome mechanism, as I mentioned above. Here at last is an utterly neutral view of the universe, waiting to have purposes given to it by sovereign fiat. The fact/value split is first a theological thesis, and God is at first the sole beneficiary. But at this stage the spiritual motivation of this view is evident. The thesis is propounded to defend God's freedom of choice.

Later something of this conception of freedom is transferred on to man. As against seeing our paradigm purposes as given to us by the nature of the cosmic order in which we are set, we find them rather in the nature of our own reasoning powers. These demand that we take control by objectifying the world, submitting it to the demands of instrumental reason. The purposes to which the surrounding world is instrumentalized are found within us. These are the purposes of life: self-preservation, and what was later called the pursuit of happiness, and as such they too are given by nature. But what confers dignity on their pursuit is that this is not to be carried on in a blind, licentious or undisciplined fashion, but under the control of far-sighted calculating reason.

The changes are well enough known: reason is no longer defined substantively, in terms of a vision of cosmic order, but formally, in terms of the procedures that thought ought to follow, and especially those involved in fitting means to ends, instrumental reason; the hegemony of reason is consequently redefined, and now means not ordering our lives according to the vision of order, but rather controlling desires by the canons of instrumental reason. Freedom consequently takes on a new meaning, and entails breaking loose from any external authorities in order to be governed solely by one's own reasoning procedures. And the source of obligation is no longer a cosmic order without, but rather my own status as a sovereign reasoning being, which demands that I achieve rational control. I owe this, as it were, not to the order of things, but to my own dignity.

Descartes was one of the founding figures of this new outlook, and virtually all its themes are present in his work. In the *Meditations*, for instance, he makes clear that my coming to understand myself as I truly am, a thinking being, involves disengaging from the usual stance wherein I perceive things through the body – see the colour as in the rose, for instance, or experience the pain as in the tooth. I must assume a stance from which I can recognize that both colour and pain are really occurrences in the soul, albeit (we have reason to believe) caused by factors in rose and tooth respectively. This is the disengaged stance in which I see the body as a mechanism, mediating causal connections between world and soul. In his later writings on morality, the correspondence with Elisabeth and *Le Traité des Passions*, Descartes reinterprets the ancient moral traditions (particularly the Stoic) in the light of this new ideal of disengaged rational control. The hegemony of reason over the passions is no longer a matter of seeing through the latter in order to render them inoperative (as for the Stoics), but of understanding them in order to make them instrumentally subordinate. The passions are no longer analysed as *opinions* (dogmata), which have to be either quite exploded (Stoics), or aligned with my whole, reflective understanding of the good (Aristotle). Instead Descartes offers a *functional* theory of them, showing us how they ought to be used. The crucial place of the new notion of dignity – which becomes explicit later with Kant – is already indicated in Descartes by the important status he accords 'generosity', which in its seventeenth-century meaning designated the aristocratic virtue one displays when one has a lively sense of one's own worth and rank and the demands it puts on one. Descartes does not in fact make a big thing of freedom, but it is clear how the later notion is implicit in his philosophy.

Descartes is in fact an excellent illustration of the criss-crossing motives I mentioned above. Of course, he was moved by the tremendous potentiality of the mechanist reading of nature, as he found it in Galileo. This scientific/epistemological motive stands out clearly. But it is also clear that he was moved by the ideal of disengaged rational control. Anthropological ideal and scientific theory collaborate, as they have throughout the modern culture of which Descartes is one of the founders.

This brings us to the point where we can say something, and perhaps raise questions, about the structure of MacIntyre's argument in *After Virtue*. What we have shown so far is that the modern meta-ethics of the fact/value dichotomy does not stand as a timeless truth, at last discovered, like the inverse square law, or the circulation of the blood. It makes sense only within certain ethical outlooks. For an Aristotelian, the sharp division between factual and evaluative claims makes no sense. Of course, at this point the defender of the split is tempted to reply that this just shows how wrong Aristotle is, whose theories the progress of science has relegated to the trash-heap. But the whole argument above has been designed to detach us from this way of seeing things. The progress of science may have refuted Aristotle's physics and his biology, but it does not rule out thinking of ethics in terms of tele, or other similar concepts. The shift in ethical outlook is underdetermined by the scientific change. Rather the split has to be seen as part of a new understanding of freedom and moral agency. The neutral world of nature waiting to have purposes imprinted on it is the correlate of the disengaged subject. Neutrality is the property he *ought* to perceive in the world, if he is to realize his potentiality as the free agent of dignity and rational control.

But then we are being sold a tremendous bill of goods by the theorists of the split. What is supposed to be an outlook-independent meta-ethical finding, setting the rules of reasoning for all possible moral positions, turns out to be just the preferred interpretation of one ideal among others. This stage of the argument is now relatively familiar to us all. It consists in unmasking the spuriously independent validity of certain meta-ethical propositions, which in fact outrageously fix the rules of discourse in the interests of one outlook, forcing rival views into incoherence.

But one can go farther. One can argue back, with all the resources of moral phenomenology, to show that this meta-ethic is not only biased but also false. All sorts of arguments have been put forward. *After Virtue* itself consists centrally in a sense of arguments for this, in pitting Aristotle against Nietzsche, whose position is thought to be the only consistent conclusion for proponents of the split. I shall not take this further here, but in general these arguments, as deployed by MacIntyre and others, attempt to convince us that in what we have to recognize as our moral reasoning we just cannot do without modes of thinking which the split rules out, for example using virtue terms which cannot be neatly segmented into descriptive and evaluative components. I refrain from going into this, because I think these arguments are now relatively familiar and I believe convincing. The difficult issue is where we go from here. Or perhaps better put, where have we got? People like MacIntyre and myself want to accuse the Hares and the Stevensons of – to put it polemically and brutally – trying to force through their own ethic of disengaged freedom under the guise of an independently established, rationally undeniable meta-ethic. Then we go on to argue for our own meta-ethic, let us call it for short 'Aristotelian'. But this is tied to another range of moral views – not, of course, narrowly to Aristotle's own detailed theory; MacIntyre shows how diverse and susceptible of development the understanding in terms of the virtues is; but nevertheless, this also makes some views more coherently statable than others. Does this mean that arguing from one's substantive view through the connected meta-ethic – for one's moral position through the implied form of moral reasoning – is after all legitimate, and that the only problem for proponents of the fact/value split was that their case was bad?

The simple answer to this question is 'yes'. If moral positions and meta-ethical theories are closely interwoven, then one ought to be able to argue in either direction. But the detailed case is more complicated. Does it follow from this that (assuming our moral phenomenology is convincing) we ought to consider the ethics of modern disengaged freedom as refuted, as the proponents of the split considered that of Aristotle? This would be too quick. All we would have shown is that in the form in which they have come down to us these moral positions are incoherent, viz., in ruling as impossible the forms of moral thinking which their protagonists nevertheless cannot help using. But perhaps the essence of the moral vision can be saved in a more sophisticated variant which takes account of this. And of course, also perhaps not; perhaps the ideal of modern freedom is so out of tune with what we are that it inevitably forces us into incoherence. But we cannot answer this question a priori. We have to give these ideals a run for their money. And the need to try is made the more urgent by the fact that for many of us in the 'Aristotelian' camp, some facets at least of the ideal of modern freedom have great appeal. Indeed, one might suspect that there is virtually no one in the modern age who is not committed to some or other of its facets. Can one build an identity in the modern world which has not to some extent been shaped by this understanding of freedom? Many of MacIntyre's critics have raised this worry. So the argument so far, once we have denounced the credentials of the spuriously independent meta-ethic, still leaves open an important issue: what can/should be rescued of the moral vision which spawned the distortive meta-ethic?

And beyond this, another issue arises. If we are right, and the

'Aristotelian' meta-ethic is the right one, in the sense of offering the forms in which we cannot help but think and construe at least good parts of our moral lives, how possible is it in fact for people to escape its forms? Presumably they can do so at the cost of abandoning those aspects of our moral lives which we cannot help casting in its terms. But how possible is this in practice? The answer we give to this question will have important consequences for our whole reading of our civilization.

If one thinks that the Aristotelian meta-ethic in fact offers the inescapable categories for anyone's moral thought, then one will see the rival package of views – say disengaged freedom, plus the meta-ethics of the fact/value dichotomy – as an unviable basis for an alternative life-form. In fact people who aspire to live by this alternative will be deluding themselves. They will be unclear in many respects about the ways that they in fact think. They will always be in truth more 'Aristotelian' than they believe, surreptitiously relying on notions like 'virtue' and 'the good life', even while they repudiate them on the level of theory. On the other hand, the more one thinks that the Aristotelian forms can be escaped, the more one will think that the modern package offers the basis for a coherent viable alternative.

Which way one goes on this issue has great importance for the critique one offers of modernity. Part of what is meant in offering the moral phenomenology which issues in the 'Aristotelian' meta-ethic is that these forms of thinking are closely tied to central features of our moral life. If one thinks that people who embrace the modern package in fact escape these forms, then one sees them as doing away with these features. One takes them seriously, and one may judge that in consequence they are sacrificing essential parts of human life and departing from the human norm. If, on the other hand, one thinks that these forms of thought are not escapable, one will be ready to convict modern culture of muddle, but be much less sure that it actually departs as much from the norm as its theory would call for.

This is a very important issue for our entire understanding of modernity, once we engage in this critique of modern meta-ethics. MacIntyre seems to lean towards the second view, that which allows that there is a viable way of being outside the 'Aristotelian' forms of thought. Consequently he tends to take modern society at the face value of its own dominant theories, as heading for runaway atomism and break-up. He speaks at times of a society organized around 'emotivist' understandings of ethics. I, on the other hand, frankly lean in the other direction. I think that we are far more 'Aristotelian' than we allow, that hence our practice is in some significant way less based on pure disengaged freedom and atomism than we realize. Of course, this does not mean that getting the right meta-ethic makes no practical difference; without doubt seeing ourselves as atoms, for instance, distorts and inhibits the practices which embed the contrary understanding. This is notably the case for the practices of citizen participation in contemporary society. But these practices nevertheless survive. Our way of life never sinks to the full horror that would attend it (I believe) if we could be truly consistent Benthamites, for instance.

MacIntyre and I lean opposite ways on this issue. (He has been heavily criticized for his stand on this question too.) The truth may be somewhere between us. But my aim here is to bring this issue to the fore. There are thus two further questions which we have to address to the line of argument that is offered in *After Virtue*. First, is the substantive ethical vision which spawned the false meta-ethic to be just abandoned, or can/ought it to be rescued in some form? Second, to the extent that it must be abandoned, is this package of inadequate views to be taken seriously in our diagnosis of modernity as what underlies a coherent but bad, dangerous and destructive practice or way of life? Or should it be discounted in part at least as confusion, rendering us blind to our actual ways of thinking and reacting, and hence no doubt potentially dangerous and destructive, but not precisely in the ways which the false theory indicates on its face?

Let me call these two questions respectively the rescue question and the diagnostic question, and plunge on to look at more serious issues of meta-ethics which MacIntyre raises.

II

I do not mean to imply that the fact/value split is unimportant. In some ways it is the most serious and fundamental claim that arises out of the new conception of modern freedom. This is why, in a sense, MacIntyre seems to give it pride of place in talking of our modern culture as 'emotivist'. It is emblematic of modern views, too, in that it issues both from the underlying ethic of freedom and from the felt pressure of that ethical scepticism which modern scientific culture tends to breed, from a mix of moral and epistemological considerations. But it is also very familiar to us, and the arguments against it have been often rehearsed; to the point where many people will now agree in laying this particular thesis to rest.

There is, however, another issue, which is close to the central theme of this paper, and which concerns the proper scope of ethical theories. In terms of the paradigm case of justice, it pits a group of thinkers, of which John Rawls and Ronald Dworkin are key figures, against another of which, say, Michael Walzer and Michael Sandel are important spokesmen. One holds that a theory of justice ought to be general,

applying across all societies, or at least all of a certain level of development. The other believes that justice is at least partly relative to the
particular culture and history of each society. Let's call these two views
the universalist and communitarian, respectively.

Now *After Virtue* seems very relevant to this issue. It offers what
appears to be a very good argument in favour of the communitarian
case. And MacIntyre specifically takes up the issue of justice in chapter
17. But the universalist might still be dissatisfied. The universalist might
think that his or her case is being side-stepped rather than confronted.
What he or she thinks is the most important point of a theory of justice,
its potential to criticize the existing reality, seems to be lost in what
appears to be a derivation of goods from existing practices.

I think that this is a misreading of MacIntyre's thesis, and that *After
Virtue* gives us an excellent basis for examining the issue between
universalists and communitarians. But confusion has arisen from running together what I think are different strands of the argument – an
elision to which proponents of modern disengaged freedom are prone.
I want to try to separate them out here. Let me take up three issues
which are or have been considered in some sense meta-ethical, and which
divide at least many communitarians from universalists.

(1) At the end of chapter 9, posing the issue of Aristotle versus
Nietzsche, MacIntyre speaks of an opposition between an ethic of rules
and one of virtue. According to the former, 'the rules of morality or law
... are not to be derived from or justified in terms of some more fundamental conception of the good for man' (p. 112). The target here is
Dworkin. Later he quotes Rawls, to show that the latter has a fundamentally derived notion of the virtues: they are defined in terms of rules
of right. He opposes this to a moral theory which would begin with the
virtues.

This is my first issue, but I shall put it in slightly different (though I
think basically equivalent) terms. I should like to oppose an ethic of
rules to an ethic whose more basic concept is the good. In effect, I think
this amounts to the same distinction. To see this, we should look briefly
at the Aristotelian notion of the relation of virtue and the good. The
term 'virtue' is often used to pick out qualities of two kinds: either
particular facets of what is seen as a good life, such as generosity (in the
modern sense), or kindness, or liberality; or else properties which have
the effect of bringing about, preserving or maintaining the good life:
courage, temperance, constancy and (on some readings) justice. Let's
call these latter 'preserving' qualities. It is central to Aristotle's theory
that while he picks out a great many preserving virtues, these are also
considered to fall into the first class, and to be proper parts of the good

life. Being a causal condition of the good does not rule out being constitutive of it.

There is a particular understanding of the good at work here, one in which the whole good life contains within it particular partial goods, but not just as an aggregation. Rather the good life puts the partial goods together in their proper order, according to their proper rank, as it were. People need the virtue of courage, and also the kind of insight he calls 'phronesis', to discern and maintain allegiance to this order; but these qualities are also goods which have their place in it, they are a part of what the virtues are meant to sustain.

Now it is a feature of many modern theories, as MacIntyre points out, that they cannot abide this kind of relation, in which one element is both cause and constituent of another. It is a central demand of one influential construal of modern reason that one clearly sort out means from ends. For utilitarians, the good is happiness, and virtues can only be good instrumentally: they are preserving qualities without being part of what is to be preserved. And something similar goes for any theory which makes rules ultimate. If the basic point of morality is to do the right actions, then the virtues must be seen as purely executive. They cannot also be seen as part of the end, because the end is not defined that way.

So MacIntyre is right to see the place accorded the virtues as a kind of litmus test for discriminating Aristotelian from modern ethical theory. But I want to make the place of the good the central issue, because I think this enables us to get faster to the motivational core of these theories. It is the same mixture as before, of epistemological and moral concerns.

The epistemological consideration is easily described, even though rather harder to justify. A theory of ethics which takes as its basic concept a notion of the human good seems to presuppose difficult metaphysical concepts, like that of a normative 'nature', which we can no longer justify. An ethic founded on rules or procedures is thought not to share this difficulty. I think this whole argument is shot full of holes, though I shall not pursue this here. (I will touch briefly on the motivation for this view below, in section III.)

The moral considerations are more interesting. They can be captured by three related qualities. The first is freedom, which we are already familiar with. An Aristotelian theory seems to determine a person's paradigm purposes from the order of nature. To be guided by reason is to be guided by insight into this order. But the modern notion of reason is of a capacity which is procedurally defined. We are rational to the extent that our thinking activity meets certain procedural standards, such as consistency, the analysis of problems into elements, the making

of clear and distinct connections, attention to the evidence, conformity
to the rules of logic, and the like. To be guided by reason now means
to direct one's action according to plans or standards which one has
constructed following the canons of rational procedure, for instance, to
be proceeding according to clear calculations, or to be obeying a law one
has prescribed to oneself according to the demands of reason. Rational
direction is therefore seen as synonymous with freedom understood as
self-direction, direction according to orders constructed by the subject,
as against those which the subject is supposed to find in nature. From
the standpoint of this understanding of freedom and reason, the Aristotelian theory – or any theory based on an antecedent notion of the
good as prescribed by nature – is profoundly repugnant. It does not
exalt the freedom of the subject as one ought, but rather pre-empts it.
If this is our predicament, then we cannot think of the best human life
as defined by the fact that we confer our own order on it. The essence
of modern dignity is lost.

To this motive is added the one directed to the other two closely
connected qualities. In its Aristotelian form (though not so much in the
Platonic as will be seen below) a theory of the good can be defined in
too close symbiosis with a particular form of life. It will lack critical
bite, and thus also universality.

On the other side, a theory which makes rules ultimate satisfies this
modern drive to freedom, universality and critical distance. To translate
it (with outrageous presumption) into Aristotelian categories, we might
say that the essence of man lies in freedom, which is the imposing of
orders on his life meeting the demands of procedural rationality. To set
up any substantive goal a priori is to bypass or downgrade this activity
of constructing self-imposed order. The norms this activity itself has to
meet are those of procedural rationality. Consequently the only a priori
standards which human life can be required to meet and which still
respect this freedom are procedural ones. What we do when we carry
out this activity in order to direct our lives is determine what we should
do, or what is right. Consequently, the proper moral theory should
make the right and not the good its fundamental category.

What I seem to have accounted for here is the supercession of theories
of the good by theories of the right. But in fact, it is evident that I am
drawing this distinction differently from the usual way; indeed, scandal-
ously so. These terms were originally introduced by the intuitionists, I
believe, in order to distinguish utilitarian from Kantian theories. 'Teleological' versus 'deontological' were other terms for this distinction. So
described, this difference is an intramural squabble within modern
philosophy. But the distinction I am drawing pits utilitarianism and
Kantianism against Aristotle and Plato.

To draw it my way you have to redefine the criterial difference. It is not just: do you determine the right from the good or the good from the right? Rather, it is something like: do you recognize a hierarchic order in goods? Everybody recognizes that humans must acknowledge de facto, non-moral goods, the objects of our needs and desires. The moral issue concerns a possible ordering of these, whether some are to be given precedence over others, as allegedly higher or more worthwhile, or truly enjoined on us, whether they are to be sought even at the expense of others, etc. The views which issue from modern freedom all shy away from recognizing this kind of good. The task of deciding the hierarchy must fall to the subject's rational construction.

The difference is that for the utilitarians, once the possibility of a higher good is excluded, the only rational procedure must be to sum de facto goods. The right solution, that which enjoys henceforth the aura of a higher or moral way, is that which emerges from the rational procedure. Kant, on the other hand, saw that utilitarianism seemed to reject altogether the hierarchy of motives; there seemed to be no qualitative distinction left between moral and prudential. For the same reason, its notion of freedom was not radical enough. It involved rejecting the spurious hierarchical orders in nature, but it did not establish the will's independence from mere de facto inclination. Kant made up both these inadequacies in one stroke: to act morally is to act from a qualitatively higher motive than the merely prudential; and this motive, being defined procedurally, independently even of de facto ends, offers an even more exalted notion of freedom.

The distinction as I draw it here, between what we could call substantive notions of ethics and procedural notions of ethics, is useful because I believe it makes criterial what were in fact the powerful motives behind these modern doctrines. As a result, it allows us to see the continuities as well as the breaks in modern ethical thought. So defined, procedural theories represent a powerful tradition, from Bentham through Kant to Rawls, Dworkin and Habermas. Indeed, if we think only of the political dimension, the move to the procedural is anticipated in Grotius's theory of legitimacy, where substantive issues about the form of the state are pre-empted by the procedural question of how it arose. I do not think it is wrong to see all these theories as affirmations, in rather different forms, of what I have been calling the modern notion of freedom.

This is what I want to identify as the first major meta-ethical issue, whether ethical theories ought to be procedural or substantive. Having said that, I just want to state baldly that procedural theories seem to me to be incoherent. Better put, that to be made coherent they require restatement in substantive form. This is not the place to argue for this conclusion, given my basic goal, which is to try to understand what the whole structure of the debate is about, and what follows from our meta-ethical insights. So I shall just take this as shown. But the weakness of procedural theories is not far to seek. It comes out when one asks: what is the basis of the hierarchy they do recognize? What makes it mandatory to follow the privileged procedures? The answer has to lie in some understanding of human life and reason, in some positive doctrine of man, and hence the good. It is greatly to the credit of Kant that he recognizes this and spells out his view of man, or rather rational agency, and the dignity that attaches to it, that is, what makes it of infinitely higher worth than anything else in the universe. This allows one to see that the logic of 'nature', 'telos' and 'the good' has not been escaped in these theories, but just displaced. For Kant we *are* rational agency. This is different from Aristotle 's rational animal, in that its 'ergon' has nothing to do with our animal existence, but only with making a certain kind of rational procedure absolutely primary. This primacy, which is equivalent to freedom, is our highest good, although the complete good requires that happiness be added to this, in the proper relation.

My contention is that any theory which claims to make the right primary really reposes on such a notion of the good, in the sense (a) that one needs to articulate this view of the good in order to make its motivations clear; and (b) that an attempt to hold on to the theory of the right while denying any such underpinning in a theory of the good would collapse in incoherence. I hope that my analysis above has made at least (a) a little more plausible.[3]

(2) The first issue concerned the very structure of a moral theory. The second touches on the nature of moral reasoning. On the first, Plato and Aristotle are together against modern procedural ethics. The second opposes Plato to Aristotle; at least Aristotle thought it did.

Aristotle thought that our moral understanding could never be fully explicit. It could not be stated in a set of rules, however long. The endless variety of the situations of action meant that we could only live well if we had some kind of insightful understanding, not reducible to rules, of the requirements of virtue in each fresh context. This is what Aristotle called 'phronesis'.

Part of one's grasp of the good lies in knowing how to act in varying circumstances. If you had to explain or communicate this knowledge you would often have to have recourse to paradigm actions, or people, or tell stories. (MacIntyre points out (p. 201) how vital stories are to our development as children.)

Sometimes our grasp of a good is through our grasp of a practice of which this is the internal good, in the sense of MacIntyre's discussion in chapter 14. In the case of something like his example, portrait painting, we may be very inarticulate, and be virtually unable to say it (as he inevitably is forced to do in his discussion), but still be excellent and discriminating at the art. But even with practices which have been much more theorized about, say that of politics as rule through citizen participation, the grasp that an experienced citizen of a modern state has, as shown by his or her sense of what practices to encourage, what to protest against, what to treat as indifferent, is far from being exhausted by the explicit theories of democracy or participatory politics. Indeed, one of the catastrophic features of the political action of a Robespierre or St Just seems to be that they made no allowance for such understanding in trying to realize a citizen republic. They expected perfect conformity with a pre-established form.

But our grasp of an existing practice is only one example of this implicit understanding. It by no means signifies that only the goods of the status quo are understood in this way. A revolutionary new value cannot be fully explicated either. We understand it partly through an imaginative grasp of the style of practice it would call for, and often it is communicated to us through model practitioners in reality or fiction. The New Testament is the outstanding example in our culture of a new spirituality which was disseminated largely through stories, both those of the Gospels themselves, and those related in the Gospels.

Of course, we are frequently called on to articulate this understanding. Disputes arise about what some good means, or what the point is of some practice. Rival formulations are proffered. But the fact that we can be convinced in some cases that some of these are more in the spirit of the previously accepted good or practice testifies to the existence of this implicit understanding.

The point made by Wittgenstein, Heidegger, Michael Polanyi and others is the by now familiar one that this process of articulation never comes to an end; it never exhausts so to speak the implicit understanding. Rules, however long and detailed, do not apply themselves. Norms and ideals always need fresh interpretation in new circumstances.

We can readily see how the ethics of modern freedom had a penchant for explicit rules. Free action was that determined by rational procedures, and these strove for exactness and explicitness in order to surmount confusion and error. We have only to think of Descartes. The same spirit that pushed for an ethic of rules over one of the substantive good tended to favour an ethic of explicit rules. What was left to phronesis seemed to be abandoned to unreason. One had rational control to the extent that one could calculate exactly, or determine one's action according to universal principles alone. All this meant that phronesis was mistrusted not just because it was not yet fully reduced to reason, but also because as a consequence it could be the domain of blind parochial prejudice. An inarticulate moral sense must be a prisoner of the existing practices, and so any concession to it amounted to a strengthening of the status quo. Freedom, universality and a critical stance all required explicit rules.

This spirit is far from dead in our day. But the sidelining of phronesis has been tremendously and effectively attacked by the authors I mentioned above, and is again by MacIntyre in *After Virtue*. This has been part of an attack across the board on the rationalist conception of the mind. But it is not surprising if, in the case of Heidegger and Gadamer at least, as well as in that of MacIntyre, Aristotle's ethical doctrines have been an important reference point.

Once again, I shall simply award victory without argument to the Aristotelian side. The value of raising this point, though, is to distinguish it from the previous issue, pitting proceduralists against substantivists. Aristotle is in both cases lined up against the defenders of modern freedom; and the motives which the latter have in taking sides on both are the same. But nevertheless, the issues are different, as the different position of Plato testifies. However, the major aim of separating out these issues is to distinguish them both from the third. To this last I now turn.

(3) The third issue is the important substantial one. It concerns how closely one's ethical theory is tied to existing practice. Once again, Plato and Aristotle can serve as models. Plato is in a sense the great revisionist. His notion of the good is such that he is ready to propose a radical break with the existing world, at least if one takes the *Republic* seriously.[4] Political life as the search for honour, family life, the accumulation of property as a basis for one's own exercise of liberality and help to one's friends – all these can be sacrificed. What people have believed to be the goods internal to these practices are reinterpreted either as neutral, or as potentially dangerous sources of corruption.

Aristotle takes Plato seriously to task for this in his *Politics* (book II). It is a fundamental error, for Aristotle, to write any of the goods out of the good life for man. This is seen as constituted by all the goods we seek, in their correct rank and proportion. This means that in some circumstances some lesser ones will almost certainly have to be sacrificed to greater ones. But the idea of ruling some in principle out as unfit to be part of the good life runs against the very essence of the *teleion agathon*, which is to include all goods, each in its rightful place. You cannot just jump out of the human condition.

This might be understood as a meta-ethical dispute, because reasons of principle can be found for believing that an ethical view must conform to each of these models. One can take the 'Platonic' view, without necessarily being as revolutionary in its application, that no existing practice is to be allowed as legitimate until it has been tested against an independent criterion of the good. Of what use would an ethical theory be unless it made possible such an independent check? Recently, for instance, Ronald Dworkin argued in somewhat this spirit against Michael Walzer that a theory of justice has to be defined independently of the particular practices of any society.

But Aristotle has his own in principle argument, as we saw. We cannot just legislate the goods people are actually seeking and finding as goods out of court. What could the highest good be if it did this? On what basis could we establish a highest good which had this property? So you have to start for your theory of justice from the kinds of goods and the kinds of common practices organized around these goods that people actually have in a given society. Ethical theory has to comprehend given practice; it cannot just abstract from it.

Now the ethical theories arising from modern freedom have naturally been 'Platonic', in the sense of revisionist. The very idea of modern freedom has entailed at least the capacity to stand aside from and put in question all our collective practices and the institutions which carry them on. In the most spectacular case, this emerges in the seventeenth-century doctrine of the social contract. And the drive for universality and the critical stance is simply the direct reflection of this conception of the task of ethics. But in addition there has been another motive for modern revisionism, which is connected with another major strand of modern thought and sensibility than the one I have been insisting on up to now. Besides this disengaged notion of freedom, there has also been what I might call the promotion of ordinary life.

'Ordinary life' is a term of art that I want to use for the life of production and reproduction, or economic and family life. In Aristotle's famous expression, 'life and the good life', it is what is covered by the first term. Now for Aristotle, as his dyad implies, this first term is simply of infrastructural significance. It is a goal of association, because you need it in order to carry on the good life. The latter is defined in terms of distinct, higher activities. In the tradition, the main candidates were the contemplation of truth and the citizen life. Aristotle integrated both into his ethical view.

A striking feature of modern culture has been a reversal of this hierarchy. One can argue that it started with the Reformers, who had a hierarchy of spiritual vocations to reverse. In denying that any specially dedicated Christians, living a life of poverty, chastity and obedience, could mediate the salvation of others, they stressed that the fullest possible life of the Christian was one led in marriage and his ordinary calling. The important issue was how, whether in a worshipful spirit, to the glory of God, or not.

This idea had important revolutionary implications, also in the social and political sense, as was evident in the Puritan revolt, and also the culture of later Puritan societies. But it also becomes secularized. One sees it as one of the underlying ideas of the Baconian revolution; and then it becomes an *idée forcé* of the Enlightenment. The life of production and reproduction is the centre of human concern. The highest life does not reside in some supposedly higher activity, but rather in living ordinary life (in my sense) rationally, that is, under rational control. This in turn spawned radically revolutionary variants, of which the theory of Marx is perhaps the most celebrated and influential. It also helped to bring about the cultural revolution which involved dethroning the ethic of honour and glory in favour of the 'bourgeois' ethic of production and rationality.

All sorts of things made the affinity a natural one between the ideal of disengaged reason and the promotion of ordinary life. Not least was their common hostility to Aristotle, and for all the hierarchical conceptions of cosmic order; their common origins in Occamist Christianity; their convergence on the supreme importance of instrumental reason. Whatever the reasons, this was one of the most important and fateful marriages of our civilization. What I might call Enlightenment humanism, and its various heirs, the doctrines of modern naturalism, are the fruits of this synthesis. It goes without saying that the resulting doctrine is firmly in the revisionist camp.

This rejection of the honour ethic is a good example for our discussion – because it involves not only a repudiation of the aristocratic way of life with its duelling and disputes *de préséance*, but also a rejection of the citizen life and the ethic of civic humanism. In this, the modern 'bourgeois' ethic stands in a long tradition of such repudiations. Plato himself can be considered the first. The competitive struggle for office and honour and fame within the framework of common commitment to the *patria*, through whose laws all the citizens enjoy the status of participants or 'equals', as they were often called – this is surely a paradigm example of a practice with internal goods, in MacIntyre's sense. Where certain other aims sought in politics, like protection of life and property, or prosperity, might properly be thought of as external goods, the goods of citizen dignity and fame for one's great deeds are essentially tied to this form of common activity. Citizen dignity attaches to one as a participant in self-rule; the fame relevant here is for the deeds appropriate to one who comes to be asked to rule over equals, basically leadership in war and counsel.

Plato condemns this competitive striving as *polupragmonein*. It is a kind of disorder, the non-recognition of limits, and it is generative of all further disorders. It turns out to be the direct opposite of justice. Here is the classic case of a revisionist doctrine. The internal goods, citizen dignity and fame, are savagely reinterpreted as a grasping after mere appearances, simulacra. The fact that fame is essentially involved with recognition, with how one stands in the eyes of others and posterity, facilitates this transvaluation, a connection beautifully reflected in the etymological connections encapsulated in the term *doxa*, meaning both 'opinion' and 'glory', and derived from a verb 'to appear', *dokein*.

Against this, as we saw, Aristotle not only wants to integrate citizen activity into the good life, but even makes politics, which he defines in terms of this activity, an essential feature of the human animal. Man is *zoon politikon*. The Stoics return us to the Platonic position, as does Christian Platonism in its Augustinian form. The modern 'bourgeois' rejection of the honour ethic is heir to all this, and it too makes a great deal of the supposed childish attachment to the merely apparent which this ethic involves. Hobbes speaks sneeringly of 'vain-glory'. Hobbes, of course, is contesting what was merely an aspiration to remake society. But since then modern Western societies have tried to recreate something like citizen politics. Low as the level of success may have been (and I would not put it as low as MacIntyre does), the repudiation of this ethic today still amounts to a rejection of the internal good of actual social practices. These internal goods are set at naught in the name of external goods, like peace, security and prosperity, which the aspiration to competitive, participatory politics allegedly jeopardizes.

III

I come to this issue now, because it's the really tough one. I do not propose simply to decide it by fiat in favour of Aristotle. Indeed, I will not be able to do more than express a few thoughts vaguely intimating the direction of some future resolution. This is because, I believe, there is no one-sided resolution of this conflict. We all must recognize allegiance both to the 'Platonic' and to the 'Aristotelian' sides of this dispute, both to the revisionist and the comprehensive approach. The important issue, about which I shall have all too little to say, is how we reconcile them.

But I also come to this issue only now because I want to distinguish it from the other two. They are understandably confused. Because of the historic confrontation of Aristotelianism with the ideal of disengaged freedom, made the more unbridgeable when this fuses with the promotion of ordinary life, it is all too easy to believe that the option for revisionism is the same as the option for a procedural ethic; that going for explicit rules against phronesis is one and the same as repudiating the status quo; and the like. A historical constellation born out of a certain set of motives is taken for a logical unity. I hope I have shown that this is not so. Certainly Plato shows how one can be a revisionist within a substantive ethic. And what I said above about the spiritual impact of the New Testament was meant to illustrate the obvious fact that revisionism in no way entails the repudiation of phronesis.

But the confusion still bedevils the debate. Two commonly held positions testify to this. For some, the supposedly intrinsic connection between revisionism and a procedural ethic makes them opt for the latter in the name of the former. I think Habermas is an example of this. He fears that an ethic of the good must inevitably forfeit universality, and hence a critical standpoint towards any and all cultural forms. From the opposite side, this same alleged connection may make others reject revisionism in the name of phronesis or in face of the obvious inadequacies of abstract, procedural rationality. Perhaps Oakeshott is an example of this.

The same confusion has led many people to misunderstand MacIntyre. His talk of the internal good of practices, and his criticism of the 'Enlightenment' project, lead some to assume that he must be in favour of whatever is, or at least that he gives himself no ground for critique of existing practices. But he clearly says the opposite. First, his concept of a tradition is actually close to the reality, and not the caricature that is bandied about in rationalist thought. Traditions, including those of practices with their internal goods, are the site of ongoing debates, internal revisions, critical turns and so on. Secondly, he says very clearly at the end of chapter 14 that 'any account of the virtues in terms of practices could only be a partial and first account' (p. 187). What we need to complement it is some notion of the good of a whole life. And there follows in chapter 15 his extremely profound and interesting discussion about the narrative unity of a human life. What I see MacIntyre as doing here is giving his own sense to Aristotle's notion of an 'architectonic' good, the good that my life as a whole must exhibit, and that determines the place and proportions of all partial goods in the totality. This is the end whose name is 'eudaimonia', and that Aristotle is concerned to define for us.

Here again I would depart somewhat from MacIntyre's way of putting the issue, although I am not far from him in substance. In fact, our moral understanding moves as it were between two poles. On the one hand, we do become familiar with certain goods by being brought up in certain practices, to which they are internal, or to which the practices contribute (on the model of Aristotelian virtues) both as cause and proper part. An example of this latter would be the practices of prayer in relation to the good of sanctity. On the other hand, some of these goods transcend all our practices, such that we are capable of transforming or even repudiating some of these latter in their name. So the prophets of Israel could radically downgrade some of the hitherto accepted ritual, and tell the people in God's name that their holocausts were an abomination, that they should rather come with a pure heart before Him. Examples of such 'transcendent' goods, besides the ones just evoked, sanctity and the fear of God, are Plato's ideal of the ordered hegemony of reason, the Stoic notion of the cosmopolis of which all men and Gods are citizens, the modern idea of disengaged freedom. (I must stress that in using the term 'transcendent' here, I do not mean to imply that these goods transcend the things of this world – only some of those in the above list do so – but rather that they transcend our practices in the above sense.)

How do we think, reason, increase our understanding of such goods? I think that modern philosophy, indeed modern culture, is in a tremendous muddle about this. It is my claim that our thought inevitably relates in part to these transcendent goods, as well as to the internal goods of practices. In a way, this was implicit in my reconstruction of the motivation for procedural ethics above. I saw them as based on a notion of the good. This comes out most clearly in the case of Kant. But modern philosophy has generated a shyness, to the point of inarticulacy, about these goods. In part, the reasons are already familiar to us: the reluctance implicit in the idea of last appeal, and the scepticism implicit in the associated epistemological doctrines about definitions of the human telos. But we can now see something more about the motives of this latter. The kind of thinking favoured by the modern understandings of freedom and reason is disengaged. That is, it is the kind which strives to draw as little as possible on our implicit understanding of the context of practice in which we act, to offer wherever possible explicit criteria of identification, so that discourse is as far as possible comprehensible independent of particular life experiences and cultural settings. The fact that the goal of total abstraction from the context of practice is a chimera should not blind us to the viability of this ideal of striving in this direction, or to the dependence on it of crucial achievements of modern culture, most especially natural science and technology.

But this ideal distorts practical reason beyond all recognition. By its very nature practical reason can only function within the context of some implicit grasp of the good, be it that mediated by a practice to which this good is internal or by practices which contribute to it as cause and constituent, or by contact with paradigm models, in life or story, or however. The error of modern rationalism is to believe that such thinking must inevitably be a prisoner of the status quo, that our moral understanding can only be revisionist at the cost of being disengaged. This more than anything else has contributed to that pernicious confusion I am trying to fight here, which has made so many believe that a critical ethic has to be procedural and explicit. And it has also contributed to scepticism, or at least to that shyness and inarticulacy I denounced above. If the only acceptable form of reason is disengaged and as far as possible context-free, then practical reasoning comes to appear impossible. You cannot prove that man is rational life, or rational agency, or the image of God, the way you show the kinetic theory of heat or the inverse square law. The gains of practical reason are all within a certain grasp of the good, and involve overcoming earlier distortions and fragmentary understanding. The certainty we gain is not that some conclusion is ultimately valid, but that it represents a gain over what we held before. The propositions of which we can be confident are comparative. What we are confident of is that our present formulations articulate better, less distorted, less partially, what we were never entirely without some sense of. Moral knowledge, unlike that gained in natural science, does not deal with the wholly new. This is what Plato was trying to say with his notion of *anamnesis*.

But once one takes the path of disengaged thought, this becomes quite lost to view. In this sense, MacIntyre seems to me entirely right that the Enlightenment project ultimately contributes to the credibility of Nietzsche. An impossible model of reasoning is proposed, and then when one sees that no rational headway can be made in this way in discerning the good, one falls into scepticism and despair. Or at least one has an extra motive for opting for a procedural ethic, on the (false) belief that one thereby can avoid the whole issue of the good altogether. This of course takes one even farther away from any understanding of the viable forms of practical reasoning, hence strengthening scepticism and despair, or at least deepening the self-willed inarticulacy about good.

The irony is that this whole position is powered originally by a vision of the good, that of disengaged, free, rational agency, one of the most important, formative transcendent goods of our civilization.

When one understands practical reason aright, one can see that the goods about which one reasons in its context-related way include transcendent ones, and that this reasoning does not by any means have to be comprehensive only, but can be highly revisionist. True, in this latter case the context will largely be provided not by established practices, but by models or stories embodying a higher perfection (like those of the death of Socrates, or the Gospels). But it will be context-related none the less, that is, not trying to frame formulae which minimally rely on context, but rather trying to articulate better what this context implies.

I should now be in a position to answer the question concerning my third big issue, between Aristotle and Plato, comprehenders and revisionists. But in fact I shall not answer it. This is partly for the good reason that it should now be evident that no global one-sided answer to this question can be accepted. The idea that it could comes from the confusion of this issue with the other two. On one side, the errors of abstract rationalism are used to discredit all revisionism; on the other, the demands of critical thought are deemed incompatible with allegiance to any internal goods. Freed from this illusion, we see that we are faced with transcendent goods which command our awed consent, and practices whose internal goals seem valuable, and a distressing amount of prima facie conflict between the two. There is no a priori way to resolve this; we have to work it out case by case. And I now turn to one such, that of justice.

IV

Our issue about theories of justice provides a good example of the kind of tension I mean, that can arise between transcendent and internal goods. MacIntyre makes a very important point in discussing the theories of Rawls and Nozick in his chapter 17. Neither of these theories has any place for the notion of desert, something which nevertheless figures in the thinking of the analogous positions which people adopt in real political discussions in our societies (represented here by A and B).

This brings us to the heart of the Aristotelian understanding of distributive justice. I shall try to summarize this in the following way:[5] to understand the demands of distributive justice for any society, one has to understand what kind of society it is. Societies are associations for the achievement of common goods; what goods are to be distributed, and to whom, will depend on what the ends of the association are, and how they are achieved. The basic intuition underlying justice is this: in any common attempt to achieve the good, all genuine collaborators benefit from the contribution of the others. They are in a sense all in each other's debt. But since some will make a more signal contribution, the mutual debt may not be entirely reciprocal. Associated for the defence of our homeland, we are all disproportionately in the debt of the valorous fighter who incurred extra risk to cover the retreat and regrouping, when we were in danger of rout, or to the far-seeing general who provided wise leadership, when we were about to make a tactical blunder. While all must share in the good – because that is the very principle of the association, and is what Aristotle means by the 'equality' which defines justice – it is clear that more is owed to these outstanding contributors. They merit more than the rest. This is Aristotle's principle of 'proportionate' equality.

This intuition of rightful distribution by desert among associates seems very deeply embedded in human consciousness. We all accept it even today for one of the goods which Aristotle singled out as a major object of just distributions: honours. Let's say that there are medals to be handed out for valour, or distinguished service. Does any one doubt that our two outstanding figures above merit them? That it would be rank injustice to give them to others instead, who had done nothing outstanding?

Yet interestingly enough, as MacIntyre points out, desert does not figure in these two highly influential contemporary theories of justice. It is deliberately set aside by Rawls, and totally swallowed up in the quite different notion of entitlement by Nozick.

Why? Part of the reason is that these theories are answering another question. It is not one tied to a particular society, and its balance of indebtedness. Indeed, Nozick abstracts from society altogether. The rules of right distribution are exactly what they would be if we weren't associated at all, but met in the state of nature, as, say, members of quite independent clans might meet at some watering-hole in the desert. Everybody would agree that the rule of right here is that each should keep his own, unless some voluntary transaction transfers ownership. Rawls in a different way wants to abstract from any particular balance of indebtedness. Stripping away the misleading method of argument through 'as if' contracts, the intuition is that men should be equal, that the only justification of A's getting more than B is B's benefiting from this.

What is at work in each case is a transcendent good. For Nozick, this is the picture of man as the bearer of inviolable rights. For Rawls, it is the ideal of the hyper-Kantian agent, capable of living by rules which utterly leave out of account his or her own advantage, and which thus could be agreed by everyone, since they are not designed for anyone's good in particular. This would be the kind of person who really could say that he or she considered his or her talents and capacities as community assets, at the service of all indiscriminately.

Now the normal way of looking at this difference between Aristotle and the two contemporary theorists is to say that only one side can be right. One or other has misconceived justice. Either desert is relevant or not. But this does not necessarily follow. At the end of the day, we may indeed want to say this; but we have some way to go before this. Because we could also understand the dispute this way: each side is pointing to a *different* good. These may indeed be rivals, and in that sense, incompatible; but they are still both *goods*. The fact that the theory designating one is valid need not mean that that designating the other is confused and invalid – although special arguments in one or the other case may show that this is so.

The fact that this possibility does not even cross some people's minds is another consequence of this mistaken modern meta-ethics. A procedural ethic of rules cannot cope with the prospect that the sources of good might be plural. A single valid procedure grinds out the rules, and if it works properly it will not generate contradictory injunctions; just as a well-ordered formal system won't generate contradictory theorems. Kant could not bring himself to face a conflict of moral laws, and in face of the obvious counter-example of the benevolent lie went to extraordinary lengths to avoid admitting it. Rawls, too, considers the reading of our moral predicament in which we face independent, unrankable goods – which he calls for some reason 'intuitionism' – as one to be avoided if at all possible. So when we grind out 'p' as the standard of justice, 'not-p' simply cannot be a good, and any theory designating it as such must be wrong-headed.[6]

By contrast the Aristotelian theory can make sense of a conflict of goods from independent sources, like one between a transcendent good and one internal to some practice. That, I submit, is how we ought to understand the issue between Aristotle on one side and Rawls and Nozick on the other. One question is how we ought to live to fulfil the integral requirements of the transcendent good as we see it. If we understand ourselves as pure rational agents in the sense of Rawls's variant of the Kantian theory, then we ought to eschew any claim to special treatment over others on any other basis but benefit to those others.

Let us suppose for a moment that we accept this as a true reading of what we are, and hence of the demands of our highest good. Nothing prevents us also recognizing – unless it be the false proceduralist meta-ethic – that some particular group of us have in fact become associated in the pursuit of some goods, that we have built up an asymmetric balance of mutual indebtedness, and hence the shared sense that some merit more than others. Of course, if we all shared the above vision of transcendent good, we would all be spontaneously willing to forgo the distribution based on merit wherever it collided with the demands of the highest good. But suppose, which is more likely, that we are fairly unregenerate creatures, but with a sense of solidarity in our society, and of fairness in distribution. Then the Rawlsians in our midst might find themselves in a dilemma.

The members of our society would expect goods to be distributed according to desert, understood in terms of mutual indebtedness in the pursuit of the common good. Let us call this distribution MD. The Rawlsian would hold that to live up to the demands of our highest good we ought to adopt distribution TD. TD conflicts, let us say, with MD. What ought we to do? The generally accepted answer is that there is no problem. If we think that Rawls's notion of the good is right, then TD is right, and so MD must be wrong. But my point is that this does not follow. The fact that TD represents what we ought to live with to conform to the best in us does not show at all that MD also does not correspond to legitimate expectations, that A having risked or sacrificed so much for the common good does really deserve more, that there would be a real wrong (yes, an injustice) involved in denying this to A against his will. Of course, in a society made up totally of convinced Rawlsians, A would happily forgo this entitlement; but if this is not our case, TD would have to be enforced against his will, in violation of his sense of right: and in this case, it would constitute an injustice. We have a dilemma on our hands.

The notion that this is not so, that TD's being a good, indeed the highest possible distribution, must mean that MD has no claim on us – this notion comes from what I have argued is a mistaken meta-ethic. If the right were prior to the good, if the rules of right were derived from the application of the correct procedure, then two incompatible principles could not be generated; unless of course they were ranked, 'lexicographically ordered', as Rawls puts it. But my case has been that this is a confused account, that the good is after all fundamental. And put this way there is no difficulty in principle in admitting that both TD and MD are valid. The fact that living up to the highest in us involves living by TD establishes its claim. But this by itself does nothing to deny that collaborators for a common good generate asymmetric relations of mutual indebtedness, and that these create legitimate expectations that the distribution conform to MD.

Part of what blinds us to this is that we are using the same term 'justice' for what underlies both distributions. But in fact we ought to recognize that the *questions* they answer are different. One is: what is the distribution corresponding to the demands of the (highest) transcendent good? The other is: what is the balance of indebtedness in our particular community? We might speak here of 'absolute' justice and 'local' justice to make the distinction.

Seeing the potential dilemma here would lead us to pose questions about justice quite differently. In fact, in any but the perfect society there is likely to be strain and tension between the demands of absolute and those of local justice. Sometimes the choice is easy to make. We might argue that in terms of the legitimate expectations of the associated Mycenaean warriors, there is a right answer to the question, who ought to have Briseis, Agamemnon or Achilles. But we would set this aside as irrelevant, on the grounds that holding people as booty or prizes of war is repugnant. Here we have the kind of departure from the demands of a transcendent good – human beings as bearers of rights – which we cannot tolerate.

But in other cases, the decision is harder. Let us say that a given society is a functioning citizen republic, one where the sense of solidarity and recognition of signal service generates the sense that some MD is right. To overrule this in favour of TD would generate a sense of injustice, would undermine the harmony and solidarity of this society, create alienation; perhaps even contribute to its downfall and replacement by some more despotic rule. Is it all that clear that we should press TD with all our might?

This consideration might give us pause: on very arguable assumptions, an ideally just distribution of wealth internationally might call for a degree of transfer with which the electorates of rich Western democracies would never voluntarily concur. Some world dictator would be needed to make the TD stick here; just as it needed Tito to force Slovenes and Croatians to share with Macedonians and Montenegrins. True justice could be purchased only at the cost of citizen rule.

Now the crucial fact that MacIntyre points out in chapter 17, that participants in real political debate speak among other things of desert, whereas this has no place in the academic theories which seem otherwise analogous to commonly held positions, can be understood, I think, in this light. Real life participants are raising questions of local justice, or of local and absolute justice together; academics speak only of absolute justice. But if I am right, then the latter are at fault in only addressing one side of the question, in ignoring what may be other relevant considerations, viz., the claims of different MDs in the context of our actual societies. To use Aristotle's expression in a slightly different way, they 'speak of a part of justice only'.[7]

Of course, one may deploy particular arguments to show that MDs should be ignored. The case of Mycenaean society above shows us one kind. But in relation to our society, other arguments can be used. Some want to argue that our society is so corrupt and/or atomized that there is barely any common search for the good left in it. Or in a converging way, one might argue that modern society is nothing but a Hobbesian association for mutual advantage, based on arm's length contracts in which everyone is entitled only to what they get in whatever free deals are swung above board. Or, from another direction, we might argue that we have lost any common understanding of a common good; and that indeed is why there is so much dissension and disagreement about distributions.

All this and more might be argued. I am bound to say that I am unconvinced by it. For me our predicament comes closer to that of the ongoing citizen republic mentioned above. For all the imperfections of our society, it does bind us together in pursuit of some common goods; this does give grounds for some MDs; and these are in some ways at variance with higher possible TDs. I think recognizing this would not only be clarifying philosophically, but healthy politically, because we could make clearer to ourselves the kind of ideal we are proposing to bring about in our society, and could measure more realistically the gap with our present condition than we do when we dress this up as *the* demands of justice, *tout court*, giving ourselves a licence to ignore all other claims.

But whether I am right here, or whether one of the more gloomy views above is correct, is irrelevant to my main purpose. This has been to show that properly understood there are at least two questions hiding under the rubric justice; that their answers may be so opposed as to place us in a dilemma; and that this is of a kind which ought to be familiar, where allegiance to some transcendent good comes into conflict with goods internal to some practice.

Even if we ignore the issue of MDs, conflicts of this kind still will arise in our search for justice in other ways. The demands of historic communities will have to be taken into account before we can finally decide what is just. This is because, as was adumbrated in the example above about international justice, communities also figure as agents among whom justice must be done, within the bounds of some wider association.

V

I have been trying in the previous section to illustrate, in terms of the theory of justice, what I think is a very common type of modern moral predicament, the tension or dilemma which may arise between the demands of some transcendent good, and the internal goals of our historical practices. (Of course I do not mean to imply that there aren't also conflicts between transcendent goods, or between the internal goods of different practices.) One of the most signal disadvantages of the modern procedural meta-ethic, in contrast to Aristotelianism, is that it makes it almost impossible to recognize and understand these dilemmas. And once we do so, its built-in tendency to self-imposed inarticulacy makes it almost impossible to address the issue properly.

In a way, one of the most important needs of practical reason today is to liberate itself from these ill-conceived inhibitions, so that we can once again talk intelligibly about goods. That is what I was struggling to do in sections II and III, with, I admit, only limited success. A more satisfactory account of practical reason than my rather brisk summary in section III is essential to the development of that argument.

Only if I managed to achieve this, and it became possible to address the issue of transcendent goods properly, could I begin to answer the questions posed at the end of section I, particularly the question what of the modern ideals of freedom and reason can be rescued from the illusory meta-ethic and the blindness to the diversity of goods which have accompanied them. My sense is that none of us could in all authenticity fully repudiate these ideals. But how to reinterpret them, and how to make them compatible with the other goods to which we cannot renounce allegiance, particularly those implicit in our historical practices? To answer this would be to say something of real use. This task is, alas, well beyond my powers.

NOTES

This chapter was originally presented as a paper at a seminar in Oxford in 1984–5.

1 Alasdair MacIntyre, *After Virtue* (Duckworth, London, 1981). All page references in the text of this chapter refer to this volume.
2 'Modern moral philosophy', *Philosophy*, 33 (1958).
3 I have argued elsewhere against the possibility of a procedural ethic in the particular case of Jürgen Habermas's philosophy, which I think is the most interesting and rich such theory ever produced.
4 I am not really sure the *Republic* should be taken seriously as a blueprint; indeed, I think it should not. And this raises questions about how revolutionary Plato really was. But I want to ignore them here. My concern is not the real historical Plato, but one way his theory has been taken, which has set one of the master types I want to debate in this section.
5 I have discussed the issue of this section at greater length in 'The nature and scope of distributive justice', which appears in my *Philosophical Papers*, vol. 2 (Cambridge University Press, Cambridge, 1985).
6 I have discussed this in my 'Diversity of goods', in *Utilitarianism and Beyond*, ed. Amartya Sen and Bernard Williams (Cambridge University Press, Cambridge, 1982); republished in my *Philosophical Papers*, vol. 2.
7 *Politics*, 1281a 10.

3

Reclaiming the Aristotelian Ruler

Peter Johnson

Reconstructing the double Aristotelian emphasis on moral character and well-grounded institutions is one of the central preoccupations of contemporary political philosophy. Aristotle articulates the natural integration of moral character and political community in language which seems alien to the dominant standpoint of modernity. It is with this refined integrative philosophy of human life that the contemporary Aristotelian wishes to engage. In direct opposition to the fractured nature of modernity Aristotle's writings and the subsequent tradition of creative interpretation represent the attempt to harmonize and bring order to multiple human activities and concerns. And yet intransigent questions of political morality remain. Is the Aristotelian vision unsettled by the recognition that political good can be achieved on occasion only by actions otherwise regarded as morally undesirable? In the dialogue between the contemporary Aristotelian and Aristotle must Machiavelli's voice strike a discordant note?

The Machiavellian claim that political seriousness entails the use of deceit and violence when necessity demands it can appear in modernity only as a shallow instrumentalism to the contemporary Aristotelian. In a world that has no sense of a political good independent of individual wants and desires Machiavelli's insight loses its moral force, and the dilemmas it identifies as part of the activity of governing are either ignored or evaded. To put the Machiavellian question is not, therefore, to side with modernity. Rather it is to suggest that Machiavelli's main preoccupation is with a more radical discontinuity between the moral and the political than modernity can address.

Now those who wish to reclaim Aristotelian modes of thinking believe that these represent a deeper grasp of ethics and its relation to politics than is available in modernity. But Machiavelli challenges us with the claim that the dilemmas of political morality do not arise solely from utilitarian necessity or from a recognition that moral principle and political good sometimes clash but are intrinsic to the activity of responsible governing. So the character of responsible rule is such that those who undertake it must face the occurrence of moral conflicts from which extrication is impossible without moral loss. The very structure of politics is morally flawed: since Aristotle considers politics to be 'the most authoritative art',[1] one which in a significant sense completes all other activities, the contemporary Aristotelian point of view must reject this conclusion. On what terms, then, does this rejection take place?

From an Aristotelian perspective political morality cannot be a utilitarian problem of matching means to ends. Political decision is not to be understood as an abstract calculation between alternative outcomes, devoid of any significant ethical reverberation for the agent. We must ask how political agents respond to the hard choices they have to make – with regret, shame or remorse. Such moral responses have a vital public place: the self-estimation of the agent is a crucial element in establishing a moral balance between goodness and harm. This provides a powerful brake on utilitarian accounts of political morality. Nevertheless, while an emphasis on the moral character of office-holders is necessary for a moral limit to be placed on their actions, it is not sufficient. Hard moral choices have their primary effect on those who are their victims. Those who are treated as a means to a political good or asked to bear burdens others do not share are acutely vulnerable if the moral character of the office-holder is their only security. Reaction to one's own dirty hands can often be extreme, ranging from evasion of responsibility to self-deception. Moral character alone does not give political agents a safe basis for trust. Commitment to just institutions and laws reduces uncertainty when hard decisions have to be made. From an Aristotelian perspective, then, a political community must avoid too wide a gap between public and private vocabulary.

Neither the utilitarian construction of politics as a technical activity nor the Sophoclean picture of it as a tragic domain seems adequate as an account of the difficulties political morality contains. Betrayal and secrecy both may on occasion serve clearly defined utilitarian purposes. One way their use may be limited without imposing an intolerable burden of guilt on those who employ such methods for the achievement of political goods is through the exercise of the Aristotelian virtues of moderation and practical wisdom.

Reclaiming Aristotle in the context of modernity is not, of course, without hazard. MacIntyre's argument that the defence of the classical view of morality and politics against modernity 'will be in *something like* Aristotelian terms or not all'[2] does not commit him to the role of uncritical follower. The question then is how Aristotle's broad understanding of the relation between virtue and polity, between the *phronimos* (man of practical wisdom) and the activity of ruling, can be extended to confront the problems raised by dirty hands.

On its own terms modernity sees political problems as soluble through the application of rational choice theory. To identify modernity's goal as the linking of means and ends in the most efficient and value-neutral way shows how opposed it is to the Aristotelian model of practical reason. For MacIntyre it is no accident that instrumentalist procedures prevail in cultures where the tight Aristotelian connection between practical reason and virtue has been lost. Furthermore, the arbitrariness which MacIntyre detects as lying behind modern political strife provokes the thought that for MacIntyre modernity can only regain a genuine sense of what it is for human beings to disagree and to face problematic moral choices by recovering a basic structure for the virtues and for a virtuous life. And MacIntyre's deployment of Weber as the supreme analyst of modern institutional and individual anxieties can be extended into Weber's examination of political morality in the modern context. In his essay on politics as a vocation Weber charts the qualities required for rule in terms of proportionality and balance. Effectively this returns us to Aristotle, suggesting that an Aristotelian perspective on political morality would repay investigation. For MacIntyre what must remain undamaged in Aristotle's moral and political thought is its central claim that the best kind of political order for human beings is one which is in accordance with virtue, and this, I will argue, is of crucial importance for understanding how political morality is treated both in Aristotle's thought and by contemporary attempts to reconstitute it.

For Aristotle the ability to achieve human excellences is closely tied to rational capacity, and both require a non-utopian attainability if they are to find social and political completion. So without the close connection between practical reason and justice human beings would lack the competence to make judgements between distinct goods, to decide between the claims of competing private loyalties, and to make the ranking decisions between different policies which public office demands. It is not the case, however, that Aristotle's close integration of virtue and politics necessarily excludes the problems with which political morality is characteristically concerned. On the contrary, Aristotle's non-instrumentalist understanding of moral and political goods enables us to see why different moral claims should matter at all to someone who faces them in a situation of political seriousness.

Virtue, law and politics each have a separate part to play here. Political morality would make little sense if the virtues which are tested by political imperatives had no intrinsic value. Likewise, without an appeal to the morality of law a community lacks a crucial recourse against offenders (both criminal and 'political'). Political agents who come to realize that it is not possible to do good in politics only by acting well may, for example, pursue their goals with such excess of bravery that what they expect of themselves may not rightly be expected of others; and then recourse to law is a necessary supplement to a morality of the virtues. Finally, the dilemmas involved in political morality require, in addition to virtue and law as distinct goods, a sense of politics as an activity with a value internal to itself. MacIntyre elucidates Aristotle's understanding of politics as meaning precisely this – 'political excellence and above all the excellence of the legislator consist in being good at ordering goods both generally and in particular types of situation';[3] by contrast with utilitarians such as James Mill, politics as Aristotle articulates it 'is a practice with goods internal to itself'.[4] In effect, then, the question we must ask here both of Aristotle and the contemporary Aristotelian is what are hands dirtied for?

Politics receives its priority over other activities in Aristotle's view because of its unique role in the achievement of human well-being. As Aristotle sees it, politics involves criteria of comprehensiveness and complexity which are not available in the same way in any other practical human activity. Political association is of value in itself *and* is the means to the attainment of non-political goods. In Aristotle's view, political action is natural because its absence renders human beings isolated and incomplete – such is the fate of Sophocles' Philoctetes. Consequentialist arguments about the relative costs of rival proposals or the extent to which private interests can be adjusted to the best advantage do play a significant part in the discussion in the *Politics*, but they cannot replace virtue and justice as the goods of excellence which provide the essential framework for politics as a form of human striving and aspiration.

Aristotle does not have an uncomplicated view of the relation between morality and politics. His difficulty is to show how virtue can enter politics and retain its character as virtue while maintaining political effectiveness. Aristotle does not approach this problem from the standpoint of those for whom 'consequentialism is the ethics of politics'.[5] If dirty hands decisions involve a sense of failure for the political agent this does not come about, in Aristotle's view, because politics is necessarily flawed. Of course, political excellence must be distinct from goods of effectiveness, but it must in some important sense also be close to the demands of political life.

For Aristotle, criteria of success and failure are variable, taking their character from the nature of the activity in question. Morality is a realm of indeterminacy and irregularity and so cannot be formulated precisely in terms of rules or precepts. It is in the nature of practice that its rules cannot encompass all its particulars, so the skill in judging particulars is to a significant degree a matter of perception and comes into play only with the possession of the virtues. The 'eye of the soul'[6] cannot acquire its formed state without the aid of virtue. Political excellence consists in ordering goods in accordance with justice both in terms of general principle and in particular situations. It aims at ensuring the stability and well-being of the political association by developing routines of moral character and constitutional forms to enable moral and political agents to see things rightly, judge differently when a relevant difference requires it, and recognize contrasting obligations to others. These aims may be missed in ways which have a bearing on political morality.

Not all political failure signifies lack of virtue. Political excellence is vulnerable to misfortune from the internal character of a political project or from the changes in circumstances external to it. Even (some might say, especially) well-intentioned political agents can find themselves facing severe moral dilemmas the intransigence of which is not entirely of their own making. A political agent may discover that a clear political good can be achieved only by dealing with the corrupt. A lie, a bribe, a blind eye turned may all allow desirable political projects to succeed. The utilitarian advantage may be gained only by sacrificing those virtues which give public grounds for trust. The risk to the political community here is high. Dissimulation is an attractive strategy for those who wish a reputation for both excellence and political effectiveness. By contrast, for those who place moral virtue before effectiveness the dilemma remains. When political goods seem to impose such choices it is Aristotle's clear view that 'he who violates the law can never recover by any success, however great, what he has already lost in departing from excellence.'[7] Alternatively, the insufficiency of virtue can arise from constraint – one good can be achieved only at the cost of another.

MacIntyre draws a morally essential distinction between those for whom expediency is the only motive for action and Aristotelian agents who are free to act expediently when occasion requires because virtue is their true aim. So for MacIntyre 'what someone takes to be his advantage depends upon what he is aiming at, and the aims of the good man are very different from those either of the vicious or the undisciplined (*akratés*).'[8] Cleverness – the disciplined ability to distinguish between goodness and expediency – is desirable when dealing with one's enemies if only because without it we may assume too readily that exchanging vice with vice is the only way of achieving a political good. Cleverness alone, however, is not enough to keep dirty hands in check. Aristotle's stress on political excellence certainly prevents the problems of political morality from appearing in an exclusively utilitarian guise but it does not eliminate them completely. Difficult and sometimes tragic choices still have to be made and it is desirable, if only from the standpoint of their victims, that there is a public measure of their moral necessity. Since public offices cannot fully script the conduct of their holders, Aristotle focuses on moral character. The moral attributes of office-holders are open to public scrutiny, which provides an essential basis for their trustworthiness. What kind of moral character is necessary for those who rule?

Aristotle thinks that rulers must possess distinctive attributes – 'the ruler ought to have excellence of character in perfection.'[9] The virtuous ruler acts moderately and justly for the well-being of the city. Magnanimity is the first virtue for honourable rule and the magnanimous ruler sees that honour is necessarily related to desert, which is in turn connected with a search for the public good. Disdainful of dishonourable conduct, the magnanimous ruler is prepared to take high personal risks in order to avoid it. Magnanimity, however, represents a target which only some can hit. Since rational deliberation and collective action are intrinsic to the political good, it is Aristotle's view that, as Irwin puts it, 'political activity should be open to everyone capable of it who values it correctly.'[10] For Aristotle, 'the magnificent man is liberal, but the liberal man is not necessarily magnificent,'[11] and it is to liberals that Aristotle must look if rule in the constitutional state is to be just and moderate. So one of the risks involved in being ruled by the magnanimous is that since they are always prepared to demand more of themselves – not to do so would be for them to rule irresponsibly – they might also require the same of others.

Prudence is described by Aristotle as the mean between cunning and simplicity;[12] it is 'the grasping of the right moment'[13] and is an admixture of right judgement and experience, which is comprehensive in nature and concerns the well-being of future generations as well as that of the whole of the city. If practical wisdom includes deliberation about means *and* ends then it is not simply the straightforward application of syllogistic reasoning: and so Aristotle has a special interest in characteristics such as astuteness and cleverness which play an important part in prudent deliberation. An Aristotelian political agent, therefore, who deliberates under constraint, who faces acting badly for the sake of good ends, will avoid both cunning and simplicity. Cleverness is an essential feature of a prudent decision (even though such a decision may in some significant respects be imperfect). What is important for Aristotle is that cleverness should be linked to a virtuous aim – 'if the mark be noble, the cleverness is laudable, but if the mark be bad, the cleverness is mere smartness.'[14] Aristotle's public measures of political excellence establish that there must be a limit beyond which well-intentioned political agents must not go; and yet, what degree of political expediency does this limit allow?

Aristotle's acknowledgement[15] that there may be circumstances in which it is right to do what is wrong shows how the presence of constraints affects our willingness to blame; it does not, however, exhaust our conception of what constitutes a constraint, which may be more variable than Aristotle can admit here. Duress can appear as advantage, reward and benefit, as well as threat; hands may be stained by attempts to reduce the moral costs of blackmail, by measures needed to reduce the incidence of treachery and betrayal. Political action may be constrained as much by what has been entrusted to our friends as kept secret from our enemies. When Aristotle recognizes a permissible wrongdoing he does so because he sees how human beings can be overwhelmed by the inescapable difficulties of the moral life, the impossibility of matching good against good, or the temptation to give way to an understandable emotion.

In politics, however, the range of allowable deceit is complicated by the presence of power and ambition as well as the need for accountability in those who are responsible for the public good. Aristotle is acutely conscious of the special risks posed by the political life. If man is separated from law and justice then he is, Aristotle thinks, 'the worst of all; since armed injustice is the more dangerous, and he is equipped at birth with arms, meant to be used by intelligence and excellence, which he may use for the worst ends'.[16] However, not to accept such risks is for Aristotle a refusal to pursue those goods which the political excellences are intended to establish. This would leave cases of discretionary non-rule-governed judgements undeliberated, and the political excellences such judgements typically involve would remain untested. Like rogues, statesmen too require ingenuity to pursue their ends, but unlike rogues Aristotle thinks their artfulness must be framed by justice if it is to aspire to excellence as well as effectiveness.

In the main, in the *Politics* Aristotle is opposed to the use of dishonest devices or 'constitutional tricks' (*sophismata*) by rulers to manipulate agreement, not simply because of the potential ineffectualness of such devices, but because, in any case, he believes a decent polity cannot be maintained entirely by fraudulent means. In one significant passage, however, Aristotle *does* justify a serious deception – to preserve the constitution the ruler who has care of it should, when it is necessary, 'invent terrors and bring distant dangers near, in order that the citizens may be on their guard, and, like sentinels in a night-watch, never relax their attention'.[17] So it is a mark of true statemen that they can more quickly perceive signs of danger and take the necessary measures to counter them. Is Aristotle being realistic here given the bounds of justice, or does political necessity license a wider range of deceits? As Newman points out,[18] Aristotle explores neither the measures necessary for such devices nor the detailed risks involved in using them. Rulers who 'make the remote come near,' in Barker's translation,[19] face the 'crying wolf' problem if false alarms are raised too often; more problematically, rulers who plead political necessity risk having to perpetuate the deceit *ad infinitum*.

Such political methods can be employed straightforwardly to deceive those who have no thought of deception themselves or in a more complicated way as countermeasures to confuse those who do. However, the Aristotelian political agent facing hard moral choices is not to be seen as a solitary chooser, an individual alone, Creon-like, bearing the existential burden of dirty hands in isolation from the judgements and companionship of others. Part of the meaning of moral character in Aristotle's terms is the ability to realize that others have moral expectations of our choices. Others have claims not only about the kinds of decisions we make, but about how we reach them – in the full recognition that there *are* conflicting goods and that sometimes it *is* necessary to override one to achieve another or to hold fast to the belief that the only important consideration is choosing the alternative that wins.

The virtues of character and rule then which flexibly govern an Aristotelian political practice form a necessary background to any unlooked-for but essential transgressions the practice may have to face. Aristotle's distinction between theoretical and practical wisdom allows him to construe politics as a form of human association with its own distinct practices and methods of rule.[20] So there is a significant difference between the deception of the Aristotelian statesman and the noble lie of the Platonic guardian. Both are serious untruths intended to deceive, and both are told by virtuous rulers who govern for the benefit of the governed and not in their own interests. But what authorizes the lie in Aristotle's view is not the philosophical nature of the rulers but their possession of practical wisdom. Given that practical wisdom is an ability which non-rulers can share with rulers, or at least learn how to acquire, it would follow on Aristotle's account that the deliberations which lead a ruler to practise a specific deception cannot be wholly inaccessible. Aristotle's perspective here encourages a common concern with the well-being of a political community when actions otherwise regarded as morally undesirable are needed to defend it; by contrast, such a concern is unavailable in Plato's political vision. The noble lie in Plato's formulation is told by a philosopher-ruler in whose nature and capacities the ruled cannot share. Both Aristotle and Plato, however, tie political deception to the kind of skill they understand ruling to be. Neither regards deception on its own as a skill which can be transferred from one political good to another, which would be to associate deception too closely with a sophistic view of ruling and, by implication, anticipate modern conceptions of ruling as a technique.

Given that there will be gainers and losers as a result of dirty hands decisions it is fruitful to examine the qualities of the Aristotelian ruler from the perspective of those who are subject to such decisions. In political circumstances of great strain, the vulnerable can sometimes be better protected and given greater inspiration by those whose moral character is not systematically ordered and stable in the Aristotelian mode. One commanding officer in World War Two was described as being 'as simple as a child and as cunning as a Maori dog' – human dispositions are not always arranged neatly proportionate one to another and the domination of two apparently incompatible features of character over others may be more likely to inspire trust and be more effective than virtues in an Aristotelian rational order.

The idea that virtues may be effective in one context and not in another is profoundly un-Aristotelian since, in Aristotle's view, a virtue is not a skill which works only in one sphere of life. This makes subjects acutely vulnerable to the moral character of those who rule – rule *is* a sphere of life in which some virtues may have to be suspended temporarily. This does not commit Aristotle to the recognition, familiar to us, that intelligence may be used for evil purposes or to the view that virtue can unproblematically coexist with vice, but it does raise the possibility that in exercising responsible rule the Aristotelian ruler must to some degree sever the connection between practical wisdom and virtue. Victims of hard choices may then face a widening gap between intelligence and rectitude, depending on the ruler's perception of the severity, intransigence and persistence of the political problem. In the absence of constraints, subjects face the risk of increasing admirable immorality by rulers who consider intelligence sufficient for success. Taking a hostage to release a hostage, countering a bribe with a bribe, or a threat with a threat, are all possibilities opened up in theory by Aristotle's defence of the ruse of deception, and taken collectively they separate political intelligence from virtue, so increasing the risks for subjects that they will themselves become victims if a specific outcome demands it. In this way, Aristotle is silenced by Machiavelli.

The Aristotelian ruler does not claim to be right all the time – practical wisdom is, in Taylor's phrase, 'a not fully articulable sense rather than a kind of science'.[21] But from the standpoint of those who may be the unwarranted victims of dirty hands decisions, this disclaimer is hardly enough. Now the Aristotelian ruler must shift from a moral to a juridical persona. A constitutional structure of rights and duties is a necessary framework of rules for establishing a limit beyond which rulers may not go and to which subjects can appeal in cases of unjustifiable wrongdoing. Good judges certainly mesh legal rules with perceptions of particular circumstances, but Aristotelian rulers cannot adapt universal to particular in the same way; their ends are political ends, not bound by exclusively legal considerations. Dirty hands decisions require of rulers a minimum recognition, first, of the harm which is caused to those who are their innocent victims, and, second, the awareness that harm may have to be unlicensed. What counts in the Aristotelian understanding of political rationality is neither the maximizing of individual preferences along a single scale nor a pragmatic intelligence devoid of virtue, but a minimum recognition of the importance to human beings of moral virtue in circumstances of political complexity and how this is tested in the problem of dirty hands. Reconstructed in the modern context, Aristotle's presuppositions and aims are more elusive: how in relation to political morality can a version of Aristotelianism be vindicated?

It would be impossible for readers of *After Virtue* and *Whose Justice? Which Rationality?* not to be aware of MacIntyre's sensitivity to the conceptual problems involved in reclaiming Aristotle in conditions of modernity. To engage with Aristotle requires in MacIntyre's view a necessary recognition of Aristotle's historical specificity. What MacIntyre does not find acceptable in Aristotle's ethics is its assumption that a telos of human flourishing can be elucidated so as to encompass the deep modern disagreement about the virtues and their place in life. That such virtues had their home in the 'now-long-vanished context'[22] of the Greek city-state means we must find a conceptually convincing way of relocating them. For MacIntyre, Aristotle's belief in the unity of the virtues and his abiding fear of stasis to an important extent diminish the permanent significance of conflict in human life. MacIntyre writes, 'it is through conflict and sometimes only through conflict that we learn what our ends and purposes are.'[23]

Nevertheless, MacIntyre does consider that 'Aristotle's account of practical reasoning is in essentials surely right.'[24] Given Aristotle's view that 'political wisdom and practical wisdom are the same state of mind,'[25] we should expect MacIntyre's defence of Aristotle to contain powerful implications for the nature of rule and its relation to moral character. Practical reason allows a margin of flexibility within which judgement is to be equitably exercised. Such rulers will be aware of differences between goods which have an absolute value and goods whose worth is relative to time, place and circumstance. In short, practical wisdom as 'a rule and a measure'[26] keeps the dilemmas of political morality in check. Seen from this Aristotelian perspective Weber's analysis of ethics and politics does not in fact leave politics stranded between the Sermon on the Mount and realpolitik. Practical wisdom contains sufficiently strong exclusion clauses to allow us to identify what kind of failure has occurred in, for example, Weber's reference to lack of objectivity as the *locus classicus* of political error; or when he refers to the political 'boss' whose obsession with power 'leads nowhere and is senseless';[27] or to that vanity which prevents the sense of distance which Weber sees as essential to sound political judgement. Walzer's image of the moral politician who 'is not too good for politics and ... is good enough'[28] ignores the ways Aristotle's understanding of practical wisdom can modify the starkly opposed alternatives Walzer's image contains. The Aristotelian notion of practical wisdom as linked with moral character provides a language of rule which avoids the abstractions necessarily contained in the modern vocabularies of utility and rights. MacIntyre's vindication of Aristotle works.

This advance creates a significant complexity. MacIntyre's defence of Aristotelian practical wisdom has been shown to have a close bearing on what it means to rule well and qualifies specific accounts of what it is to have dirty hands in politics. But can this be done without addressing Aristotle's claims regarding the human good as such? Is it possible to identify political wisdom without those goods which Aristotle takes to be essential for human flourishing? For MacIntyre, 'the activity of the skillful, but unvirtuous achiever is always parasitic upon the activity of those who by the exercise of the virtues sustain the practice in which he or she participates.'[29] Thus dissimulation for a morally desirable political end, a temporary suspension of a moral imperative, must always pay tribute to virtue valued for its own sake. But can this be elucidated independently of the moral telos which Aristotle takes to be the end of human life? In order to keep policy-making within morally tolerable bounds must we have an account of the moral purpose of the political community itself? MacIntyre recognizes, of course, that answers to this question variously reflect the plurality of standpoints in moral and political life, and, indeed, the problem raised here appears to threaten the Aristotelian project.

But it is not just because we lack agreement on the conditions which Aristotle claims are essential for morally decent rule that such conditions may actually be unrealizable. Rulers must be virtuous and have the rational capacity to identify just ends and assess competing choices; they must have external goods – money and property – to provide the leisure needed for wise reflection; they must be in good health and avoid misfortune both in terms of external hazard and the ill-luck which is found in badly formulated projects. For Jacques Maritain, however, this aim is simply impossible for human beings. So 'our moral life, all our effort and striving towards rightness and virtue, are suspended from an End which, in fact, eludes us, vanishes within our grasp';[30] this is for Maritain 'the first defeat suffered by Aristotelian ethics'.[31] In this way, dirty hands signifies the strain which is placed on political agents by the existence of multiple goods which cannot be satisfied without loss. It is true that practical wisdom on occasion can check the intractability of some dilemmas, but generally it yields to 'the perception of qualitative hetero-geneity',[32] between virtue and virtue, good and circumstance, virtue and good, on which Aristotelian agents pride themselves. The variety of independent excellences pursued in the Aristotelian good life means greater conflict and perplexity for those who attempt to pursue them. At the limits of justification of choice there will be increased arbitrariness and at the point of connection between intention and outcome there will be greater indeterminacy. Practical wisdom, which Aristotle thinks of as a skill for the reduction of complexity, appears to succeed only in increasing it.

MacIntyre's revised Aristotelianism must therefore supply, first, an account of the telos of human life, which has been wrecked in modernity; second, a method of vindicating this telos in Aristotelian terms, even though such terms will not be those used by Aristotle; and, third, recognize the permanent existence in human life of moral and political conflicts which cannot be explained exhaustively by reference to flaws in character or defective political structures. Aristotle's teleology of politics can respond to the Weberian demarcation of political morality only at the high cost of increased perplexity and uncertainty. MacIntyre reads Weber as supplying 'the key to much of the modern age';[33] can MacIntyre's revised Aristotelianism avoid perplexity and still provide an effective response to Weber's view of political morality as being ultimately a matter of existential choice – 'one cannot prescribe to anyone whether he should follow an ethic of absolute ends or an ethic of responsibility, or when the one and when the other'?[34]

The turn towards practice in MacIntyre's thought is the initial stage in the development of what he calls 'the core conception of virtue';[35] it is followed successively by the ideas of narrative order, and a moral tradition, each stage playing a necessary part in the moral telos which MacIntyre aims to recover.

The shift to practices as an anti-Kantian method of grounding virtues is common to both MacIntyre and Oakeshott,[36] both of whom interestingly claim a degree of Aristotelian authority for this strategy. As Rorty points out, however, this move 'makes it impossible to think that there is something which stands to my community as my community stands to me, some larger community called "humanity" which has an intrinsic nature'.[37] If, as MacIntyre claims, practices are arenas within which new ends and means arise but have no substantive ends of their own, we must ask how, apart from an unwanted utilitarian adjustment, ends and means can be scrutinized in a way both adequate to the criteria of the practice and effective for the moral aim at hand.

The range and depth of conflict here are, of course, considerable. MacIntyre refers to T. E. Lawrence[38] as someone caught up in a situation where his commitments pull in different ways, someone for whom the search for a morally authoritative 'outside' is, in fact, ultimately self-destroying. Arendt, too, is concerned with the nature of Lawrence's predicament. For her it signifies the problematic character of moral sincerity in the context of modern politics – Lawrence was a party to multiple betrayals and false allegiances – 'never again was the experiment of secret politics made more purely by a more decent man.'[39] Lawrence's failure may be emblematic of modern insecurity: if there is no way of reconciling competing goods at the level of practices, what can prevent the reappearance 'of the modern self with its criterionless choices'?[40]

This question reappears in MacIntyre in a different way - if we have no telos of human life as such, we have no rational way of ordering different virtues or deciding at what point a virtue such as patience ceases to be admirable and becomes a simple failure to identify incapacity or stupidity. MacIntyre asks whether patience always requires that we wait on a particular person or activity or whether there are certain situations – 'if the material is just too refractory, the pupil too slow, the negotiations too frustrating'[41] – in which we should 'give up in the interests of the practice itself'.[42] The idea of a practice must place some limit on agents' choices and, *a fortiori*, on the choices open to those who face the quandaries of political morality. But without some conception of a telos we cannot discriminate sufficiently between the virtues when they conflict and we cannot take adequate account of the possibility raised by MacIntyre that a virtue like integrity can only be predicated of life treated as a whole.

The account MacIntyre gives of what it means to treat life as a whole brings us to the second stage of the human telos he aims to identify. The unity of a life is found in its narrative course: its goodness is found in those vulnerable attempts human beings make to bring their lives to completion, to discover what sense their lives have, what direction they should take, what priorities they should have. It is a fruitful idea that human conduct can be made intelligible through narrative. How the problems of political morality begin, how they impose burdens on those who are caught up in them, how commitments change circumstances, and how a politically necessary immorality may be survived by a political community are discussed not by reference to an abstract standpoint, but in the narrative of a human life or that of a society. Starting points and endings can both be seen as having immense political significance. Arendt, for example, construes the notion of an origin in relation to natality – a sense of founding or starting anew as a key moment in the political. The redemptive values – mercy, pardon and forgiveness – show how political communities survive or succumb in the face of hard choices by those who rule. 'Human beings', as MacIntyre notes, 'can be held to account for that of which they are the authors; other beings cannot.'[43] Accountability is an essential feature of all but the most straightforward narratives and is suggestive of the idea that narrative is in its essence a democratic mode. The idea of a link between narrative and democracy suggests a richer perspective on the dirty hands problem than that provided by utility or rights-based political philosophies which depend on abstract starting points for their premises. And yet, narrative as a suitable mode for virtuous conduct or political decency does contain serious difficulties.

There is, first, the Sartrean claim that as narrative can only be understood retrospectively it must falsify life. In life we are uncertain about the outcomes of our actions – as Roy Pascal explains Sartre's position, 'we are unsure of effects, and we ignore what is happening elsewhere and in the minds of the people around us.'[44] Now it is certainly true, as MacIntyre points out, that retrospection is at times a condition of intelligibility – 'it is only retrospectively that hopes can be characterised as unfulfilled or battles as decisive'[45] – but is this enough to counter the Sartrean objection? What narrative falsifies on the Sartrean view is the force of contingency in life, the unavoidable presence of accident and the unforeseeable, lacunae and interstices in conduct which retrospection renders overdetermined and overexplained. How can this point be accommodated without slipping into the kind of temporal dislocation which the absence of narrative structure seems to involve? For Gallie,[46] narrative, and the retrospection it must involve, far from denying contingency actually rescues it from isolation, from having no recognizable incorporation in a human life. It may be, of course, that in dirty hands cases the part played by contingency in relating moral intention and political outcome, moral character and political circumstance, will be substantial. But the point of narrative is not to destroy the contingent, but to show how it has meaning.

A second area of difficulty concerns the problem of evaluating rival narratives.[47] Why should a narrative expressed in terms of an Aristotelian telos be superior to, say, Machiavelli's political story-telling? It seems question-begging to look to philosophical deficiencies in Machiavelli when his grasp of character, incident, strategy and speech in politics is so substantial and rich. Indeed, Machiavelli's 'I love my native city more than my own soul'[48] can be read as expressing a republican political narrative which over time develops into a tradition of political thinking and action. For Arendt, for example, the problem posed by Machiavelli 'has always been the crucial decision for all who devoted their lives to politics'.[49] Recognition of this real problem of rival narratives is a driving force behind MacIntyre's three-stage conception of virtue.

Third, it may be argued that the retrospection which is essential to narrative limits it as a complete account of political discourse. In Aristotle's view, narration plays a minor role in political language; 'to govern', as Merleau-Ponty writes, 'is to foresee';[50] – 'nobody', Aristotle asserts, 'can "narrate" what has not yet happened.'[51] This gives deliberation *the* crucial political sense – what is deliberated is a course of action to be performed – and it questions the sufficiency of narrative as a mode of political communication. These complexities come about when narrative is considered as a mode of politics. In MacIntyre, of course, it plays a wider role as a necessary stage in the development of virtue. Nevertheless, both narrow and wide lenses focus on the same problem – how can narrative relate past and future judgements?

Moral individuals exercise virtue in the context of practices which exist in time and are, therefore, the bearers of moral traditions. A moral inheritance is a complex amalgam of practice and narrative re-enactment, an amalgam which cannot be identified or maintained by the individual alone. What MacIntyre means by the 'embedding'[52] of virtue is a hierarchy of distinct levels of meaning, ranging from individual actions, institutional and social practices to deeply laid and larger traditions of behaviour. What corrupts traditions, what weakens them, is, primarily, the absence of those moral excellences which have animated MacIntyre's revised Aristotelianism all along – a 'lack of justice, lack of truthfulness, lack of courage, lack of the relevant intellectual virtues'.[53] In so far as a political agent faces a world in which rival traditions clash, in which new ways of behaving are emerging, in which old forms of conduct die out, then, as MacIntyre stresses, a necessary virtue is 'an adequate sense of tradition [which] manifests itself in a grasp of those future possibilities which the past has made available to the present.'[54]

The virtue referred to here is the skill in judgement needed to match specific virtue to situation, enabling the effective pursuit of firmly held beliefs in severe political circumstances. MacIntyre's 'tragic protagonist',[55] whose moral dilemma in disturbed political times is how to act effectively on his principles without abandoning them, does not face an existential choice, devoid of moral resource. What may be drawn on is the narrative of a life and a tradition of moral understanding which give sense both to the virtues and to the way they are made subject to political test. Thus MacIntyre's 'tragic protagonist may behave heroically or unheroically, generously or ungenerously, gracefully or gracelessly, prudently or imprudently'[56] – although he cannot escape historical irony. Here we see the reappearance in uncertain times of the Aristotelian standard of practical wisdom, expressed in regard to future possibilities by political agents who possess the self-awareness and historical discernment necessary for the wise deployment of the tradition of virtue to which they owe their allegiance.

Of course, it is MacIntyre's claim that the politics of the modern world rejects precisely the tradition of the virtues to which this Aristotelianism belongs. The modern world lacks the practical agreement on the nature of justice which Aristotle considers necessary if justice is to be the primary virtue of a political community. Our sense of the dirty hands problem is correspondingly impoverished. To those who understand governing as a technical exercise, the dirty hands problem cannot exist. To those who see politics as the adjustment of means to ends it is a cost open to rational calculation in the same way as any other strategy. MacIntyre believes, however, that 'the Aristotelian tradition can be restated in a way that restores intelligibility and rationality to our moral and social attitudes and commitments.'[57] We have seen what form this takes in relation to political morality; in conclusion, what problems remain?

The first concerns the status of MacIntyre's Aristotelianism. The Thomist view of the relations between politics, the virtues and practical rationality which MacIntyre elucidates in *Whose Justice? Which Rationality?* involves both an indebtedness to, and departure from, Aristotle by incorporating his views on practical rationality into an essentially Christian picture of the virtues and their place in the world. This shift requires an investigation of how a Thomist standpoint in the modern context would address the problems of political morality. For example, MacIntyre acknowledges Aquinas's view that lying is inherently evil, and is not made good by the circumstances in which the lie is told or by any benefit which may be produced by it,[58] but it remains true, nevertheless, that Aquinas was much preoccupied with the distinctions, qualifications and practical exigencies which surround untruths often in times of political emergency. Differences between being silent about the truth and intentional falsehoods, lies made under oath and self-incrimination, between deception and pretence, between a deliberate falsehood and a prudent dissimulation are not matters of interest only in Christian apologetics.[59] They go to the heart of all discussions of political morality because they concern the range of justifiable deceit. We would further need to examine Aquinas's concept of political prudence on the basis of which he argues that 'there is no good counsel either in deliberating for an evil end, or in discovering evil means for attaining a good end';[60] thus, we would need to investigate how Aquinas construes the virtues in relation to caution, how the responsibilities of rule are undermined by negligence and ignorance, and what kinds of consequential costs are disallowed in this view of governing.

The second general problem concerns the nature of political morality when seen from the perspective of *After Virtue*. To ask MacIntyre how political morality is to be conceived philosophically is to require initially an understanding of political morality as a historical phenomenon, gaining its sense from the kinds of conflicts in politics and morality which characterize particular historical contexts. We would be interested in showing how political morality changes in form with the emergence of the modern state – not just changes in the doctrine of reason of state, but in changing understandings of the idea of prerogative, and the attempts to provide a conception of the state which satisfies the requirements of sovereignty and gives a rational formulation of procedural justice and the rights and duties of citizens. MacIntyre's emphasis on the tradition of the virtues and his association of the language of rights with modern individualism does not mean that he is unable to give an account of the perspectives of those who are victims of dirty hands decisions, but it is necessary to ask how virtues and rights are related, how the rights and duties of citizens are related to the requirements of virtuous rule. Thomas Nagel's remark that 'the great modern crimes are public crimes'[61] suggests, however, that in the modern world political morality typically presents itself as a problem of scale, and it might be argued that as a response to this an Aristotelian politics must be inadequate.

Quentin Skinner's reclaiming of republicanism[62] raises a third problematic area, which concerns the relation of political morality to those broad traditions of moral and political thought which provide the intellectual frameworks for its discussion. Towards the close of *Whose Justice? Which Rationality?* MacIntyre distinguishes between one for whom traditions of enquiry are irrelevant to the aim of constructing an impartial standard of rational judgement, and another for whom traditions of thought and action, including those which are alien, are occasions for, and objects of, 'self-recognition and self-knowledge'.[63] This reference has important affinities with MacIntyre's discussion of the idea of a quest for meaning in *After Virtue*,[64] but here I want to bring out its importance for understanding issues in political morality. Caught up in the dilemmas of political morality, what political agents deny in their judgements is as important as the truths those judgements are intended to convey. Political morality pictured in this way must surely be illuminated by precisely the kind of receptivity to traditions which MacIntyre stresses. For example, Melville's *Billy Budd* would seem to find an appropriate interpretive location within the conflict between purity and evil represented respectively by Billy and Claggart, and the strain such a conflict places on Vere as a figure of Aristotelian virtue and experience. But this does not enclose the text within one tradition of interpretation. Merleau-Ponty's remark that 'we do not have a choice between purity and violence but between different kinds of violence'[65] suggests how Vere's dilemma, Billy's goodness and fate, and Claggart's envy may be read as requiring, and setting limits to, political transformation.

The idea of political morality providing a focus for distinct traditions of political thought – liberal, utilitarian, Aristotelian, Marxist – raises a fourth problem, that of the intrinsic complexity of political morality in relation to the different accounts these traditions give of the nature of rule. Aristotle's notion of the complexity of politics, testing human ingenuity, challenging human intelligence and rationality, does not mean that the only significant complexities are those of scale. Political morality involves perplexities which all political communities, of whatever size, which lay claim to any kind of intellectual and moral refinement, must face. Indeed, Aristotle does recognize the difference between a deception intelligently employed for necessary political purposes and a ruse which is merely foolish – 'to have no walls would be as foolish as to choose a site for a town in an exposed country, and to level the heights; or as if an individual were to leave his home unwalled, lest the inmates should become cowards.'[66] In the Aristotelian tradition, too, Aristotle's insistence that 'the conditional action is only the choice of a lesser evil . . . not the foundation and creation of good'[67] is not forgotten and seems to keep the instrumentalities of politics firmly in their place.

However, the intransigence of political morality does not come about because its conflicts are between moral imperatives alone. From an Aristotelian perspective the complexity of politics consists in part in how rule imposes special burdens on moral character, how a political community can on occasion tolerate the suspension of its own moral understanding for its own defence, and how it judges which actions are appropriate in which circumstances. In the Aristotelian tradition political morality does not appear as an intractable dilemma, although there will be times when it comes to that, or more straightforwardly as a conflict between moral principles; for Aristotle the problem of dirty hands is to a significant degree the political one of how anticipation and clear deliberation can avoid, reduce or dispel the situations in which it occurs.

The final problem concerns possible tensions between MacIntyre's defence of practical wisdom and his elucidation of virtue in terms of the three-stage core conception. For example, MacIntyre thinks of ruthlessness as a quality which is linked to practices – there are specific circumstances in which aims cannot be achieved without the kind of unconditional single-mindedness which ruthlessness involves. Ruthlessness is not, however, a virtue because it cannot satisfy the requirements of narrative order and deep reflection on tradition which the search for moral direction and moral telos demands of the virtues. MacIntyre distinguishes ruthlessness from 'the phronetic quality of knowing when to be ruthless',[68] but in relation to political morality this leaves a number of difficulties. Political life is such that the need for ruthlessness cannot be entirely discounted. If ruthlessness means being prepared to set aside the sufferings of others, then there will always be circumstances in politics where this is precisely what is required. Does this mean that ruthlessness is a virtue here? If politics is construed as a Hobbesian practice which aims at collective survival or the achievement of some minimum political good, then ruthlessness is a card which it is open to the phronimos to play. But someone like Odysseus whose political choices are made strategically in accordance with the realities of the situation will play that card when necessary and think nothing of it. Another for whom ruthlessness is neither in moral character nor a tactic willingly engaged may put aside the benefits ruthlessness promises. Another may simply be incapable of ruthlessness in any circumstances.

The ruthlessness of the phronimos – who is ruthless when necessary – is certainly different from that of the tyrant, but in politics, when it is necessary to deal with the evil, the unjust, the ambitious and the base, that 'when necessary' can slip into when beneficial or when advantageous to the individual or the political movement the individual stands for. If politics is not understood as a practice but as a narrative order open to reflection in the fullest Aristotelian sense (what is the best state?), then we need to know how a narrative logic – what it is for a political life to have or lack direction – can limit ruthlessness in the way practical rationality can in the context of practices, and how, in the absence of the full structure of the Aristotelian ethical scheme, a political telos modelled on Aristotle can achieve this. In MacIntyre's diagnosis of modern politics such moral and political values are devoid of traditional support, lack agreement and have no shared application. To show how Aristotelianism can be vindicated requires that we show, first, that *our* world is not entirely morally resourceless, and, second, the task I have attempted here, that Aristotle's political philosophy is not as remote from the problems of political morality as is sometimes thought.

NOTES

1 Aristotle, *Nicomachean Ethics*, trans. W. D. Ross (Oxford, 1940), 1094a 28–9.
2 Alasdair MacIntyre, *After Virtue*, 2nd edn (Duckworth, London, 1985), p. 118.
3 Alasdair MacIntyre, *Whose Justice? Which Rationality?* (Duckworth, London, 1988), p. 107.
4 *After Virtue*, p. 227.
5 R. F. Holland, *Against Empiricism* (Blackwell, Oxford, 1980), p. 135.
6 *Nicomachean Ethics*, 1144a 29.
7 Aristotle, *The Politics*, ed. Stephen Everson (Cambridge University Press, Cambridge, 1988), 1325b 5–8.

8 *Whose Justice? Which Rationality?*, p. 108.
9 *Politics*, 1260a 17.
10 T. H. Irwin, *Aristotle's First Principles* (Clarendon, Oxford, 1988), p. 433.
11 *Nicomachean Ethics*, 1122a 29.
12 Aristotle, *Eudemian Ethics*, trans. J. Solomon (Oxford, 1940), 1121a 12.
13 Ibid., 1250a 33–4.
14 *Nicomachean Ethics*, 1144a 27–8.
15 For mixed acts see ibid., 3.1; see the excellent discussion in Michael Stocker, *Plural and Conflicting Values* (Clarendon, Oxford, 1990), pp. 51–85; for *sophismata* (constitutional tricks or devices) see *Politics*, 1297a35, 1308a2.
16 *Politics*, 1253a 34–6.
17 Ibid., 1308a 28–30.
18 W. L. Newman, *The Politics of Aristotle*, vol. 4 (Clarendon, Oxford, 1902), pp. 386–7; Newman cites Xenophon: 'Confidence breeds carelessness, slackness, disobedience: fear makes men more attentive, more obedient, more available to discipline. The behaviour of sailors is a case in point. So long as they have nothing to fear they are, I believe, an unruly lot, but when they expect a storm or an attack, they not only carry out all orders, but watch in silence for the word of command like choristers' (*Memorabilia*, III, V, 5–6).
19 Ernest Barker, *The Politics of Aristotle* (Clarendon, Oxford, 1946), p. 226.
20 For extensive discussion of Aristotle's priorities here see Richard Kraut, *Aristotle on the Human Good* (Princeton University Press, Princeton, 1989).
21 Charles Taylor, *Sources of the Self* (Cambridge University Press, Cambridge, 1989), p. 125.
22 *After Virtue*, p. 163.
23 Ibid., p. 164.
24 Ibid., p. 161.
25 *Nicomachean Ethics*, 1141b 24.
26 Ibid., 1117b 17–19.
27 Max Weber, 'Politics as a vocation', in *From Max Weber*, ed. H. H. Gerth and C. Wright Mills (Oxford University Press, Oxford, 1958), p. 116.
28 Michael Walzer, 'Political action: the problem of dirty hands', *Philosophy and Public Affairs*, 2 (1973), p. 168.
29 Alasdair MacIntyre, 'Bernstein's distorting mirrors: a rejoinder', *Soundings*, 67 (1984), p. 37.
30 Jacques Maritain, *Moral Philosophy* (Geoffrey Bles, London, 1964), p. 48.
31 Ibid.
32 See Martha C. Nussbaum, *Love's Knowledge: Essays on Philosophy and Literature* (Oxford University Press, Oxford, 1990), p. 67.
33 *After Virtue*, p. 86.
34 Weber, 'Politics as a vocation', p. 127.
35 *After Virtue*, p. 186.
36 See Michael Oakeshott, *On Human Conduct* (Clarendon, Oxford, 1975), p. 110.
37 Richard Rorty, *Contingency, Irony and Solidarity* (Cambridge University Press, Cambridge, 1989), p. 59.
38 *After Virtue*, p. 201.
39 Hannah Arendt, *The Origins of Totalitarianism*, new edn with added prefaces (Harcourt Brace Jovanovich, New York, 1973), p. 218.
40 *After Virtue*, p. 202.
41 Ibid.
42 Ibid.
43 Ibid., p. 209.

44 Roy Pascal, 'Narrative fictions and reality', *Novel*, 11 (1977), pp. 40–50, at p. 40; see the discussion of the issues raised by the Sartrean claim in Frank Kermode, *The Sense of an Ending* (Oxford University Press, Oxford, 1979).

45 *After Virtue*, p. 212.

46 W. B. Gallie, *Philosophy and the Historical Understanding* (London, 1964), p. 41; see also Pascal, 'Narrative fictions and reality', pp. 45–6.

47 This second difficulty may be extended to cover the separate problem of how to detect hidden or secret meanings within narrative discourse.

48 Alan Gilbert (ed.), *The Letters of Machiavelli* (New York, 1961), no. 225.

49 Hannah Arendt, *On Revolution* (Faber, London, 1963), p. 290.

50 Maurice Merleau-Ponty, *Humanism and Terror*, trans. with notes by John O'Neill (Beacon, Boston, 1969), p. xxxiii.

51 Aristotle, *Rhetoric*, 1417b 12; see the discussion in Ronald Beiner, *Political Judgement* (Methuen, London, 1983), pp. 89–91.

52 *After Virtue*, p. 222.

53 Ibid., p. 223.

54 Ibid.

55 Ibid., p. 224.

56 Ibid.

57 Ibid., p. 259.

58 *Whose Justice? Which Rationality?*, pp. 203–4.

59 For a discussion of this see Perez Zagorin, *Ways of Lying, Dissimulation, Persecution and Conformity in Early Modern Europe* (Harvard University Press, London, 1990), pp. 28–31.

60 *Summa Theologica*, II-II, Q.51, art. 1.

61 Thomas Nagel, 'Ruthlessness in public life', in *Public and Private Morality*, ed. Stuart Hampshire (Cambridge University Press, Cambridge, 1978), p. 75.

62 Quentin Skinner, 'The republican ideal of political theory', in *Machiavelli and Republicanism*, ed. Gisela Bock, Quentin Skinner and Maurizio Viroli (Cambridge University Press, Cambridge, 1990), p. 308.

63 *Whose Justice? Which Rationality?*, p. 394.

64 *After Virtue*, p. 219.

65 Merleau-Ponty, *Humanism and Terror*, p. 109; see *After Virtue*, p. 238, for MacIntyre's explicit contrast between Jacobinism and Aristotelianism as modes of re-establishing the idea of public virtue.

66 *Politics*, 1331a 5–10.

67 Ibid., 1332a 17–18.

68 *After Virtue*, p. 275.

4

MacIntyre and Aquinas

Janet Coleman

This paper is arranged in two parts, the first of which tries to outline some of the basic tenets of Thomas Aquinas's ethical theory and the foundations on which it rests. This outline is attempted because I want, thereafter, to examine whether Alasdair MacIntyre adequately presents Thomism as it stands, not only as a theological philosophy written in the thirteenth century but as it was meant to be, a universal explanation of how things are for mankind throughout history. I am less interested in what appears to have been MacIntyre's personal itinerary from Aristotelian to Thomist, although I think the changes are more apparent than real, than in his interesting assertions not only that Thomism provides social and political humans with a preferred and inclusive systematic account of the ways things really are for us, but that Thomism deserves serious consideration in liberal societies where other traditions of discourse have, until now, been dominant.

In *After Virtue* MacIntyre outlined a history of apparently incompatible and changing notions of virtue as these related to changing social orders from Homer, to Aristotle, the New Testament, Aquinas, to Jane Austen and the modern liberalism of Ben Franklin and beyond. He asked: can we disentangle from these rival versions a unitary core concept of the virtues? He believed we could and so sought to give an account of a unitary core which would be more compelling than *any* of the rival versions discussed.[1] This was a deceptive way of putting it, because his new account was an attempt to provide the revised account of an already discussed version – the Thomist and therefore Aristotelian account of virtues as 'practices' with a telos or goal which transcends any of the limited ends of particular practices by encompassing a whole human life.[2]

In *Three Rival Versions of Moral Enquiry* he went on to sketch two incompatible and opposing rival versions of morality, which he called the Nietzschean genealogical approach and the abstract and unitary rationalist approach of Encyclopaedists, opposing these to a third view, made explicit in the papal encyclical letter *Aeterni Patris* (1879) which 'summoned its readers',[3] as MacIntyre puts it correctly, to a renewal of the Thomist tradition, a tradition he believes is lost to modern liberal society, but a tradition which he partially and indirectly outlined in *After Virtue*. That *Aeterni Patris summoned* rather than *invited* readers to look again at a unified tradition of thought completed in the thirteenth century is of crucial significance to this discussion because MacIntyre takes considerable trouble to address the problems of progress in history and does not want to argue that Aquinas was brilliant in his own time but cannot enter the twentieth century with any coherence. But as we shall see, MacIntyre does not believe that those not already educated in a tradition of practices, here, it seems, of Catholicism as it has been shaped not only by Aquinas but by the historical, institutional Church, are in a position to judge of its intelligibility.[4] As I see it, the problem with MacIntyre's immensely stimulating account is his understanding of human practices that are determined by the standards achieved 'so far' by historically situated practitioners, an understanding of human excellence that is open to change but that is determined by authorities at a particular time,[5] rather than human excellence being determined by a timeless definition of what constitutes the essence of human nature in its existence.

My aim in what follows is to clarify what I take to be Aquinas's positions in order to highlight what I see as MacIntyre's divergence from both Aristotle and Aquinas in his discussion of traditions which encompass a multiplicity of practices with a multitude of ends.[6] By knowingly altering certain aspects of Aristotle's discussion of the virtues as means to ends, MacIntyre has, I think, distorted Aristotle *and Aquinas*[7] in order to address what he sees as certain liberal dilemmas, not least the existence of incommensurable value systems accepted by pluralist societies. There is little time here to treat whether or not MacIntyre adequately describes liberalism. My purpose is, in the first instance, to examine whether he adequately presents Aquinas's philosophical theology and the Aristotelianism on which it is based. I contend that he misunderstands how an Aristotelian and a Thomist regard definitions which grasp the natures of things absolutely, so that his discussion of historical practices and traditions is neither Aristotelian nor Thomist. Lastly, I ask whether, as a consequence of finding Thomism satisfying as we well might, we need to conclude that liberal principles are to be rejected as MacIntyre claims.

Let us begin with the question: how do you have to see the world and come to know it as it purportedly is if you are to call yourself a Thomist? This question – what is reality like and how do we know it as it is, constituted one of the major thirteenth-century scholastic set questions with which every university student and teacher had to deal. Aquinas's *Summa Theologiae* was an encyclopaedic exposition of an agenda of questions and answers that he did not himself set. Throughout his works MacIntyre has made Aquinas sound more unique and even marginal to the scholastic enterprise than he was. But Aquinas systematized the questions and answers given by others and himself in a more thorough way than did most of his contemporaries, and in that systematization he was able to include more answers linked to one another and thereby fitting into a whole than anyone else in his generation. This achievement, and it was extraordinary, was only possible, I believe, because Aquinas was a tremendously sophisticated Aristotelian, being as he was a member of that first generation to have nearly all of Aristotle's works available to him in Latin translation. In terms of man's purpose and the means to its achievement in *this* life, Aristotle had provided the full analysis in the *Nicomachean Ethics* (preceded by his various works on logic and epistemology) and Aquinas absorbed it completely. To become so astute a commentator on Aristotle in the second half of the thirteenth century you had to make a choice that many intellectuals had not yet explicitly made: the choice was between being a Christian Platonist or a Christian Aristotelian, and Platonism was by far the more fundamental and long-lived underpinning of Christian philosophy and theology from the time of the early Church Fathers – especially Augustine – until Aquinas's own lifetime. Aquinas and his Dominican Order chose Aristotle and he and they would suffer for it at the hands of contemporary Franciscan Platonists. Christian Aristotelianism of the Thomist and subsequent varieties would continue to be opposed by Christian Platonism well beyond the thirteenth century, not least by its variant in Lutheran Protestantism and its legacy into the eighteenth century and beyond. My view is that Aquinas's Aristotelianism subsumed the then current Platonism of Augustine's philosophical theology into an account that was incommensurable with Platonism, and Aquinas's account thereby denatured Augustine's insights rather than, as MacIntyre would have it, combined an Aristotelian philosophy with an Augustinian theology in one overarching and more satisfying and inclusive vision.[8]

Reality and the Universality of Thought

When Aristotle and Aquinas following him speak about reality they assume that nature, that is the natural world, the cosmos, and man as part of that natural whole, is somehow ordered to natural ends. Human beings are part of a reality that is given, ordered, not chaotic or unknowable, and humans happen to think about it and then talk about what they think about. Both Aristotle and Aquinas believe that it makes no difference to the reality or occurrence of a thing whether when one person has affirmed that it will happen, another should have denied it. As Aquinas says in explaining Aristotle's *Perihermenias*, I, 14.4 (*Categories*):

> things will be the same whether this has been affirmed or denied since the course of reality or something's existing or not existing does not change just because of our affirming or denying. This is because it is not the truth of our indicative sentences that causes reality but rather reality causes the truth of our statements. So it makes no difference to what is happening now whether somebody affirmed or denied it a thousand years ago or indeed ever.[9]

Aquinas interprets Aristotle as having argued correctly from the truth about things to the truth about indicative sentences,[10] so that truth in expressions is related to the way things are or are not in reality. An expression is true or false according to whether what it refers to exists or not.[11] Whereas some interpret Aristotle to be speaking of an ordered reality as it appears to humans and that therefore Aristotle's account of what there is is an anthropocentric one, believing as he probably did that all we can *say* about what there is is what there is for *us*, Aquinas takes the observation that we experience the world and then think about what we experience in terms of cause and effect to be evidence that we are enclosed in a meaningful whole which extends *beyond* our intellectual capacities to grasp this whole solely through the efforts of self-motivated thinking. But both Aristotle and Aquinas accept that reality is fixed and ordered and is as it is and also that humans share a particularly human way of thinking about what there is so that there is a species-specific uniformity in how we know what there is to know. At the level of conceptualizing reality, human thinkers know the same universals and this demonstrates to both thinkers that there is a universal language of thought that is species specific, prior to any conventionally established language, be it written or spoken.[12]

For both, however, all our conceptualization, all our general knowledge has its origin in sense experience. Both insist on the importance of 'observation' by the senses as the origin of our knowledge. But they do not hold as do empiricists that this is the end of whatever knowledge we can have. For both Aristotle and Aquinas the human intellect has knowledge whose origin is in sensing, but such knowledge is not limited to the manipulation and combination of concepts derived from sense particulars. Intellect is active and acts in ways specific to it.

Furthermore, Aquinas like Aristotle assumes there is some kind of unconscious metaphysics that humans as humans share and use when they know things and that this is presupposed in our subsequent descriptive theories of knowing.[13] Epistemology rests on a prior unconscious metaphysics; the logic of thinking and speaking rests on a metaphysics. What does this mean?

For Aquinas there is a notion of actual existence that is more basic than logical existence. Whenever we say that something exists in the sense of 'is true' or 'is the case', or that there is something that belongs to the kind we are talking about, there is a prior sense of being which is implied which is akin to 'is there or alive'. Aquinas notes that the Latin verb *esse* can be used to express existence in many ways. But beyond what is or can be named truly is actual existence. For both Aristotle and Aquinas actual existence is intuited as a first principle that is indemonstrable; or as Aristotle puts it in the *De Interpretatione*, 'the necessary and not necessary are first principles of everything's either being or not being and it is clear that what is of necessity is in actuality, so that if things which always are, are prior, then also actuality is prior to capability [possibility].'[14] Now not all things necessarily are. But, we ask, what kinds of 'things' always and necessarily are and so are actual existents in their own right?

We can best answer this by recalling that anyone in the thirteenth-century university began his studies with grammar and logic based on late antique Latin grammarians and Aristotle's logical writings, which had already achieved centrality in the arts course well before the thirteenth century and the beginnings of universities. Aquinas, like many others of his time, but not all, insisted that naming does not have signification by nature; nouns or names are conventionally imposed, thinking came before grammars, but conventional signification does fit the natures of things.[15] Every name (where a name or noun like 'man' is predicated, as a universal, of many) signifies some determinate nature, for instance human being, and there needs to be an individual in the mind as a concept to which the name or noun refers, the concept itself referring to something in the world.[16] Nouns for Aristotle and Aquinas signify first our concepts and thereafter the world, and such signification is *without time* so that it makes no difference to the truth of a sentence at what time a name or noun is applied. Nouns or names are conventionally and historically imposed but are ahistorical in their signification; they signify something as if it were something that exists in its own right. For Aquinas that which exists in its own right is an actual existent, not merely a logical existent, and such an actual existent is a genuine individual, a human being or any other individual substance that is a something. Nothing can just be, it must be a something even though something that exists actually can come to exist in another way: a stone as a something can become a statue as a something else. Like Aristotle, Aquinas distinguishes between that which exists potentially and that which exists actually. For a particular something to be a something it must have the (universal) nature of all somethings named by the noun.

Natures and Definitions

Now when nouns as conventionally established signifiers of the natures of things do their job, just what kind of 'thing' are they signifying to be a thing's nature? Aquinas starts from reality rather than from language and says that there is a something in virtue of which Socrates or any other named individual is a human being. The essence or nature of man, human nature, is not a Platonic form separable from individuals; natures do not float separately in or above the world. Aquinas insists that it is useful to speak of the nature of a thing but not as a something which we extract and display and point to as a thing, but rather the form or essence or nature of a thing is a functional expression signifying, for instance, what being a man is.[17] Human natures are actual only when they exist in an individual who actually exists and acts in a peculiarly human way. We can speak of human nature as a consequence of observing the capacities of and tendencies in human behaviour, behaviour that is not simply moved by unconscious drives that men share with lower animals, but behaviour that is voluntarily undertaken, deliberated upon, thought of and actively chosen to achieve certain goals or ends. It is by observing human tendencies, acts, 'practices' that we grasp the nature of what it is to be human and, therefore, are able to give a definition of what is human. This definition does not change over time. No definitions change over time for Aristotle or Aquinas and this is what MacIntyre seems to have omitted in his discussion of practices, which, he says 'never have a goal or goals fixed for all time'.[18] For Aristotle and Aquinas a definition is 'a set of words [*logos*] which indicates the essence [of a subject]'.[19] Hence, the nature of definition is a mirror in conventional language of the nature of essence. It is fundamental to Aristotle and to Aquinas that a single definition is possible, that it has no history, and when one gives a definition – of man or doctor – one is predicating a genus of a subject, one is placing the thing to be defined in a genus and adding the differentiae. For Aristotle genus and differentiae are among those things that are without qualification more intelligible and so absolutely universal,[20] and therefore the elements of a definition must be prior and more intelligible absolutely than any subject whose essence is thereby expressed. This realist understanding of definition is fundamental to Thomism. For Aquinas there can only be one definition of a subject and in describing the fixed and universal nature of a thing which is timeless and not open to historical alteration, we are allowing definition to function by providing us with unitary subjects of discourse. What being a doctor is is not determined by a historical tradition of practitioners but by the definition of doctor. We shall return to this later.

Now when we observe human capacities and tendencies in order to define human nature we are doing something more than passively observing what happens in acts; Aquinas says we are observing tendencies or intentions that are there and not only created in our minds from constant repeated conjunctions of events. The nature of something is not to be confused with a thing's accidents, a nose being snub or red for instance, and accidents are not existents at all and certainly not in their own right. When we speak of human nature then, we are referring to what is essentially human according to a *definition* of human being, and for Aquinas as for Aristotle, this definition includes a person being a material thing. Humans are composite beings; as a species they have what he calls souls joined to bodies. The essence of human being includes matter but not *this* matter. The nature or essence of the human being is a combination of a life force that is subject to mortality, an unconscious set of natural, biological drives which keep all the individuals alive, fed and procreating, a capacity to desire and to reflect rationally or consciously on experience and deliberately to make choices concerning various means to achieve what are recognized as peculiarly human ends, and even to think beyond ourselves and to conclude that we are not the centre of the universe. All this is actualized, put into active life, when we are born as individual bodies which are constantly changing. Hence, the essence of the human race is made individual in Socrates, whose material body is constantly changing, growing older, balder, fatter, so that Socrates' individual essence, the nature of his humanness, cannot be defined to include this matter now but matter or body in general. Nor is Socrates his intellect; he is a man who wills and knows and acts.

Now anything of a certain kind or essence or nature has the properties, powers and tendencies which belong to that essence and from these follow the thing's specific or essential activities. Aquinas like Aristotle says the only way *we* can describe or think of human capacities and tendencies to act in certain ways is by observing specific performances or practices, and therefore tendencies are described teleologically by means of a series of causes leading to an end which is implicitly or explicitly grasped by the agent prior to the performance.[21] I shall say something more about this teleology later.

Substantial Form and Individuals

One last concept needs to be explained, that of substantial form, before
we can proceed to Aquinas's discussion of what the world is like and
how we know it as it is. The concept of substantial form is crucial to any
subsequent discussion of whether Aquinas's philosophy can be made
compatible with liberal theories of personal identity. Understanding
Aristotle correctly, Aquinas explains how matter is not anything specific
and separable and different from made-up substances. Matter is not a
kind of thing; indeed he says we cannot properly be aware of matter in
itself except by considering change, as Aristotle notes in his *Physics*.[22]
Matter is that in anything which can become something else. At any
time matter will be some substance in virtue of what Aquinas calls some
substantial form; the form is defined as that in virtue of which this lump
of matter is a substance of this kind and not of another kind. According
to Aquinas the substantial form of humans as well as of animals is the
psyche or soul. Aristotle called it the *entelechy* of the body, entelechy
being the formative principle of the body.[23] Each of us is a human being
in virtue of the substantial form or soul. But what individuates you from
me, what makes us different human beings is that as different individuals
of the same kind we are different lumps of stuff with the same human
form; the form in virtue of which we are human is an individual too,
when individualized in a single person, being the substantial form of this
distinct lump of matter. Matter then, is the principle of individuation.[24]
As a form the substantial form is formally identical with all others of
the kind, so that in so far as we are human we are not different from one
another; our difference is in the fact that we are different lumps of
matter that are informed by a human psyche, which has no gender as
such. Matter is not, then, a this something except in virtue of its form
by which it comes actually to exist. As was said, nothing can just be, it
always must be a something and what it is is a substantial form immattered
in this individual. Note the difference between a substantial form of a
distinct lump of matter, which is Socrates, and the nature or essence of
Socrates which functionally defines what his being a human is, which
includes Socrates having a body but not this body now. The nature of
humanness is not the peculiarly human soul. The nature of humanness
is a certain way of acting and tending in the world, which is grasped by
its definition.

If we now turn to Aquinas's discussion of human nature in relation
to how each of us lives our lives, a discussion which is elaborated especially in the central parts of the *Summa*, we shall see that he presents a
massively impressive recapitulation of themes and variations on Aristotle's

Categories, De Interpretatione, Topics, the *De Anima* and, as a consequence of a discussion of psyche, he shows it working in the world of Aristotle's *Nicomachean Ethics.* Aquinas wrote the middle parts of the *Summa* about the same time as he wrote his commentaries on the *Ethics* and it seems to me that what he does is agree with Aristotle but he also goes beyond him but only where the Greek left certain issues undecided in the final, tenth book.

Perception and Conception

Aquinas provides a coherent re-presentation of Aristotle's discussion of perception and conceptualization in the *De Anima* when he treats the question: how can we ever think conceptually of our sensual experiences?[25] How do we intellectually respond to what we feel? It is not a question of how sense data get into our heads from outside, but rather a discussion of what has to happen in us when we are affected by the world. In short, what is called the sensitive part of the soul is caused to change by objects which it apprehends or perceives. The cause is outside but the alteration is inside. In response to the material characteristics or external accidents of external things, the psyche's senses and imagination set up an outline or image of the thing. As Aristotle explained, sensing and imaging are re-presentations according to the capacity of sense perception. It all happens within the soul, which is diffused throughout the body, and an image is set up which is like the thing sensually experienced out there. Aquinas says as does Aristotle that it is not necessary that a likeness have the same manner of existing as that of which it is a likeness. Through the soul's sense powers we are aware of an individual thing through our sense organs having been affected by something's determinate dimensions, colour, etc., but these are not *in* the sensitive soul as colours etc. but as their representations. But to say that someone has an image or likeness of what his organs have experienced is not to say he *knows* what he experiences. For to know or be intellectually aware of something is to have a concept, a thought, a form which is universal like the concept man. When we think intellectually we think in terms of the inmost *nature* of that *kind* of thing which is to be found in the individuals sensed. We think about natures of things and we sense particulars. This means that when we think we have an immaterial awareness of material things. Our thoughts are *of* the world by means of representative likenesses; the intellect is aware of the nature or essence of a thing by means of its likeness, which is its own medium of awareness, a creation of intellect in response to what there is beyond itself. We think of the nature, the form, the essence and its tendencies as something existing in flesh and bone but not in this flesh or these bones. When we think we think in kinds and their tendencies to behave in specific ways, and this means that for Aquinas mind cannot be aware directly of the individual as a material thisness. So too for Aristotle the mind gets involved with individuals coincidentally as a consequence of our sensing particulars. The only way *we* can be aware of anything and think about it is by first having sensed it; but thinking is not sensing, although they are related.

When the intellect forms natures as conceptual likenesses of things, it then goes on to judge the thing it has grasped, this judgement being its own activity and not found in things. The first judgement made is as to whether something exists or does not. Intellectual judgement is characterized as the formation of *definitions* the correct or incorrect application to reality of which decides whether the definition is true or false. The true is a match of thing and intellect.[26] But we must remember that there is a difference between the way things exist and the way we as humans come to know them. We have to start from the senses; that is simply how we operate in the world. But the real, as actual existents, already is whether or not we perceive it or affirm it or deny it. Reality comes before us. Following Aristotle's *Metaphysics*, Aquinas then places the things of nature as existents before the divine intellect, that is, the creator cause of there being the kinds of existents that there are. Existents are true according to their match first with the divine intellect, by which is meant that they fulfil what is ordained for them by a first ordering cause of what there is. Hence, if we then go on to ask whether our thoughts are congruent with the world, the answer for Aquinas is that they certainly can be but the truth of existents does not depend on their relation to the human intellect and its ways of coming to know. Aquinas and Aristotle both insist that all our knowledge arises originally from our knowledge of the first unprovable somehow intuited principles concerning existence, and it is an *awareness* of these principles that *arises* in us from the senses.[27] We are part of what there is, not outside it or over it, and we exist in a manner that is peculiar to being human in a world in which other things exist according to their own natures.

Aquinas believes as does Aristotle that our awareness starts with the senses, so we are more easily aware of the things that are more available to the senses. But by nature things are more easily known which are by nature more fit for our awareness and these are the things that are most existent and most actual.[28] These are less available to our senses. Naturally we think in universals but we sense particulars and what links these parallel but interrelated capacities to sense and to think is the soul's representative likenesses from corporeal images to universal concepts or natures which are judged existent and actual by reason.

According to Aquinas, human beings are naturally appreciative of human good and evil as a natural consequence of our rationality, by which he means our being able to think in the way he describes. Hence the object of reason is the true universally[29] and we saw that the true expresses a relation between an existent and some thinking mind. When we reason we move from principles naturally known, which does not mean innate but does mean universal natures, existing or not existing, to particulars – that is we think deductively. The reason we can conceptualize in the first place is because we first experience things sensually. But once we have thought, we turn back, as it were, from the concept of dog to Fido represented in our imaginations.[30] When the intellect conceptualizes it does not perceive of our existence only under the aspect of 'now' as do the senses but rather it conceptualizes existence absolutely, without qualification, existence in general. When humans grasp existence without qualification, Aquinas says there is then set in motion a desire to exist without qualification.[31] Hence we can define complete human well-being as continuous and perpetual existence. *Here is the nub of the issue.* Taking Aristotle's definition of *eudaimonia* as the human end for which all other things are done, the ultimate object of human desire to be achieved through a series of means ordered to a given species-specific end, Aquinas says that because of the way intellect thinks, humans conceive of and then desire immortality. But this desired end is not achievable as we are mortal and mortality is part of the definition of human nature. In our present life complete well-being is impossible; we cannot live forever. But there is, as there is for Aristotle, a well-being which *is* possible in this life which is distinctly human and therefore mortal and it is realized only when a human being continues peculiarly human good performances or practices as a human being throughout his whole life.[32] Well-being then, in this life, is a series of end-related performances specific to human beings according to excellences judged in accord with a completely human life. A completely human life is not one lived by lurching from one impulse to another, one unconsciously determined preference to another. Nor is a completely human life lived in accord with standards historically established by cultures or by practitioners admired by certain cultures and taken as authorities, as MacIntyre seems to think.

Knowing and Willing

Human souls or psychologies can be spoken of in two ways, one of which emphasizes our capacity to be aware and another our capacity to desire.[33] Now Aristotle defined the good in the *Ethics* as that which all things desire so that the object of our desire is simply the good. But the object of our awareness is defined as the true, by which is meant that we become aware, as we have seen, when the thinker creates a representative but universal likeness of what he has sensually experienced. The existent should match the intellectual conception of it for it to be true. Those things not perceived by the senses cannot be grasped by the human intellect in the way it grasps things through representative universal thought, and this means for Aquinas that God cannot be grasped essentially, in his nature, by human minds operating normally.[34] What is the relation between these two ways of speaking about the soul's powers, its awareness and its desire? As Aristotle said, everything in nature moves and acts for an end that is its good, since by definition the end of something acting naturally is the result of natural appetite. But do we, can we desire something before we have some intellectual grasp of its nature – even if we then judge it wrongly? No. It is the intellect which moves the appetites by first proposing their objects to them.[35] There is thereafter an intellectual appetite which is called the will, what Aristotle called *prohairesis*, and it in turn moves the sense appetites of passion, what Aristotle called *orexis*. We have to want to or will to obey our passions; we do not *as humans* simply act on passionate impulse alone. And the object proposed to us as desirable is first grasped by intellect. Once the will (intellectual appetite) consents to its proposed object, the sense appetites then move the body.

Hence, in order to act in a way that is fully human it is not the sense appetites that need training but the will, the intellectual appetite, and this means that training unconsidered habits, becoming acculturated to a tradition, is insufficient for one to act truly humanly. One must be aware of what one does, what one desires and its purpose. As Aristotle says, social laws that are rational *can* be considered coercive in the training of the young but someone who voluntarily does what a rational law commands actually does something that is natural to what being a man fully means.[36] As Aquinas puts it: only those actions of man are properly called human which are characteristic of man as man (and not man as animal). The difference between man and irrational creatures is that humans are masters of their actions, through reason and will, through thinking and desiring and acting on these in a peculiarly human way, that is through free judgement of choice. Actions deliberately willed are properly called human and actions are willed because their end or purpose has been thought of.[37] Every agent acts for an end, even non-intellectual agents; an agent does not move unless it intends an end and the determination of an end by rational agents is made by the rational desire or will rather than by biological impulse or instinct. Men apprehend an end, they grasp what they are aiming at and they direct themselves there doing this rather than that as means to that end.[38] Hence, acts are called human since they are deliberately willed.[39] The capacity deliberately to will something is what Aquinas means by man being a morally responsible choice-making agent. When a man has a grasp of what it means to be human, not acting on impulse but on reasoned desire, whose natural object is the good universally and absolutely, he acts with an unchanging and timeless rational end in view. Through thinking and experiencing he discovers an already existent truth about ordered reality, a truth that has no historical dimensions.

Reasoning towards what is universally and absolutely true is not an alien command imposed on recalcitrant human nature: rather, it is a consequence of what Aquinas insists is a natural desire in all humans to know the cause of what they see, and thus man by nature desires to know the first cause of all that there is and why it is so. This is God. Not only does experiencing and then reasoning from effect back to cause lead the human mind naturally on a search to find out about beginnings as the ultimate end of all intellectual search. This knowledge of the ultimate end of all enquiry, Aquinas insists, is actually available to all men who are sufficiently reflective to think of the world order as a whole and wonder how it came to be and how it is sustained.[40] Knowledge of the ultimate end of intellectual enquiry – that first cause of all the effects – is not a knowledge of an innate idea. Rather the first cause is the extrinsic end or goal of all rational enquiry. A natural theology which reasons from effects back to cause can show us *some* of the main attributes of what Aquinas calls God, our ultimate end, the first cause of all, but it is just the beginning. It must be supplemented by revelation in Scripture, but it is a necessary and natural beginning. A serious study of natural theology requires a rigorous philosophical training which includes a study of epistemology, logic and their metaphysical underpinnings, a study for which Aquinas says most men have neither leisure nor inclination but for which all have the potential as humans because we have a natural appetite for such knowledge of the true.[41] Given their human natures, humans are capable of being perfected; they can come to know God as the first cause in his very nature but only through divine assistance and not through an intellectual search, because all man's thoughts have their origin in the senses and God essentially, in his nature, cannot be sensed. True human happiness as man's ultimate end therefore exceeds created nature.

It is not clear to me that someone who is not interested in logic, epistemology and philosophy ever gets this far, so that Aquinas's message to MacIntyre's average man is not obvious to me,[42] because it requires not simply that humans have a capacity for reflection but that men actively be reflective about the cause of all effects they experience.

If human happiness is not simply being alive but rather consists in living actively as a human being, actualizing oneself as a deliberating agent with a natural end in view that is given, then intellectually we do naturally seek the true and we naturally will what we desire, our good. An ultimate end must by *definition* absolutely satisfy man's natural desire that there is nothing left for him to desire or know.[43] Aquinas insists there is by nature one ultimate end for all men – to know all the answers and to achieve the satisfaction of all desires. He says all humans agree in desiring the ultimate end since all humans desire their good to be complete, which is what the ultimate end is.[44] That in which this is realized, of course, differs from human to human but there *is* a *suitable* good for humans as such which is their happiness or human well-being and this essentially brings desire to rest, a desire for such an end which is first apprehended by the intellect as the possessing of an essential and present knowledge of God, the cause of all, which man as man cannot achieve through his natural powers.[45]

If man himself *were* his own ultimate good then the consideration and ordering of his actions and passions would be his happiness, ethics would be our end, that is, the cultivation of virtues that enabled us to live a satisfying private and political life. But Aquinas insists that with some effort we are capable of grasping, although not fully, that ultimate human happiness is an extrinsic good, where intellectual searches to know and continuous desiring cease.[46] Man's ultimate perfection has to be through a knowledge of something like but above the human intellect, or, as Aristotle put it at the end of the *Nicomachean Ethics*: 'the activity of God which is supremely happy must be a form of contemplation and among human activities that which is most akin to God's will be the happiest. The life of the gods is altogether happy and that of man is happy in so far as it contains something that resembles the divine activity.'[47] Aquinas says it in his words: 'In man's present state of life his ultimate perfection is in the activity whereby he is united to God but this activity cannot be continual because we are human not divine.'[48] Hence the good we can achieve by ourselves is mixed with sadness and worry that it will be disturbed. Humans cannot have complete and continuous happiness in this life because of what they are – souls in bodies, mortal, rational animals. Accept it, we have no choice as to our natures. 'Hence the Philosopher, when considering man's happiness concludes "we call men happy but as men".' Aquinas adds: 'but God promised us complete happiness when we shall be like the angels in heaven.' And without this promise Aquinas seems to suggest that humans will never be completely at peace because their minds will always be thinking and their wills desiring infinitely. Under such conditions, imperfect social and political happiness is our lot, with intellectual effort, in order that we may be as fully human as we can possibly be. But Aquinas says we want more and we know it. We want immortality and the cessation of desires, we want the end of the search to know the cause of everything absolutely and essentially. If Christ had not appeared, according to Aquinas, we would simply have to accept that we die at the end of all this intellectual effort and activity in which we must as humans engage anyway. There may indeed be two ends for man, one in this life as a full human being and in the next as saved, but Aquinas never argues that *unless* we make that effort to be fully human we will not be rewarded with heaven where there is an end of desire and intellectual search.

In other words, the social, moral and political realm as described by Aquinas looks remarkably the same as Aristotle's whether we believe in a Christian revealed God or not. The metaphysic remains, the teleology remains, the placing of humanness in a hierarchy of ordered existents even remains back to perhaps an extrinsic initiating cause, and then we do politics, where we are constantly reminded from social experience how we are not alone but interdependent, economically but more importantly psychologically and morally: in this life we need friends. We come to see that there are all these other humans requiring optimum environments in which to express their natures, their peculiarly human acts and tendencies according to their individual talents and their willingness (or not) to assume social responsibility for the general good. This general good all men *can* naturally see because that is what conceptualization and willing are: the activities of thinking a mind's natural object – the unqualified and universally true; and the activity of desiring the will's natural object – the universal and unqualified good.[49] As Aristotle says in *Metaphysics*, Z 3, 1029b 3–12: 'intellectual advance occurs when, starting from what *we* find intelligible, we come to find intelligible that which is so without qualification.' But thinking is not doing. You have to follow through on your thought by means of intentional acts to be human, and human acts are judged, says Aquinas, by their ends. The same act, such as killing a man, can, he says, be ordered to diverse ends, for instance upholding justice or satisfying anger. In the first way it will be an act of virtue, in the second, of vice.[50] Human acts which are deliberately willed *by definition* have as their natural ends or objects the unqualified universal good.[51] If someone acts for an end that is not the good he acts against his nature and is to be held morally responsible for so doing, effectively for being wilfully ignorant of what human nature is, thereby harming himself and others. Such a man has given in to evil, he has not ordered his acts to natural ends defined as the good. There is not a multiplicity of natural ends. The one end to which natural human practices lead is the unqualified and universal good.

And so when Aquinas answers the question: does man have to do good deeds in order to receive happiness from God, he goes back to considering the nature of man, which realizes itself through action. He says that to possess one's end, the perfect good *by definition*, without movement belongs to one who has it by nature and this belongs to God alone; it certainly does not belong to us. No creature can attain its natural end without some activity natural to it by which it tends towards its end.[52] Deeds on the part of man are required for happiness, he says, not because of any inadequacy of the divine power that bestows happiness, but for preserving the order in things, that is, for maintaining reality which will not be affected by our not acting to natural type, but if we do not so act we will be uncomfortable in our skins, we will not be at home in the world, and if we find ourselves in this condition it will be because we chose to be uncomfortable with our natures. Whatever we choose, we as humans are the initiating and controlling principles of our individual and collective futures because we deliberate and act in whatever ways we do.[53]

As far as human affairs are concerned, Aquinas says Aristotle

> shows that it is obvious that human beings are the originating principle of those things in the future they do as the controllers of their own acts and that they have in their power to do or not to do. They do not only act by natural instinct but by deliberating and judging what is to be done. If you deny this originating principle, you remove the whole structure of human intercourse and all the principles of moral philosophy.[54]

If you deny this, he says, 'there is no point in persuasion, or threats, or punishment or reward by which people are encouraged to do good and discouraged from doing evil and so the whole science of society becomes vain.'[55] 'People who do what they do not want to do', says Aquinas, 'may not have freedom of action but they do have freedom of choice.'[56] Indeed, Aquinas makes it clear that 'if one lives in a society whose customs and traditions are not in accord with what a reasonable nature would consider appropriate, then by deliberating a person who is accustomed to do something can, indeed should, act against custom and tradition.'[57] It seems to me that this is one of the many things MacIntyre has altered in his account of both Aristotle and Aquinas in order to focus on a multiplicity of practices and traditions with a multiplicity of ends or goods that he sees as developing historically.

After Virtue charts a history of apparently rival and changing notions of virtue and their presumed incompatibility with one another. When he speaks of Aristotle MacIntyre says correctly that Aristotle treats the acquisition and exercise of virtues as means to an end and the relationship of means to end is internal not external. But then he reverses the order Aristotle gives; MacIntyre tells us he calls means internal to a given end when the *end* cannot be adequately characterized independently of a characterization of the means.[58] Aristotle's position, which is also that of Aquinas, is that means are internal to a given end where the *means* cannot be adequately characterized independently of a characterization of the end. As we saw, Aquinas said acts (which are means to an end) are judged by their ends. The same act can be virtuous or vicious depending on what was intended – killing to uphold justice, or killing out of anger. If someone acts for an end that is not the good, he acts against his nature in not having ordered his acts to their natural end, defined as the good. Ends are natural, given, universal goals for species, knowledge of which must be prior to and therefore internal to means by which they are to be achieved.

MacIntyre believes that we can find a unitary core concept of virtues, which are means to ends, and thereby give an account that is more compelling than the rival versions he has discussed, including Aristotle's. What we require, he says, is a background account of a practice, in the first instance, and a definition of goods that are internal to practices like virtues.[59] Without specifically referring to natural and universal, peculiarly human ways of behaving and intending, MacIntyre speaks of an internal good which itself is pleasurable and derived from the practice itself, so that a practitioner discovers the good of a certain kind of life and therefore living a life as a certain practitioner is also a good internal to the practice. He notes that practices involve standards of excellence and obedience to rules as well as the achievement of goods. To enter into a practice is to accept the authority of those standards and the inadequacy of one's own performance as judged by them. So far so good and Aristotelian and Thomist. But then he adds: 'it is to subject my own attitudes, choices, preferences and tastes to the standards which *currently* and partially define the practice, [for] practices have a history.'[60] For Aristotle and Aquinas there may indeed be a history of practices, a history of the means to ends, but the defining standards by which they may be judged have no history, they are universals absolutely, they are the natures or essences grasped by the definition of their goal. Hence MacIntyre, in asserting that standards are not immune from criticism, misunderstands how Aristotle and Aquinas define practices in terms of what they aim to achieve, their ends. A definition is not culture bound nor is it temporal. Both names and definitions which grasp the essence of a subject have no temporality. Hence MacIntyre is not a Thomist when he says 'we cannot be initiated into a practice', that is, into what men who are considered virtuous in a particular historical culture consider good practice, 'without accepting the authority of the best standards realized so far'.[61] This places definition in the hands of cultures with

conventional codes of self-expression. But definitions are the set of words
that grasps the nature of something thought of which is, as a thought,
not conventional but species specific, universal and timeless. The definitions of practices which are human do not depend on the variability of
taste but rather on universal thought which words in different languages
represent. Instead of practices requiring that we subordinate ourselves
within the practice in our relationship to other practitioners, we ought
to subordinate ourselves as practitioners to a fixed definition of what is
required to be a human practitioner. We do not compete with bad flute
players, we compete only with the best according to its definition; a
wise man does not compete in virtue with the unvirtuous or less virtuous but against the goal of virtuous behaviour. Virtues are goods only
as intermediaries or means to the final end, the good for man. And for
Aquinas as for Aristotle, virtuous habits are not in themselves strictly
goods; they are dispositions or states relative to their goal and are consciously known and willed dispositions seen as means to the human
good. What virtuous men share is an intention to act well; they do not
share precise ways of so doing in contingent circumstances. MacIntyre
seems to think that ends being immanent in the means by which ends
are achieved requires that the practices themselves somehow be identified and therefore they are recognizably rule bound *as these rules are set
by practitioners as authorities.*

What emerges from this is a much more authoritarian perspective
than is found in Aristotle or Aquinas, because MacIntyre seems to insist
that not only are definitions fixed successively by different generations
of practitioners within cultures, but also that the means to their attainment are also fixed by discrete traditions. This would not allow Aristotle's or Aquinas's scope for a pluralism of individual responsible ways
of acting virtuously towards the same universal and specifically human
end within discrete cultures, ways which are dependent on circumstances
and character. Traditions for a Thomist or an Aristotelian do not constitute practices as definitions; traditions are subordinate to definitions,
because traditions or cultures are bad or good realizers in practice of the
definition, which is itself a universal, is timeless and stands as a conventionally uttered representation of human universal conceptions concerning peculiarly human behaviour. Where MacIntyre says that we must
be willing to trust the judgements of those whose achievements in the
practice give them an authority to judge, this can only be true if they do
not set the standards. Being a doctor *qua* doctor is defined simply as he
who uses his knowledge to cure the ill, bringing them back to health
where possible, and not as practised in fourth century BC Greece or in
thirteenth-century Paris. When MacIntyre says that practices never have
a goal or goals fixed for all time but goals themselves are transmuted by

the history of the activity so that every practice (read virtue) has its own history,[62] he is saying something that neither Aristotle nor Aquinas could say. For them the only history there is is of individual men engaging a variety of means to ends, not a history of ends. And a man of virtue in the fourth century BC would *essentially* exhibit the same virtues in the thirteenth century, for Aquinas. What a doctor is does not change over time definitionally. The particular subject is dominated by and given meaning through that which is absolutely and unqualifiedly intelligible, the universal, be it the human essence or the essence of doctor. For Aristotle and Aquinas there is only one tradition of professional practitioners that should be invoked as judge of practices and this is not any old tradition that may fall prey to internal corruptions. You do not define a doctor in terms of the actual practices of a historically and culturally specific set of doctors. Rather, the skill of medicine is defined in terms of its aim, whether or not a tradition actually exists which recognizes its true aim, and the aim of medicine is the health of the patient's body. Accordingly, a historically specific medical community that puts its budget before the healing of the ill at all costs is a tradition with a deformed practice. Particular cultures and traditions are not existents in their own right; they are, as Aquinas insisted, the effects of what exists in its own right, and as such they are determined by the choices made by humans, choices for which they are responsible and which indeed may be vicious and incompatible with their definition. The definition of a doctor is one who heals the ill no matter what status the patient has in society. The definition of doctor does not include the privilege of judging relative merits of patients as political participants or in any other way other than in terms of their health.

Where for Aquinas and Aristotle there is a distinction between natural ends or goals and coincidental or accidental ones, and this is mirrored in MacIntyre's distinction between internal and external goods, the crux of their argument is that there are in reality those entities that are existents in their own right as opposed to those things that are contingent effects of what exists in its own right. Furthermore, there are activities or practices which help to define the nature of humanness, and other activities which are, as it were, accidental, not essential to being human. Earning money, once money is established culturally as a means of exchange, is not essential to being human. It merely facilitates human existence in a way that could be replaced by another utilitarian exchange convention. What *is* essential to humanness is to expend energy in deciding how, amongst alternatives, one might stay not only alive but content in a peculiarly human way, and to achieve human well-being requires the exercise of reason and will in forging one's own private and collective future, given that human nature is social and political rather than solitary.

But historically specific cultures or traditions are not existents in their own right; they are derivative of voluntary choices made by deliberating men and they may be vicious as well as virtuous. They are vicious if they wilfully misperceive means for ends and if they enshrine external goods to the detriment of internal ones.

Now, I suspect MacIntyre would be in part offended by this account of the Thomist position because it is epistemologically centred and this is his complaint against certain Thomisms of the past.[63] Furthermore, MacIntyre wants to argue that there is a tradition of thought which allows no fundamental dissent[64] and is embodied in a community which was exemplified and brought to completion by Aquinas, a tradition which does not start from man but from God. In a sense, this is, of course, correct. But on MacIntyre's own account of Aquinas's Aristotelianism, man can only come to know the kind of nature he has and that there is a God by acting in a human way, acting according to his essence, which tends towards an unchosen end, freely choosing means to that end, and learning from sense experience and thinking on it. That man observes and thinks about effects demonstrates to Aquinas man's tendency to reason back to a first initiating cause of effects, which shows the whole of reality tied up and interrelated. Men, Aquinas says, naturally seek beginnings even if they cannot grasp the essence of their source. God may indeed be there just as reality is there but *we* only come to learn of both through living human lives. That we cannot define God and therefore grasp his essence absolutely does not mean that we cannot define man.

MacIntyre rightly says that 'Aquinas, like Aristotle, can find no room for any question as to why, given that one recognises that something is one's true good, one should act so as to achieve it.'[65] Indeed, for both Aristotle and Aquinas this is just the way things are; there are natural ends of human actions and when recognized we must as humans move towards them. But humans do not act unthinkingly or by faith or by the coercion of a tradition when they realize their natures because if they did so they would not by nature *be* voluntary deliberators about the true or their good, an observed tendency and activity which constitutes what being human is. You are not expressing your humanness if you are simply educated into practices within a household or a community, learning to be habitually virtuous without raising philosophical questions about the rightness or wrongness of such customs.[66] Even in *After Virtue*, which is perhaps not so explicitly Thomist as it is Aristotelian, MacIntyre wanted to focus on a tradition of faith to which Aristotelian metaphysics offered no access. 'We have', we are told without the slightest justification, 'every reason to reject Aristotle's physical and biological science'[67] – which we must note, Aquinas never did and had he done so his notion of substantial form and the ethics which follow from it would have dissolved. Furthermore, MacIntyre says 'the part of Christian theology which concerns man's true end and which is not Aristotelian metaphysics is, on Aquinas's own account, a matter of faith not reason.' This, to my mind, distorts Thomism beyond repair for there is no way of accepting the faith, except through forceful imposition, if it is not seen as a continuity with metaphysics and reason. Aquinas insisted in his most famous remark that grace does not destroy nature but perfects it. And as MacIntyre rightly notes, take away or reject the Aristotelianism in the Thomist account but leave the despair of moral achievement and the gratuitousness of grace and you get Luther.[68] Faith in a grace *ad extra* does not impel you to act according to your human nature. Humans just do act in ways that are peculiar to the kind of substance they are. Part of what it means to be human is the exercise of intellectual judgement concerning the truth or falsity of thought and statements about actual existents and hence to exercise intellectual judgement within a scheme where there is a background set of indemonstrable first principles which constitute a metaphysics of existence. Human cognition and action simply are already in the real and Aquinas's insistence on this metaphysics was not only not unique to him but was shared by virtually all contemporaries and perhaps still is shared, although not explicitly, by all philosophical enquiry that is not limited by the narrowness of the self-imposed parameters of language theory. For Aquinas there *is* a fullness of knowledge that takes place in faith but man, *naturally*, has a foretaste of this kind of knowledge.

Aquinas insists that the knowledge that directs man to his final end should be very certain since it is the basis of all his actions that are aimed at achieving his final end. And the principles which are known to man by nature are, he says, of the greatest certainty. Something is known with the greatest certainty either because it is self-evident, such as the first principles of argument, or because it is derived from things that are self-evident, such as conclusions from self-evident principles. Since what is proposed to us from God to be held by faith is *not* self-evident, exceeding as it does the capacity of the human intellect, Aquinas says that it should be proposed to man by someone to whom it *is* self-evident and this is Christ, not some other authoritative teacher within a community of traditional practitioners. Christ then makes it known to all in a way similar to the way we know things with certainty by resolving them into indemonstrable first principles.[69] There is, then, a continuity between man's natural knowledge and a knowledge of divine things and this is through similarities and likenesses. God instructs man, he says, so that man can receive a knowledge of divine matters *in a human way*.

Now here we see, I believe, a confusion in MacIntyre between the

historical Church's authority as a traditional community and the authority of the truths of faith, and this has important repercussions for
secular governance as well. According to Aquinas, man receives instruction in the truths of faith from God himself as Christ; this is, for Aquinas,
the divine law of Scripture, God's revealed word. The Church is required to be a universal schoolroom in which God's law is pronounced.
But Aquinas recognizes that if the Church as an institution is to be
united the *faithful* must *agree* on the faith and since there are many
questions concerning matters of faith and different *opinions* (not truths)
on such matters, the Church must be kept in unity by the decisions of
one person following Christ's command that Peter be over the Church.[70]
This does not and cannot mean that authoritative pronouncements by
the archetypical, expert practitioner within the tradition express the
highest standards 'so far achieved' and are standards as yet unknown by
less expert practitioners. Rather, added to the divine scriptural law
which men understand in a *human* way can only be universal utterances
signifying the true and the good as human ends, ends which are already
there and graspable as such by rational human agents who think the true
and desire the good but who, none the less, cannot attain their ends
without divine aid.

In terms of the *human* good they can attain in social and political life,
based as it is on an account of what human nature is, derived from
observation of human voluntary and deliberative acts and tendencies
towards ends, then the *opinions* in the social world are also best unified
by a public person, an elected ruler who is an organizer of the general
good.[71] It is not the ruler's unique capacity to know and desire peculiarly human ends; it *is* his unique public capacity, a constitutional capacity, to represent and to implement what is known and desired by all
men who bother to reflect on what being a man is. There is a principle
of unanimity here and not a majoritarian principle. As a public representative he is accountable to reason. For Aquinas the best constitutions
are those dominated by men of intellectual rectitude, where true rulership
or kingship is *defined* not by birth but by exemplary humanness,
knowing and willing the universally true and good for mankind in its
care. Natural rulers are those who have made the philosophical effort to
achieve a superior intellect, he says, not ruling by physical force or
because they have been given authority out of some men's sensual affec-
tion for them.[72]

If, as MacIntyre insists, we read the *Summa* not by domesticating it
to our own prejudices and therefore distorting it, nor by translating it
into our own language, but rather by reading it within what he calls the
tradition which Aquinas reconstituted in the course of writing it,[73] then
that tradition, I submit, is not that of an already trained Catholic in

Catholic families and Catholic societies post *Aeterni Patris*; the tradition is initially the more abstract and general Aristotelian one which attempts a holistic account of what the world is like and how humans who are social and political agents come to know it as it is, whatever customary culture they happen to inhabit. Reason overrides custom. And if this is the case, then instead of a tragic Aristotle, which MacIntyre says results from Thomism, we get something much more positive, certainly than MacIntyre, because there is no presumption that all men are knaves despite their *tendency* to sin and be stupid for themselves and others. MacIntyre rightly argues, following Aquinas, that man's acts are determined by there being a goal beyond themselves which is their ultimate good. But he is not a Thomist when he describes the *consequences* for the soul without faith, finding itself directed beyond all finite goods, unsatisfiable by those goods and yet able to find nothing beyond them to satisfy them. Permanent dissatisfaction would be its lot. What, MacIntyre asks, would such a soul become? He says it would become a Hobbesian for whom there is no *finis ultimus*.[74] But that is not what Aquinas says it would become. Humans naturally know and indeed are what they are because they know and desire a *finis ultimus*: to know the cause of all and to satisfy all desires. Rather, the searching and ever desiring soul would become an Aristotelian for whom the objects of philosophical, intellectual pursuit are *not* unsatisfying in themselves. They are simply, in our human state, not continuously present as we would wish them to be, because we are by nature mortal and in bodies.

If, in the end, we now ask whether liberal principles are incompatible with Thomism, I think we can answer 'no'; there is a compatibility with a certain Millian liberalism but only if we insist on resurrecting the notion of human nature as essential to ethics and politics and include in our definition something more than a materialist description of human action based on impulsive pleasure and pain. We would also need to agree that there is a level of conceptualization, thinking of universals, which is the species-specific language of thought, and here culture holds no sway. Cognitive scientists have been doing just this for most of this century, as have neuroscientists when they investigate how the human mind thinks. Above or beyond cultural habituation, way above irrational, subjective appetite and beyond the bickering of philosophical sects, there is, as Collingwood once said, 'a melody sung in unison by the great philosophers; this melody, *philosophia quædam perennis*, is not a body of truth revealed once for all but a living thought whose content, never discovered for the first time, is progressively determined and clarified by every genuine thinker.'[75] Aquinas could have said that, but not, I think, MacIntyre's Aquinas, whose Thomism is somehow intelligible only to a closed tradition of practitioners.

Lastly, to make Thomism compatible with liberalism we would have to spend rather more time than we have done in ethical and political theorizing on accommodating ourselves to the fact that we die. *Is* the living of a human life, with its endless and restless search to know and desire something we *want* to end through knowing all and possessing everything we ever desired? Calculating the greatest happiness of the greatest number on the basis of unexamined individual sense preferences makes the subject of politics a kind of animal culture rather than human beings. But for Aquinas, specific cultures and traditions are accidental not essential. Cultures are coincidental, they are not properly speaking existents in their own right; they are effects of what exists in its own right. Cultures are possibles, but humans are necessary existents, and for a Thomist, human nature is the subject of politics. Can liberalism survive this?

NOTES

1 *After Virtue*, 2nd edn (Duckworth, London, 1985), p. 186.
2 Ibid., p. 203.
3 *Three Rival Versions of Moral Enquiry: Encyclopaedia, Genealogy, and Tradition* (Duckworth, London, 1990), p. 25. In order not to produce an essay of unreasonable length I have focused on an earlier work (*After Virtue*) and a late work (*Three Rival Versions*). This stresses an essential continuity in MacIntyre's thoughts on Aquinas. But see also his *Whose Justice? Which Rationality?*
4 *Three Rival Versions*, see p. 60: 'that membership in a particular type of moral community, one from which fundamental dissent has to be excluded, is a condition for genuine, rational enquiry and more especially for moral and theological enquiry'; p. 65: 'at any particular moment the rationality is inseparable from the tradition through which it was achieved . . .'; also see p. 82; pp. 128–9: 'the concept of having to be a certain sort of person morally or theologically, in order to read a book aright – with the implication that perhaps, if one is not that sort of person, then the book should be withheld from one – is alien to the assumption of liberal modernity that every rational adult should be free to and is able to read every book'; p. 171: 'the universality of a capacity to make what was framed in the light of the canons of one culture intelligible to those who inhabit some other quite alien culture [is (wrongly) taken for granted]'; pp. 202–3; see p. 205 on the Thomist appeal to standards implicit in and partially definitive of dialectical and confessional activity.
5 Ibid., pp. 63–5.
6 *After Virtue*, p. 196.
7 He acknowledges his criticism of Aquinas's account of the unity of the virtues in *After Virtue*, p. 179, in part because it reiterates an Aristotelian cosmology.
8 *Three Rival Versions*, p. 123.
9 Where possible, I have used the translations of Aquinas's writings from the excellent book by Christopher Martin (ed.), *The Philosophy of Thomas Aquinas: Introductory Readings* (Routledge, London, 1988). Aquinas, *In Perihermenias*, I, lectio 14.4.
10 Aquinas, *In Perihermenias*, I, lectio 15.1.

11 Ibid., I, lectio 15.4; Aristotle, *Categories*, c.5, 4a 22f; c.12, 14b 9f; *De Interpretatione*, c.9, 18b 26f; and 19a 23. Translation used here is *Aristotle's Categories and De Interpretatione*, trans. J. K. Ackrill, Clarendon Aristotle series (Oxford, 1974).

12 Aristotle, *De Interpretatione*, c.1, 16a 3f; Aquinas, *Summa Theologiae*, Ia Q.76 a.2 especially ad 3. See Janet Coleman, *Ancient and Medieval Memories: Studies in the Reconstruction of the Past* (Cambridge University Press, Cambridge, 1992), pp. 422–60.

13 See C. Martin, 'Aquinas on metaphysics', ch. 3 of *The Philosophy of Thomas Aquinas*, pp. 49–76.

14 Aristotle, *De Interpretatione*, c.13, 22b 29f; 23a 21; *Posterior Analytics*, 76a 38, 77a 26–31, 76b 3–22, 76a 31–77a 4. Aquinas, *In Perihermenias*, I, lectio 14.8 and lectio 14.11.

15 Aquinas, *In Perihermenias*, I, lectio 4.11.

16 Ibid., lectio 4.13; Aristotle, *De Interpretatione*, c.4, 16a 19, c.7, 17a 38. Also Aquinas, *Commentary on the Metaphysics*, V, lectio 9.12 and 13.

17 Aquinas, *Commentary on the Metaphysics*, VII, lectio 2 *passim*.

18 *After Virtue*, p. 194.

19 Aristotle, *Topics*, A 5 101b 38f. Aquinas, *Commentary on the Metaphysics*, V, lectio 10.4.

20 Aristotle, *Topics*, Z 1, 141b 25–8; Aquinas, *Commentary on the Metaphysics*, V, lectio 10.5.

21 Aquinas, *Commentary on the Metaphysics*, VII, lectio 2.16–36; also Aquinas, *De Veritate*, Q.10 a.4.

22 Aquinas, *Commentary on the Metaphysics*, VII, lectio 2.16.

23 Aristotle, *De Anima, Books II and II*, notes and trans. D. W. Hamlyn (Oxford, 1968).

24 See Martin, 'Aquinas on metaphysics', pp. 65–9; Aquinas, *Summa Theologiae*, Ia, Qq.75–6; see Coleman, *Ancient and Medieval Memories*, pp. 425–32.

25 Aquinas, *De Veritate* Q.10 a.4–6. (For discussion of Aristotle on perception and conception in the *De Anima*, see Coleman, *Ancient and Medieval Memories*, pp. 15–38). For the mature presentation of perception and conception, Aquinas, *Summa Theologiae*, Ia, Qq.75–83, the 'Treatise on man', vol. 11 in Blackfriars' edn, Latin text and trans. Timothy Suttor (London, 1970).

26 Aquinas, *De Veritate*, Q.1 a.1 response.

27 Ibid., Q.10 a.6 response; Aristotle, *Posterior Analytics*, 76a 31–77a 4.

28 Aquinas, *Commentary on the Metaphysics*, VII, lectio 2.32–3.

29 Aquinas, *Summa Contra Gentiles*, II, c.25. *De Malo*, Q.6 response, and *Summa Theologiae*, Ia, Q.83 a.1.

30 Aquinas, *De Veritate*, Q.10 a.5 response.

31 Aquinas, *Commentary on the Nicomachean Ethics*, I, lectio 10.12.

32 Ibid., lectio 10.13.

33 Aquinas, *De Veritate*, Q.1 a.1.

34 Aquinas, *Summa Contra Gentiles*, I, c.3.

35 Ibid., III, c.3 and c.25.

36 Aristotle, *Nicomachean Ethics*, I, 13, 1101b 32–1102a 17; III, 5, 1113b 21–1114a 8; V, 1, 1129a 21–1129b 30.

37 Aquinas, *Summa Theologiae*, Ia IIae, Q.1 a.1 response. Translation used with modifications, *Treatise on Happiness* (*ST*, Ia IIae, Qq.1–21), trans. John A. Oesterle (University of Notre Dame Press, Notre Dame, Ind., 1983), p. 4.

38 Ibid., Q.1 a.2 response, p. 5.

39 Ibid., Q.1 a.3 response, p. 7.

40 See Peter Geach, 'Aquinas', in G. E. M. Anscombe and P. Geach, *Three Philosophers: Aristotle, Aquinas, Frege* (Blackwell, Oxford, 1973), p. 125 and *passim*.
41 Aquinas, *Summa Contra Gentiles*, III, c.25; c.63; IV, c.54; *De Regno*, I, c.1, (4) and (6), trans. G. B. Phelan (1949), revised T. Eschmann, 'On kingship' (Pontifical Institute of Mediaeval Studies, Toronto, 1982), pp. 3–5; *Summa Theologiae*, Ia IIae, Q.1 a.4 response and replies to 1 and 2.
42 *Three Rival Versions*, 'the plain person', p. 136. See Aquinas, *Summa Contra Gentiles*, I, c.4.
43 Aquinas, *Summa Theologiae*, Ia IIae, Q.1 a.5 response.
44 Ibid., Q.1 a.7 response; *In Perhermenias*, I, lectio 14.24.
45 *Summa Theologiae*, Ia IIae, Q.2 a.6 response; *Summa Contra Gentiles*, I, c.8.
46 *Summa Theologiae*, Ia IIae, Q.2 a.8 response.
47 Aristotle, *Nicomachean Ethics*, X, 1178b 7–29.
48 Aquinas, *Summa Theologiae*, Ia IIae, Q.3 a.2 reply to 4 referring to Aristotle, *Nicomachean Ethics*, I, c.10, 1101a 20. *Summa Theologiae*, Ia IIae, Q.2 a.8 response; *Summa Theologiae*, Ia IIae, Q.2 a.5 and Q.3 a.4 response; *Summa Contra Gentiles*, III, c.63.
49 *Summa Theologiae*, Ia IIae, Q.4 a.3. 3 and response.
50 Ibid., Ia IIae, Q.1 a.3 reply to 3.
51 Ibid., Q.1 a.1 response and reply to 1 and 2; Q.1 a.2 reply to 3.
52 Ibid., Q.5 a.7 and reply to 1.
53 Aquinas, *In Perihermenias*, I, lectio 14.5.
54 Ibid.
55 Ibid.
56 *De Malo*, Q.6 reply to 22.
57 Ibid., Q.6 reply to 24.
58 *After Virtue*, p. 184.
59 Ibid., pp. 187–8.
60 Ibid., p. 190, my emphasis.
61 Ibid., pp. 191–3.
62 Ibid., p. 194.
63 *Three Rival Versions*, p. 75.
64 Ibid., p. 60; see note 4 above. On MacIntyre's avowed partisanship, pp. 117–18.
65 Ibid., p. 154.
66 Ibid., pp. 128–9; p. 137. MacIntyre also says: 'A knowledge of God is, on Aquinas's view, available to us from the outset of our moral enquiry' (p. 141). But as Aquinas shows, we are not originally aware of this; we have a natural desire to know the truth, including, ultimately, about God, but that we can have some knowledge of God depends on first having lived a human life and then having reflected on it and on the causes of what there is, back to an initiating cause.
67 *After Virtue*, p. 179.
68 *Three Rival Versions*, p. 141.
69 Aquinas, *Summa Contra Gentiles*, IV, c.54.
70 Ibid., IV, c.76.
71 Aquinas, *De Regno*, I, c.1 (8), c.6 (42) and (49); II, c.3 (103), (106).
72 *Summa Contra Gentiles*, III, c.81.
73 *Three Rival Versions*, p. 43; p. 135; pp. 171–3.
74 Ibid., pp. 117–18.
75 R. G. Collingwood, *Speculum Mentis, or the Map of Knowledge* (Oxford, 1924), p. 13.

5

MacIntyre's Thomist Revival: What Next?

John Haldane

It has ever been a cause of deep and heartfelt sorrow to honest folk, and above all to good loyal sons of the Church, that the judgments of mankind in the sphere of religion and morals should be so variable, and so apt to stray from the truth . . .
[F]alse evolutionary notions, with their denial of all that is absolute or fixed or abiding in human experience, have paved the way for a new philosophy of error. Idealism, immanentism, pragmatism, have now a rival in what is called 'existentialism'. Its method, as the name implies, is to leave the unchanging essences of things out of sight, and concentrate all its attention on particular existences.
There is, too, a false use of the historical method, which confines its observations to the actual happenings of human life, and in doing so contrives to undermine all absolute truth, all absolute laws, whether it is dealing with the problems of philosophy or with the doctrines of the Christian religion.

Pope Pius XII, *Humani Generis* (1950)

Introduction

Alasdair MacIntyre is a welcome presence within a philosophical community that is becoming increasingly scholastic in its theoretical enquiries and superficial in its practical applications. He combines conceptual creativity with broad scholarship, in a form shaped by a Celtic sensibility and appetite for constructive debate. No one who has read MacIntyre's works can fail to feel challenged by them. Indeed, even sympathizers are apt to find that just as they thought the argument was running their way, there is a quick twist or turn and some thesis is being vigorously defended which they took to be at odds with their cherished position.

This raises the question of whether MacIntyre's many twists and turns may even lead *him* in a direction counter to that in which he is claiming to be moving. And the thought of this unsettling possibility suggests a further question of where, if a course correction is necessary, MacIntyre may go next. Such speculations might have arisen in response to reading *After Virtue*[1] and *Whose Justice? Which Rationality?*,[2] but whatever the response to those books, they can hardly fail to arise in the mind of a thoughtful reader of *Three Rival Versions of Moral Inquiry*.[3] In this most recent volume, MacIntyre makes explicit his commitment to Roman Catholicism and to Thomistic Aristotelianism. Of themselves, these attachments are likely to prove uncongenial to many who have hitherto been fellow travellers along the road away from 'modernity'. But it will now seem that this road quickly divides, and that whereas one branch leads forward into postmodernity, the other – now walked by MacIntyre – doubles back towards premodern ideas. Indeed it remains to be seen how many of those who cited MacIntyre (along with Sandel and Taylor) in criticism of 'deontological liberalism', 'enlightenment rationalism' and 'the project of modernity' are likely to feel comfortable when presented with papal encyclicals and mentions of original sin. But there is also a question, I believe, of whether those who are sympathetic to Thomism should feel happy about MacIntyre's historicist version of it. Here I shall only be concerned with this second issue.

In what follows, I first recall the origins of MacIntyre's central themes in the work of Elizabeth Anscombe, recount something of the development of MacIntyre's view through the three books mentioned above and register some worries about what I take to be the relativist tendency of this. Next I look at the characterization of Thomism presented in the second and, especially, the third volume. Then I reflect upon further worries about the coherence of MacIntyre's present position and consider the question of where, if these worries are well founded, he might go next in his continuing enquiry. Needless to say there are many interesting aspects of these impressive writings which I shall not even mention. Also when I spoke above of 'worries' I chose my word deliberately. I should not be surprised to learn that I have misread aspects of his view, but if so it would be good to have that misreading corrected.

By implication, I shall be arguing that what has so far been a *trilogy* needs to be, at least, a *tetralogy*. MacIntyre ended *After Virtue* acknowledging the need to provide an account of practical reason. This led to *Whose Justice? Which Rationality?*, which itself ended with the thought that competing traditions need to demonstrate their explanatory resources. There then followed *Three Rival Versions*, which ends with the injunction to devise institutions within which Nietzschean and neo-Thomist critics of modernism might be heard. My suggestion, however, is that what is next required is a clearer statement than has so far been offered of what distinctive ideas the Thomist tradition might be able to contribute, and I shall argue that this must be a matter of developing certain metaphysical claims – perhaps under the title *The Truth in Thomism*, or more generally, *The Requirements of Truth*.

A History of Ethics

MacIntyre's dominant idea is, as he acknowledges, not a new one. In 'Modern moral philosophy',[4] Elizabeth Anscombe presented three theses: first, that moral philosophy should be shelved until we have an adequate philosophy of psychology; second, that the distinctively moral vocabulary of deontological terms and uses is a surviving remnant of an outlook that has largely been abandoned; and third, that English-speaking moral philosophy has a single general character.

The substance of Anscombe's argument is that we find ourselves educated in the use of a range of terms and tones, for the evaluation and direction of character and of conduct, which derive principally from a legalistic view of morality – more precisely, from a Judaeo-Christian Divine Law ethics. Since the philosophical and theological presuppositions of this way of speaking have long since ceased to hold sway, the vocabulary is devoid of meaningful content – notwithstanding that, psychologically, it retains a commandatory force. Having mistaken force for content, modern moral philosophers set about trying to explain how the use of this moral vocabulary might be warranted. Unsurprisingly, one of the possibilities that soon occurred was that its purpose and warrant are not the stating of facts but the expression of preferences. All of this being so, the enterprise of moral philosophy needs to rid itself of the old legalistic terms and start afresh to think about how the evaluation and guidance of action might be rationally warranted. At this point Anscombe reintroduces Aristotle and suggests that questions of conduct might be approached via consideration of the habits of action and avoidance it is necessary to cultivate if one is to lead a good life. What a good life is might itself be determined by investigating the natural teleology of human kind. To know what a good X is one considers the kind of existence naturally characteristic of Xs and projects forwards into an idea of what flourishing for that kind of entity would consist in. This is a matter of developing an account of a natural form of life, or equivalently of a kind of animating principle *psuche* – hence the need for an 'adequate philosophy of psychology'.

It has often been supposed that Anscombe was encouraging the complete abandonment of a deontological vocabulary of absolute requirements and prohibitions, but this is a mistake. Her point, I take it, is that, *pace* Kant (and, by implication, latter-day neo-Kantians), pure prescriptive deontology only makes sense on the assumption that there is a transcendent legislative authority – God or (perhaps) Cosmic Order – and that unless one believes this, one should abandon that kind of moral thinking. Like MacIntyre, however, Anscombe is a traditionally minded Roman Catholic and *does* believe in the Law of God. Consequently she can find a place for absolutist language, *but not*, I think, as the kind of talk whose use might be warranted simply by a neo-Aristotelian theory of virtue. Better then not to use the term 'moral' in connection with both natural virtue and ordained law; or if one does, then it is essential to remember that these uses are not univocal but only analogous.[5]

I have set out Anscombe's theses in part as a reminder of the extent to which MacIntyre has been carrying on a project already begun, and in part to serve as a relevant basis for comparison and contrast between members of a class of philosophers, *viz.* Roman Catholic neo-Aristotelians, who might be thought to hold very similar views.[6] Clearly, anyone who wanted to follow Anscombe's suggestions and work out a broadly Aristotelian theory of virtue while retaining a Divine Law account of moral absolutes would have to make intelligible and defend two sets of controversial assumptions: one set *metaphysical*, having to do with human nature; the other *theological*, concerning God, His commands and the means of their reception.

Given that MacIntyre begins with something very close to Anscombe's analysis of modern moral philosophy, it is interesting to see how he places himself with respect to these two sets of assumptions. However, since his commitment to Christianity is only made explicit in the second and third volumes of the trilogy, the question of theological presuppositions is best delayed. Beginning with *After Virtue*, then, we are given a similar account of the separation of our moral vocabulary from the historical sources of its life. The account differs from Anscombe's discussion both in wealth of detail and in presenting Aristotelianism itself as one of those major sources. Furthermore, whereas Anscombe refers to a 'philosophy of psychology' and offers certain parallels involving the life of non-sentient organisms, MacIntyre sides with the critics of Aristotle's naturalistic philosophical anthropology, speaking of it as involving an untenable 'metaphysical biology'.[7] What is retained, however, is the Aristotelian idea that an ethics of virtue *requires* a teleology of agency. If certain act-dispositions are rationally to be encouraged (and others discouraged) then it must be possible to specify an end of action towards which these dispositions will lead us. Disavowing the effort to identify a natural *telos* for man as such, MacIntyre introduces the idea of a historically developed social nature, and within this the notion of a narrative history and a life of self-definition.

Later, he emphasizes that the rationality of cultivating a particular set of virtues in relation to a given end, and the rationality of that end's being prescribed, is not to be thought of as determinable from outwith the tradition of socially constituted norms and broadly moral practices in which the agent finds himself. On one interpretation of this suggestion, it seems to introduce an element of relativism. This will be worrying to those who saw the appeal to Aristotle as marking the adoption of a kind of naturalism that would begin with an empirical-cum-philosophical anthropology and move from this to an account of the virtues as rational habits which it is necessary to possess always and everywhere – variation only appearing at the level of their application in diverse circumstances.

The general question of relativism will be returned to, but for now the interest attaches to MacIntyre's internalist account of rationality. The supposed failure of liberalism has been due not to any accident of history – such as the existence within the political community of groups who are antagonistic to its neutralism or, more specifically, to its toleration of what they regard as intolerable. Rather, it was doomed to fail by virtue of its philosophical presuppositions. In MacIntyre's analysis, liberalism rests on an incoherent account of rational agents, that is, one which sees them as constituted as persons independently of their social context and which takes their deliberations to be answerable to ahistorical, transcendent norms of reasoning. Since these presuppositions are incoherent[8] it follows that reliance on them must lead to further incoherencies – including the disintegration of social practice. What is offered by way of fundamental reconstruction is the idea of practical rationality as emerging and developing through forms of social exchange. But of course there is not just one community, there are many. Similarly any given community has a history through which it has developed. Thus there will be as many forms of rationality as there are distinct communities, where the latter are individuated by reference to the forms and norms of social life.

Although I cannot pursue the point here, it is important to note that there are difficulties facing the idea of radically distinct communities. What exactly, for example, are the criteria of identity for cultures and societies? Where do *we* stop and *others* begin? Certainly, geography and time may separate communities but this empirical fact is, in itself, philosophically trivial. What has to be shown is that there are points of separation beyond these spatio-temporal ones which constitute incommensurable differences. A line of reasoning familiar from Wittgenstein and Davidson suggests that this may not be possible.[9] MacIntyre is dismissive of Davidson's interpretative argument but yet invokes a linguistic criterion of cultural difference: roughly, a culture is distinct from one's own to the extent that understanding what speakers belonging to it are saying involves learning the meaning of their words as terms in a second language. But this suggestion invites a reapplication of the Davidsonian argument: either such learning involves translation of terms from one language into those of another or it does not. If it does, then in what sense did the foreign language represent an incommensurable cultural difference, as opposed to an interesting variant of a common human culture? If it does not, then how does one know what one is saying, or indeed that one is saying anything coherent at all? It is worth adding that, in fact, MacIntyre manages to say a good deal about the meaning of the terms of the languages, and *ipso facto* about the concepts and practices, of supposedly alien cultures and traditions.

Suspicions of Relativism

Even allowing the thesis of the plurality of rationalities, questions arise as to what forms of practical rationality are or have been operative, of how cognitive progress within any given form occurs and, most importantly, of how any socially constituted rational order can be judged superior to any other. Here I say 'most importantly', not only for the special interest that question has for philosophical theorists, but because MacIntyre himself makes clear that the account of rationality as tradition dependent is being developed for a practical purpose:

> [W]e must first return to the situation of the person to whom, after all, this book [*Whose Justice? Which Rationality?*] is primarily addressed, someone who, not as yet having given their allegiance to some coherent tradition of enquiry, is besieged by disputes over what is just and about how it is reasonable to act, both at the level of particular immediate issues ... and at the level at which rival systematic tradition-informed conceptions contend.[10]

In a moment I shall consider what MacIntyre has to say about the way in which proponents of one tradition may come to judge another to be superior. But it is worth dwelling on the situation envisaged in the quoted passage. Here we are to imagine someone who has not yet subscribed to 'a coherent tradition of enquiry'. That immediately raises the question of how such a person can choose between rival suitors for his or her mind and conscience. It would seem that his or her choice must either be rooted in reason or else be non-rational. But the former is excluded if rational norms are only available to a participant within a coherent tradition, for, *ex hypothesi*, the addressee is a complete outsider. If the latter, however, then one may be hesitant to speak of a 'choice' as having been made, and certainly it could not be seen as other than arbitrary viewed from *all* rational perspectives. In *Three Rival Versions*, MacIntyre draws upon Aquinas's account of the metaphysical preconditions of learning in order to resolve a paradox of knowledge arising with respect to the introduction of a tyro to the craft of moral enquiry.[11] But the present difficulty concerns someone who is supposed to understand what he hears presented to him but does not know how or whether to commit himself. Given the other assumptions it is doubtful that the envisaged situation is even intelligible. But if it is, then it seems to imply that MacIntyre's position on the present case is either contradictory or else lends support to a relativist conclusion. We are prohibited from saying that the rootless addressee can choose on the basis of transcendent norms of practical reason, so that excludes a realist resolution. This returns us to the thought that all choosing is from within a tradition, but if so there is after all nothing to be said by or to such a person, and *a fortiori* he cannot make a rational choice. Indeed, earlier in *Whose Justice? Which Rationality?* MacIntyre says as much himself:

> The person outside all traditions lacks sufficient rational resources for enquiry and *a fortiori* for enquiry into what tradition is to be rationally preferred. He or she has no adequate relevant means of rational evaluation and hence can come to no well-grounded conclusion, including the conclusion that no tradition can vindicate itself against any other. To be outside all traditions is to be a stranger to enquiry; it is to be in a state of intellectual and moral destitution.[12]

But this contradicts the suggestion that such a person stands to be helped by what MacIntyre has to say. One might suppose, however, that the addressee's deficiency is not in respect of reason *as a whole* but only in regard to moral rationality. This would make intelligible the idea that he can understand something of what is being urged upon him without yet being able to assess the rival specific and general claims. But if that is so then he, the outsider to moral traditions, has reason to regard the disagreement between the rival suitors as being, for him, rationally undecidable. Of course, from *within* the competing traditions, rival, purportedly conclusive, demonstrations may be advanced. But nothing can be made of these either from a perspective of transcendent moral rationality – for there is none – or from the perspective of speculative or scientific reasoning, not because the latter does not exist but because, *ex hypothesi*, its concepts and criteria of rationality find no place for moral notions and reasoning. Viewed from this second perspective, the situation of competing traditions seems precisely that which invites a relativist description. A rational enquirer finds himself confronted by rival accounts of *moral* reasoning between which it is said to be impossible for him to make a rational choice. This suggests either that the rival accounts lack any kind of rationality, or that their rationality is internal to them. Thus we arrive at either non-rationalism or relativism.

MacIntyre discusses relativism, not in connection with the case of the outsider (generally conceived of as the disinherited product of Enlightenment individualism) but as it seems to arise directly from the claim that rationality is only constituted within traditions of enquiry. Ironically, indeed, the second of the passages just quoted occurs in this discussion. His strategy for dealing with relativism is twofold. First, he considers how participants in different traditions might come to recognize the superiority of a rival through experiencing an epistemological crisis which the rival has more effective means of diagnosing and treating.

(This becomes the central theme of *Three Rival Versions* – the victor being Thomism.) But since he allows that events might not take this course and traditions could persist in irresoluble conflict he turns to a second consideration. This takes the form of the earlier dilemma which he uses to confront someone who moves from the claims he, MacIntyre, accepts, that is, *that norms and requirements pertaining to morality are always tradition dependent and that there are rival (and incommensurable) traditions*, to the claims that he rejects. that is, *that one's own evaluative deliberations are rationally undermined by these facts and that truth is shown to be, at best, relative to a system of enquiry.* The dilemma is intended to reveal the incoherence of the presupposition of these latter claims. Given the immanence of practical reasoning, someone must either be within a tradition and hence operating with its standards and so committed to their correctness, or else outside it and hence not equipped to take a view one way or the other.

The point of my previous remarks was to suggest, firstly, that the second disjunct defeats MacIntyre's educational aim and so he must either abandon it or this disjunct; and, secondly, that the very composition of the disjunction overlooks a possibility implied by MacIntyre's own characterization of the outsider. Since he hears and understands he is possessed of reason, even though he is a moral alien. And what this reason tells him is that the matters placed before him are not ones that his or any other 'external' rationality can investigate. A further worry now arises concerning the structure of MacIntyre's defence against relativism. Although he begins by considering this as the challenge that his position is relativistic, he proceeds to treat it as if it were a challenge made *by* a relativist who regards MacIntyre as holding back from relativism.

For convenience, let me speak of the Cartesian-cum-Kantian view of reason as *universalism*, of MacIntyre's tradition-constituted rationality as *immanentism* and of the idea that is now under consideration as *relativism*. (These correspond to the Encyclopaedist, Thomist and Genealogical conceptions explored in *Three Rival Versions*.) Employing these terms, the present charge is that immanentism, as MacIntyre presents it, either is, or implies some version of, relativism. It is curious, therefore, that his defence is concerned with demonstrating the incoherence of relativist claims. For that is not likely to be an issue between MacIntyre and his present critic, be he a universalist or some other sort of immanentist. What is actually needed is a demonstration that immanentism neither is nor implies relativism. Certainly one indirect way of going about this would be to start by deriving a contradiction from relativism and tracing its roots to assumptions which are demonstrably absent from immanentism. But MacIntyre's argument falls short of that. The dilemma he presents to the relativist invites two responses. One is to argue that it does not refute relativism, and so cannot serve the role in the defence of immanentism mentioned above. The other response is to observe that even if it does refute it, the task of showing that MacIntyre's immanentism is not incoherent remains incomplete until it has been established that it is not itself a version of relativism or a position that leads to it. One way of developing my previous argument would be to say that while the dilemma may prevent a participant in a moral tradition from simultaneously affirming its norms and denying them any special authority, that is compatible with occupying a theoretical stance from which they are seen relativistically. Whatever we think about that, however, there remains the question of the philosophical status of immanentism and this issue leads me to MacIntyre's revival of Thomism.

MacIntyre and Thomism

MacIntyre has many very interesting things to say about the structure of traditions of enquiry, about how an individual might make his way through these and extend them, and about how rival traditions can engage with one another and what it would mean for one of them to emerge from such engagement as recognizably superior. Here I can only consider the last of these aspects as it bears on the way in which MacIntyre discusses Thomism.

In *Whose Justice? Which Rationality?* and in *Three Rival Versions* it is argued that the absence of transcendent norms of enquiry does not exclude the possibility of one tradition being judged better than another. *Ex hypothesi*, that judgement cannot be made from outwith the competing traditions and hence it can only be rooted within one or more of them. However, it is neither likely nor ultimately intelligible that anyone involved in moral enquiry would take the claims to superiority on behalf of a rival at their own estimate. How then can the proponent of one position possessed of its own criteria of rationality defer to the superior rationality of another view? MacIntyre's answer involves the idea of a tradition running into difficulties and finding that it lacks the means to understand those difficulties and/or to resolve them. A rival may then offer a historical-cum-philosophical analysis and solution – both, of course, couched in terms generated from within itself. Real progress comes when the tradition in crisis recognizes *by its own lights* that the rival has the conceptual and argumentative resources it lacks. In *Whose Justice?* MacIntyre develops a history of such engagement and victory, leading from Homer to Aristotle to Augustine to Aquinas, and in *Three Rival Versions* this process is explored more fully in relation to competing nineteenth-century conceptions and their contemporary descendants. Besides saying more about the logical character of relations between these rivals, the latter book also devotes much space to characterizing what MacIntyre takes to be the most successful tradition of enquiry, *viz. Thomism.* For many readers, myself included, this will be its point of greatest interest and innovation.

Earlier I named several philosophers who are both Roman Catholics and, in a broad sense, neo-Aristotelians. These are distinguished figures but they are few in number, and fewer yet would be willing to be described as Thomists. Indeed in Great Britain I doubt that there are sufficient Thomists to constitute a football team (even assuming age and infirmity were not disqualifications). In the United States matters are certainly different, mainly because of large-scale immigration from Catholic countries and the existence of seminaries, colleges and universities established in consequence. Even so, Thomism has been in decline throughout this century as younger Catholics lost either their faith, or the traditional taste for philosophy – or having retained it took to a diet of continental thought ranging from existentialism to deconstructionism and beyond. Ironically, these French, German and Italian inspired schools are major participants in one of MacIntyre's rivals to Thomism, *viz.* the *genealogical* tradition. This might be dismissed as a sociological curiosity, but given MacIntyre's historicism he needs to explain why Thomism has lost out to Nietzsche in North American Catholic institutions of learning (or equivalently, why Gilson, Maritain and Simon have been neglected while Gadamer, Levinas and Derrida have been taken up with enthusiasm). The same is true on the continent itself. In Louvain, for example, the site of the nineteenth-century Thomist revival, Thomism has largely given way to phenomenology and critical theory. At one point MacIntyre speaks with admiration of Grabmann, Mandonnet, Gilson, Van Steenberghen and Weisheipl. But these are dead authors whose influence is confined to the most scholarly members of the neo-scholastic community, and though I share something of MacIntyre's admiration for such men they could hardly be said to have produced a renaissance of Thomistic philosophy. For good or ill (very much the latter, I think) in those places where Thomism can be found, the *zeitgeist* would suggest that if any conception has emerged victorious from an engagement of rival conceptions it is postmodernity rather than premodernity.

There are 'neo-Thomist' viewpoints from which this might not seem a bad thing, such as those which reinterpret Aquinas through the methodologies of postmodern thought. In his *Le Point de depart de la métaphysique* (1926), for example, Joseph Maréchal argued that if the Thomist synthesis was to have any chance of being 'revalidated' in the context of modern philosophy it would have to develop its methodology of inquiry. So while the metaphysical and epistemological realism of St Thomas need not be departed from, it was necessary to adopt the Kantian method of Transcendental deduction in order to address the new epistemological 'problematic'. This tradition of 'Transcendental Thomism' has continued and been developed in North America by Bernard Lonergan and others,[13] and on the continent by its most distinguished proponent Emerich Coreth. Moreover, Coreth's major work *Metaphysik* has been abridged and translated for North American college students by Joseph Donceel, another proponent of this continuation of Thomism.[14] What should come as no surprise, however, is that the content of this philosophy stands in direct opposition to the realism of Aquinas himself. So this 'revalidation' of the perennial philosophy has resulted in its transformation into one of the many anti-realisms of post-Cartesian thought. MacIntyre makes a similar point about the revival of Thomas via Kant attempted by Rosmini in the nineteenth century. Subsequently he also mentions Maréchal, but not the later figures whose influence is still active, and continues:

> And if this were the whole story of Thomism it would at least appear as, and perhaps be, a story of defeat. But happily *Aeterni Patris* [Pope Leo XIII's encyclical commending the study of Aquinas] also generated a quite different set of intellectual enterprises, those which, in retrieving stage by scholarly stage the historical understanding of what Aquinas himself said, wrote, and did, recovered for us an understanding of what is distinctive about the mode of enquiry elaborated in its classical and most adequate form by Aquinas.[15]

The 'different set of intellectual enterprises' is that associated with the historians of Thomism quoted earlier. As I remarked, however, their work – like that of English historians of philosophy writing about Lockean empiricism, for example – has produced exegetical and interpretative insights but not generated a living philosophy generally acknowledged to be able to engage with and be proven superior to Davidsonian philosophy of action, Nagelian moral psychology or Parfitian moral theory.

I also suggested, however, that the growing dominance within academic philosophy of 'postmodern' ideas and methods might not be universally unwelcome among some of those with an interest in Aquinas, for they might see in it a way to reinterpret what is at any rate not a modernist philosophy and thereby give added historical weight to the case against universalist rationalism.[16] A further example of this is suggested by MacIntyre's own discussion of the fourteenth-century fate of Aquinas's reinterpretation and synthesis of earlier traditions. He mentions

Meister Eckhart and describes his mystical theology as a repudiation of the Thomist achievement but allows that it may not have been seen as such:

> Eckhart may well have believed that he was only carrying certain strands of Aquinas's thought further. When in 1325 he was accused of heresy, he claimed to be a Thomist. But it is precisely because and insofar as he was not that he has exerted such influence on a variety of later non-Thomistic and anti-Thomistic thinkers, most notably on Hegel and Heiddeger.[17]

Several aspects of this discussion are of interest. MacIntyre goes on to quote John Caputo's interpretation of Eckhart as a kind of mystical existentialist, but charges none the less that he (Eckhart) was guilty of an erroneous appropriation of the Thomist language of 'being' for irrationalist purposes, and that Heidegger's interest in Eckhart was precisely because of this anti-Thomist stance. In an earlier book which, however, MacIntyre does not mention (entitled *Heidegger and Aquinas*) Caputo seeks 'to undertake a confrontation of the thought of Heidegger and of Thomas Aquinas on the question of Being and the problem of metaphysics', and offers a MacIntyrean sounding rationale for doing so: 'The cutting edge of this confrontation lies in the fact that each thinker is included in the other's history of the oblivion of Being.'[18] The conclusion of this study is a thesis about what lies at the heart of Aquinas's work: '[B]ehind the discursive arguments, the conceptual distinctions, the whole impressive display of *ratio* . . . there lies the experience of Being . . . a profound, if implicit mysticism. In the end, St Thomas is properly understood only by converting the coin of his metaphysical theology into its religious and alethiological equivalent.'[19]

In short, Aquinas is not so far from Eckhart and Heidegger. Clearly this conclusion is at odds with MacIntyre's interpretation, and it is a further reminder that to the extent that Aquinas is discussed by those among whom a revival might be expected he is seen in quite different historical and philosophical terms from those presented in *Three Rival Versions*. This fact also raises a general methodological question. According to MacIntyre, the superiority of Thomism consists in its ability to construct a rational narrative within which the advances and crises of other traditions can be described and transcended. But the construction of such a narrative – of self and other – is liable to be controversial. In *Whose Justice?*, MacIntyre invokes something like the theory-ladenness of observation:

> There are no preconceptual or even pretheoretical data, and this entails that no set of examples of action, no matter how comprehensive, can provide a neutral court of appeal for decision between rival theories . . . To put the

same point another way: each theory of practical reasoning is, among other things, a theory as to how examples are to be described, and how we describe any particular example will depend, therefore, upon which theory we have adopted.[20]

Applying this thesis to the present issue suggests that the competition between the Genealogist, the Encylopaedist and the Thomist, and the disputes between different proclaimed continuations of Thomism itself, such as the Kantian, the Heideggerian and the Rationalist, cannot be resolved by reference to empirical histories. In relating the sort of narrative with which MacIntyre is concerned, at least two kinds of theoretical formation will feature (perhaps inseparably intertwined). First, events will be related historically (I do not say causally); and second, history will be articulated into passages of ascent and descent, of progression, retrogression and stagnation, etc. Clearly it is a matter of contention whether the work of an author represents advance or confusion in the development of an enquiry, and such matters are not resolvable without reference to a *philosophical* investigation of the issues and arguments. But that casts doubt on the very idea that history or narrative can, of themselves, play a major part in determining the standing of a tradition. MacIntyre writes:

> The standards of achievement within any craft are justified historically. They have emerged from the criticism of their predecessors and they are justified because and in so far as they have remedied the defects and transcended the limitations of those predecessors as guides to excellent achievement within that particular craft ... So it is within forms of intellectual enquiry, whether theoretical or practical ... because at any particular moment the rationality of a craft is justified by its history so far, which has made it what it is in that specific time, place, and set of historical circumstances, such rationality is inseparable from the tradition through which it was achieved.[21]

What need to be assessed, however, are arguments and concepts considered in their own right and largely independently of their role in any recorded sequence of debates. This thought prompts worries about the historical conception and methods of enquiry which constitute the framework of MacIntyre's project, but it also directs attention on to the philosophical character of the Thomism he favours.

Given MacIntyre's criticism of Rosmini and others, it would be ironic if he were guilty of a similar revisionist tendency. But as I read his trilogy I find myself worrying about this, and the main worry is related to the earlier concern about relativism. There is not the opportunity here to enter into detailed debate about the interpretation of Aquinas or the status of the arguments and theses MacIntyre advances. But perhaps I may register a doubt about the general character of the position. In

several places in *Whose Justice?* and *Three Rival Versions*, MacIntyre
sets out elements of the Thomist view. This is done in ways which contribute to the establishment of that view as a *via media* between the
radical relativism of the genealogist and the universal rationalism of the
encyclopaedist.

One way of viewing this third tradition is as a mode of thinking
that recognizes the truth in each of its rivals while rejecting the false.
The genealogist insists on the historically situated and open-ended character of enquiry and concludes that its objects are similarly immanent –
that they are, in some sense, constructions or projections of thought
rather than independent features detected by it. The encyclopaedist, by
contrast, takes the objects of reason to be transcendent and assumes that
the means of engagement with them are likewise independent of historical conditions of enquiry. In response to these opposing assertions one
might try to construct a *via media* by combining the idea of the immanence and open-endedness of the means of enquiry with that of the
transcendence of its objects. In places MacIntyre seems to offer just this
view of the Thomism he espouses. That is to say, he presents it as a form
of theistic philosophical realism committed to a view of the objects of
reason as mind-independent, but a realism which maintains that reason
itself is shaped and advanced through traditions of enquiry.

At least four questions now arise in my mind. First, whether this is
an accurate description of MacIntyre's view. Second, whether it is faithful to the character of Aquinas's epistemology and metaphysics. Third,
whether this combination of ideas is a coherent one. And fourth, whether,
if it is coherent, it does not trivialize, or at least diminish the philosophical interest of, the historical-tradition model of the circumstances of
enquiry. Needless to say, these questions are related to one another. As
regards its accuracy to MacIntyre's intentions, consider the following:

> The temporal reference of reasoning within a craft thus differs strikingly
> from that of either encyclopaedic or genealogical reasoning. The encyclo-
> paedist aims at providing timeless, universal, and objective truths as his
> or her conclusions, but aspires to do so by reasoning which has from the
> outset the same properties. From the outset all reasoning must be such as
> would be compelling to any fully rational person whatsoever. Rationality,
> like truth, is independent of time, place, and historical circumstances ...
> [For the genealogist] to treat tradition as a resource is one more way of
> allowing the past to subjugate the present. And the central symptom of the
> sickness of this type of social existence, from the genealogical standpoint,
> is that, despite its historical recognition of the historical situatedness of
> all reason-giving and reason-offering, it understands the truth to which it
> aspires as timeless. Hence the rationality of craft-tradition is as alien and
> hostile to the genealogical enterprise as is the encyclopaedist's to either.[22]

This sounds like the *via media* I described, incorporating a realist metaphysics, and certainly MacIntyre cites Aquinas in terms which affirm both writers as realists. Elsewhere, however, truth is characterized in ways that suggest a pragmatist version of anti-realism: 'The mind is adequate to its objects [i.e. attains to truth] in so far as the expectations which it frames on the basis of [its] activities are not liable to disappointment and the remembering which it engages in enables it to return to and recover what it had encountered previously, whether the objects themselves are still present or not.'[23]

Subsequently he explicitly criticizes the identification of the concept of truth with that of warranted assertability on the grounds that what is warranted at one stage of enquiry may not be so later: 'The concept of truth, however, is timeless.'[24] But two points are relevant to this. First, an anti-realist need not seek to identify truth with warranted assertability. He may not be looking for conceptual analyses, anyhow; but even if he were, the relevant notion would be something like Hilary Putnam's 'idealized rational acceptability'[25] and that looks to be what MacIntyre's inquiry-based account suggests. Second, given the conceptual connections between rationality and truth, and the claim that the former is immanent within, and constituted by, traditions of enquiry, it is difficult to see how truth itself can be tradition-transcendent, which is what metaphysical realism requires.

The latter issue concerns the coherence of the combination offered by the *via media*. No such question would arise if the claim that practical and theoretical enquiries are tradition-immanent were to be interpreted as saying no more than that the forms and progress of enquiries are shaped by history. This removes a philosophical worry but at the price of turning the major thesis of MacIntyre's trilogy into a commonplace of humane learning. And certainly he is claiming something more: 'It is no trivial matter that all claims to knowledge are the claims of some particular person, developed out of the claims of other particular persons. Knowledge is possessed only in and through participation of dialectical encounters.'[26]

My persistent worry is that any interpretation of this claim which makes it out to be more than a version of the commonplace of scholarship must lead to a relativism quite at odds with what I take to be the philosophy of Aquinas. Like MacIntyre, I view the work of St Thomas with interest and admiration and look to it as a source for the articulation of a credible form of philosophical realism.[27] I very much hope, therefore, that we will see a future volume by MacIntyre setting out the truth in Thomism – in ways which make clear why such worries as I have presented here are unfounded.

NOTES

Work on the essay was done during the period of a Visiting Fellowship at the Institute for Advanced Studies in the Humanities, University of Edinburgh. I am grateful to the Director (Professor Peter Jones), staff and co-fellows of the Institute for making my time there agreeable and educative. I am also indebted to the Carnegie Trust for the Universities of Scotland for financial support.

Epigraph from the introduction to Pope Puis XII, *Humani Generis* (1950), paras 1, 6, 7; translated under the title *False Trends in Modern Teaching: False Opinions which Threaten to Sap the Foundations of Catholic Teaching* (rev. edn, Catholic Truth Society, London, 1959).

1 *After Virtue* (Duckworth, London, 1981).
2 *Whose Justice? Which Rationality?* (Duckworth, London, 1988).
3 *Three Rival Versions of Moral Inquiry* (Duckworth, London, 1990).
4 G. E. M. Anscombe, 'Modern moral philosophy', *Philosophy*, 33 (1958); reprinted in *Ethics, Religion and Politics: The Collected Philosophical Papers of G. E. M. Anscombe*, vol. 3 (Blackwell, Oxford, 1981).
5 In fact her view may be more complicated than this, see 'Authority in morals', in Anscombe, *Ethics, Religion and Politics*, vol. 3; *Contraception and Chastity* (Catholic Truth Society, London, 1977); and 'Morality', in *Pro Ecclesia et Pontifice* (London, 1982).
6 It is interesting to note in passing how many of those associated with an influential cognitivist movement within moral philosophy belong within this broad grouping: Elizabeth Anscombe, John Finnis, Peter Geach, Germain Grisez, Alasdair MacIntyre, Charles Taylor and Henry Veatch.
7 *After Virtue*, ch. 12. I try to defend the appeal to naturalistic philosophical anthropology in support of normative enquiry in 'Metaphysics in the philosophy of education', *Journal of Philosophy of Education*, 23 (1989).
8 I cannot discuss this aspect of MacIntyre's work here but I believe that the radical case against individualism is overstated by MacIntyre and its other well-known critics, *viz.* Charles Taylor and Michael Sandel. I discuss something of this in 'Individuals and the theory of justice', *Ratio*, 27 (1985), and in 'Political theory and the nature of persons: an ineliminable metaphysical presupposition', *Philosophical Papers*, 6 (1992). By the same token, a modest communitarian conclusion seems warranted by consideration of the conditions of reflective agency. This is explored in 'Identity, community and the limits of multiculture', *Public Affairs Quarterly*, 7 (1993).
9 See Donald Davidson, 'On the very idea of a conceptual scheme', in *Inquiries into Truth and Interpretation* (Clarendon, Oxford, 1984).
10 *Whose Justice? Which Rationality?*, p. 393.
11 *Three Rival Versions*, ch. 3, p. 63; ch. 6, p. 130. I discuss the same issue from an avowedly realist interpretation of Aquinas in 'Chesterton's philosophy of education', *Philosophy*, 65 (1990).
12 *Whose Justice? Which Rationality?*, p. 367.
13 See B. Lonergan, *Insight: A Study of Human Understanding* (Longman, London, 1957). For an appreciative analytical account of Lonergan see Hugo Meynell, *An Introduction to the Philosophy of Bernard Lonergan* (Macmillan, London, 1976).
14 *Metaphysics*, ed. and trans. J. Donceel (Herder and Herder, New York, 1968).

15 *Three Rival Versions*, p. 77. For the text of *Aeterni Patris* and interesting discussions of the development of Thomism since its publication, see V. Brezik (ed.), *One Hundred Years of Thomism* (Center for Thomistic Studies, Houston, 1981).

16 I should note my considerable reservations about the use of such terms and expressions as 'postmodernism', 'the project of modernity' and so on. My own use of them is broadly quotational. For a development of these reservations see 'Cultural theory, philosophy and the study of human affairs', in *Postmodernism in the Social Sciences*, ed. J. Doherty, E. Graham, M. Malek and D. Riches (Macmillan, London, 1991).

17 *Three Rival Versions*, pp. 165–6.

18 See John D. Caputo, *Heidegger and Aquinas: An Essay on Overcoming Metaphysics* (Fordham University Press, New York, 1982), pp. 1–2.

19 Ibid., p. 283.

20 *Whose Justice? Which Rationality?*, p. 333.

21 *Three Rival Versions*, pp. 64–5.

22 Ibid., pp. 64–6.

23 *Whose Justice? Which Rationality?*, p. 356.

24 Ibid., p. 363.

25 I think there are interesting resemblances between MacIntyre's position and the subtle ideas developed by Putnam. See the latter's *Representation and Reality* (MIT Press, Cambridge, Mass., 1988), 'Internal realism as an alternative picture', pp. 113–6, and 'Realism with a human face' in *Realism with a Human Face* (Harvard University Press, Cambridge, Mass., 1990).

26 *Three Rival Versions*, p. 202.

27 I try to develop some of the elements of this in 'Brentano's problem', *Grazer Philosophische Studien*, 35 (1989), and in 'Mind/world identity theory and the anti-realist challenge', in *Reality, Representation and Projection*, ed. J. Haldane and C. Wright (Oxford University Press, New York, 1993).

6

Projecting the Enlightenment

Robert Wokler

I

In three chapters of *After Virtue* Alasdair MacIntyre describes what he terms 'the Enlightenment Project' whose breakdown underlies the chaos of moral values in contemporary culture. That project was in his view centrally concerned with providing universal standards by which to justify particular courses of action in every sphere of life, and although Enlightenment thinkers manifestly did not agree as to exactly *which* principles might be acceptable to rational persons, he claims they nevertheless collectively propagated the doctrine that such principles must exist, and that moral conduct must therefore be subject to intelligible vindication or criticism. Many post-Enlightenment philosophers have continued to pursue that aim, but in the absence of any prevalent framework of values within which moral judgements could be agreed, they have only shown, according to MacIntyre, that this ideal cannot be attained. The legacy of the Enlightenment has therefore been to render our morality confused – to divide our allegiances between different competing doctrines and to foster disagreement about what is right and good, even when we seek to make our standards plain. Without already settled moral beliefs, we have come to identify our principles only in terms of abstract notions of the self and individual choice, freed from the contingencies of social roles or historical tradition. In such a world every person may legislate his or her own code of conduct. Adrift in the democratic sea of modernity, we clutch at values which are incompatible, incommensurable and arbitrary.

A similar argument, albeit with different emphases, also informs both *Whose Justice? Which Rationality?* and *Three Rival Versions of Moral Inquiry*. Six chapters of *Whose Justice?* are devoted to seventeenth- and eighteenth-century themes, mainly concerned with the peculiar blend of Calvinist Augustinianism and Renaissance Aristotelianism deemed to be centrally distinctive of the background to the Scottish Enlightenment, and with Hutcheson's and Hume's conceptions of practical reason and justice, all in the context of an overarching image of the Enlightenment, whose 'central aspiration' is described there (p. 6) in much the same terms as in *After Virtue*. In *Three Rival Versions* MacIntyre offers a critical assessment of a universalist framework of moral discourse which he associates especially with the ninth edition of the *Encyclopaedia Britannica*, dating from 1873, inspired, in turn, by principles of science, reason and progress, and by an allegedly 'unified secular vision of the world' (*TRV*, p. 216) such as had already been infused in the Enlightenment *Encyclopédie* of Diderot and d'Alembert.

If pride of place among moral philosophers seems to pass slowly from Aristotle to Aquinas in his three most canonical writings, MacIntyre's Enlightenment Project, by contrast, remains largely unreconstructed, unredeemed and undiminished in its failure, even after substantial embellishment. His three principal works comprise an extraordinary indictment of the theoretical and practical legacy of eighteenth-century philosophy, as comprehensive as any among the numerous critiques produced over the past half-century, and among the most trenchant since Burke's *Reflections on the Revolution in France* and Hyppolite Taine's *Origines de la France contemporaine*. His account projects the Enlightenment's implications and influence as they stem from its aims. He holds it to blame for some of the most sinister aspects of a morally vacuous civilization, cursed by the malediction of unlicensed Reason. His intellectual history of the period forms one of the mainsprings of his own philosophy.

Of course opposition to a putative Enlightenment Project figures conspicuously in many other doctrines, including perhaps all of the most prominent ideologies of the past two hundred years. Conservatives and Romantics have characteristically condemned the scepticism, atheism and generally critical temper of eighteenth-century speculative philosophy for bringing into question the very foundations of the *ancien régime*, thereby allegedly inspiring the French revolutionaries with their anti-authoritarian spirit and a zealous determination to transform the world, which culminated in the Jacobin Terror. Marxists, radicals and communitarians have judged its commitment either to utilitarianism or to natural rights as heralding the age of bourgeois liberties, appropriate to a world of independent producers engaged in maximizing their separate interests, under bureaucratic authorities following principles of instrumental reason. Modern liberals and libertarians have instead judged the Enlightenment's espousal of at least some of the rights of man as conducive to institutions of popular sovereignty and democratic control which have prompted state interference in the private domain and have proved hostile to the interests of commercial society. Such images of the Enlightenment are of course scarcely compatible, and they ill accord with the substantial intellectual debt which the same ideologies are also said to owe to eighteenth-century philosophy. But MacIntyre's account owes little to them. Although he seems to share certain misgivings about the loss of public engagement and the moral fragmentation of modern life with communitarian critics of the Enlightenment (like Charles Taylor and Michael Sandel), and although he may appear to have come to such views by a similar route, passing above all from Hegel, his objections in fact have a rather different focus and, by and large, as I hope to indicate, a strikingly distinct pedigree.

In retracing that pedigree and thus attempting, as it were, to reproject the steps of his own construal of the Enlightenment Project's trajectory, I mean to show how his interpretation of an intellectual tradition depends above all on his assessment of its impact. And while most of my remarks here stem from a quite different understanding of the Enlightenment which leads me to take issue with MacIntyre's claims, I should first like to give due weight to what I take to be the chief merits of his approach. In *After Virtue* and elsewhere he puts a compelling case for the integration of moral philosophy with moral behaviour and conduct, rejecting the demarcations of academic disciplines which, on the one hand, keep the metaphilosophy of morals uncontaminated by historical and sociological commentary, and, on the other, leave down-to-earth historical discourse uninformed by theoretical analysis. Overcoming the double barrenness of detached philosophy and mindless history has been an admirable aim promoted by MacIntyre throughout his career, and he has pursued it in this context by recounting how certain speculative presuppositions gave rise to consequences which have shaped the lives of persons and indeed the character of whole societies, even when their members are scarcely aware of their own fundamental moral uncertainties spawned by such beliefs. As the title of the fifth chapter of *After Virtue* makes plain, the Enlightenment Project of justifying morality which MacIntyre portrays not only failed, but 'had to fail'. The chaos of values prevalent in democratic society is the negation in concrete form which springs from the negativity of its philosophy. Corresponding in the world of ideas to a defunct institution which fetters the development of a new productive force, it had to be annihilated, and it was.

Claims of such magnitude are seldom made by philosophers, least of all by those whose analytical skills were sharpened as his were by the scalpels of post World War II Oxford. MacIntyre's philosophy of history is on a grand scale, scarcely attempted in this century since Oswald Spengler and Arnold Toynbee, and far more persuasive – not to mention intelligible – than either. In its attempt to thread the unity of theory and practice within the morals of modern civilization it is boldly conceived and splendidly incautious – indeed profoundly reminiscent in its nature of the Enlightenment Project he holds in such low esteem. In a sense, it might even be described as that Project turned upside down, or back to front, inspired as it is by a deep religious conviction and a profound sense of faith of a kind from which eighteenth-century sceptical philosophers, themselves missionaries in reverse, endeavoured to liberate peoples enthralled by them. MacIntyre's philosophy of history, moreover, forms a richly textured tapestry drawn from an impressively wide range of reading, both of primary sources and modern authorities, most notably, perhaps, with regard to the Scottish Enlightenment, but also on Aristotle, medieval conceptions of morality, nineteenth-century ethics, and contemporary French and American philosophy. If *After Virtue* remains his principal work, because of its depth and scale, *Whose Justice? Which Rationality?* and *Three Rival Versions* make more substantial contributions to the history of ideas on account of their scholarship, increasingly remarkable for its historical specificity and attention to detail. These works do not recapitulate the all too glaringly obvious errors so unfortunately evident in his *Short History of Ethics*; in taking stock of his philosophy of history as a whole, current readers must learn to grapple not only with the subtle turns of his argument but also with the both dense and delicate contextual treatments of the writings and authors he investigates. It is a formidable achievement, demanding close scrutiny. The Enlightenment Project portrayed at its heart is, nevertheless, profoundly misleading.

II

In *After Virtue* that Project is reconstructed from its nineteenth-century dénouement to its seventeenth-century source by the regression of a lineage of concepts not unlike Alex Haley's search for his ancestral family in *Roots*. MacIntyre begins with the publication of Kierkegaard's *Enten–Eller* (*Either–Or*) in 1842, a work which is found to herald the capriciousness of moral choice in contemporary culture, in that it provides an account of two contrasting ways of life – the ethical, or the realm of duty, and the aesthetic, or the realm of pleasure and satisfaction – without offering any grounds to justify one over the other. What makes the argument of Kierkegaard seem so disturbing is the apparent incommensurability of two distinct value systems, and the arbitrariness and irrationality of any moral choice between them. That perspective, according to MacIntyre, was largely inspired by Kant, whom Kierkegaard had read with care, and whose ethics provide the essential background for his own philosophy (*AV*, p. 42). Kant, that is, while making compliance with duty a morally binding principle, had provided no logical grounds for doing so, leaving the performance of duty for duty's sake indefensible to anyone who elected to act in accordance with self-interested prudence rather than disinterested reason (*AV*, pp. 44–5). Kierkegaard merely appropriated Kant's doctrine to show that the precepts of reason could not themselves be rationally vindicated. Kant, moreover, had put forward his own conception of duty as a universal law largely to overturn a hedonistic morality whose principles prescribed that duty stems from passion or interest. No moral code, he contended, could be based on the pursuit of happiness or personal benefit, since our duties would then hold only conditionally, overturned without contradiction when our advantage changed.

The two central Enlightenment figures whom MacIntyre identifies as subscribing to the sort of principles Kant deemed immoral are Diderot, on the one hand, and Hume on the other. In *Le Neveu de Rameau*, Diderot, speaking in his own voice, propounds the view that the conservative rules of bourgeois morality conform to conscientious desire and passion, while speaking as the nephew of the dialogue, he acknowledges that such rules are just sophisticated disguises for our devious and predatory abuse of one another. The logic of any ethic of desire which corresponds with feelings obliges him, claims MacIntyre, to recognize that there are incompatible desires which may be ordered in rival ways (*AV*, pp. 45–6). Hume, independently and more philosophically, is deemed to have put forward much the same thesis. Convinced that morality must either be the work of reason or of the passions, he contended that it had to be attributable to the passions, since they alone form the springs of human action. Of course he allowed that moral judgements required the invocation of general rules, but, like Diderot, he sought to account for such rules by explaining 'their utility in helping . . . to attain those ends which the passions set before us' (*AV*, p. 46), and in both his *Treatise of Human Nature* and his *Enquiry Concerning the Principles of Morals* he sought to explain how persons might feel bound to adhere unconditionally to certain rules by discriminating between desires and feelings according to normative criteria of a kind which could not themselves be feelings (*AV*, pp. 46–7). In this sense, Hume and Kant may be understood as exact philosophical counterparts within the Enlightenment Project, the one deriving his morality from reason, the other from passion – in one case, indeed, laying the groundwork for all subsequent rights-based deontological moral philosophies, in the other promoting the consequentialist and utilitarian ethics of the post-Enlightenment world.

In drawing this group portrait to its close, MacIntyre concludes that Hume may even have found inspiration in the Jansenism of Pascal, whose conception of reason as a merely calculative faculty which cannot inspire action or belief anticipated his own view that it could serve as a means but never prescribe the ends of human endeavour. According to MacIntyre, Pascal stands at a seminally important point in the history of the Enlightenment Project (*AV*, p. 52), since his account of reason, so attuned to the innovations of seventeenth-century philosophy and science, excluded the Scholastic essences conceived as potentialities to act which had been inherited from Aristotle. At the heart of the Enlightenment Project, as he describes it in *After Virtue*, lay a rejection of teleology so central to Aristotle's developmental notion of man's perfection. In abandoning that idea of self-fulfilment, philosophers of the Enlightenment left no place for the classical ethics of virtue, which articulated qualities that promoted the excellence of character. They regarded the nature of humanity as uniform and constant, thus dismembering the moral consciousness of man by cutting off the contingent and unfolding truths of his experience from the realm of duty and obligation. Whether rooting morality in reason or passion, their diremption of one from the other entailed the loss of reason's capacity to control what the passions pursued. It divorced the precepts of morality from the facts of human nature, leaving individuals as sovereign masters of their own conduct. In this sense Pascal's conception of reason as incapable of prescription heralds Kierkegaard's notion of the irrationality of moral choice. The Enlightenment Project can be seen to have cast moral philosophy adrift by its rejection of the classical ethics of virtue and the entelechies of Aristotle and Scholasticism.

In *Whose Justice?* MacIntyre's portrait of the Scottish Enlightenment takes shape by contrast in the opposite direction – that is, forward, from the mid-seventeenth century, by reconstituting the deconstructed tradition described in *After Virtue* with much fuller embellishment and greater elaboration within a particular tradition, now inaugurated rather than consummated by the rejection of Aristotle. His refashioned and refocused argument, of substantially greater length than in *After Virtue*, proceeds in the following way. As a result of the 1707 Treaty of Union with England, Scotland lost her sovereignty but not her identity, sustained against Anglican cultural forces by the Presbyterian order of its Calvinist Church, by the institutions and practitioners of Scots law, and by its unique and relatively homogenous educational system which promoted a peculiarly Scottish ethos of Protestant civility (*WJ*, p. 220). In this closely knit nexus of legal, theological and educational systems, the five national universities (at a time when England had just two) filled a central role, both spiritual and practical, in the articulation of a Scottish identity, and MacIntyre devotes most of his attention to that role, and especially to the contribution made within it by professors of moral philosophy, as 'one of the most important bearers of a distinctly Scottish tradition' (*WJ*, p. 251).

The coexistence of Augustinian theology with the revived study of

Aristotelianism had been sustained in seventeenth-century Scottish universities through the influence of men like Robert Baillie, Principal of Glasgow University after the Restoration, and Viscount Stair, Lord President of the Scottish Court of Session, but the political settlement with England, and the need perceived by Scottish educationalists to contend with the pretensions of the new sciences and metaphysics of their day, put the adherents to what is termed 'the central Scottish intellectual tradition' (*WJ*, p. 254) under strain to reaffirm both their faith and their principles. According to MacIntyre, Frances Hutcheson, appointed to the Glasgow Chair of Moral Philosophy in 1730, felt a special responsibility to meet such needs because he assumed himself entrusted with the task of secular instruction in Christian theology as well. In his lectures and publications based upon them he attempted to refine the philosophical principles of morality he had inherited partly from Aristotelian Scholasticism and partly from Calvinism, mainly in the light of Shaftesbury's psychological account of the passions. From Shaftesbury he developed an idea of the *moral sense* as a kind of inward rationale for principles which could no longer be shown to be true in the light of either Reason or Revelation, but which corresponded closely with the religious feelings of his contemporaries, who had grown both politically and spiritually vulnerable to moral conflict. Hutcheson's doctrine was thus espoused with enthusiasm by his students, and ministers, merchants, advocates and the gentry all rushed to subscribe to his posthumously published *System of Moral Philosophy*. As MacIntyre observes, it had been his remarkable achievement to provide 'new foundations both for moral theology and for the philosophy of law and justice, and in doing so preserving the distinctive characteristics of the Scottish presbyterian and intellectual tradition' (*WJ*, pp. 278–9).

That achievement, however, proved short-lived and unstable, for on the subversive road leading from the lowlands of Perfidious Albion there soon appeared Hume. Cosmopolitan philosopher and historian of England, Hume, says MacIntyre, writes of his native Scotland 'as if it were a foreign country' (*WJ*, p. 320), uncultivated, uncivilized, barbarous. Although he was in certain respects indebted to Hutcheson – partly for his own account of the passions in his *Treatise of Human Nature* and above all in his acceptance of the claim that reason is practically inert (*WJ*, p. 285) – he shared none of Hutcheson's attachment to a Scottish Presbyterian social and intellectual tradition. He spoke for himself, in the first person, and turned to Hutcheson, together with Hobbes, Shaftesbury, Mandeville and others, only to provide an account of the complex intentionality of human passions which was superior to theirs (*WJ*, p. 293). That account imputes to the self a social identity shaped in reciprocal relations with and expectations of other persons, and it provides

the framework of a moral philosophy whose evaluative principles accord with human passions and not with any standards of right reason
independent of men's judgement.

Yet on inspection it transpires that the conservative principles of
justice, property, order and rank which Hume in fact endorses are most
distinctive of the social order, embracing landowning classes and their
clients, which he inhabited himself and of which he approved, so that
what his philosophy presents as human nature turns out to be eighteenth-
century *English* human nature and, indeed, only the dominant variant of
that (*WJ*, p. 295). Whereas Hutcheson's moral philosophy had sought to
renew as well as preserve a Scottish inheritance in religion, law and
education in the face of new challenges, Hume had grasped that Scottish
theology and law could not survive such change. He therefore under-
took to refute the conceptual foundations of Scotland's past. Its
unphilosophical culture, he came to believe, stood in the way of philosophical enquiry and a general science of human nature. Together with
other thinkers of the Enlightenment, as was once remarked, although
not about Hume,[1] he thus threw dust in our eyes even while pointing
in the direction he wished us to follow. He has made those persuaded
by him blind to what we in fact need to recover, that is, 'a conception
of rational enquiry ... embodied in a tradition', whose standards of
justification emerge from and are vindicated within it (*WJ*, p. 7).

III

What are we to make of this? To my mind, it is all wonderfully confused, both in method and substance, generally and in detail. An Enlightenment Project shaped by a mid seventeenth-century Jansenist
(Pascal) and a mid nineteenth-century Christian existentialist
(Kierkegaard), with an encyclopaedic romantic (Diderot) and a motley
crew of Scots and Germans between them, needs more justification to
pass muster than MacIntyre provides. It may be thought that the diversity of thinkers linked with that whole assemblage is too great, or the
tensions between them too profound, to allow any ascription of a ge-
neric identity or common purpose to them, and eighteenth-century
scholars who have failed to uncover any such 'project' or 'movement' or
even 'the Enlightenment' after a lifetime's research devoted to the subject could be forgiven their exasperation when confronted by so great a
leap and quick fix.

But let us grant that the idea of an 'Enlightenment Project' is credible.
Even if our terminology was not employed by eighteenth-century
thinkers themselves (the expression 'Scottish Enlightenment', for instance,
was apparently invented in 1900), what we have in mind may indeed

have formed part of the self-image of that age. The literary salons and
academies, the moral weeklies and journals, the *Encyclopédie* and other
dictionaries of the arts and sciences, the association of philosophy with
kingship which in the eighteenth century was already described as 'en-
lightened despotism', all lend warrant to the notion of shared principles,
a campaign, an international society of the republic of letters, a party of
humanity. Its friends and critics would not perhaps have been surprised
to hear its name, but they would have been entitled, as are MacIntyre's
readers, to learn what the Project was about. What was its political
economy, its anthropology, its conjectural history or philosophy of
science? Allowing that it failed, and perhaps even had to fail, would it
not have been appropriate first to explain what it set out to achieve?
And would it not also have been sensible to identify its central figures?
Montesquieu is nowhere mentioned in *After Virtue* or *Whose Justice?*,
while Rousseau receives only the most scanty attention and Smith hardly
much more. How is it possible that Voltaire – the godfather of the
Enlightenment Project on any plausible interpretation of its meaning –
is altogether missing from MacIntyre's cast? Readers anticipating that
after the Scots he must address the French may be disheartened to discover from *Whose Justice?* (p. 11) that the only tradition of practical
reasoning in the Enlightenment which MacIntyre deems worthy of similar attention is that of Kant, Prussian public law and Lutheran theology.

At least part of the explanation of his neglect of French thinkers is
that he regards them as relatively insignificant by comparison with the
intellectual range and variety of the Scots, contending, furthermore,
that their general lack of a secularized Protestant background and the
absence from their country of a politically influential intelligentsia which
might have read their works, or progressive universities that might have
been attentive to them, left them alienated from their own society, as
Scottish, English, Dutch, Danish and Prussian intellectuals were not
(*AV*, p. 36). I confess my failure to comprehend the significance of their
lack of Protestantism, but put baldly in this way each of these points
is in fact false. The *philosophes* of the Enlightenment characteristically
exercised a great deal *more* influence in France, and over the political life
of their nation, than did intellectuals in other European countries, not
least because France enjoyed by far the most substantial reading public
in the eighteenth century, *outside* the universities which resisted their
ideas, though they also had allies among scholars and scientists within
universities and in the academies, as well as among liberal theologians,
of whom several contributed to the *Encyclopédie*.

Yet supposing that MacIntyre's inaccurate claims about the institutional marginality of French Enlightenment thinkers were true, his
premise about the depth and range of their influence would still be false.

In so far as the *philosophes* of the French Enlightenment were self-employed writers, they were often *more* free to speak their mind, unconstrained by the obligations of office or the duties of teaching a prescribed syllabus. Their apparent licence to comment on topical issues of the day made their influence all the greater, not only in France but in French-reading circles throughout Europe and even America. When, as often happened, they were judged to have abused their freedom, they were not just excluded from university appointments but imprisoned or exiled, which enhanced their reputations still more. MacIntyre appears to subscribe to the view that only holders of public positions, with socially rooted responsibilities, can exercise any real impact on their followers. But that is surely absurd. To the extent that the Enlightenment was indeed a critically subversive movement, as MacIntyre portrays it, its estrangement from the settled institutions of its day, in France and elsewhere, enhanced its power. By deliberately excluding a French focus from his study, MacIntyre offers his readers an account of peripheries without a core. His Enlightenment Project has been shorn of its projectionist.

Only two French eighteenth-century figures attain any prominence in his work – Diderot and the Chevalier de Jaucourt. *Three Rival Versions* contains several paragraphs devoted to Jaucourt's articles 'Morale' and 'Moralité' for the *Encyclopédie*, which embrace the proposition that morality is a matter of general rules independent of religious faith, inviting MacIntyre's comment that 'it is striking how far other thinkers of the Enlightenment agree' with him (*TRV*, p. 175). If he had added that Jaucourt was of Huguenot background he might have judged his influence even greater, but what in fact is most striking about the judgement of Jaucourt's contemporaries was their agreement that he was just an indefatigable compiler of the views of others. Diderot himself, who had cause to be grateful to him for completing more than one-quarter of the *Encyclopédie* single-handed, wrote precisely this. Jaucourt of course drew most of his material from other encyclopaedias, including those of Moreri, Chambers and Brucker, and in the case of 'Morale' and 'Moralité' he may have relied most of all upon Bayle. It was not at all difficult to be persuaded by a man who spoke on behalf of so many others.

Diderot is introduced by MacIntyre not as a contributor to his own *Encyclopédie* but as the author of the *Neveu de Rameau*. The main point MacIntyre elicits from that work, as we have seen, is that the older Diderot, the bourgeois moralist in the dialogue, cannot legislate between his own moral preferences and those of the bohemian nephew, thus admitting that there are irredeemably incompatible orderings of desire (*AV*, p. 46; see also *WJ*, p. 346). This thesis is contrasted by MacIntyre with the proposition advanced in the *Supplément au voyage de*

Bougainville, where Diderot instead acknowledges the superiority of natural desires (such as exercise free rein in Polynesia) over the corrupted desires characteristic of Western civilization. That distinction, states MacIntyre, cannot survive the proposition – in short, that we have no grounds for discriminating between desires – which in *Le Neveu de Rameau* Diderot at last forces himself to recognize (*AV*, p. 46). But this is a misreading of the *Supplément*, whose central claim is that a morality in accordance with nature is preferable to one that combats it. Western civilization is found to repress natural desires rather than to espouse different ones. The *Supplément* does not discriminate between desires but between moralities, and it commends only what is compatible with the promptings of nature. There are, moreover, reasons to doubt whether the unresolved dramatic tensions between the two fictional protagonists of *Le Neveu de Rameau* express the fundamental moral scepticism of their author's own philosophy. In any case, the *Supplément* was drafted more than ten years after *Le Neveu* and, in conjunction with several other writings, it appears to reflect Diderot's considered judgement that moral principles should accord with both public utility and physiology, which he does not see as giving rise to a conflict of desires. MacIntyre's forays into eighteenth-century French moral philosophy, in short, do not carry sufficient conviction.

Neither, regrettably, do his comments about Scotland. The six Scottish chapters of *Whose Justice?* shed much illumination on a society whose legal and religious institutions, buttressed by its educational curriculum, reinforced a sense of national identity which was and remains among the most remarkable in Europe. If MacIntyre's elegiac tribute to a noble and indigenous tradition of practical reasoning seems sometimes to approximate a Scottish Nationalist Party broadcast of the songs of Ossian, I do not wish to quarrel with him for that, even though the civic culture and ethics of virtue which he portrays before the Union of 1707 strike me as unduly uniform and unlikely to have been quite so prevalent as he suggests. What I cannot detect is any evidence that Hutcheson assumed the responsibilities for sustaining that tradition which MacIntyre entrusts to him after his appointment to the Glasgow Professorship of Moral Philosophy. For one thing, his principal writings, including those which Hutcheson himself judged most original, had already been completed and published before he took up his Chair. His theory of the *moral sense* was thus fully articulated prior to the ascribed occasion of its composition.

In so far as his philosophical works reflect a specifically national focus, moreover, they appear less Scottish than Irish, not only on account of their having been drafted in Ireland by a native Ulsterman, but more notably because they were intended principally for the Presbyterian students of the private academy he had established in Dublin in 1718, and they figure in a campaign waged out of that city in the 1720s by the circle of Viscount Molesworth to inculcate among Irish youth a respect for liberty and virtue, which it was thought were inadequately embraced in Scottish universities. Hutcheson was to take up his Glasgow appointment not as a conservative adherent to a Scottish tradition of higher education but as a vigorously critical reformer. His widely attested popularity as a lecturer in Glasgow, partly due to his casual style of delivery in English rather than by way of Latin readings, was even more attributable to the zealotry of his preaching a joyously uplifting moral philosophy in accordance with benign nature and providence, that contrasted with the gloomy precepts around original sin of Augustinian Scholasticism. The Scottish theological tradition which MacIntyre claims Hutcheson reaffirmed was actually rejected by him, and indeed rejected with as much determination as, for other reasons, still in the same period of his life, he opposed the jurisprudence of Pufendorf and the epistemology of Locke. If in apparently espousing Christian Stoicism Hutcheson eventually proved more morally conservative than he might have wished, this was not because of his resolve, as a professor, to keep alive a peculiarly Scottish intellectual inheritance, but almost the opposite – that is, because the pedagogical demands of his office required him to teach by way of textbooks and compendia in accordance with a prescribed syllabus which, by and large, was not of his choosing. The two major works he produced after 1730, the *Synopsis metaphysicae* and the *System of Moral Philosophy*, were deemed by him, in the first case, 'a trifle ... foolishly printed', and, in the second, 'a confused book ... a farrago'. This distinguished university professor, according to MacIntyre a bearer of a great Scottish tradition, could in fact prove a bore, even to himself, when weighed down by the burdens of his office.

While he portrays Hutcheson as having deliberately aimed at reaffirming the values of a beleaguered past, MacIntyre sometimes depicts Enlightenment thinkers as instead unwitting adherents of circumscribed social practices, advocating ideals which really serve only particular interests as if they were of universal validity. Hume, whose favourite principles are found to be specially well-suited to the interests of the landed gentry, is represented in just this way, and so too are both Diderot and Kant. Each of these figures is depicted as ostensibly radical in his philosophy but in fact conservative as a moralist – Diderot mainly on account of his concern with the responsibilities of parenthood, Hume and Kant largely because of their uncompromising views on the need to keep promises. But do such moral standpoints really reflect the settled social institutions by which philosophers of a certain disposition feel bound? Diderot's anxieties about his daughter, to whom MacIntyre refers, were largely inspired by his rage and frustration at the morally reprobate conventions of a system of marriage which required intricate negotiations to ensure her dowry, while the fastidious respect for promises shown by Hume and Kant may just exemplify the awesome esteem for marriage vows felt by two shy bachelors psychologically incapable of undertaking them.

The connections between normative principles and social institutions which MacIntyre seeks to draw seem to me elusive and inconsistent. Why, for instance, did the Enlightenment Project issue in the moral disorder of contemporary culture but not noticeably in the chaos of the French Revolution? MacIntyre makes a point of challenging certain writers, among whom he names J. L. Talmon, Isaiah Berlin and Daniel Bell, who have traced the origins of totalitarianism and the Jacobin Terror to the Enlightenment. Jacobinism, he claims, was inspired not only by the virtues of liberty, equality and fraternity, but also by patriotism, productive labour and a simplicity of manners which owed much to the influence of Rousseau and, more distantly, to Aristotle. Such benign communitarian sources manifestly could not have been responsible for violence. Indeed, MacIntyre doubts whether any commitment to virtue could have been 'so powerful as to be able to produce of itself such stupendous effects' as the Terror, which he ascribes instead to the political institutionalization of virtue through desperate means employed by men such as Saint-Just (*AV*, p. 221).

But how is it that the institutionalization of virtue during the French Revolution exculpates the moral philosophy which Saint-Just and others sought to implement, whereas in the post-revolutionary world that philosophy may be deemed responsible for the conduct of persons unaware that they were endeavouring to put Enlightenment moral ideas into practice? Allowing, with MacIntyre, that the abstractions of philosophy may be dangerous, why should his treatment of the insidious influence of Enlightenment principles carry greater conviction than Burke's or Hegel's accounts of how such principles unfolded into revolutionary violence? Why should eighteenth-century doctrines have had greater impact on the remoter march of modernity than on the more proximate course of the French Revolution? Can the influence of ideas, like the putative progression of certain historical epochs, actually skip stages? Readers of MacIntyre's philosophy of history are too often tempted with richly appetising food for thought, but then denied the required sustenance. If the Enlightenment Project had to conclude in failure, was its inception equally necessary?, they are entitled to ask. How, indeed, according to MacIntyre, did the Enlightenment Project come to arise at all? And if abstract ideas are generally so deeply intertwined with social conventions as he claims, how has it come to pass that the contemporary practice of history remains, on his own testimony, so little contaminated by philosophical issues as to be almost mindless, and the practice of philosophy so similarly insular as to lack any pertinent social focus?

IV

At least some of these issues, it seems to me, can be best understood in terms of the Enlightenment's more strictly philosophical legacy, as MacIntyre explains it, and against the background of his own intellectual biography. In the second and third chapters of *After Virtue* – that is, the chapters immediately preceding his discussion of the Enlightenment Project – MacIntyre asserts that the lack of rational criteria for securing moral agreement in contemporary culture is largely attributable to a prevalent philosophical doctrine, according to which all evaluative judgements are at bottom nothing but statements of preference which by their nature cannot be shown to be either true or false (*AV*, pp. 11–12). This doctrine he calls 'emotivism', following the terminology of its principal exponent, C. L. Stevenson. It is in confrontation with emotivism in its various philosophical guises, MacIntyre contends, that his own thesis must be defined (*AV*, p. 21). That confrontation, already evident from the final chapter on modern moral philosophy in his *Short History of Ethics*, dating from 1966, was indeed elaborated even earlier in a course of lectures he gave at Oxford entitled 'What was morality?', and it forms part of a very wide debate with numerous contributors among mainly British moral philosophers of the post World War II period. Much of the material in that debate was first published in *Mind* or in the proceedings of or supplementary volumes to the *Aristotelian Society* in the late 1940s and 1950s, and some of it has since been reassembled in such collections as *The Is–Ought Question* edited by W. D. Hudson in 1964 or *Revisions: Changing Perspectives in Moral Philosophy* edited by Stanley Hauerwas and MacIntyre himself in 1983.

Among its heroes or heroines from the professedly anti-emotivist point of view adopted by MacIntyre are Philippa Foot, Elizabeth Anscombe and Stuart Hampshire – the first because she attempted to show that it was impossible to extract from the meaning of moral terms such as 'good' some evaluative significance that was externally related to the object so defined; the second because she placed particular emphasis on the Christian tradition in which our moral discourse and values were once embedded; and the third because he drew special attention to Aristotle's ethics and to the extraordinary gulf that had arisen between classical moral philosophy, concerned with moral choice and judgement, on the one hand, and modern meta-ethics, divorced from evaluative claims and devoted only to problems of language and meaning, on the other.

MacIntyre's villainous doctrines, moreover, are by and large the same as those which Philippa Foot, Elizabeth Anscombe and Stuart Hampshire had in mind. They embrace the prescriptivism of R. M. Hare and his divorce of the language of moral imperatives from that of description, as well as the logical positivism of A. J. Ayer, which divided judgements into a threefold classification of logical, factual and emotive, relegating moral principles, together with theology, to the emotive category. From both Ayer's sceptical Humeian perspective and Hare's reformulated Kantian doctrine, it thus transpired that moral judgements were of necessity distinct from matters of fact. Ayer and Hare appear to have been condemned, each by the logic of his philosophy, to fall victim to the irreconcilable conflict between the morality of passions and the morality of reason which had been characteristic of their eighteenth-century forbears, described by MacIntyre in *After Virtue*. As he furthermore makes plain in his *Short History of Ethics* (pp. 249–65), both of their doctrines may be understood in connection with C. L. Stevenson's emotivism, dating from his seminal work of 1944, *Ethics and Language*. According to Stevenson, the proposition 'this is good' means little else than 'I approve of it' – a claim which in yet another idiom reinforced the positivist and prescriptivist disjunction of facts from values. Stevenson, for his part, apparently developed his moral philosophy out of the intuitionism of H. A. Prichard and especially G. E. Moore, who in his *Principia Ethica* had portrayed all attempts to define the attributes of goodness as a naturalistic fallacy, on the grounds that goodness was a simple and indefinable property of which nothing could be rationally predicated as true or false. Following both Henry Sidgwick and William Whewell, Moore supposed that goodness could only be intuited, never justified, a view which Whewell in turn drew essentially from the younger Mill, who had decoupled the moral injunctions of utilitarianism from their unconvincing psychological foundations devised by Bentham, while Bentham's mistake had been due to the general failure of the Enlightenment Project, for the reasons I have already advanced. As MacIntyre remarks in *After Virtue*, 'The history of utilitarianism thus links historically the eighteenth-century project of justifying morality and the twentieth century's decline into emotivism' (*AV*, p. 63).

The is–ought distinction of modern moral philosophy is in this fashion explained as emanating, through intuitionism and emotivism, from Moore's criticism of the naturalistic fallacy, in its turn heralded by the passage from Book III, part 1, section 1 of the *Treatise of Human Nature* in which Hume had challenged the erroneous deduction of propositions with the word 'ought' from statements containing the word 'is' in all the systems of morality known to him. In a notable commentary on that passage first published in *The Philosophical Review* in 1959, MacIntyre contends that Hume did not himself believe in the autonomy of morals, as so many of his interpreters have alleged, and that he in fact derived 'ought' from 'is' in his own theory of justice. Moore's intuitionism, moreover, was only indirectly indebted to Hume, who is unmentioned anywhere in the *Principia Ethica*. But Hume, Moore and the other moral philosophers whom MacIntyre names as proponents of the fact–value distinction are nevertheless collectively deemed responsible for the Enlightenment Project and its legacy. That Project failed in its unwarranted bifurcation of 'ought' from 'is', in cutting off moral principles from their moorings in human nature, thereby releasing them to drift, with every passing current of philosophical fashion, into arbitrariness and irresolution.

MacIntyre is not the first interpreter of ethical naturalism to have reconstructed the history of objections to that alleged fallacy and to have traced them to the Enlightenment. Among others, both David Raphael, in *The Moral Sense*, dating from 1947, and Arthur Prior, in his *Logic and the Basis of Ethics* of 1949, had addressed this subject long before MacIntyre and had each chronicled its seventeenth- and eighteenth-century prefigurations in the works of Hutcheson and Hume, but also Ralph Cudworth, Samuel Clarke, Thomas Reid, Richard Price and others, through their contrasting accounts of the place of feelings and reason in morals. The various texts which invite such treatments of ethics and of the fitful appearance of a certain principle within a speculative tradition had already been assembled even earlier by L. A. Selby-Bigge in his *British Moralists* at the end of the nineteenth century and are now available in a new format, with a somewhat different cast, in the collection compiled under the same title by Raphael. Yet in his initial reflections on emotivism, MacIntyre turned his attention, not to its Enlightenment origins, but to its philosophical underpinnings and influence. Readers hard-pressed to keep up with the permutations of his faith may therefore be comforted to learn that the principles of his clash with emotivism, as explained in *After Virtue*, have always informed his outlook on the world. They constitute the moral bedrock of his philosophy, unaffected by the great or subtle modulations of his views on Christianity, Hegelianism, Marxism or irrationalism.

His critique of the emotivist theory of ethics is substantially prefigured in the M. A. dissertation he completed at the University of Manchester, under the title *The Significance of Moral Judgements*. Already then, in 1951, he challenged the presuppositions of the intuitionist and emotivist ethics of Moore and Stevenson. Already then, he found fault with the logic of contemporary moral discourse in its misconceived appeal

to categorical truths and universal standards. Already then, in comment-
ing on Hume's distinction between 'ought' and 'is', he stressed that our
notions of what is right and good, shaped by concrete and conditional
circumstances, must fill a place within the structure of socially prescribed behaviour. 'Moral judgements', he claimed – still as a young man
of twenty-two – form 'part of a pattern of language and action, continually to be adjusted and criticised.' The arguments we employ 'are not
just about the applications of . . . principles, but also about which principles to apply . . . not just about the relation of the facts to . . . judgements, but also about which facts are relevant to our decisions'.[2] It is
salutary to find such durable and enduring precepts at the dawn of his
career. They provide a solid foundation to his life-long censure of
emotivism. But only with an almighty, unfounded and uncalled for leap
of the imagination can MacIntyre bring that censure to bear upon his
projection of the Enlightenment. His comments on the legacy of
eighteenth-century moral philosophy, portrayed as if it were a peripa-
tetic long day's journey into night, only render it obscure.

The Enlightenment did *not* confront the entelechies of Aristotelian
Scholasticism with a new metaphysics and epistemology drawn from
Descartes and Locke. Aristotelianism had been largely discredited in
most European universities – especially the progressive institutions
accorded popular significance by MacIntyre – long before the eighteenth
century, and the curriculum which Hutcheson and other professors of
moral philosophy and related subjects felt obliged to offer included a
great deal more Stoicism and rather more civic humanism, more natural
jurisprudence in the tradition of Grotius and Pufendorf as explained by
Carmichael, Barbeyrac or Brucker, than MacIntyre allows. The ethics
which serious eighteenth-century academic commentators thought it most
essential to refute – in Germany and Scotland as well as France – was
first that of Hobbes, then Spinoza's and then perhaps Mandeville's. After
around 1750, the figure who began to command the greatest attention
and praise was Montesquieu, rather like John Stuart Mill in British
universities of the late nineteenth century. To the extent that Jansenist
doctrines were prevalent in secular studies, it was less because of the
continued irradiation of Augustinian theology than because of the still
intellectually fashionable standing of Antoine Arnauld's and Pierre
Nicole's *Logique, ou l'art de penser* and of the Port-Royal *Grammaire
générale*.

Neither is MacIntyre correct to claim that Enlightenment thinkers
characteristically believed in the uniformity of human nature and of the
moral laws that govern it. Many eighteenth-century moral philosophers,
including Helvétius and Kant, did subscribe to such views, but those
that did generally agreed with Hume that men might change their

situations and circumstances and thereby improve or worsen their conduct. Others, like Turgot or Adam Smith, adopted more manifestly developmental notions of human nature and character, deemed to pass through stages, like the epochs of civilization. Still others endorsed biological models of mankind's perfection or corruption, along lines intimated by the natural historians of humanity, most notably G. L. Buffon. Rousseau not only adopted yet another evolutionary perspective, but in fact invented the term *perfectibilité* to encapsulate his understanding of the malleability of human nature, in a potentially benign but in fact humanly blighted providential framework somewhat akin to that of Pelagius. Teleological conceptions of man's moral metamorphosis such as Aristotle had put forward are not absent from eighteenth-century philosophy, even if Aristotle himself was no longer widely acclaimed for such notions. MacIntyre's account of the Enlightenment Project is on this point far too blunt and shallow.

In need of most substantial revision is his disregard of one principle which lies at the heart of that Project, however else it may be conceived – that is, the principle of toleration. Eighteenth-century thinkers, a few of whom became globetrotters themselves, had greater access than ever before in European history to reports by explorers, merchants and missionaries on primitive and unChristian societies. They recognized the sophistication and utility of moral traditions different from their own, and sometimes, as with Diderot, called for anti-colonial policies to preserve the integrity of other cultures. If the Christian moral tradition predominant in Europe did not win their universal approbation, that was because, with Voltaire, they deemed so many of its principles hypocritical, bigoted or intolerant, and the practices of its political and priestly powers despotic. For the *philosophes* of the eighteenth century it did not follow from the moral specificity of our disparate cultures that persons from one community were unable to grasp the values of another, still less that their differences must render them enemies. Religious and moral diversity, they believed, did not entail dreadful crusades against infidels. Rather, they thought it possible for the whole of humanity to engage in peaceable assembly, like the traders at the London Stock Exchange, each a faithful follower of his church, but also capable of dealing with other men as if they were of the same religion. In such circumstances, remarked Voltaire in his *Lettres philosophiques*, the Presbyterians trust the Anabaptists, but in Scotland, where they are supreme, they affect a solemn bearing, behave as pedants and preach through their nose.

Having summoned St Benedict to return in *After Virtue* (p. 245), MacIntyre concludes his *Three Rival Versions* with an appeal for the reconstitution of the Thomistic university as a place of 'constrained disagreement' following the failed experiment of unconstrained agreement in contemporary liberal universities (*TRV*, pp. 230–3). It is difficult to imagine that under such constraint Hume would have fared any better than he did in his candidacy for the Edinburgh Chair of Moral Philosophy in 1745 (*WJ*, pp. 286–7). Whatever Hutcheson's actual reasons for opposing Hume's appointment, there can be little doubt that, both in the interests of the Scottish intellectual tradition as described by MacIntyre and on behalf of a Thomistic principle of constrained disagreement, he ought to have found Hume unfit for that post and to have stood in his way. Hutcheson, after all, had trained as a minister. Indeed, on the 'enforced exclusion' principle which MacIntyre himself expressly commends, the successful candidate (Cleghorn, also trained for the ministry) had been 'rightly preferred to Hume' (*TRV*, p. 224). But would not natural reason, common sense or justice suggest otherwise? Was the Enlightenment Project's attachment to the translatability of foreign languages and the intelligibility of other cultures not more compelling than MacIntyre's own portrayal of such languages and cultures as 'alien'? (*TRV*, pp. 171–2.) The merest hint of theological correctness, like political correctness, is a potentially most dangerous thing. It may kindle the fires of orthodoxy, and eventually fan the flames of heresy and persecution, even while observing the pieties of confraternity. A cosmopolitan spirit of tolerance and goodwill would be a welcome antidote to the fractious fundamentalism of many contemporary religious movements and the all-too-persistent ravages of ethnic and civil wars. The moral chaos of the modern world stems not from the failure of the Enlightenment Project but from its neglect and abandonment.

NOTES

This paper was first drafted for the Morrell Conference on 'After MacIntyre' at the University of York and then revised for the University of Manchester Political Thought Conference on 'Truth and Rationality' in March 1992. I am grateful to Keith Graham, John Horton, Geraint Parry and Maurizio Passerin d'Entrèves for various comments on my views of MacIntyre's philosophy; to Istvan Hont and Jim Moore for their reflections on Hutcheson; and above all to Dorothy Emmet for pointing me in the direction of MacIntyre's M.A. dissertation, which she supervised.

1 John Plamenatz, *Karl Marx's Philosophy of Man* (Oxford, 1975), p. 472.
2 University of Manchester Library, M.A. thesis 7580, April 1951, pp. 1, 47–8, 81 and 92.

7

MacIntyre's Critique of Utilitarianism

Paul Kelly

[Utilitarianism] may not be the most loved but it is certainly the most discussed moral theory of our time.

James Griffin, 'Modern utilitarianism'

The important issues that utilitarianism raises should be discussed in contexts more rewarding than that of utilitarianism itself. The day cannot be too far off in which we hear no more of it.

Bernard Williams, 'A critique of utilitarianism'

Introduction

In a period of just over a decade and in three important and controversial books,[1] Alasdair MacIntyre has mounted a distinctive and concerted assault on the practice of modern moral philosophy. By crossing the disciplinary boundaries of philosophy, sociology, anthropology and history, he has attempted to shake modern moral philosophy from its technical complacency and restore a sense of vitality and urgency to moral enquiry. Few who have read MacIntyre's work can have failed to be impressed by the boldness of his arguments. That said, the impact of his writings on the course of philosophical debate has not been as significant as the notice his books have attracted. In the field of ethics, the liberal individualism to which MacIntyre takes such exception in both its utilitarian and deontological guises, continues to hold centre stage. Indeed a review of the most significant recent defences of a utilitarian or consequentialist[2] moral theory shows almost no reference to his work at all, let alone a sustained critical examination of his main theses.[3] One obvious response to this fact might be to argue that it simply reinforces MacIntyre's critique of the redundancy of so much of our philosophical culture, and in particular its inability to accommodate any criticism of the fundamental terms of moral enquiry as it is practised in the Anglo-European philosophical community. Modern moral theory cannot even recognize the challenge implicit in MacIntyre's recent work. But what exactly is that challenge? And should it alter the course of contemporary moral theory? These are the questions I wish to examine by focusing on MacIntyre's critique of utilitarianism.

However, my reason for focusing on utilitarianism is not simply that it provides a case study for assessing the success of his critique of modern moral philosophy. The point of concentrating on utilitarianism is that, according to MacIntyre, it occupies a dominant position in post-Enlightenment philosophy. Indeed, one of the main elements of the early narrative chapters of *After Virtue*[4] is to show how the apparent debate between the deontological and utilitarian versions of liberal individualism actually masks the dominance of instrumental reasoning, which receives its most familiar manifestation in the utilitarian tradition. MacIntyre therefore draws heavily on one of the main theses of Elizabeth Anscombe's influential paper 'Modern moral philosophy'.[5] Anscombe argues for three main theses: firstly, that ethics should be abandoned until we have an adequate philosophical psychology; secondly, that the obsession with a vocabulary of deontological terms is a remnant from a world that has largely been abandoned; and finally, that English-speaking moral philosophy, at least since Sidgwick, has a single general character. All of these theses are reflected in MacIntyre's critical enterprise, and all are interconnected, but the most important from the perspective of this paper is the claim that English-speaking moral philosophy has a single general character.[6] Anscombe's diagnosis of the failings of contemporary ethics is also shared by Charles Taylor,[7] but what is distinctive about MacIntyre's argument is the way in which he provides a more detailed philosophical history showing how the single general character of contemporary ethics goes back to the Enlightenment project of modernity, and his development of a rival conception of tradition-based moral enquiry, which he argues allows us to transcend the limits of contemporary ethics. If MacIntyre and Anscombe are right in claiming that English-speaking moral philosophy is of a single general character, then recent liberal political philosophy with its attempts to defend theories of justice[8] as a critical response to the claims of utilitarianism amounts to nothing more than a series of pseudo arguments. My concern is not strictly with liberal individualism, but given the centrality of utilitarian arguments to the history of the liberal tradition, my conclusions will have implications not simply for the viability of utilitarian theories but also for liberalism.

By concentrating on this critical aspect of MacIntyre's enterprise and the assessment of his account of utilitarianism, I will undoubtedly have to ignore much of what is distinctive and challenging about his arguments. Nevertheless, I will necessarily cover some of his most important arguments, for he is not simply concerned with defending a rival conception of moral enquiry, but rather, with showing how this rival conception allows us to transcend the inadequacies of utilitarianism. But before turning to these arguments I need to provide a brief review of MacIntyre's account of modern ethical debate, in order to explain his critique of utilitarianism.

Utilitarianism and the Culture of Emotivism

One of the most important features of MacIntyre's argument is his reassertion of the centrality of history to moral enquiry. He argues forcefully, following Vico,[9] that the concepts, arguments, judgements and maxims of morality are nowhere to be found except as historically embodied in particular social groups and communities. This history shapes both their institutions and forms of discourse. In so far as moral philosophy employs moral concepts, these must necessarily be the concepts of some particular historical community.[10] Thus when he turns to a critique of contemporary moral debate he advances both a philosophical narrative and a historical sociology of modernity.

This sociological thesis focuses on the public moral discourse of modern liberal societies. MacIntyre claims that what is distinctive about public moral and political discourse is its interminable character. He illustrates this claim with examples such as the debate over abortion. Here the character of debate is polarized around particular groups claiming a 'right to life' or a 'right to choose', with no possibility of a rational determination of such issues. Consequently, a central character in modern politics is the protestor. But this polarization of political debate has transformed the character of protest. Where once protest involved the positive attitude of bearing witness to a cause or principle, it has now taken on a negative character as a form of utterance addressed only to someone who shares the same fundamental commitments.[11] Major issues of public debate become dominated by the incommensurable voices of rival protestors all expressing a judgement, but only addressing their own constituencies.

The interminability and incommensurability of public moral debate is reflected in the similar inconclusiveness of philosophical discussions of ethics. The reasons for this inconclusiveness are due to the 'emotivist' character of modernity. Emotivism as a philosophical thesis asserts that the authority of moral judgements is derived solely from the personal expression of preference. As a thesis about the meaning of moral discourse it is untenable, but as an account of moral debate it is essential. For it is MacIntyre's contention that the interminability of moral debate is the result of the parties acting as if 'emotivism' were true and merely exchanging conflicting fundamental preferences. The point is that if moral judgements are merely expressions of preference then they can be neither true nor false and there can be no assessment of the ultimate rationality or value of these various preferences; they are just basic. The fundamental role of preferences and commitments in our 'emotivist culture' means that there can be no ultimate authorities which are external to the preferences of the subject. Thus MacIntyre writes:

> [T]he self that I have called emotivist, finds no limits set to that on which it may pass judgement for such limits could only derive from rational criteria for evaluation and ... the emotivist self lacks any such criteria. Everything may be criticised from whatever standpoint the self has adopted, including the self's choice of standpoint to adopt.[12]

At the heart of his diagnosis of our 'emotivist culture' is a Humean conception of instrumental rationality. This conception of instrumental reason, which achieves primacy in the utilitarian tradition, is however not unique to utilitarianism. MacIntyre's thesis that all of modern moral philosophy has a single general character involves the claim that this conception of reason is equally crucial to deontological liberalism, which aims to prioritize authentic choice and autonomy by justifying certain absolute rights or principles which will promote these values. But here again MacIntyre argues that the values of autonomy and authentic choice cannot be grounded but are themselves only the preferences of an individualist culture. The values on which deontology depends are arbitrary and the conception of *right* which follows from them is merely a means to these pre-given and non-rational ends. The result is a utilitarianism of rights.[13]

One way of responding to this state of affairs might be to argue that we can nevertheless decide in cases of moral and political conflict by summing the various preferences and deciding in favour of the majority. This is the paradigmatic utilitarian solution. However, this is unlikely to resolve debates because it presupposes that individuals regard their preferences as of equal weight. The whole point about contemporary moral debate is that its participants merely express conflicting preferences which each claim are of ultimate value. Thus the adherents of any one cause could not have a reason for accepting any other preference as being of more value than their own, and therefore could not have a reason for accepting a majority decision in such cases. This leads on to the other important element of MacIntyre's diagnosis of modernity. The values and principles which are adopted by various groups or individuals as the basis of their ultimate commitments have to come from somewhere. Because emotivism is merely an account of the meaning of moral judgements it cannot provide an account of where the various vocabularies of value come from. This introduces another of the main themes of *After Virtue*, namely, that the interminability of contemporary public moral debate is due to the incommensurability of the concepts, values and principles deployed, and this is because they are merely surviving fragments of incommensurable moral traditions. These incommensurable values incorporate parts of such traditions in their meanings, and therefore cannot be reduced to some universal rational standard. Thus many of the concepts of liberal deontology are not reducible to utility because their meanings originated in the Christian natural law tradition. It is this tradition which provides the peremptory character of deontological concepts such as obligation and right, and these understandings permeate the use of such concepts even by those who no longer believe in God as a Lawgiver.

Nevertheless, it might be argued that although these concepts and values have a history which is often one of radically incommensurable moral traditions, we can reconstruct these concepts in a way that enables us to discriminate among the various preferences that are expressed. Thus the enterprise of moral theory since the Enlightenment has not been a simple retreat in the face of seemingly interminable conflict, but has endeavoured to reconstruct either a new categorical basis for morality or else to develop a new naturalistic teleology. The first course gives rise to the Kantian project, the second to utilitarianism. However, MacIntyre goes on to argue that the Enlightenment project not only failed, but had to fail. He does this with a brief review of the arguments of Bentham and J. S. Mill on the utilitarian side and of Alan Gewirth's *Reason and Morality*,[14] as an example of the failure of Kantianism. In the course of five pages the whole utilitarian tradition is dismissed.[15]

MacIntyre's critique of utilitarianism focuses on a number of issues; firstly, Bentham and J. S. Mill's hedonistic psychology; secondly, the attempt to derive the principle of utility from psychological hedonism; and finally, how self-interested agents could be motivated to pursue impartial benevolence. He concludes that utilitarianism failed in the nineteenth century, although it was responsible for many social reforms.[16] The failure of utilitarianism is linked to the emergence of 'intuitionism' in the latter nineteenth and early twentieth century, which eventually gave way to the 'emotivism' of A. J. Ayer and C. L. Stevenson. However, another story could be told featuring the likes of W. S. Jevons, F. Y. Edgeworth, Alfred Marshall, G. E. Moore, R. F. Harrod and contemporary theorists such as J. C. Harsanyi, R. M. Hare, Derek Parfit and James Griffin, which takes the utilitarian tradition into contemporary moral and political thought. Such an alternative narrative would illustrate how the utilitarian tradition attempts to accommodate the criticisms that MacIntyre raises. So how damaging is MacIntyre's criticism of utilitarianism? If we take his accounts of Bentham and Mill seriously then his argument is next to worthless: firstly, because the utilitarian tradition did not begin or end with Bentham and J. S. Mill; and secondly, even though the criticisms he makes are familiar from standard histories of ethics, he does not address any of the recent utilitarian scholarship which shows how even Bentham and Mill had the conceptual resources to answer or avoid these difficulties.[17] One response to MacIntyre might be to show how Bentham and Mill did not fail in their own terms. But I doubt that MacIntyre really places much weight on these historical arguments for these only show that a version of utilitarianism failed, and not that the enterprise underlying utilitarianism must fail. MacIntyre wants to show that utilitarianism must fail, and to do this he needs a stronger philosophical critique. The elements of that critique are implicit in his diagnosis of the 'culture of emotivism' which I have just reviewed. We can now examine them in turn and see whether they prove fatal to utilitarianism. The issues to be discussed in the next three sections are: the nature of the moral agent, the problem of incommensurability, and method of normative ethics.

Individuals, Agents and Narrative Selves

The attempt to reconstruct a rational basis for morality cannot be discredited simply by showing how Bentham, Mill, Kant or Gewirth failed to provide such a basis. MacIntyre's argument has to be stronger than that if he is to show why the Enlightenment project must fail. Thus the question at issue is what is it about that project which is so fundamentally misconceived? The clue is to be found in the character of the 'emotivist self'. In *After Virtue* MacIntyre writes: 'to be a moral agent is . . . to be able to stand back from any and every situation in which one is involved, from any and every characteristic that one may possess, and to pass judgement on it from a purely universal and abstract point of view.'[18]

This conception of the detached self is common to all forms of liberal individualism. Thus MacIntyre's main argument against the Enlightenment project is that it assumes a subject as a rational agent who can be radically separated from his or her particular circumstances. It is a version of the communitarian rejection of the atomistic individual in favour of a socially constituted moral identity. Before discussing MacIntyre's alternative conception of the 'narrative self' it is worth asking whether utilitarianism requires a radically detached conception of the agent.

Act-utilitarianism[19] argues that actions are good if they maximize happiness or welfare and bad if they do the reverse. Consequently, if the principle of utility is the standard of right and wrong, then it follows that individuals are under an obligation to act so as to maximize happiness or welfare. This obligation is both negative and positive. The positive obligation involves the injunction to actively pursue utility in the course of acting, which is a stringent enough requirement, but the negative requirement is more stringent still, requiring the agent to be responsible not simply for what he does, but also for what he does not prevent.[20] Act-utilitarianism does indeed require a detached self, in the sense that any attachments to community, family or particular individuals must be contingent to one's identity as a moral subject, for these ties must be easily overcome if the concept of obligation is to remain coherent. This account of utilitarianism may seem particularly crude, but it captures a feature that is common to many more sophisticated versions. If one turns to R. M. Hare's two-level theory, it is clear that at the level of critical moral thought the individual[21] must be able to detach himself from his particular circumstances and reason from a universal standpoint. Indeed, it has been argued that Hare's account of universalization is so strong that the identity of the subject disappears.[22] Admittedly, at the intuitive level of moral thinking Hare does not require that subjects be so cavalier about their attachments and commitments, but if it is possible to move between the two levels, as it must be if Hare's theory has any coherence, then the indifference to particularity which is so characteristic of level-two thinking will invade the intuitive level and both levels will collapse into act-utilitarianism. Radical detachment, therefore, does seem to be an essential feature of utilitarianism. But what is wrong with this idea?

Bernard Williams has argued that the corncept of negative obligation, which makes us as responsible for what we allow as for what we do, undermines the integrity of the person.[23] This is because individuals have fundamental projects and commitments which they take seriously and which give coherence and meaning to their lives. His argument is that utilitarianism is psychologically unrealistic if it simply assumes that we can easily detach ourselves from these goals and projects. This is one way of attacking utilitarianism's detached subject, but is it a good argument? It surely depends upon what those projects and commitments are: if they are wicked or despicable then one might want to argue that a bit of personal reorganization is just what is called for. But this raises an important issue for Williams and MacIntyre. Do they want to argue for a strongly constituted self in which such personal reorganization is impossible, or do they allow some concessions to the idea that individuals can both criticize their inherited identities and be under an obligation to do so? If they opt for the latter, can this stance be maintained without opening the door to a version of the Enlightenment project? Before I can address this question it is necessary to say a little more about MacIntyre's conception of the narrative self and its connection with moral agency.

As with other communitarians, MacIntyre argues that man is a self-interpreting being.[24] This self-interpretation takes the form of providing a narrative 'that runs from my birth to my death'.[25] It is this narrative structure which connects the otherwise discontinuous elements of experience and allows one to give an account of one's life as a unified whole. However, it is important for MacIntyre that while we tell these stories about ourselves, we are not their sole authors for we enter society 'with one or more imputed characters ... and we have to learn what they are in order to be able to understand how others respond to us and how our responses to them are apt to be construed.'[26] Furthermore, these narratives are embedded in the narratives of communities which form the roles and characters on which we draw in uncovering the narrative structures of our own lives. The identities of persons are related in complex ways to the historical narratives of the communities which constitute them, thus MacIntyre writes: 'I inherit from the past of my family, my city, my tribe, my nation, a variety of debts, inheritances, rightful expectations and obligations. These constitute the given of my life, my moral starting point.'[27]

MacIntyre introduces the idea that communities constitute the self by providing the resources from which the self's narratives must be constructed. But does this imply the strong thesis that the individual is constructed by the community, that is, that his identity is bounded by these communal narratives such that we could not identify the 'individual' independently of his communally given roles? If this is so the implication would be that the detached self would be unidentifiable: detaching the agent from his communally given roles and character would render him so transparent that he would disappear altogether. Yet it is not clear that MacIntyre does want to claim this, for despite arguing that conceiving of oneself in the individualist mode would 'deform my present relationships'[28] and that such an idea would have painful consequences, he also argues that: 'the fact that the self has to find its moral identity in and through its membership in communities such as those of the family, the neighbourhood, the city and the tribe does not entail that the self has to accept the moral limitations of the particularity of those forms of community.'[29] This implies that the self is not strongly constituted by its communally given roles and characteristics. The individual can be distinguished from the collectivity and can separate himself from the particularity of his circumstances and adopt a critical stance towards those communities. This is just as well, for individuals quite clearly do separate themselves from such imposed identities without completely disintegrating. One only has to think of those brought up in religious communities who lose their faith. But is this distancing enough to help the utilitarian project? MacIntyre argues that it is not, because although the individual might adopt a critical stance to his heritage, he cannot totally abandon it and adopt a stance free from all particularity.

However, the argument only works if utilitarianism requires that we adopt a strictly universal and impartial standpoint in determining our obligations. And it is unclear even in the case of Hare's model of critical thinking that the possibility of adopting this strictly universal standpoint is required, for Hare writes: 'The most that human beings can ask for, when they are trying to do the best critical thinking they can, is some way of approximating, perhaps not at all fully, to the thought-processes of an archangel.'[30] All that is necessary is that we can detach ourselves from as many of our constitutive projects as possible, and certainly not necessarily all at once. After all, we can approach the requisite degree of impartiality in a way less rigorous than Hare requires and still retain sufficient distance from any one particular standpoint to get the project of a utilitarian morality off the ground. In many instances this is not going to be easy,[31] and it may be psychologically demanding, so that the questions that Williams raised about whether this is an appropriate method for moral theory remains. But for the purposes of this argument, all that matters is that it is possible even on MacIntyre's argument. For as long as it is possible the project of a rational morality along utilitarian lines is not ruled out, although it might prove a much more difficult enterprise than the likes of Bentham envisaged.

However, MacIntyre has a response to this line of argument. For even if the individual can detach himself from some particular communally identified role, he can only do this by adopting another particular perspective from which to judge those roles. Detachment would only allow for the utilitarian project if individuals could detach themselves and adopt a critical stance that was independent of a particular conception of moral enquiry, and it is a further thesis of MacIntyre's that this is not possible. Thus the point is not simply that the individual moral subject is socially constituted, but that the rational criteria a detached subject might appeal to in criticizing a community or practice are themselves socially and historically constituted. It is precisely this point about the social and historical constitution of rationality which underlies his thesis about incommensurability. As utilitarianism is based on the possibility of value commensurability, this is an issue to which we must turn.

Incommensurable Traditions versus Commensurable Values

There are two questions facing us in this section; firstly, whether all rational criteria are historically and socially constituted, such that there is no impartial criterion on the basis of which a detached subject can pass judgement; and secondly, whether value commensurability is a coherent thesis. MacIntyre links the discussion of these separate issues as part of his assault on utilitarianism. If there is any thesis to which all utilitarians must subscribe, it is some version of the thesis of the commensurability of values, and it is this which distinguishes utilitarianism from any other variety of liberal individualism. Recent critiques of utilitarianism have challenged this thesis,[32] but they have done so on the basis of the assertion of value pluralism. What is wrong with utilitarianism is that it reduces this plurality to one monistic value concept, namely welfare or utility. This thesis has not involved the assertion of incommensurable rationalities. Indeed one can assert value pluralism without making any reference to the historical contingency of rational criteria.

MacIntyre does not simply assert value pluralism as a way of rejecting the claims of utilitarianism. Like other neo-Aristotelians he acknowledges a plurality of goods within the individual life, but as a Thomist he also wants to claim that we can discriminate amongst these socially constituted goods: not all goods are *Good*. The morality of the virtues has to be supplemented by a moral law,[33] which becomes Divine Law in his move towards a full-blooded Thomism.[34] So there is a reason why he does not merely resort to the *fact* of moral pluralism as a response to utilitarianism. One way of avoiding such a recourse to pluralism while retaining the Thomistic account of Divine Law on the basis of which we discriminate amongst *goods* is by appealing to a tradition-based conception of rationality such that all moral concepts and rational criteria are historically and socially particular. Thus it is my thesis that MacIntyre resorts to historicism to undermine utilitarianism, and avoids resorting to the simple assertion of value pluralism found in anti-utilitarians such as Williams and Raz.

But need one resort to such a thesis to explain MacIntyre's historicist argument about the incommensurability of traditions? Not if he is simply offering the weak historicist claim that all concepts have a history and all language belongs to some linguistic community. However, he wants to make a stronger claim about moral language and canons of reasoning as being constituted by radically distinct communities. This stronger thesis cannot simply be grounded in Wittgensteinian ideas about shared languages implying shared judgements, or allusions to Vico, Hegel or Collingwood.[35] On the other hand, very little argument is offered for anything other than a weak historicism. His thesis that there are radically distinct rationalities emerges through the narratives he presents in *Whose Justice? Which Rationality?* While these are impressive pieces of scholarship, they are a precarious foundation for the strong historicist thesis. For the justification of criteria of rationality that are not particular to some community does not commit us to making simplistic comparisons across history. The fact that there have been different answers to ethical questions, does not entail that we cannot discuss such questions from a non particular standpoint. We can accept a weak historicism without adopting MacIntyre's communitarian thesis.

In fact there are considerable difficulties in making the strong historicist case. MacIntyre argues that moral language is always the discourse of some particular historical community. Thus he relates his discussion of the various forms of practical rationality in *Whose Justice? Which Rationality?* to accounts of the history of the forms of community in which these rationalities functioned. But he has not shown that these forms of community are radically distinct. Obviously, Homeric Greece is not eighteenth-century Scotland, but what form of difference is necessary to show that these are radically distinct communities? Temporal and geographical separation are obvious but trivial, so MacIntyre provides a linguistic criterion of difference. What makes the concepts and practices of such communities radically incommensurable is that they have to be learnt as part of a second language. However, following Davidson[36] one might argue that the learning of a second language involves the translation of concepts from one language into another. If we can do this then in what way is the language of one community radically incommensurable with another? Surely if the concepts of one community were genuinely incommensurable with those of another culture then we would be at a loss to understand them at all, and past societies would remain completely mysterious to us. Despite this MacIntyre is able to say a lot about such practices as *taboo.*

Another important point which is obscured by focusing on communal rationalities that are so temporally separated is the degree to which the boundaries of these communities are not fixed. The history of moral discourse is one of development and transformation. We can easily identify the history of ancient Greek culture because the texts on which our understanding is based are relatively few in number. But if we want to say anything about radically distinct communities in Europe we have more of a problem. The boundaries around distinct languages and traditions are much more indeterminate and are constantly being redrawn in the light of changing political circumstances. Certainly, Aquinas and Hume have distinct conceptions of practical reasoning, but before we can say that they are radically incommensurable we need to be sure that we cannot provide a philosophical and historical narrative which allows us to see why one gave way to the other. The radical incommensurability thesis would be more plausible if MacIntyre could provide an account not simply of why the Enlightenment project had to fail, but why there had to be such a project in the first place. If we can provide such a narrative we can surely say something about those respective theories that is independent of a particular tradition but part of a culture which is informed by many theories. It is certainly the case that we cannot pass judgement on one or other theory from no perspective at all, but the perspective we adopt in passing such a judgement does not have to be constituted by one particular theory of practical reason. Indeed, even if we adopt one particular account of practical reason it is likely to be significantly modified by its engagement with other theories. And this raises a further problem about the socially constituted meaning of moral terms. For even though many terms of moral discourse have an origin in distinct traditions, this does not entail that the meaning of these terms cannot be transformed as the traditions engage with and are transformed by others. Thus learning the use of a term does not simply involve learning a determinate set of rules for its application. Learning the use of these concepts has to have a context, but that does not mean that we cannot use concepts in new and innovative ways. Quite clearly the history of ethical and political thought is full of examples of such transformations in the meanings of moral concepts as they are applied to changing political and social circumstances, and as the boundaries of the communities in which they originally functioned become blurred.

Where does this leave the detached subject? We can conclude that he or she is not faced with a choice between radically distinct communities that one can only enter on the basis of a leap of faith. Rather the communities merge into one another in a culture that while not being wholly transparent is not wholly opaque. Thus the agent is faced with a variety of perspectives and a host of different values and principles all claiming priority. The response the agent makes to these circumstances will depend on the way in which this historical legacy can be ordered by a constructive theory. This theory is not simply plucked out of the air, but emerges through the process of criticizing components of this historical legacy using other parts of that legacy. Out of this process it may be possible to ground a set of near universal values. What we cannot conclude along with MacIntyre is the radical incommensurability of socially embodied traditions which entails that there cannot be such an impartial standpoint.

However, even if it is possible to engage in rational criticism from outside some particular socially constituted tradition, might there not still be something in the other incommensurability thesis: namely the incommensurability of values. For if this thesis can be maintained then there would still be grounds for rejecting utilitarianism as a possible rational morality. While MacIntyre focuses most of his discussion on the incommensurability of traditions, he does have arguments which call into question the utilitarian reliance on commensurability in practical reasoning.

As part of his account of the virtues MacIntyre emphasizes the concept of a practice and the goods internal to practices. He defines a practice as: 'any coherent and complex form of socially established cooperative human activity through which goods internal to that form of activity are realised in the course of trying to achieve standards of excellence which are appropriate to and partially definitive of that form of activity.'[37] Practices provide the context for exercising the virtues, but they are also important as part of his critique of utilitarianism because the ideal of commensurability underlying utilitarianism cannot recognize any distinction between internal and external goods. The good of any practice must be the instrumental external good of how far it contributes to utility or pleasure. MacIntyre's point is that practices are important to understanding many forms of social activity which involve the recognition of a non-subjective authority, but the individualism and instrumentalism of utilitarianism can only provide the weakest caricature of the value of these practices. The internal goods of practices are therefore incommensurable in the same way that the fundamental projects underlying Williams's conception of *integrity* are incommensurable. We can only reduce them to a single measurable standard by eviscerating their social meaning and personal significance. We can hold on to this account of the nature and significance of practices without accepting MacIntyre's thesis about the incommensurability of traditions, so does he still have a good case against utilitarianism?

There are two points that can be made on behalf of utilitarianism. In the first instance utilitarians often attach a considerable value to practices and institutions which provide the conditions of interest formation and satisfaction, and this involves cultivating and sustaining attitudes to these practices which do not regard them as merely instrumental, but as constitutive of individual well-being. This still leaves the goods of practices as instrumental in promoting well-being, but by regarding some practices and their internal goods as constitutive of well-being, the utilitarian's attitude to them can be seen to be much closer to MacIntyre's position. We do not have to regard well-being or welfare as a simple hypergood like pleasure; rather it can be a more complex concept approaching the Aristotelian notion of 'eudaemonia'. Secondly, if we move from a simple model of utility as hypervalue to an account of what value is, then commensurability does not involve the problem of looking for one particular value in all practices and activities and one which is identified as valuable independently of those practices. This leaves a sufficient degree of instrumentalism in appraising practices, but only sufficient to allow us to prioritize practices and their internal goods, which of course is something that MacIntyre and the Aristotelians wish to do by appeal to the *Good* and the Moral Law.[38]

The difficulties in working out an account of the commensurability of values in either the prudential or moral sphere does not undermine the utilitarian enterprise,[39] it only shows that the construction of a theory of moral reasoning is much harder than Bentham or J. S. Mill envisaged. In which case we can hardly criticize utilitarianism because the enterprise of doing normative ethics is difficult. In some cases comparability is possible and in a very precise fashion, in others it may be difficult, in others still it may be practically impossible. But to cover the problems of strict commensurability, utilitarian theorists have always relied on rules, practices and institutions, which often create strict obligations of a near peremptory character. Both Bentham and J. S. Mill placed great emphasis on legal rights and law, as a way of coordinating social interaction, thus providing a utilitarian justification for these institutions and practices, but without needing recourse to particular assessments of the obligatoriness of these rights in each case of action.[40] If Bentham and J. S. Mill were aware of the value of such social and political practices then it can hardly be beyond the resources of modern utilitarian theory to accommodate the limits of value commensurability.

All of the points made so far have tended to undermine MacIntyre's arguments that utilitarianism must fail, but by criticizing him I have not referred to one particular version of utilitarianism, but have rather alluded to the ways in which aspects of utilitarianism might be construed so as to avoid his criticisms. This still leaves open the question of how one might defend a fully worked-out utilitarian theory, and this raises questions about method in normative ethics.

Conclusion: Utilitarianism and Method in Normative Ethics

The best way of undermining MacIntyre's critique of utilitarianism would be the articulation of a fully worked-out theory which does not fail for the reasons that he suggests. I have not provided such a theory, and certainly could not in the space available were it within my powers to do so. But that is not to say that such a theory could not be provided. What I can do by way of conclusion is to say something about the method for providing such a theory. We began this discussion of utilitarianism by focusing on MacIntyre's rejection of Bentham and Mill and the account of why their theories must fail. The key feature of his critique of Bentham and Mill was their inability to provide an adequate foundation for the principle of utility and a way of connecting moral motivation with a psychology of self-interest. How is a modern version of utilitarianism going to overcome these difficulties? And what in outline is a revised utilitarianism going to look like?

Firstly, there is the problem of justification. To try and derive the principle of utility from the psychology of self-interest, as MacIntyre argues Mill did, is not a realistic possibility. The reason for this is that the psychological theory does not provide a firmer foundation for the principle than a direct justification of the principle independently of the psychology. If we leave J. S. Mill and turn to Bentham's theory we get a much more promising suggestion. Bentham unlike Mill asserted that no proof of the principle was possible and there could be no deductive argument leading up to the principle.[41] However, he did not think there could be no reasons for supporting the principle as foundational. It is just that these reasons could only be provided by a full defence of a utilitarian theory and a criticism of rival theories, in terms of premises provided by the utilitarian theory, a test against intuitions, and an assessment of the internal inadequacies of rival theories. Admittedly, Bentham was not particularly good at the internal criticism of rival positions, and there is a futher problem of delimiting a class of rival theories to utilitarianism. But we can at least see a method of justification, namely 'constructivism', which enables one to avoid the problem of recourse to a single foundational premise about which nothing more can be said.

The most important recent version of this method is John Rawls's procedure of 'reflective equilibrium'.[42] With Rawls the theory begins with unreflective moral intuitions and works up through the process of theory construction to a position in which these intuitions can be transformed into a political morality which provides criteria for prioritizing the claims of intuition and setting boundaries around the demands of particular moral beliefs and principles. At each stage the process is designed not simply to reflect what we already believe, but to show though a process of critical reflection on those intuitions what we might come to accept as public moral rules. What I want to suggest is important here is not the details of Rawls's method of 'reflective equilibrium', but rather the role of constructing a theory within that conception of 'reflective equilibrium'. The point being made here is that we can only assess the question of justification when we have a fully worked-out normative theory. Thus we cannot do meta-ethics independently of providing a substantive normative theory, and it is only in terms of the way in which the theory is able to complement, complete or overthrow rival views that we can start to assess the question of ultimate justification. For it is only in the process of constructing such a theory that we can actually get a clear view of the philosophical questions that the theory is supposed to resolve. Similarly, we can also conclude that we cannot do normative ethics independently of other areas of philosophy, as an adequate theory of prudential and moral reasoning will rely on an adequate moral psychology and theory of action, and a theory of personal identity as well as an epistemology. So the enterprise of justifying a utilitarian ethic is going to be enormoulsy complex, but that should hardly be very surprising, or indeed particularly worrying given the importance of the issues at stake.

What we can conclude contrary to MacIntyre is that such a method is possible, as individuals are not strongly constituted by their communal attachments and the weak historicism which he can justify does not support the case for incommensurable values and rationalities. We can also conclude that the enterprise is not vitiated simply because past attempts have failed. Indeed it is precisely because of past failures that we can develop an account of the direction of moral inqiry. The weakness of previous theories helps us to clarify the issues that have to be developed in terms of advancing rival theories. This does not merely collapse into the development of a distinctive and exclusive utilitarian tradition, because the context in which utilitarian theories are being articulated is one that is populated by neo-Kantian theories as well as Aristotelian and Hegelian versions of communitarianism. The conceptual resources available to each cannot but be available to all given MacIntyre's inability to sustain the strong historicist thesis. Therefore, the articulation of a utilitarian theory must also address the claims and arguments of rival theories. The plausibility of such criticisms will depend on the extent to which they are dependent on arguments internal or external to one particular theory. This is always going to be a matter of degree, but that fact does not rule out the possibility of public justification.

In response to MacIntyre's other criticism of Bentham and Mill, namely their inability to connect obligation with a psychology of self-interest, we can argue that this argument only works if we also accept such a psychological theory. This raises many difficult questions in philosophical psychology about the nature of internal and external reasons for action.[43] But again there are two points that we can make here: firstly, the plausibility of a theory of action which relies on either internal or external reasons can only be judged in terms of its coherence and completeness – we cannot simply rule out such a theory; and secondly, we need not assume that utilitarianism requires an account of the motivational force of moral obligation which is internal to an individual's self-interested motivations.[44] All of this is not to show that utilitarianism *is* an adequate moral theory or one that *can* be rendered coherent. This is something that cannot be judged independently of the assessment of particular theories. It is perhaps this fact which explains why modern moral philosophy continues to proceed by the articulation and criticism of rival theories and positions. Equally, we cannot rule out the possibility that an adequate utilitarian theory can be provided. If this is the case then what force does MacIntyre's critique of utilitarianism have?

The conclusions drawn in the earlier sections show that whatever form of theory might be justifiable, it is unlikely to be an unrestricted act-utilitarianism. Instead it is more likely to be a version of indirect utilitarianism which recognizes the constitutive role of various social practices and institutions in an account of human well-being. This is particularly important in that the primary focus of modern utilitarianism is as a political morality concerned with the justification of public rules, and not necessarily as a comprehensive morality which extends to all areas of individual life. Also any account of value commensurability will need a more complex version of welfare or well-being than pleasure or the avoidance of pain. Furthermore, it may not even offer welfare or well-being as a single hypervalue, but rather as an account of what it is for something to be prudentially or morally valuable. In terms of outcomes, a utilitarian political morality may converge with deontological theories. What distinguishes them is their method of justification and their attitude to the question of whether values ought to be promoted or respected. All of these points can be derived from responding to MacIntyre's critique, and important though these qualifications are to an adequate utilitarian ethic, they are not as devastating as he suggests. In fact they are part of the common currency of utilitarian ethics. Modern moral philosophy may still seem interminable and hold out no chance of resolving questions of the good or the right once and for all, but then unless one is actually predisposed to the idea of the *Good* as sanctioned by Divine Law, then the closure of debates on certain moral issues can seem either repugnant or foolish. Thus we can conclude that in ethics, redundancy arguments are almost always premature, and reports of the imminent death of utilitarianism are greatly exaggerated.

NOTES

This paper grew out of an earlier paper presented at the Morrell Conference, 'After MacIntyre', and a departmental research seminar in the Department of Political

Theory and Government, University College Swansea. I am grateful to the participants on both occasions.

Epigraphs from J. Griffin, 'Modern utilitarianism', *Revue Internationale de Philosophie*, 36 (1982), pp. 331–75; B. Williams, 'A critique of utilitarianism', in *Utilitarianism For and Against*, ed. J. J. C. Smart and B. Williams (Cambridge University Press, Cambridge, 1973), p. 150.

1   *After Virtue* (Duckworth, London, 1981), *Whose Justice? Which Rationality?* (Duckworth, London, 1988), and *Three Rival Versions of Moral Enquiry* (Duckworth, London, 1990).
2   I do not propose to make any significant distinctions between consequentialist and utilitarian theories.
3   See R. M. Hare, *Moral Thinking* (Clarendon, Oxford, 1981), D. Parfit, *Reasons and Persons* (Clarendon, Oxford, 1984), S. Kagan, *The Limits of Morality* (Clarendon, Oxford, 1989), or R. Hardin, *Morality Within the Limits of Reason* (University of Chicago Press, Chicago, 1988). An exception is J. Griffin in *Well-Being* (Clarendon, Oxford, 1986). However, even Griffin's discussion is brief and confined to the footnotes.
4   *After Virtue*, chs 1–9.
5   G. E. M. Anscombe, 'Modern moral philosophy', reprinted in *Ethics, Religion and Politics: The Collected Philosophical Papers of G. E. M. Anscombe*, vol. 3 (Blackwell, Oxford, 1981), pp. 26–42.
6   Ibid., p. 34.
7   C. Taylor, *Sources of the Self* (Cambridge University Press, Cambridge, 1989) and *The Ethics of Anthenticity* (Harvard University Press, Cambridge, Mass., 1992).
8   See J. Rawls, *A Theory of Justice* (Oxford University Press, Oxford, 1971), R. Nozick, *Anarchy, State and Utopia* (Blackwell, Oxford, 1974), R. Dworkin, *Taking Rights Seriously* (Duckworth, London, 1977) and B. Ackerman, *Social Justice in the Liberal State* (Yale University Press, New Haven, 1980).
9   *After Virtue*, p. 265.
10 Ibid., pp. 264–72.
11 Ibid., p. 71.
12 Ibid., p. 32.
13 This is most clearly the case with Dworkin, see *Taking Rights Seriously*, chs 6, 7 and 12.
14 A. Gewirth, *Reason and Morality* (University of Chicago Press, Chicago, 1978).
15 *After Virtue*, pp. 61–6.
16 Ibid., p. 65.
17 Among the recent works of Mill scholarship see, inparticular, J. Gray, *Mill On Liberty: A Defence* (Routledge, London, 1983), and F. Berger, *Happiness, Justice and Freedom* (University of California Press, Berkeley, 1984). For recent revisionist Bentham scholarship see G. J. Postema, *Bentham and the Common Law Tradition* (Clarendon, Oxford, 1986), and P. J. Kelly, *Utilitarianism and Distributive Justice: Jeremy Bentham and the Civil Law* (Clarendon, Oxford, 1990).
18 *After Virtue*, p. 32.
19 See D. Lyons, *The Forms and Limits of Utilitarianism* (Clarendon, Oxford, 1965), and J. J. C. Smart, 'An outline of a system of utilitarian ethics', in *Utilitarianism For and Against*, ed. Smart and Williams.
20 See Williams, 'A critique of utilitarianism', pp. 100–18.

21 Hare, *Moral Thinking*, pp. 45–64.
22 J. L. Mackie, 'Rights, utility, and universalization', in R. G. Frey, *Utility and Rights* (Blackwell, Oxford, 1985), pp, 86–104.
23 Williams, 'A critique of utilitarianism', pp. 108–18.
24 See C. Taylor, 'Interpretation and the sciences of man', in Taylor, *Philosophy and the Human Sciences: Philosophical Papers*, vol. 2 (Cambridge University Press, Cambridge, 1985), pp. 15–57.
25 *After Virtue*, p. 217.
26 Ibid., p. 216.
27 Ibid., p. 220.
28 Ibid., p. 221.
29 Ibid.
30 Hare, *Moral Thinking*, p. 122.
31 For an excellent discussion of the issues and difficulties involved in adopting an impartial perspective see, T. Nagel, *The View from Nowhere* (Clarendon, Oxford, 1986) and *Equality and Partiality* (Clarendon, Oxford, 1991).
32 See I. Berlin, *Concepts and Categories* (Hogarth Press, London, 1978), B. Williams, 'A critique of utilitarianism', and J. Raz, *The Morality of Freedom* (Clarendon, Oxford, 1986).
33 *After Virtue*, p. 200.
34 MacIntyre's Thomism is most explicit in *Whose Justice? Which Rationality?* and *Three Rival Versions of Moral Enquiry*.
35 *After Virtue*, p. 265.
36 D. Davidson, 'On the very idea of a conceptual scheme', in Davidson, *Inquiries into Truth and Interpretation* (Clarendon, Oxford, 1984).
37 *After Virtue*, p. 187.
38 Ibid., p. 200.
39 See for example the arguments of J. Griffin, *Well-Being*, and Russell Hardin, *Morality Within the Limits of Reason*.
40 See P. J. Kelly, 'Utilitarian strategies in Bentham and John Stuart Mill', *Utilitas*, ii (1990), pp. 245–66, and H. L. A. Hart, 'Natural rights: Bentham and John Stuart Mill', in *Essays on Bentham: Jurisprudence and Political Theory* (Clarendon, Oxford, 1982), pp. 79–104.
41 Jeremy Bentham, *An Introduction to the Principle of Morals and Legislation*, in *Collected Works* (Athlone, London, 1968), p. 13. He writes: 'To give such a proof is as impossible as it is needless.'
42 Rawls, *A Theory of Justice*, pp. 48–51.
43 See the discussion in B. Williams, 'Internal and external reasons', in *Moral Luck* (Cambridge University Press, Cambridge, 1981), pp. 101–13.
44 Griffin, *Well-Being*, pp. 157–62.

8

MacIntyre and Historicism

Robert Stern

In one of his more recent papers, Hilary Putnam makes the following observations regarding the origins and outcome of historicism:

> Hegel contributed two great and formative ideas to our culture, ideas between which there is some tension. On the one hand, he taught us to see all our ideas, including above all our ideas of rationality, as historically conditioned ... On the other hand, Hegel postulated an *objective* notion of rationality which we (or Absolute Mind) were coming to possess with the fulfilment of the progressive social and intellectual reforms which were already taking place ... Thinkers who accept the first Hegelian idea, that our conceptions of rationality are all historically conditioned, while rejecting the idea of an end (or even an ideal limit) to the process, tend to become historical or cultural relativists.[1]

Putnam is here giving expression to what is I think a popular and widespread view, namely that once one drops Hegel's nineteenth-century faith in the progressive development of consciousness through history, and merely retains his contextualized conception of rationality, then historicism collapses into some form of relativistic scepticism, as there is now no standpoint at the end of history from which previous outlooks can be judged, and in which their culmination can be assured. For Putnam, it seems, without support from Hegel's philosophy of history, historicism must inevitably slide into Nietzschean scepticism.

My aim in this paper is to argue that it is precisely such a slide that MacIntyre hopes to avoid, while none the less only endorsing Hegel's first idea and abandoning the second. Thus, while accepting the central historicist thesis, that 'human understanding is always a "captive" of its historical situation,'[2] and allowing that our form of rationality is not the outcome of some inevitable historical advance, he none the less sets out to resist the turn that many recent historicists have taken towards relativism, thereby setting himself at odds with the more Nietzschean camp of (for example) Richard Rorty and Michel Foucault.[3] It is the cogency of this non-sceptical form of historicism developed by MacIntyre that I wish to explore.

I

Much of the impetus for MacIntyre's historicism, together with that of other contemporary thinkers such as Charles Taylor, Michael Sandel and Michael Walzer, can be seen to stem from their shared hostility to the methods of liberal theorists such as John Rawls. In his book *A Theory of Justice*, Rawls attempted to revive the fundamentally Kantian project, of arriving at an ethico-political system by appealing to the supposedly universal principles of practical reason. Rawls, like Kant, wanted to found an ethical and political system (a system of justice) by appealing to the principles that would be agreed to by a subject who had adopted the standpoint of a universal lawgiver, legislating for a republic of similarly abstract and rational selves. In *A Theory of Justice* Rawls calls on the reader to consider what social system they would rationally choose if they did not know what position they would occupy in it (thereby ironing out the distortions of self-preference and perspective), and by so doing Rawls hoped to arrive at results that would be universal in their application.

Now, Rawls rejects any 'representational' model of truth in a characteristically Kantian fashion, together with the crude realism of moral facts, and the intuitionist claim that we have direct knowledge of what those facts are. None the less, Rawls does appear to hold that the principles of justice arrived at by individuals in the 'original position' do have a strong claim to objectivity, in so far as this Archimedean standpoint gives them a timeless, transhistorical validity, being principles that any individual, *qua* rational moral subject, must adopt.[4]

Now, it is precisely this last claim that is rejected by the historicists like MacIntyre, Taylor, Sandel and Walzer, on the following grounds. Firstly, it is argued, Rawls is working with an insufficiently historicized and contextualized conception of the self. Secondly, Rawls is accused of having an insufficiently historicized conception of reason. Thirdly, Rawls is accused of having an insufficiently historicized conception of justice. Let me examine the charges levelled at Rawls in a little more detail.

First, then, there is the charge that Rawls is working with an insufficiently contextualized and historicized conception of the self. This claim marks the common ground between historicism and the more narrowly political philosophy of *communitarianism*, with which MacIntyre, Sandel et al. are also associated. The claim here is that Rawls shares the mistaken liberal view of individuals as being (in Sandel's phrase) 'unencumbered':

that is, as being able to abstract from the particular time and place in which they live, and the roles and attachments which they have, and to adopt some universal outlook, some Archimedean standpoint, freed from the perspectival distortions of their concrete situation. By contrast, the historicist claims that the liberal conception of the self that encourages this kind of picture is mistaken, because it underestimates the way in which any individual is embedded in a particular, historically 'local', framework. Sandel puts this point as follows:

> to have character is to know that I move in a history I neither summon nor command, which carries consequences nonetheless for my choices and conduct . . . As a self-interpreting being, I am able to reflect on my history and in this sense to distance myself from it, but the distance is always precarious and provisional, the point of reflection never finally secured outside the history itself.[5]

Rawls, like liberalism in general, is said to have overestimated the capacity of the individual to rise above his or her historical, cultural and social situation, and reflect upon it *sub specie aeternitatis*.

This point has been used by Sandel and others to mount an attack on the strong conception of autonomy that is so central to the outlook of Kantian liberals like Rawls. For Kant in the *Grundlegung*, autonomy requires not only that individuals be capable of making choices (that is, have free will in the philosophical sense), but also that they be capable of reflexivity, rationality and integrity in making those choices (where by integrity I mean that the grounds for making those choices be theirs and no one else's). Now it is precisely this that the historicist characteristically denies: that is, he or she denies that moral agents do (in fact) have the capacity to reason about the preferences, values and beliefs they use to make their choices to the extent the Kantian implies; and that they could or should do so. The Kantian, the historicist argues, over-emphasizes the way in which the individual is capable of reasoning and reflecting *outside* of the set of values and beliefs available to him or her in any specific historical period or social position. The Kantian, it is claimed, has not sufficiently acknowledged the way in which all individuals are dependent for their outlook on the social and historical situation in which they find themselves, and this circumscribes their capacities for the full rational reflexivity and autonomy on which the Kantian conception depends. This aspect of historicism is graphically captured in Hegel's claim that 'Each individual is the son of his own nation at a specific stage in this nation's development. No one can escape from the spirit of his nation, any more than he can escape from the earth itself.'[6]

Having attacked the Kantian/Rawlsian conception of the individual as insufficiently historicized, the same charge is also levelled at Rawls's account of reason. The claim here is this: the Kantian liberal like Rawls is mistaken in assuming that there is *one* determinate mode of theoretical or practical reasoning that is shared by all individuals and cultures, in terms of which all human practices can be understood and governed. Against this the historicist stresses the multiplicity of rational procedures and modes of thought, and the contrast between them. The historicist argues that the Kantian liberal like Rawls is misled into thinking there is only one system of rationality because, as we have seen, he assumes that it is possible to step outside the rationality of particular cultures and times, and arrive at an account of 'rationality as such': in this way (it is argued) Rawls's first two errors play into each other's hands. Thus, as MacIntyre puts it, this 'conception of ideal rationality as consisting in the principles which a socially disembodied being would arrive at illegitimately ignores the inescapably historically and socially context-bound character which any substantive set of principles of rationality, whether theoretical or practical, is bound to have.'[7] MacIntyre himself identifies three different accounts of practical rationality,[8] of which the Rawlsian notion is only one, the implication being that Rawls underestimated the variation and divergence to be found within our conceptions of reason, all of which have been embodied in past ethical practices.

MacIntyre then goes on to argue (as the title of his book – *Whose Justice? Which Rationality?* – implies) that the fact of divergence in our historical conceptions of practical rationality means that we face a connected divergence in our accounts of justice, in so far as the latter are based on the former. Thus, it is claimed, Rawls's third error is to believe that there is only *one*, transhistorically valid system of justice that would be accepted by all rational individuals; for in so far as what it is to be a rational individual is historically and culturally variable, so too is the associated system of justice. Thus, given (as we have seen) the historicist rejection of some Archimedean standpoint from which all such systems of justice can be judged, on the grounds that no such standpoint is intelligible for us as historically situated individuals, then no neutral, absolute grounding for our principles of justice can be supplied, as no principle of practical reason can lay claim to timeless validity and universality. The systems of justice that have been endorsed within particular periods and cultures are treated by the historicist as fundamentally *local* practices, that have a meaning and legitimacy relative to their local standards of practical rationality: the contention is that Rawls is mistaken in seeking some grounding for these practices in a universal framework of rational thought, the idea of which the historicist rejects as untenable.

II

There are, however, well-known problems raised by the outlook I have just outlined, and it is these problems that I now wish to consider.

The principal problem faced by the kind of historicism just discussed may be put as follows: how can the superiority of one ethical conception to another be judged, if there is no objective criterion in terms of which they can be assessed? And how can the change from one ethical conception to the next be said to represent *a progressive development* if no such judgement can be made? And, if the change does *not* represent progress, how can the change be explicable on a rational model? How can the change be rationally justified or motivated? By taking the notion of an objectively valid ethical system to be unintelligible, historicism seems to make such questions unanswerable, as it is this notion that appears to underlie any conception we may have of progress, rational theory-change and transhistorical and transcultural comparative judgements.[9]

Now, the situation faced here by historicism may be usefully compared to the situation faced by post-Kuhnian philosophy of science, which increasingly abandoned the connection between truth, rationality and progress,[10] and began to speak more perspectivally of different and (possibly) incommensurable world-views, which cannot be compared to one another using the criterion of truth, because in order to ascertain the latter we would have to attain some absolute conception of 'the way the world really is', a notion that is rejected as 'transcendent' and unintelligible. Just as the historicist insists that the individual be set within some culturally and historically local practice, so Kuhn, Feyerabend and others insisted that the scientist be seen as working within a particular theoretical framework; and just as the historicist insists that there is no objective basis for this practice that would make it timelessly valid, so the philosophers of science insisted that it makes no sense to talk of a theory 'corresponding to reality', and so as absolutely true; for just as the historicist insists that justice and rationality are culturally relative, so the philosophers of science insisted that truth can only be relative to theories, giving us no neutral and transcendent basis on which to base a claim for absolute, timeless validity.

The further developments of the philosophy of science also show interesting parallels to the further developments of historicism. Just as some (like Rorty and perhaps Foucault) seem to move beyond historicism and to embrace relativism, the irrationality of conceptual change and the unintelligibility of progress, so some (like Feyerabend) seem to do the same with respect to science. Similarly, while some historicists have tried to find ways of resisting the radical scepticism of Rorty and Foucault, so some philosophers of science have tried to avoid the anarchism of Feyerabend. In both cases, the challenge the 'moderates' have faced has been this: how can we explain a change in one ethical or scientific conception to the next as *progressive* if we abandon the notion that there is any ultimate goal towards which such change ought to aim; and how can we understand such a goal if we do not allow talk of absolute validity or transcendent truth, either in ethics or in science? For if we abandon such a transcendent standard (which, according to the historicist and the Kuhnian, we must), how can progress, as the successive approximation to this goal, be judged? And if we abandon in turn the notion of progress towards an absolutely valid conception, how can the historical changes in outlook, either in ethics or in science, be deemed *rational* if these changes are no longer said to represent a progressive convergence on some absolutely valid truth?

Now it turns out that a moderate historicist like MacIntyre and the more moderate philosophers of science have both made a similar move at this point, a move that seems to offer a way out of the Nietzschean scepticism that appears to threaten their position. The strategy adopted by MacIntyre and the moderate philosopher of science is to try and show how conceptual change can still be rational, even *without* any claim that one is thereby adopting an outlook that has a greater degree of absolute validity. Instead, it is argued that we can use here an 'internal' notion of rationality, whereby it is rational to change from one outlook or theory to another *not* because the latter possesses the transcendental predicate of 'truth' or 'absolute validity', but rather because it represents a resolution of the problems, incoherences, anomalies, inconsistencies and limitations of the *previous* scheme or theory, and so constitutes an advance on it, in relative but not absolute terms.

In the philosophy of science, aspects of this approach can be found in Popper and Lakatos, but it is adopted most clearly by Larry Laudan, in his book *Progress and its Problems* and subsequent articles. Adopting a more sceptical position than either Popper or Lakatos, in so far as he abandons all talk of truth or verisimilitude, Laudan is none the less interested in capturing what is progressive about science, and why theory change in science is still rational. His answer is to argue that its rationality lies in the way in which the change to a new theory is made in order to solve the empirical and conceptual problems unresolved by its predecessors, claiming that we should take this advancement in problem-solving capacity as constituting scientific progress, rather than 'truthlikeness'. He argues that the advantage of the former account over the latter is that it enables us to hold on to the notion of progress and rational theory-change in science without being committed to 'such transcendental properties as truth or apodictic certainty'.[11] Laudan argues that it is rational to change a theory only when the new theory is a more effective problem solver, and insists against the relativist that this *is* a transcultural and transtemporal criterion of rationality, and that the development of science through history shows that this criterion has been generally applied. The only truth in relativism lies in the fact that different periods and different cultures may quite legitimately vary in what they take to be problems, and how they can possibly be solved: but that does not undermine the general criterion of rationality that Laudan applies.

Turning now to the approach adopted by MacIntyre, some remarkable parallels emerge. As we have seen, like Laudan MacIntyre abandons any talk of such transcendental properties as universal validity or timeless truth for ethical systems, arguing that there is no Archimedean point in practical reason that could give ethical thought the necessary absolute foundation. However, also like Laudan, he seeks to uphold the rationality of ethical change on the grounds that such change is progressive (and therefore rational) in so far as the new ethical system overcomes the problems, inconsistencies and limitations of its predecessors, and thereby represents a gain on the latter. MacIntyre sets out this position as follows, explicitly comparing his approach to that of post-Kuhnian philosophy of science:

> when rival moralities make competing and incompatible claims, there is always an issue at the level of moral philosophy concerning the ability of either to make good a claim to rational superiority over the other.
>
> How are these claims to be judged? As in the case of natural science there are no general timeless standards. It is in the ability of one particular moral-philosophy-articulating-the-claims-of-a-particular-morality to identify and to transcend the limitations of its rival or rivals, limitations which can be – although they may not in fact have been – identified by the rational standards to which the protagonists of the rival morality are committed by their allegiance to it, that the rational superiority of that particular moral philosophy and that particular morality emerges. The history of morality-and-moral-philosophy is the history of successive challenges to some pre-existing moral order, a history in which the question of which party defeated the other in rational argument is always to be distinguished from the question of which party retained or gained social and political hegemony. And it is only by reference to this history that questions of rational superiority can be settled. The history of morality-and-moral-philosophy written from this point of view is as integral to the enterprise of contemporary moral philosophy as the history of science is to the enterprise of contemporary philosophy of science.[12]

Understood against the background of developments in recent philosophy of science that I have outlined, MacIntyre's position seems to be strikingly similar: the rationality and progressive nature of moral philosophy lies not in its gradually moving towards some goal of timeless validity, but in the fact that each moral system can be seen to 'transcend the limitations' of its predecessors, and thus represent an advance on it. Like Laudan, therefore, MacIntyre emphasizes that the rationality of a change in moral theory can only be judged (so to speak) *internally*, as a response by one moral outlook to the problematic of its predecessors, and this judgement is not to be grounded in some appeal to a set of objectively valid norms of moral reasoning.

For both recent philosophers of science like Laudan and a historicist like MacIntyre, this 'internalist' approach to conceptual change (whether scientific or moral) is associated with a strong defence of the relevance of historical understanding to the rational appraisal of scientific theories on the one hand and moralities on the other. The position here is this: given that the realist is wrong in thinking that any theory can have validity *sub specie aeternitatis*, from the standpoint of timeless truth, the progressive (or regressive) character of any conceptual change can only be judged by reference to the historical problematic of which it is part; for the issue as to whether or not it represents an advance on its predecessors requires that we have an understanding of the historical tradition in which it has a place. As Collingwood had it, in a dictum that Laudan used as a motto for one of the chapters of *Progress and its Problems*, 'The revolutionary can only represent his revolution as a progress in so far as he is also an historian':[13] that is, only from a historical perspective, and not from the perspective of objective truth, can the progressive nature of a conceptual change be understood.

Thus, by judging theories in historical terms, MacIntyre and Laudan hope to overcome the challenge of scepticism, while at the same time abandoning the apparently naive assumptions of dogmatic absolutism. They both suggest that what enables us to make a rational and objective choice between competing theories (whether moral or scientific) is *not* by applying absolute standards, but only historical ones: namely, whether or not the theory represents an advance on its predecessors compared to its rivals, by more successfully overcoming the problems which the previous theory had faced.[14] MacIntyre and Laudan argue that once this historical perspective is introduced, it enables us to give rational grounds for moving from one theory to the next, without having to show that it is valid in absolute terms; as a result, MacIntyre claims, 'it is only when theories are located in history, when we view the demands for justification in highly particular contexts of a historical kind, that we are freed from either dogmatism or capitulation to scepticism.'[15] This, then, is the strategy MacIntyre has adopted in order to show that when the problematic assumptions of absolutism are abandoned, the collapse into Nietzschean relativism can still be avoided.

III

Can this strategy succeed, however? Does this appeal to 'historical reason'[16] represent a coherent *via media* that will enable the Scylla of dogmatism and the Charybdis of scepticism to be avoided? It is this worry about MacIntyre's strategy that must now be discussed.

One immediate worry is how far MacIntyre's approach represents a genuine third option, and whether it can avoid collapsing into either dogmatism or scepticism. On the one hand, it could be argued, Mac-Intyre's position remains in effect indistinguishable from scepticism, for although MacIntyre insists that an ethical outlook is to be preferred to another when it 'transcends the limitations of its predecessors', he makes clear that what one perceives these limitations to be, and how one might take them to be transcended, is relative to one's particular perspective;[17] and when the choice is not just within *one* tradition of enquiry, but between *conflicting* traditions, then the criterion is so vague as to be empty. On the other hand, it could also be claimed that MacIntyre's position incorporates an unsupported element of dogmatic absolutism, in his apparent assumption that in solving the problems of one theory by moving to another, we are thereby making some sort of epistemic gain, by *ipso facto* acquiring a better understanding of how things are.[18]

Does MacIntyre have the resources with which to maintain the stability and distinctiveness of his position, and resist attempts at assimilation on both these fronts? The difficulty for MacIntyre is that in the case of ethics and science, his *via media* is bound to look unstable, as in these areas the search for absolutes has tended to blur the distinction between historicism and relativism. The case for MacIntyre strategy would be strengthened, therefore, if a field of evaluation could be found in which historicism can clearly be shown to be a distinctive option. In order to see how this might be possible, the following way of thinking about the issue may help in assessing MacIntyre's approach.

Consider the histories of the arts, of painting, architecture, music, literature and so on, and then ask yourself the question: is it meaningful to claim that transition from one style, one period, to the next can constitute progress? To some people (call them sceptics) it is obvious that this question must be answered negatively, for they deny that we can possess a transhistorical set of criteria by which we can judge whether one period is better than another. To other people (call them dogmatists) it is obvious that this question can be answered positively, for they think there *are* such absolute criteria, using which aesthetic advances can be appraised. It could be argued, however, that neither of these options is particularly appealing: while it is hard to admit that the dogmatist is right to claim that we can postulate absolute standards against which art objects can be judged and progress can be measured, it is equally difficult to agree with the sceptic that there is no sense in which we can make judgements regarding periods of advance (or decline) in the development of the arts. It seems, then, that it would be sensible to make room for a third position: namely, a position that would still enable us to talk of some style, period or art object in terms of progress or decline, without assuming that we have access to some set of absolute criteria in terms of which this development can be assessed.

In outline, this third position could claim the following: that in the histories of the arts, one style, period or art object represents an advance on another in so far as it 'transcends the limitations of its predecessors', by being better able to solve some aesthetic problems (for instance, of representaiton, of composition, of characterization) that had frustrated those which went before, by adopting some fresh stylistic approach or through the discovery of some original artistic form.[19] This conception of progress is essentially *historical*, for only in the context of the artistic tradition of which it is part can one period be said to constitute some developmemt over its forerunners: it is only from a historical perspective that one can understand how it was that some new development overcame limitations in what was possible so far. In response to the outlook of the sceptic, therefore, this position can claim that it *is* reasonable to say that a new artistic period constitutes an advance on its predecessors in historical terms, without thereby resorting to the dogmatist's assumption, that there are absolute criteria against which the respective merits of each style and art object can be judged. This conception of the arts is distinctive, in that it requires some historical context in order for the process of evaluation to proceed: abstract this evaluation procedure from this context (as both scepticism and dogmatism do in different ways), and you cannot then say wherein the merit or demerit of a new art form might consist.

Now, if it is legitimate to think of the histories of the arts in this way, there are several lessons to be learnt. First, by setting styles and art objects in their historical context, it is possible to talk of progress without assuming (as in a Hegelian conception) that some end-point of artistic development is or can be attained: to do so would be to revert to some form of dogmatism. Secondly, we can none the less use the notion of artistic development to show that this style or art object has evolved beyond the limitations of its predecessors, and can meaningfully claim that this is where its value lies. Thirdly, we can allow that this value would be missed by anyone who lacked any understanding of the historical context in which this evolution occurred, or who viewed the art object from an artistic tradition in which a different historical problematic could be shown to apply. Finally, it could be argued, that to this approach the labels of neither scepticism nor dogmatism can be meaningfully applied.

This approach is also very close to MacIntyre's, to the extent that he too uses historical considerations with which to assess moral theories, by looking to see whether they constitute any sort of advance on the ethical systems adopted so far. Just as someone might argue that (for example) landscape painting in our time is lacking in any merit, because it does not take this tradition any further, so MacIntyre likewise argues that modern moral theories are inadequate, in so far as they have failed to make any positive contribution to the way in which the tradition of moral enquiry has evolved. For MacIntyre, a moral theory, like a scientific theory or work done within a craft (*techne*),[20] can be judged in terms of its contribution to the tradition of which it is part, and it is on this that his historical critique of modern moral theories, and his 'historicist defence of Aristotle',[21] relies.

Of course, I do not wish to suggest that because a historicist approach can provide coherent grounds for aesthetic evaluation the historical development of the arts bears any very exact analogy to the historical development of scientific and moral theories. In particular, as Collingwood stressed, it may well be argued that in science and philosophy it is more common to set out with a very clear and conscious desire to solve the problems of one's predecessors, while in the case of the arts this is rarely the case.[22] However, whether or not a particular artist does *in fact* overcome the limitations of what went before can be assessed independently of his or her intentions, and can still provide a perfectly intelligible basis for assessment in aesthetics. Nor am I suggesting that historical progress represents the *only* possible grounds for comparative judgement in the arts, for obviously we *can* be guided by considerations that we recognize to be purely subjective: all I wish to claim is that here we have a clear case where historicism provides support for our rational evaluations, without collapsing into either absolutism or scepticism.

Moreover, although it may be straining the parallel too far, it is interesting to speculate on whether another feature of MacIntyre's historicism may also gain support when considered from the perspective of the arts: namely, his claim that an important feature of any advance must be that it enables us to account for the breakdown and stagnation of the outlook that preceded it. In the case of theoretical progress (as in the sciences or philosophy), this is likely to happen because the introduction of some new set of concepts or intellectual framework allows us to see how the previous conception was inadequate, and thus why it came to fail.[23] At first sight, it might appear that no such phenomenon is intelligible in the case of the arts. However, I think it could possibly be argued that even here, when a progressive development occurs, we will then be able to understand the limitations that had to be transcended if any further advance was to take place. Thus, to take one example, only with the development of Cubism was it possible to see *why* the constraints of naturalism had led into a cul-de-sac, although *that* they had may have been obvious to the naturalists themselves. This is not to say that Cubism is any closer than naturalism to realizing some aesthetic ideal: that would be to revert to absolutism. It is rather to suggest that the historicist approach shows how aesthetic evaluations can be made in terms of the notion of progress, in a way that enables us to do *without* such ideals, by showing how one art form or object overcomes the limitations inherent in its predecessor. Clearly there can still be debate over what one takes those limitations to be, and whether they are successfully overcome: but what makes this debate resolvable is the evidence of the subsequent history.

In conclusion, then, it seems to me that MacIntyre's strategy does offer a way out of Putnam's conundrum: namely, how can the historicist avoid relativism without being a full fledged Hegelian? As MacIntyre makes clear,[24] he does not see historical change as necessarily progressive and unitary, nor does he believe that it has reached its culmination in modernity; he thereby abandons two central features of nineteenth-century historicism, features that protected it from scepticism. As I hope to have shown, MacIntyre is thereby forced to adopt a more subtle position, one that seeks to escape relativism by retaining the idea that historical change can still be evaluated using the notion of progress ('the transcending of limitations') as a criterion. I have suggested that in the case of the arts, this idea can be coherently applied, as we can use the concept of an aesthetic advance to give us an objective, rational evaluative standard, and thereby escape relativism, while at the same time insisting against the dogmatist that no advance could ever coherently be taken to be 'final'; and if this strategy can be successfully employed in our assessment of works of art, why can't we also follow MacIntyre in applying it in our assessment of moral theories?

NOTES

1 Hilary Putnam, 'Beyond historicism', in *Realism and Reason: Philosophical Papers Volume 3* (Cambridge University Press, Cambridge, 1983), pp. 287–303, pp. 287–8. Cf. also Putnam, *Reason, Truth and History* (Cambridge University Press, Cambridge, 1981), p. 158.
2 Robert D'Amico, *Historicism and Knowledge* (Routledge and Kegan Paul, London, 1989), p. x. Cf. Richard J. Bernstein, *Beyond Objectivism and Relativism*

(Blackwell, Oxford, 1983), pp 3–4: 'We have been told that it is an illusion and a deep self-deception to think that there is some over-arching framework, some neutral descriptive language, some permanent standards of rationality to which we can appeal in order to understand and critically evaluate the competing claims that are made, and that we are limited to our historical context and to our own social practices. The dream or hope that many philosophers have had – to grasp the world *sub species aeternitatus* – is, we are told, a deceiving illusion that leads to dogmatism and even terror.' In using the term 'historicism' to characterize this position, I am employing it in its traditional sense, and not in the manner adopted by Karl Popper, who defined historicism as 'an approach to the social sciences which assumes that *historical prediction* is their principal aim'. Karl Popper, *The Poverty of Historicism*, 2nd. edn (Routledge, London, 1960), p. 3.

3   See, for example, MacIntyre's attempt to meet what he calls the relativist and perspectivist challenges in *Whose Justice? Which Rationality?* (Duckworth, London, 1988), pp. 362ff.

4   The reservation 'appear to hold' is necessary because Rawls's actual position, as expressed in his more recent papers, is considerably less universal in its implications than this. He now merely claims that the principles of justice arrived at in the original position articulate *our* conception of justice. Moreover, even in *A Theory of Justice* itself, some of Rawls's comments are more historicist in tone; see, for example, *A Theory of Justice* (Oxford University Press, Oxford, 1972), p. 548: 'Of course, in working out what the requisite principles [of justice] are, we must rely upon current knowledge as recognized by common sense and the existing scientific consensus. But there is no reasonable alternative to doing this. We have to concede that as established beliefs change, it is possible that the principles of justice which it seems rational to choose may likewise change.' Richard Rorty has stressed the historicist and pragmatist side of Rawls's work in 'The priority of democracy to philosophy', in *The Virginia Statute for Religious Freedom*, ed. Merril D. Peterson and Robert C. Vaughan (Cambridge University Press, Cambridge, 1988), pp. 257–82 (reprinted in *Reading Rorty*, ed. Alan R. Malachowski (Blackwell, Oxford, 1990), pp. 279–302), and *Contingency, Irony and Solidarity* (Cambridge University Press, Cambridge, 1989), pp. 57–8.

5   Michael Sandel, 'The procedural republic and the unencumbered self', *Political Theory*, 12 (1984), pp. 81–96, pp. 90–1; cf. Michael Sandel, *Liberalism and the Limits of Justice* (Cambridge University Press, Cambridge, 1982), p. 179.

6   G. W. F. Hegel, *Lectures on the Philosophy of World History: Introduction*, trans. H. B. Nisbet, with an introduction by Duncan Forbes (Cambridge University Press, Cambridge, 1975), p. 81.

7   *Whose Justice? Which Rationality?*, p. 4.

8   'To be practically rational, so one contending party holds, is to act on the basis of calculations of the costs and benefits to oneself of each possible alternative course of action and its consequences. To be practically rational, affirms a rival party, is to act under those constraints which any rational person, capable of an impartiality which accords no particular privileges to one's own interests, would agree should be imposed. To be practically rational, so a third party contends, is to act in such a way as to achieve the ultimate and true good of human beings. Ibid., p. 2.

9   Cf. Rorty, *Contingency, Irony and Solidarity*, p. 48: 'To accept the claim that there is no standpoint outside the particular historically conditioned and

temporary vocabulary we are presently using from which to judge this vocabulary is to give up on the idea that there can be reasons for using languages as well as reason within languages for believing statements. This amounts to giving up on the idea that intellectual or political progress is rational, in any sense of "rational" which is neutral between vocabularies.'

10 Larry Laudan has explained this connection as follows: 'Specifically, it has normally been held that any assessment of either rationality or scientific progress is inevitably bound up with the question of the *truth* of scientific theories. Rationality, it is usually argued, amounts to accepting those statements about the world which we have good reason for believing to be ture. Progress, in its turn, is usually seen as a successive attainment of the truth by a process of approximation and self-correction.' Larry Laudan, *Progress and its Problems: Towards a Theory of Scientific Growth* (Routledge and Kegan Paul, London, 1977), p. 125.

11 Larry Laudan, 'A problem-solving approach to scientific progress', in *Scientific Revolutions*, ed. Ian Hacking (Oxford University Press, Oxford, 1981), pp. 144–5. Cf. Thomas S. Kuhn, *The Structure of Scientific Revolutions* (2nd edn, University of Chicago Press, Chicago, 1970), p. 206: 'A scientific theory is usually felt to be better than its predecessors not only in the sense that it is a better instrument for discovery and solving puzzles but also because it is somehow a better representation of what nature is really like. One often hears that successive theories grow ever closer to, or approximate more and more closely to, the truth. Apparently generalizations like that refer not to the puzzle-solutions and the concrete predications derived from a theory but rather to its ontology, to the match, that is, between the entities with which the theory populates nature and what is "really there" ... [But] There is, I think, no theory-independent way to reconstruct phrases like "really there"; the notion of a match between the ontology of a theory and its real counterpart in nature now seems to me illusive in principle. Besides, as an historian, I am impressed with the implausibility of the view. I do not doubt, for example, that Newton's mechanics improves on Aristotle's and that Einstein's improves on Newton's as instruments for puzzle-solving. But I can see in their succession no coherent direction of ontological development.'

12 *After Virtue*, 2nd edn (Duckworth, London, 1985), pp. 268–9. For a similar attempt to compare the history of moral systems to the history of scientific theories, see J. B. Schneewind, 'Moral knowledge and moral principles', in *Revisions: Changing Perspectives in Moral Philosophy*, ed. Stanley Hauerwas and Alasdair MacIntyre (University of Notre Dame Press, Notre Dame, Ind., 1983), pp. 113–26, pp. 122–3.

13 R. G. Collingwood, *The Idea of History* (Oxford University Press, Oxford, 1946), p. 326; cited Laudan, *Progress and its Problems*, p. 121. Cf. MacIntyre's claim that 'scientific reason turns out to be subordinate to, and intelligible only in terms of, historical reason', and that 'the theory of scientific rationality has to be embedded in a philosophy of history.' Alasdair MacIntyre, 'Epistemological crises, dramatic narrative and the philosophy of science', *The Monist*, 60 (1977), pp. 453–72, pp. 464, 467.

14 Cf. MacIntyre, *After Virtue*, p. 268: 'What rendered Newtonian physics rationally superior to its Galilean and Aristotelian predecessors and to its Cartesian rivals was that it was able to transcend their limitations by solving problems in areas in which those predecessors and rivals could by their own standards of scientific progress make no progress. So we cannot say wherein the rational

superiority of Newtonian physics consisted except historically in terms of its relationship to those predecessors and rivals whom it challenged and displaced. Abstract Newtonian physics from its context, and then ask wherein the rational superiority of one to the other consists, and you will be met with insoluble incommensurability problems.'

15   MacIntyre, 'Epistemological crises', p. 471.

16   Ibid., p. 464.

17   'What each person is confronted with is at once a set of rival intellectual positions, a set of rival traditions embodied more or less imperfectly in contemporary forms of social relationship and a set of rival communities of discourse, each with its own specific modes of speech, argument and debate, each making a claim upon the individual's allegiance. It is by the relationship between what is specific to each such standpoint, embodied at these three levels of doctrine, history and discourse, and what is specific to the beliefs and history of each individual who confronts these problems, that what the problems are for that person is determined.' MacIntyre, *Whose Justice? Which Rationality?*, p. 393.

18   Charles Taylor appears to make this claim on behalf of the sort of reasoning that MacIntyre employs: 'Practical reasoning . . . is a reasoning in transitions. It aims to establish, not that some position is correct absolutely, but rather that some position is superior to some other. It is concerned, covertly or openly, implicitly or explicitly, with comparative propositions. We show one of these comparative claims to be well founded when we show that the *move* from A to B *constitutes a gain epistemically*. This is something we do when we show, for instance, that we get from A to B by identifying and resolving a contradiction in A or a confusion which A relied on, or by acknowledging the importance of some factor which A screened out, or something of the sort. The argument fixes on the nature of the transition from A to B. The nerve of the rational proof consists in showing that *this transition is an error-reducing one*.' Charles Taylor, *Sources of the Self* (Cambridge University Press, Cambridge, 1989), p. 72; last two emphases added.

19   Of course, it might be said that some advance in the arts was due to other factors, such as the discovery of new materials or techniques, but I take it that while this may *aid* aesthetic development, it does not *constitute* it.

20   Cf. *Three Rival Versions of Moral Enquiry* (Duckworth, London, 1990), pp. 64–5.

21   *After Virtue*, p. 277.

22   Collingwood, *The Idea of History*, pp. 330, 333–4. Richard Bernstein has claimed that 'A scientist is always under the obligation to give a rational account of what is right and wrong in the theory that is being displaced and to explain how his or her theory can account for what is "true" in the preceding theory (when adequately reconstructed) and what is "false" or inadequate' (*Beyond Objectivism and Relativism*, p. 68). Although this obligation obviously does not apply to the artist, it does not follow from that that we are not entitled to use the idea of progress as a basis for aesthetic evaluation.

23   Cf. Alasdair MacIntyre, 'The relationship of philosophy to its past', in *Philosophy in History*, ed. Richard Rorty, J. B. Schneewind and Quentin Skinner (Cambridge University Press, Cambridge, 1984), pp. 31–48, p. 43.

24   Cf. *Three Rival Versions*, pp. 58–9. For critical comments on Hegel's absolutism, cf. *After Virtue*, p. 270, and *Whose Justice? Which Rationality?*, pp. 360–1.

9

MacIntyre's Fusion of History and Philosophy

Gordon Graham

In the *Critique of Hegel's Philosophy of Right* Marx criticizes Hegel's account of the state in the following terms.

> Hegel has done nothing but resolve the constitution of the state into the universal, abstract idea of the organism; but in appearance and in his own opinion he has developed the determinate reality out of the universal Idea. He has made the subject of the idea into a product and predicate of the Idea. He does not develop his thought out of what is objective, but what is objective in accordance with a ready-made thought which has its origins in the abstract sphere of logic.[1]

Though this remark is made about Hegel's treatment of the state, it may be read, in fact, as a summary of a general objection to Hegelian idealism, namely its fashioning an account of history and social reality not according to the findings of empirical investigation into 'what is objective', but 'in accordance with a ready-made thought' drawn from the philosophical manipulation of ideas and concepts. In short, Hegel's method of uncovering 'determinate reality' is aprioristic, and blindly so.

This familiar objection may or may not be justified; Hegel himself is aware of the charge and makes great efforts to rebut it in the Introduction to the *Philosophy of History*. But it certainly strikes at the heart of the Hegelian enterprise. For Hegel's philosophy, and especially his philosophy of history, is predicated on the supposition that 'what is actual is rational and what is rational is actual'[2] and that 'the history of the world ... presents us with a rational process',[3] so that a proper understanding of reality must consist in the exploration of ideas, or as Hegel would prefer 'Spirit', which, though eternally 'Now' makes itself manifest in different historical forms. It is this approach that makes Hegel's philosophy of history historicist. It construes history as a 'rational necessary course' and bids us not merely establish how things were, but explain why they must have been so.

Marx attempts to escape the historicism by turning the Hegelian dialectic on its head, by making material reality rather than philosophical
concepts the driving force of history. But if Popper's well-known criticisms are sound, he does not succeed in escaping it. In Marx, at best, the
Idealist historicism is replaced by a materialist version. But no less than
Hegel's philosophy, the fundamental economic and social 'laws' that
Marx's theory of history relies on tell us how the past must have been
and outline the necessary development of the future.

My concern here, however, is not with Marxist social theory but with
Hegelian Idealism. In its Idealist form, critics allege, historicism arises
from the confusion of history and logic, or more broadly factual and
conceptual questions.[4] Necessary relations are the province of logic
and of concepts; historical fact is concerned with what is contingent. To
claim that some historical change or development *had* to happen is to
go beyond anything history proper could establish. Claims of this sort
seem plausible in Hegel, as Marx alleges in the passage quoted, because
Hegel purports to derive 'determinate reality' from a 'universal idea' and
of course the discussion of ideas in this sense is a properly philosophical
activity and hence properly concerned with necessary relations. But
whatever appearances may suggest, the truth is that philosophical ideas
are one thing and the social and historical realities that may be described
in terms of them another.

This line of criticism is very familiar and has been generally persuasive. There are not many enthusiastic supporters for Hegel's philosophy
of history in contemporary philosophy, even among those who are
broadly sympathetic to Hegel. But despite this widespread consensus, it
is not at all clear to me why contemporary philosophy rejects the Idealist approach to history. This is because the objection I have just elaborated briefly – that we must not confuse the empirical and the logical, the
historical and the conceptual – rests on a thesis that Quine has famously
declared a dogma of empiricism, the thesis that there is a radical distinction between conceptual questions and matters of brute fact. And Quine's
rejection of this distinction has also found widespread support in contemporary philosophy. But if this is a dogma, and an indefensible one,
what then is Hegel's fault?

One suggestion is this. Hegel is not wrong to think in terms that
deny a logical gap between the conceptual and the factual. But he tries
to bridge it in the wrong way. He brings philosophy to bear on history,
rather than bringing history to bear on philosophy. Philosophical concepts have a history; that is why philosophy cannot ignore their historical development. But Hegel speaks as though history can be construed
as a philosophical development. To abandon Hegelian philosophy of
history, therefore, is not to suppose that there is after all a radical gulf

between history and philosophy, but only that Hegel goes the wrong way about bridging it.

This suggestion, it seems to me, has the merit of being in accord with much current opinion. If there is little enthusiasm for approaching historical questions in the grand philosophical manner, there is considerable enthusiasm in contemporary philosophy for the idea that a proper understanding of philosophical questions requires an understanding of their historical genesis. One of the leading proponents of this idea over many years is Alasdair MacIntyre.[5] In this essay I want to ask whether, in the end, MacIntyre's subversion of the philosophical/historical distinction is any more successful than Hegel's.

I

The belief that philosophical questions require historical illumination runs through all of MacIntyre's writings. It is the guiding thought behind *A Short History of Ethics*, as he makes plain at the start, and he reiterates his belief in the preface to *After Virtue*.

> A central theme of much of [my] earlier work (*A Short History of Ethics*, 1966; *Secularisation and Moral Change*, 1967; *Against the Self-Images of the Age*, 1971) was that we have to learn from history and anthropology of the variety of moral practices, beliefs and conceptual schemes. The notion that the moral philosopher can study the concepts of morality merely by reflecting, Oxford armchair style, on what he or she and those around him or her say or do is barren.[6]

Accordingly, *After Virtue* begins with a sociohistorical hypothesis, that contemporary morality is a collection of fragments of earlier moralities which, taken together, cannot be welded into a coherent whole. There is, MacIntyre claims, widespread moral disagreement in our society because there is a deep incommensurability between moral views. Nor is this the full extent of the cultural chaos by which we are beset. Any idea that we might employ principles of reason to adjudicate between these rival moral views founders on the fact that our culture employs incommensurable conceptions of practical reason also. This is the theme of his next book *Whose Justice? Which Rationality?*.[7]

Plainly this is a historical hypothesis, an account of where we are and how we got here. But it also has philosophical implications. The fragmented nature of our morality, according to MacIntyre, explains the peculiar staying power of emotivism in twentieth-century moral philosophy. Though analytical philosophers rejected emotivism by and large, the emotivist analysis of moral language continues to attract attention, albeit largely critical attention. This is because its analysis of moral language as having a purely emotive use in fact reflects fairly accurately an important strand of much contemporary use of moral language. As moral theory, however, it is none the less defective. Its fault lies in its failure to understand the historical dimension of moral concepts. If many moral concepts are currently used merely to express personal feelings, it was not always so. And this ahistorical character explains emotivism's inability to accommodate another, equally important strand of modern morality, namely its continuing aspiration to moral reasoning. In short, emotivism takes itself to be concerned with moral language and moral concepts *as such*, whereas its account of morality is fashioned merely by contemporary morality. It thus cannot allow for the fact that the confrontational character of contemporary moral disagreements is the result of a long historical process and that at other times and places the use of moral language and the role of moral concepts, and hence their philosophical analysis, were quite different. If this is true of emotivism, it follows that the history of moral philosophy can show a philosophical doctrine to be inadequate.

According to MacIntyre, emotivism (and indeed all its rival metaethical theories) is poor moral philosophy in another respect also, namely in its attempt to be value neutral. Moral concepts are not fixed and final; that in part explains the necessity to understand their history. But

> philosophical inquiry itself plays a part in changing moral concepts. It is not that we have first a straightforward history of moral concepts and then a separate and secondary history of philosophical comment. For to analyze a concept philosophically may often be to assist in its transformation by suggesting that it needs revision, or that it is discredited in some way, or that it has a certain kind of prestige.[8]

An adequate moral philosophy, then, must combine both the historical and the normative. MacIntyre recognizes that this second dimension presents something of a problem for his own position. If our moral world is as chaotic as he alleges, and if the incommensurability between rival moralities reaches the depths he suggests, to what rational basis can philosophical criticism appeal? Providing an answer to this question is the central task of those writings subsequent to *After Virtue*. This problem, and his solution to it, are not my immediate concern here, however. For the moment I want to stress only that what he is calling for is not merely more attention to the history of ideas, or greater honesty about evaluative commitment in philosophy, but a conception of moral philosophy in which the historical and the critical are *fused*. My question is whether we have good reason to regard it as real fusion rather than a very sophisticated form of what in Hegel is generally agreed to be confusion.

II

To explore this question let us look more closely at the basis of MacIntyre's contention about modern society. There is of course an important question about the identity of anything called 'modern society', and a corresponding one about what the expression 'our morality' might refer to.[9] But even when these are solved, or left aside, considerable difficulties remain. How can we establish or refute the thesis that modern morality is deeply fragmented? In *After Virtue*, MacIntyre rehearses a number of familiar moral arguments – about war, abortion and social justice. He makes two claims about them, first that though the conclusions they support are in conflict, each argument can be made logically sound, and second that these arguments are to be heard and found not merely among professional moral philosophers, or even 'articulate expert spokesmen' such as the Pope and Milton Friedman, but 'in newspaper editorials and high-school debates, on radio talk shows and letters to congressmen, in bars, barracks and boardrooms'.[10] It is this ubiquitousness that is important, showing as it does the extent of moral disagreement across contemporary society.

His diagnosis is thus concerned both with philosophical questions – the soundness of moral arguments – and with sociological ones – the social extent of moral disagreement. But a historical dimension also enters in. If we are to understand how it is that incompatible arguments are equally sound, we will have to explore the difference of approach each adopts, the larger set of assumptions each relies on. To do this is to be steered into an exploration of traditions of moral thought and inquiry and into the study of their development over time. In this way MacIntyre's argument in favour of his 'disquieting suggestion' about the modern world is itself a good illustration of his belief that a proper understanding of contemporary morality cannot rely on analytical philosophy alone, but must employ the resources of historical and social inquiry as well.

But does the existence of these different arguments and their rival proponents bear out the contention about modern morality? Consider first the relation between the philosophical question of incommensurability and the fact of social disagreement. To claim that the foundations on which these various moral arguments are based are irresolvably incompatible is to make a claim about the *possibility* of rational agreement. It is of course consistent with the impossibility of rationally conclusive proof that all moral agents should *as a matter of fact* agree, and even that their agreement should be the result of rational argument between them. It could be, for instance, that once the foundations of the various arguments have been laid bare, those who are in dispute settle their differences by abandoning some of the beliefs that led to dispute. In such a way, perhaps, agreement might be reached between deontologists and consequentialists, not by rational proof in favour of one side, but by their all becoming one thing rather than the other. Conversely, as many have argued, a belief in the possibility of rationally conclusive proof in all moral matters is logically compatible with the fact of widespread disagreement because, just as with some simple matters of fact which are easy enough to settle, some of the disputants may persist in error.

So, if we are to connect the absence of widespread agreement with its conceptual impossibility, as MacIntyre's argument aims to do, it will not be enough to gesture towards a certain consonance between the two, about which, probably, everyone will agree. We will have to show first that both are in fact the case, and secondly that the latter is the explanation of the former. Similarly, if we are to connect the emergence of a philosophical doctrine such as emotivism with the fact of widespread social disagreement, we must show that the former is a result of the latter, that there is widespread disagreement just because of the incommensurability of the concepts we employ. In short, even if we accept that what MacIntyre alleges about modern morality is true, there is another level of historical and social investigation required before we can claim with confidence that moral philosophy and cultural history are connected in the ways that MacIntyre's philosophy requires.

Now what is important about this observation is that it seems to introduce the possibility of fission where MacIntyre requires fusion, because the most obvious way of connecting the two is by means of the beliefs of participants. It is the common experience of most teachers of philosophy that without much prompting students starting out in moral philosophy espouse some elementary version of emotivism. It is also the case that they normally disagree about war, abortion, social justice and so on along the lines MacIntyre describes. These two facts might be connected in either of two ways. It may be that students subscribe to emotivism because in their experience they rarely reach moral agreement with others. Or it may be that their subscription to emotivism leads them to abandon moral argument at an early stage, in the belief that rational resolution of disagreement is impossible. If the first is the case, their experience does not of course show that emotivism is true; it only shows that they believe it on the basis of their experience. If the second explanation holds, it does not hold because emotivism is true, but only because they believe it to be so. Let us suppose that the mentality of students such as these may be said to be typical of the modern mind. In explaining its existence in either way we do not need to engage in argument about the philosophical adequacy of emotivism. We need only record the beliefs of existing people in the round. That is to say, we need not fuse our philosophical and sociological inquiries, but engage in the latter alone. Similarly, if what interests us is the truth or falsehood of emotivism, we can consider this in the abstract and need not concern ourselves with any given social context. It seems, then, that in investigating the accuracy of MacIntyre's account of the modern condition, the separation of philosophy from history and sociology is possible after all.

III

It might be argued that this conclusion follows only if we ignore the normative aspect of moral philosophy which MacIntyre stresses. We have also omitted an important element in his description of contemporary morality. Though students may readily accept emotivism, they also embrace moral causes and engage in debate in a way that has point only if emotivism is *not* true. To arrive at a critical assessment of contemporary morality, then, we do need to concern ourselves with the truth or falsity of emotivism (and other philosophical positions), as well as sociohistorical conditions. More importantly, this involves a critical consideration of the grounds on which judgements of philosophical truth and falsehood are to be based.

As it stands, however, this rejoinder is not enough to secure the fusion of history and philosophy. Consider a parallel. To decide whether modern medicine promotes health we need to investigate *both* the evaluative concept of health *and* the effectiveness of doctors, hospitals, drugs and so on in securing the ends which that concept implies. But it does not follow that the two investigations are conceptually unified in any interesting sense. To assemble relevant information on the second point – effective means – involves a quite different sort of inquiry than does arriving at a clearer view of the end.

MacIntyre, I think, would deny this, certainly in the case of morality but probably in medicine as well. This is because the objection is itself victim to a failing in contemporary philosophy which, precisely by trying to consider concepts as rational abstractions, ignores the singular importance of tradition. The suggestion that in looking at the state of medicine or morality we can separate the concepts and the methods it employs relies on a distinction between ends and means which is inapplicable within a coherent tradition.

To appreciate fully this rejoinder to the argument so far, more needs to be said about MacIntyre's account of the contemporary condition of morality. In his latest book, *Three Rival Versions of Moral Enquiry*, the rival versions he distinguishes are the encyclopaedist, the genealogist and the traditionalist.[11] The first of these conceives of rational inquiry and the pursuit of truth on the model of compiling an encyclopaedia such as the *Encyclopaedia Britannica*. On this conception the pursuit of knowledge is progressive and accumulative. By the consistent application of methods of a sort that must commend themselves to any rational inquirer, humankind has gradually amassed more and more of the truth. Science is unified and its aim is the growth of knowledge. The genealogist, by contrast, sees truth as an impossible ideal and intellectual endeavour as an exercise of power in defence of interests; its self-professed character as the pursuit of knowledge is nothing more than an amalgam of distortion and illusion which moral thinkers, such as Nietzsche, can at best work to dispel. In contrast to both these, traditionalists, those who self-consciously work within a historical tradition of inquiry, see the pursuit of understanding as requiring not merely knowledge of but membership of that tradition, and as consisting chiefly in the exploration of coherent self-understanding.

For the genealogist there is no truth as traditional epistemology understands it; for the encyclopaedist truth is external to the method of inquiry. On both conceptions it is possible to specify the end of intellectual endeavour independently of its methods, and possible therefore to ask irrespective of the content of those ends whether the methods are effective. But from within a given tradition, ends and means cannot be specified independently in this way, because those things we might identify as the means of achieving the ends at which the tradition aims are necessarily embedded in states of character which are themselves constitutive of the ends. This means that the central source of legitimation and justification in a tradition of inquiry is neither the end result – truth – nor principles of inquiry – Cartesian-type rules – but the authoritative practitioner, the one who has mastered the tradition.

All human practices can be thought of in this way, and thus the practice of rational inquiry also. In *Three Rival Versions* MacIntyre says this:

> The authority of a master is both more and other than a matter of exemplifying the best standards so far. It is also and most importantly a matter of knowing how to go further and especially how to direct others towards going further, using what can be learned from the tradition afforded by the past to move towards the *telos* of fully perfected work. It is thus in knowing how to link past and future that those with authority are able to draw upon tradition, to interpret and reinterpret it, so that its directedness towards the *telos* of that particular craft becomes apparent in new and characteristically unexpected ways. And it is by the ability to teach others how to learn this type of knowing how that the power of the master within the community of a craft is legitimated as rational authority.[12]

It is now possible to see how tradition fuses historical understanding and normative judgement.

[B]ecause at any particular moment the rationality of a craft is justified by its history so far, which has made it what it is in that specific time, place, and set of historical circumstances, such rationality is inseparable from the tradition through which it was achieved. To share in the rationality of a craft requires sharing in the contingencies of its hisory, understanding its story as one's own, and finding a place for oneself as a character in the enacted dramatic narrative which is that story so far.[13]

If we apply this line of thought to moral reasoning, we can readily see how different it looks once we begin to think in terms of tradition. Determining the right course of action will not now be a matter of applying abstract principles of practical rationality (Kant) or estimating likely consequences for happiness (Mill), or exposing the forces which, while masquerading as deliverances of truth and rationality, are really devices to suppress the exercise of individual will (Nietzsche). Rather practical reason will be a matter of relying on the judgements of those well versed in the moral traditions of specific times and places, and by emulation coming to be able to make judgements in our turn. We are accustomed to define the morally good agent as one who performs right actions; on this way of thinking the morally right act is to be defined as that which would be performed by the good agent.

The Aristotelian character of this line of thought is evident. Yet MacIntyre has expressly denied that his aim is to restore a 'morality of the virtues' in preference to a 'morality of rules'. The difference is to be found in the last sentence of the passage just quoted, for his account goes beyond Aristotelianism precisely in its appeal to history. The master of a tradition, including a tradition of rational moral inquiry must find a place 'as a character in the enacted dramatic narrative which is that story so far'. To do so, obviously, requires a knowledge of what that story is, in short a knowledge of history.

This is an addition of the greatest importance to MacIntyre's enterprise because conscious participation in a tradition could be wholly ahistorical. Mastercraftsmen must be inducted into the craft by a master, and have their judgements informed by experience reflected upon, but the form of this reflection need not be expressly historical. The origins of the craft, or of a specific project, the names and contribution of predecessors, and indeed the historical development of the craft itself could be quite unknown to a contemporary master. This, I assume, was the case with the engineers, architects and stonemasons who contributed to the building of the great Gothic cathedrals of Europe. They were masters of a craft engaged in a project with its special telos, one which they sought to bring to fulfilment and perfection, but without any formulable knowledge or understanding of the past.

MacIntyre would argue, I think, that such ahistorical understanding of a moral tradition or a tradition of inquiry is impossible, since these crucially employ concepts, and the use of concepts implies conscious reflection on a cultural reality and historical legacy, chiefly that of one's language.

> Every tradition is embodied in some particular set of utterances and actions and thereby in all the particularities of some specific language and culture. The invention, elaboration, and modification of the concepts through which both those who found and those who inherit a tradition understand it are inescapably concepts which have been framed in one language rather than another . . .
>
> The conception of language presupposed in saying this is that of a language as it is used in and by a particular community living at a particular time and place with particular shared beliefs, institutions and practices.[14]

It is this view of language that makes MacIntyre critical of the ahistorical semantics that has dominated philosophy in general, and philosophy of language in particular, over the last few decades. To understand language is to understand *a* language in a sociohistorical context. Each tradition of inquiry must employ such a language and hence this context is a condition of the tradition's existence. For this reason the understanding of that tradition, by practitioners themselves as much as by inquirers from other traditions, has to be reflectively historical. So MacIntyre's appeal to the idea of tradition in his account of moral reason and rational inquiry in general is not merely Aristotelian; it is Hegelian. The important point about it is that it requires masters of the tradition to know its story and to see for themselves a place in it and this is close to the way in which Hegel conceives understanding.

One of the things most people find objectionable in Hegel, of course, is the place that he seems to see for himself in the story of philosophy, namely that his endeavours are its fulfilment. Whether this is a just reading of Hegel I shall not now stop to inquire. More important for present purposes is the general question which MacIntyre's appeal to tradition raises; how are masters of a tradition to ascertain what the story of their tradition is and their place in it?

IV

Among the types of historical study that Hegel identifies in his introduction to the *Philosophy of History* is 'pragmatical' history, which is to say a study of history intended to produce lessons for present political and social conduct. A little further on, in the course of defending himself from the charge of apriorism, Hegel contends that some historians introduce '*a priori* fictions of their own into the records of the Past'.[15] One of the examples he gives is that of an original primeval people, and this example shows that it really is baseless fictions that he is concerned with. But it is easy enough to see that pragmatical history might also read a priori classifications into the records of the past. Consider, for instance, a notion like 'the German people'. Arguably, when Fichte issued his *Addresses to the German Nation*, there was no German nation in existence to be addressed. Indeed, along with many other nationalist writers, part of the point of his *Addresses* was to awaken consciousness of nationhood precisely because the disparate territories of what we now know as Germany had no sense of common identity. Of course, to speak of 'awakening consciousness' is to suppose that there is a reality waiting for the awakened consciousness to recognize, and hence this very way of speaking concedes what many would want to dispute; perhaps the proper description is not 'awakening' but 'creating'. Fichte himself thought that the ideal of education to which he was drawing attention was a regulative one, something that never was or would be, but only 'eternally ought to be'. But other writers have been less clear on this point and supposed that such entities as Mazzini's 'Rome', whose principal significance is pragmatic, can be simply discovered in the course of historical investigation.

But this is not so. Faced with the mass of material which historical study of any sophistication will supply, practical concerns are chiefly important, as Hegel saw, in providing one method of selection. This does not mean that pragmatical history can be quite cavalier with respect to the facts of the past; some pragmatic 'histories' are entirely fanciful and can be recognized to be such. But it does mean that the practical ideas which we bring to history are, so to speak, active in our understanding and not merely the passive products of a detached investigation into the past. As a consequence, there inevitably enters into pragmatic history an a priori element.

Consider the example of Christianity. If our concern is to chart the development of the Christian religion we can observe that Quakerism was among its products. We may also observe its reception on the part of other denominations, without considering whether that reception was right or wrong. But suppose, from the point of view of our own religious endeavours, we want to decide whether Quakerism is to be regarded as a development of orthodox Christianity or a deviation from it, we must bring to ecclesiastical history a conception of orthodoxy which, though it may be informed by history, cannot be determined by it. In short, we have to have a 'ready-made thought' about Christianity of the sort that Marx condemns in Hegel.

These remarks about pragmatic history are intended as a preliminary to raising a question about MacIntyre's appeal to the idea of tradition. It needs to be remembered here that if the appeal to tradition is to do work in moral philosophy, the tradition in question must be a living one, and not merely a historical curiosity. People sometimes speak of, for example, preparing food 'in the traditional manner' where what this means is 'as it used to be prepared at some time in the past'. There may of course be reasons for doing this (it makes for variety, or has advertising value, perhaps), but anyone who does so is not participating in a tradition as MacIntyre means it. This is not to say that a tradition cannot be revived, but to participate in a tradition is not merely 'to know its story' but 'to see a place for oneself in it'. It is thus an exercise in pragmatic history. But if this is so, how do we avoid the charge that we are not letting history speak for itself but bringing to it 'a ready-made thought'? The most plausible answer to this question, I shall argue, shows that the fusion of history and philosophy to which MacIntyre aspires must be abandoned. It will be easiest to see this by first considering an example.

Suppose that a Christian is concerned about right and wrong in sexual relations and wants to know what the correct attitude should be to premarital sex. It is commonly thought that on the traditional Christian view premarital sex is as much a case of fornication (that is, proscribed sex) as extramarital sex. As a matter of fact the New Testament says almost nothing on this question and if we investigate the history of Christian attitudes we will discover that the attitude to premarital sex has changed over the last few centuries. Before the middle of the eighteenth century, marriages solemnized in church were in the minority and marriages by habit and repute widely recognized. Moreover, betrothel, that is a relationship formed by the intention of two people to marry, was regarded as legitimizing sexual relations. Arguably, the social pre-eminence of solemnized marriage as the sole ground for legitimate sex came about as a result of the desire of kings and princes to secure lines of inheritance, rather than as a result of moral or theological reflection and teaching.[16] For the inquiring Christian this historical knowledge may make a difference, and premarital sex come to be viewed in a different way.

This looks like a good example of the sort of thing MacIntyre has in mind – the way in which a better knowledge of a tradition has a bearing on the judgements of right and wrong of its members. But even in this example, the historical knowledge does not of itself require a change of attitude or belief. There are a number of ways in which the historical facts adduced in it might be interpreted. It might be argued for instance that solemnized marriage, that is, express commitment in the presence of God, is the Christian ideal, the argument being based on the relation between certain concepts in Christian theology (the nature of God, of commitment and of blessing, for instance), and hence that both betrothal and common marriage fall short of that state at which the Christian should aim. This falling short may be tolerable, but the fact that at some time in the past it was widespread does not make it any less a falling short. To take this view, based on a theological understanding, is at one and the same time to take a view about the historical tradition, namely that the tradition is more fully perfected in strict Victorian attitudes to sex than in more liberal Elizabethan or Georgian ones. In its turn, this implies a revised view of our place in that tradition.

There are, then, at least two ways in which the historical facts about Christian attitudes can be understood by those who seek to follow the tradition; they can see Victorian attitudes as a deviation from the tradition which it is their duty to correct, or as a progressive advance on earlier attitudes, an advance that the contemporary world is in danger of losing. Which of these interpretations they ought to take will depend, not on the historical facts, which can always be made to be neutral between the two, but on the validity of the theological argument which purports to determine the ideal.

The details of this example are not important for my argument. What it shows is that even where we are clearly working within a moral tradition, historical knowledge may inform but will not determine the resolution of normative disputes. Even so, it would be wrong to describe this case as one in which historical understanding is distorted by a ready-made thought. The thought – about the Christian ideal of marriage – is not a ready-made one, but one based on an abstract consideration of theological concepts. The charge of distortion can be rejected, then, but only by acknowledging an alternative rational basis for normative conceptions of historical change, that is to say, a basis other than the appeal to the story of that tradition.

The point may be generalized as follows. In order to tell the story of a tradition and understand one's place in it, we must have conditions of identity for the continuation of that tradition, both in the past and for the future. But these conditions of identity, though they will be informed by historical knowledge, cannot be determined by them. For precisely how we tell the normative story – as one of progress, decline, purification or deviation – will depend on what we identify as the tradition's normatively necessary elements. If we are to avoid arbitrary stipulation on this point (which is what the 'ready-made thought' criticism comes to) and at the same time preserve the normative character, we have no alternative but ahistorical argument of the kind MacIntyre aims to escape.

I have argued that one of the most persistent and most interesting aspects of MacIntyre's philosophy is its attempt to put historical flesh on the dry bones of conceptual argument. In trying to fuse the historical and the philosophical, MacIntyre is appealing to a contemporary aspiration which his own writings have helped to make widespread. Central to his attempt is the idea of traditions of inquiry, through which past and participant are united. But I have argued that, whatever may be true of 'scientific history', normative stories of the past require us to have an independent conceptual grasp of the relevant, identifying norms. We require a philosophy in order to tell the story. If this is true, and if MacIntyre's project is to succeed, philosophy must take the lead in telling historical stories, and interestingly, to conclude in this way is to call for more, not less Hegelianism.

NOTES

1 Karl Marx, *Critique of Hegel's Philosophy of Right*, ed. Joseph O'Malley (Cambridge University Press, Cambridge, 1972), p. 14.

2 G. W. F. Hegel, *The Philosophy of Right*, trans. T. M. Knox (Oxford University Press, Oxford, 1952), p. 10.

3 G. W. F. Hegel, *The Philosophy of History*, trans. J. Sibree, (Dover, New York, 1956), p. 9.

4 Whatever we think about the charge of historicism I am not myself persuaded that this analysis of its cause is based on a proper understanding of Hegel and I am inclined to subscribe to T. M. Knox's gloss on Hegel's dictum about the rational and the actual. 'Hegel is not saying that what exists or is "real" is rational. By "actuality" he means the synthesis of essence and existence. If we say of a statesman who accomplishes nothing that he is not a "real" statesman, then we mean by "real" what Hegel calls "actual". The statesman exists as a man in office, but he lacks the essence constitutive of what statesmanship ought to be, say effectiveness. Conversely, and in Hegel's view no less important, if effectiveness were never the quality of an existing statesman, then it would not be the rational essence of statesmanship, but a mere ideal or dream. Hegel's philosophy as a whole might be regarded as an attempt to justify his identification of rationality with actuality and vice versa, but his doctrine depends ultimately on his faith in God's Providence, his conviction that history is the working out of His rational purpose.' Translator's Notes to Hegel, *Philosophy of Right*, p. 302.

5 Among more recent advocates are Richard Rorty in *Philosophy and the Mirror of Nature* (Blackwell, Oxford, 1980), and Stephen Toulmin, *Cosmopolis: The Hidden Agenda of Modernity* (Free Press, New York, 1990).

6 *After Virtue* (Duckworth, London, 1981), p. viii.

7 *Whose Justice? Which Rationality?* (Duckworth, London, 1988).

8 *A Short History of Ethics* (Routledge and Kegan Paul, London, 1967), p. 2.

9 Are conservative Southern Baptists who find themselves quite at home in a high-technology culture, part of 'modern society'?

10 *After Virtue*, p. 7.

11 *Three Rival Versions of Moral Enquiry* (Duckworth, London, 1990).

12 Ibid., pp. 65–6.

13 Ibid., p. 65.

14 *Whose Justice? Which Rationality?*, pp. 371–3.
15 *The Philosophy of History*, p. 10.
16 On this subject see Christopher Brooke, *The Mediaeval Idea of Marriage* (Oxford University Press, Oxford, 1989).

Liberal/Communitarian: MacIntyre's Mesmeric Dichotomy

Philip Pettit

One of the most striking contributions of Alasdair MacIntyre's later work is his emphasis on the role of the Enlightenment in the evolution of our political and ethical ideas. That emphasis was badly needed in a context of discussion where participants were often insensitive to the historical provenance of their intuitions and modes of argument. But the emphasis has also done damage. It has foisted upon us a perspective from which it is easy to register only a limited range of ideas: those associated respectively with the Enlightenment, the counter-Enlightenment and the post-Enlightenment. It has shaped our intellectual imaginations, as a new departure can too easily do, so that we now see only the alternatives that it makes salient. So, at any rate, I shall argue.

I shall argue this, in particular, with reference to the main dichotomy that emerges in MacIntyre's thinking about politics. This is the dichotomy between liberal thought, represented as continuous with the Engligh-tenment project, and communitarian thought, represented as Aristotelian in inspiration but associated characteristically with the counter-Enlightenment, Romantic tradition.[1] I ignore the post-Enlightenment way of thinking inspired by Nietzsche, as this is of limited relevance to politics. I believe that the dichotomy between liberal and communtarian politics which shines out in MacIntyre's work is misleading, because it blinds us to further, interesting possibilities. Specifically, I believe that it has the effect of eclipsing the possibility of a preliberal, republican politics – a politics of great importance prior to the Enlightenment – and that this sort of politics is worthy of serious reconsideration.

The paper is in three sections. In the first I describe how the liberal and communitarian pictures are drawn by MacIntyre and I indicate their connections, respectively, with the Enlightenment and counter-Enlightenment traditions. I suggest that if the liberal–communitarian dichotomy is found compelling, that may be because of the rhetoric of Enlightenment–Romantic oppositions which dominates our thinking. In the second section I describe the republican tradition of political thought which is invisible within MacIntyre's perspective, and perhaps within any perspective that is dominated by the dialectic of Enlightenment and counter-Enlightenment. I maintain that this older, historical tradition offers a distinct alternative to the liberal and communitarian options. And, finally, in the third section I offer some reasons for holding that this republican mode of thought is a resource which we should explore further. My belief is that republicanism can be developed to provide a genuinely attractive political perspective.

Before proceeding further, I must make one important disavowal. I am a philosopher and theorist, not a historian of ideas, and I do not intend this essay as an original piece of historical research; my main aim is to open up the possibility of the republican way of thinking I describe, not to establish its historical roots. I occasionally deal in general, ideal-typical characterization of the past, as in discussing the Enlightenment and counter-Enlightenment, but I hope that the lines I take will be more or less uncontroversial, at least among readers of MacIntyre. At other times I associate myself with more striking historical claims, as in the identification of the long tradition of republican politics, but here I generally rely on the authority of well-established historians; in particular I rely on the work of John Pocock and Quentin Skinner.[2] Skinner explicitly accuses MacIntyre and other communitarians of neglecting the republican tradition of politics and, if you like, my essay can be seen as an attempt to provide a construal of liberalism, communitarianism and republicanism which supports that accusation.[3]

Liberalism and Communitarianism

The Enlightenment, as we have learned to think about it from MacIntyre and others, is characterized by the aspiration to go beyond tradition and, relying on the universally valid dictates of reason and method, to lay bare the nature of things: the nature of the world in general but, in particular, the nature of human beings and human society. Enlightenment thinkers had scant regard for established, more or less religious traditions of thought and they looked for a rational, neutral foundation on which to build a future consensus. They hoped that this consensus would extend to evaluative matters and they espoused the project of rationally deriving ethical and political principles which would be found compelling by all. As MacIntyre puts it in writing about the period, 'the project of an independent rational justification of morality becomes not merely the concern of individual thinkers, but central to Northern European culture.'[4]

This project of justification was pursued by thinkers as various as Hume and Kant and Bentham. It failed, in the sense that no scheme of justification became accepted as a compelling framework for ethical and political thought. It failed and, according to MacIntyre, it had to fail. He argues, controversially, that the project would have had to assume a teleological conception of human nature – a conception of human beings as they would be if they fully realized their essence – and that the scientific world-view that informed the Enlightenment denied its protagonists any such teleological vision; teleology had been lost with the demise of Aristotelianism which was occasioned by modern science.[5]

Whether or not it had to fail, the failure of the Enlightenment project of justification had distinctive results for our modes of ethical and political argument. According to MacIntyre it meant that, whatever traditional meanings haunt our evaluative and normative language, those of us who live in the wake of the Enlightenment came to use that language just to express our feelings, with little or no expectation of being able to resolve any important differences between us. He puts this point in *After Virtue* when he says that we all now conform to emotivism; we take our value judgements to express preferences, not to record any facts that we might expect others equally to acknowledge.

But though the Enlightenment project of justification failed, the Enlightenment ideal of providing a neutral foundation for political principles is alive and well. The aspiration to neutrality, the aspiration to provide a basis for political agreement between the adherents of different traditions and different conceptions of the good life, is maintained in the liberal way of thinking about politics. Sustained by liberal thought, the aspiration is influential in actual social and political affairs; it constitutes nothing less than 'the project of modern liberal, individualist society'.[6] Neutrality is to be secured in this way of thinking, not by establishing a common ethical foundation, a common, rationally compelling account of what is good for human beings, but by devising a way of organizing political life which is not committed to any particular conception of the good. 'No overall theory of the human good is to be regarded as justified.'[7]

How is politics to be conducted in this liberal vision: this vision to which the Enlightenment has more or less inexorably driven us? MacIntyre has a distinctive account, which many liberals may wish to contest; it fits with economistic versions of liberalism but not with other variants. In the world of liberal politics, according to MacIntyre, people do not reason about what they should do from the desirability of this or that situation, let alone try to debate with one another in terms of such considerations; perhaps to do this would be to import, too explicitly, a particular conception of the good. Rather they support their practical deliberations and their political persuasions by open and honest avowals of what they each want: of what they each brutely and indefensibly desire. 'I want it to be the case that such and such' is the only allowable major premise in 'this characteristically modern form of practical reasoning'.[8]

The nature of this reasoning reveals the deeply anti-communitarian character of the liberal vision, as that vision is understood by MacIntyre. Political agents are depicted as individuals for whom it is incidental that they belong to this or that country, culture or class. Membership in such communities is incidental in the sense that it does not serve as a determinant of any of the considerations that weigh with agents. The fact that a person belongs to this or that community will not ensure, for example, that considerations to do with its welfare will count with her. More generally, the fact that a person belongs to a particular community does not mean that the considerations which are normative there will engage her. The only reasons that weigh with agents, at least in the political context, are affiliation-free considerations to do with what they individually happen to desire. 'In Aristotelian practical reasoning it is the individual *qua* citizen who reasons; in Thomistic practical reasoning it is the individual *qua* enquirer into his or her good and the good of his or her community; in Humean practical reasoning it is the individual *qua* propertied or unpropertied participant in a society of a particular kind of mutuality and reciprocity; but in the practical reasoning of liberal modernity it is the individual *qua* individual who reasons.'[9]

If political agents each reason and argue from their own desires, of course, then there is no room for debate between individuals as to what it is best to do in cases where their interests conflict. So what happens in the liberal order?

What will often happen – presumably in political contexts – is that people bargain with one another as distinct from conducting a debate: they each state their ideal outcome and they make the minimal concessions necessary in order to get one another's cooperation.[10] But presumably bargaining cannot be hailed as a general panacea, since it is sensitive to differences in people's bargaining power and is going to leave many unsatisfied. And so MacIntyre says that the liberal order is forced to look for general principles of conflict resolution: general principles of justice, which do not themselves presuppose any particular conception of the good. It is a matter of consensus among liberal theorists, he says, that we need principles of this kind for the tallying and weighing of people's different preferences, so that each individual can acquiesce in the way conflicts are resolved. But no common, compelling principles are to be found, according to MacIntyre, for there is no way of establishing them without reference to an agreed conception of the good.

And so, in practice, liberal politics comes down to the rule of a legal system which is driven now by this set of principles, now by that. 'The lawyers, not the philosophers, are the clergy of liberalism.'[11]

Does liberalism succeed in realizing the Enlightenment ambition of providing politics with a neutral foundation? No, says MacIntyre. Far from being neutral, there are many conceptions of the good under which the institutions and forms of activity prescribed by liberalism will be anathema: 'its toleration of rival conceptions of the good in the public arena is severely limited.'[12] We have to say that liberalism is a tradition in its own right and that it represents its own non-neutral conception of the good: it represents a conception of social life which finds value in characteristically liberal institutions. 'The overriding good of liberalism is no more and no less than the continued sustenance of the liberal social and political order.'[13]

Not only does liberalism fail in its original, neutralist ambition. It also fails as one tradition amongst others, for the conception of the good that it purveys is not likely to be found compelling by the adherents of other traditions. As we shall see later, liberalism fails to encourage a regime of social practices in which people are challenged to develop appropriate virtues and are given the chance to flourish; it generates a culture in which virtue is replaced by technical expertise.[14] More generally, 'liberalism can provide no compelling arguments in favour of its conception of the human good.'[15] One tradition will generate compelling arguments and win out over another, according to MacIntyre, so far as it can do better at resolving problems that arise within the other. Liberalism holds out no great promise in this regard. On the contrary, it generates serious problems of its own: the self is required, perhaps impossibly, to order and know its own wants; and the good of the overall liberal order is required, unrealistically, to command a stronger allegiance than the sectarian and conflict-generating goods to which different groups are attached.[16]

I hope that these remarks will serve to remind readers of the liberal vision of politics that is conjured up in MacIntyre's work. Many will not endorse this representation of liberalism; many will associate liberalism, for example, with something closer to the republican image I will be presenting in the next section. But I propose, for present purposes, to use 'liberalism' to identify roughly the sort of doctrine on which MacIntyre focuses. Like him, I take liberalism to be essentially an Enlightenment tradition, focused on the prospect of a neutral state and distinctively atomistic in its assumptions, even if I do not believe that it has to be so economistic as his account of practical reasoning suggests. What unites the tradition, as I will urge later, and what distinguishes it from republicanism, is the particular ideal of negative liberty which it is committed to endorsing.

MacIntyre's communitarian alternative is the negative image of the liberal picture. The main feature of this alternative, unsurprisingly, is that political agents are represented as deeply social. In MacIntyre's ideal blueprint, as in Aristotle's, 'it is the individual *qua* citizen who reasons.'[17] The individual takes as given her membership of this or that community or communities. In particular, she takes as given the concepts whereby people make sense of what they do, and identify what they should do, within the practices in which she participates: these are the concepts associated with the conceptions of the good projected in those practices. There is no question of the individual reasoning from premises that are valid just for her – premises to do with the state of her desires, for example; the individual always reasons from premises that must appeal to anyone who participates in the same practices.

The linkage between the individual and the community in this picture is not of the sort that calls to be made voluntaristically intelligible by reference to a currency of non-social reasons: say, by reference to the satisfaction of the individual's desires. There are no reasons more basic than the social reasons whereby people make sense of themselves and one another in communal exchange. If those reasons presuppose that the individual belongs to the community, and leave the bond between individual and community itself incapable of being rationalized, then so be it; that is merely to say that the individual belongs to her community in the same intimate and constitutive way that she belongs to this or that physical body.

Where the liberal image of political agents is distinctive of Enlightenment thinking, with its penchant for breaking wholes down into parts, and its image of individuals as the parts whereby society is constituted, the communitarian image is characteristic of the heterodoxy of Enlightenment: the Romantic tradition fuelled by Vico and Rousseau, which developed in Germany with figures like Herder and Schiller and which reached its most systematic expression in the work of Hegel.[18] The crucial contribution of this counter-Enlightenment movement was to provide reasons for thinking of individuals as dependent on their social relations with one another for the appearance of the very capacities that mark them off as human.[19]

Assume that the ability to think is the most distinctive of human capacities; this idea would have come naturally to people in the wake of Descartes's representation of the self as a *res cogitans*. In Enlightenment circles, thought was taken as a capacity of the individual that she exercises without being in the logical debt of others; she may causally require others for training and stimulation but this is only a contingent form of dependence. Thus, in the Enlightenment tradition, individuals were presented as logically self-sufficient thinkers whose association in this or that community is a contingent affair.[20]

In the Romantic critique of the Enlightenment, one of the main principles was that while thought is certainly a capacity of the individual, it depends constitutively on participation in a public language and in other means of expression.[21] Without language, no thought; without society, no language. This break with the orthodox view meant that individuals were presented in the counter-Enlightenment tradition as creatures whose most characteristic ability logically requires mutual involvement and communal belonging. Society no longer appeared like a contingent association of freestanding individuals, like an amalgam of separable parts. It manifested itself as a whole from which parts could be detached only at the cost of losing their species characteristics. It began to look, in the imagery of the day, like something organic rather than mechanical.

So much for MacIntyre's communitarian characterization of political agents and its counter-Enlightenment connections. Given such a characterization of agents, the question arises as to what forms of social relationship and activity, in particular what political arrangements, are best. MacIntyre takes this question in an Aristotelian way as a question as to what arrangements are best fitted for the flourishing of human beings: for the highest realization of human capacities. 'If a premodern view of morals and politics is to be vindicated against modernity, it will be in *something like* Aristotelian terms or not at all.'[22] MacIntyre argues, at an extremely abstract level, that what we should look for in the ideal society is the presence and preponderance of that kind of social activity which he describes as a practice.

A practice is any socially established human activity such that to participate in it is to recognize certain things as goods and to internalize standards of excellence in achieving those things.[23] Chess is a practice because one cannot play the game without recognizing the goods of strategy and success which are internal to the game and without admitting the standards appropriate for attaining those ends: standards which rule out cheating, for example. The goods attained in a practice are only intelligible and available via that practice: they are internal to it in the way in which the pleasure of checkmating is internal to chess but the pleasure of spending the prize money is not. And the standards of excellence associated with a practice are non-discretionary for someone who wishes to take part. In the context of the practice it is almost silly to think of flouting them, as it would be silly to want to play chess without always abiding by the rules.

MacIntyre believes that practices in this sense abound in social life. 'The range of practices is wide: arts, sciences, games, politics in the Aristotelian sense, the making and sustaining of family life, all fall under the concept.'[24] He contrasts practices with technical skills and with institutions. Such capacities and such organizations are designed for the achievement of certain goods, as practices are, but the goods which they are meant to achieve are external to them. A skill facilitates the achievement of a good, as keen sight facilitates reading, but is not necessary to understand it. An organization furthers a certain aim, as a central bank furthers financial stability, but the aim is intelligible to someone who knows nothing of the organization.[25]

Why does MacIntyre think that practices are so important? He suggests in one place that they are necessary for any society that is to escape the fate of Hobbes's state of nature: any society that is to avoid the rule – better perhaps, the anarchy – of complete and continual competition.[26] His more general theme, however, is that virtues in an Aristotelian sense are necessary for human flourishing and that practices are necessary for virtues. This theme becomes a matter of definition, as virtue is associated with the realization of goods internal to practices. 'A virtue is an acquired human quality the possession and exercise of which tends to enable us to achieve those goods which are internal to practices and the lack of which effectively prevents us from achieving any such good.'[27]

The preference for practices suggests an argument that bears directly on the sort of society, and in particular the sort of state, which we should want. If it is impossible to achieve a neutral politics, as MacIntyre believes he has shown in his critique of liberalism, then he thinks that the only attractive alternative is to look for a state which does best by human beings in something like the Aristotelian sense. And that means that we should look for a state which facilitates those practices, whatever they are, by means of which virtue and human fulfilment are best promoted.

MacIntyre does not say much on which practices are likely to achieve this result but two things are worth noting. One is that he thinks there is no picking and choosing among ideal alternatives, as we must all begin from the particular practices and traditions into which we are born. 'Without those moral particularities to begin from there would never be anywhere to begin.'[28] And the other is that, for all that he actually says, he may be utterly pessimistic about the possibilities available to us in the modern world; he may think that the particularities available in this world offer no hope for the future. He often sounds such a resigned, nostalgic note. 'Modern systematic politics, whether liberal, conservative, radical or socialist, simply has to be rejected from a standpoint that

owes genuine allegiance to the tradition of the virtues: for modern politics itself expresses in its institutional forms a systematic rejection of
that tradition.'[29]

Although we have not done much by way of specifying the Aristotelian sort of society and politics which MacIntyre embraces as an alternative to liberalism, and although he does not do much himself to this
end, one theme at least should be clear. This is that as he rejoins the
counter-Enlightenment tradition in stressing the social nature of political agents, so too he rejoins that tradition in developing his image of the
good society and the good polity. Two features underline the connection with the Romantic tradition. One is his assumption that politics
cannot stay detached from the historical practices of the local society; it
must start from such practices and try to identify those that best serve
the purpose of politics. The second is an assumption about that purpose:
that the point of politics is to facilitate the self-development and self-
realization of citizens – to facilitate their virtue and flourishing – if not
actually to provide the forum in which they achieve self-expression.

The first feature reflects the Romantic preference for wholeness, in
particular for the wholeness manifested when the politics of a society are
a natural outgrowth of the other areas of social life. Liberal theorists
would put aside the different social practices, and the different conceptions of the good, which characterize a society, and seek to define a
distinct, neutral goal for the state to pursue. Romantic thinkers insisted,
as MacIntyre does, that the state must make contact with at least some
of the social practices and traditions that govern a society; it cannot find
a distinct province of its own. 'They could not abide the idea', Charles
Larmore writes, 'that what is relevant in one domain need not be so in
another. They longed for an all-pervading spirit of community that (they
imagined) religion had once provided and that a distinction-drawing
Enlightenment had dismissed.'[30]

The second feature of MacIntyre's vision connects with the Romantic
emphasis on the importance of individual self-expression and self-
realization, in particular on the sort of expression and realization that is
allegedly possible through active involvement in various forms of social
life. This emphasis connected with the general theme, stressed for example by Herder, that expression of the self is inevitably what human life
is about. 'Herder seeks to demonstrate', according to Isaiah Berlin, 'that
all that a man does and says and creates must express, whether he intends
it to do so or not, his whole personality; and, since a man is not conceiv-
able outside a group ... conveys also the "collective individuality".'[31]

MacIntyre's affiliation with this Romantic idea becomes especially
striking in his critique of the instrumentalism to which liberalism, in his
view, reduces politics. The communitarian politics for which he looks

would facilitate forms of human behaviour that involve the non-instrumental realization of certain goods: the realization of goods that are internal to the behaviour in the way in which the good of checkmating is internal to chess, or indeed the good of resting internal to lying down. It would encourage virtuous fidelity to practices, and the good life that this fidelity produces, where 'the exercise of the virtues is a necessary and central part of such a life, not a mere preparatory exercise to secure such a life'.[32]

But the liberal version of politics, MacIntyre complains, would sever human behaviour from whatever good it is supposed to realize. Liberal politics consists in bargaining with others on matters of common interest or debating about the principles that ought to govern conflict resolution and these pursuits are causally and extrinsically related to the good they are designed to achieve; they have not, or at least need not have, any value in themselves. 'Politics, as Aristotle conceives it, is a practice with goods internal to itself. Politics, as James Mill conceives it, is not.'[33]

And not only is politics instrumentally demeaned in this way within liberalism; it is also marginalized, as non-political forms of expertise are preferred to political. In the liberal vision, the main role goes, not to the politician, but to 'that central character of the modern social drama, the bureaucratic manager'.[34] This manager is not expected to display virtue in the Aristotelian sense but rather technical skill in the devising of whatever means are thought most effective for the furtherance of the goals assigned to him. Not only does he rob others of the goals that they might have pursued and virtuously made their own; he does not even enjoy the challenge of virtue himself. His profession is conceived without reference to any common practice of achievement: any common conception of the good or any common standards of excellence.

But MacIntyre's dirge over the modern, liberal world goes further still. Not only is political activity instrumentally degraded and bureaucratically marginalized. 'Moreover the kind of work done by the vast majority of the inhabitants of the modern world cannot be understood in terms of the nature of a practice with goods internal to itself.' Why so? Because such work has been moved outside the household, and disconnected from the activity of sustaining the family and community. It has been moved to the production line where 'the means–end relationships ... are necessarily external to the goods which those who work seek'.[35]

I have been stressing the Romantic, counter-Enlightenment provenance of MacIntyre's communitarian vision. Not only does his social characterization of political agents pick up on a Romantic theme, his suggestions about the shape of the best social and political arrangements, undeveloped though they are, fit naturally with the Romantic idea that politics should facilitate socially mediated self-expression and self-realization. But if his ideas are so much of the counter-Enlightenment, why the constant reference to Aristotle? MacIntyre is clearly a committed and informed Aristotelian but even in this aspect of his thought, he remains faithful to the Romantic role in which I have cast him. One of the most distinctive features of the counter-Enlightenment was the tendency to look back nostalgically to the lost world of the Greek polis and its theorists. Charles Taylor makes the point. 'Many Germans in this period – among them Hegel – saw in the ancient polis a summit of human achievement yet unequalled. They saw in it a society whose public life was the locus of all that was of greatest importance to its citizens.'[36]

The upshot of this line of consideration should be clear. MacIntyre presents us with a sharply drawn dichotomy in his characterization, respectively, of the liberal and communitarian alternatives. But we should be suspicious, for the dichotomy is all too resonant of the tired dialectic of Enlightenment and counter-Enlightenment. That dialectic expresses itself in a series of oppositions that appear and reappear, mesmerically, in contemporary political thought: atomistic–holistic, individualistic–collectivistic, mechanical–organic, natural–cultural, analytic–synthetic, instrumental–expressive, man–citizen, private–public, egocentric–virtuous, and so on through familiar changes on the theme. If the same dialectic is at work in generating the liberal–communitarian dichotomy, then we can understand why it should seem so unavoidable and compelling. But if it seems unavoidable and compelling for this sort of reason – because it reflects a rhetoric that dominates our political thinking – that is all the more reason to look at the dichotomy again and see whether it is really exhaustive of relevant options. I turn to this task in the next section.

The Republican Alternative

The full historical range of the republican or civic humanist tradition has come to be appreciated only recently. John Pocock has argued that, originating in Roman times, the tradition offered a currency of political analysis and critique which dominated Western political thought from the time of the Renaissance down to that of the American and French revolutions.[37] The tradition is linked with names like Cicero, Machiavelli, Harrington, Montesquieu, and even de Tocqueville, though it often received its most trenchant applications in less celebrated authors, as in the eighteenth-century volume published as *Cato's Letters*.[38]

What are the themes that characterize republicanism? Three apparently distinct themes stand out. The most salient nowadays is the anti-monarchical motif: the idea that a republic is a state without hereditary rulers, in particular a state without royalty. But this idea is perhaps nothing more than an expression of the deeper idea that republics are meant to be governed by laws, as it used to be put, and not by men: that they require the rule of law, in which there is no room for the caprice of the autocrat. It would have been natural for republicans at many periods, and in particular for republicans in eighteenth-century France, to think that monarchy must go, since they would have seen monarchy as inconsistent with the rule of law.

The notion of the rule of law goes back explicitly to Roman sources, though many legal commentators speak as if it were a byproduct of English common law. A second theme that is associated with republicanism also has explicit Roman antecedents. This is the idea that the republic not only requires a rule of law, it also requires a rule of check and balance. Where there is a rule of law, there is no one who stands above the law. Where there is a rule of check and balance, the authorities who hold power under the law are institutionally constrained so that they cannot easily abuse their position. They hold office for short periods, they are subject to public scrutiny and accountability – in particular accountability in public, democratic debate – they are forced to share power with parties who may be of a different mind, and they are liable to impeachment for any failures of duty.

The third and last theme that stands out in the weave of republican ideas is that not only does the republic require a rule of law, and a rule of check and balance, it also needs the rule of virtue. The eighteenth-century French aristocrat, the Baron de Montesquieu, summed it up nicely: in despotisms, fear is the spur; in monarchies, honour; in republics, virtue. Republics need citizens who can be relied on to take a part in public life, to stand for public office, and to do their very best in execution of any official duties that are allotted to them. They need people who are free from the lethargy that disables the masses, and the ambition that diverts the few. They need people who can stand against the tide of corruption which is always ready to wash over the affairs of state.

It will be more or less widely agreed that the long republican tradition described by Pocock is a reality and that participants in that tradition do display a distinctive concern with the ideas just mentioned. They speak a political language, as Pocock likes to put it, in which the great desiderata are civic order and civic virtue and the great dangers corruption and invasion. That language is quite different, for example, from the language of state legitimacy and individual obligation that emerged about

the seventeenth century with the social contract way of thinking and
that had such an influence on later liberal ideas.[39] Equally, it is very
different from the nineteenth-century liberal language in which the great
desideratum is the laissez-faire ideal of non-interference, often an ideal
sanctified in the notion of natural, individual rights, and the great danger
the threat of an overweening state.

But not only is republicanism widely recognized, and widely associated with the themes I have mentioned. There is also a general consensus
that the unifying and motivating idea behind the tradition is a certain
ideal of liberty. The reason why laws, and checks and balances, and civic
virtue are needed is that they represent the means whereby republican
liberty is achieved. But what then is republican liberty? What, in the
other languages of republicanism, is *libertas, liberta, liberté*? And what
exactly are the connections between this ideal of freedom and the three
themes identified?

The striking thing about the Enlightenment and the counter-
Enlightenment is that they conspired to project an answer to this question,
which continues to affect our reading of the republican tradition. In
effect, they project an answer which makes the republican tradition
more or less invisible as a genuinely alternative source of political ideas.
This claim is a variant formulation of something argued with historical
authority by Quentin Skinner but I think that we can make it plausible
without recourse to detail.[40] The claim is relevant to my concerns here,
since MacIntyre exemplifies the blindness to republicanism that the
Enlightenment perspective generates.

In discussing the opposition between liberalism and communitarianism,
I tried to avoid talk of liberty. But it will be clear that the doctrines can
be represented, and of course have been represented, as alternative
explications of the ideal of liberty. The ideal of liberty advanced in the
liberal tradition casts liberty in a negative light, as Isaiah Berlin has
argued. [41] It represents liberty as the condition enjoyed when others do
not interfere with someone in the pursuit of those activities that lie
within the normal person's power: others may accidentally get in her
way but they do not intentionally or negligently do anything to obstruct or frustrate or coerce the choice of the agent.[42] Liberalism is the
doctrine according to which the state should assume such a form that
negative liberty is maximally advanced within a society.[43] Liberalism in
that sense may put an intrinsic value on negative liberty or it may value
it for associated benefits: for the happiness its realization produces, for
example, as in the utililitarian view. Again liberalism in that sense may
take a libertarian/classical liberal form, acknowledging no political value
besides negative liberty, or it may see liberty as one desideratum among

many, as in more left-of-centre versions of the doctrine. I abstract from such matters here.

The ideal of liberty advanced in the communitarian or Romantic tradition casts liberty in a positive light, to continue to use Berlin's metaphor. It sees liberty as a positive achievement that requires more than the non-interference of others: more than the absence of external obstacles. It is taken to require elements like the absence of internal obstacles – strength of will and the like – the presence of external powers, in particular the power of sharing in the governance of one's community, and even the realization of a certain moral ideal.[44] Charles Taylor gives this account of the development: 'the standard Enlightenment view of freedom was that of independence of the self-defining subject in relation to outside control, principally that of state and religious authority. Now freedom is seen as consisting in authentic self-expression. It is threatened not only by external invasion but by all the distortions that expression is menaced by ... Not every author will make freedom his privileged description of the goal, but it is always one available description.'[45]

The opposition between negative and positive liberty is yet one more example, then, of the contrasts put in play by the dialectic of Enlightenment and counter-Enlightenment. With that opposition in place, how are we to understand the republican ideal of freedom?

Unsurprisingly, those who take an Enlightenment perspective have always been forced to see the republican notion of freedom as an adumbration of the counter-Enlightenment ideal. The Romantics themselves, with their attachment to the classical world and to classical ideas, claimed the republican notion of freedom as their own. How could liberty link up with ideas like that of the rule of law, the rule of check and balance – in particular, the checks and balances of democracy – and the rule of virtue? On the Romantic conception of liberty there is no problem.[46] Such instruments are the means whereby people achieve the positive sort of emancipation to which the Romantics looked: the sort of emancipation in which the full personality flowers and attains its essence.

The Romantic appropriation of the republican ideal was given an important boost on the other side, as Enlightenment figures endorsed the Romantic reading of ancient liberty and proclaimed their own negative notion as the distinctively modern ideal of liberty. Here the most important contribution was the famous 1819 lecture by Benjamin Constant, 'De la liberté des anciens comparée à celle des modernes'.[47] Constant argues in this essay that whereas modern liberty has to do with the subject's being able to determine matters pertaining to her own life, ancient liberty had to do with the subject's being part of a self-determining

community: a democratic community in which each has a part in making decisions for all. Constant himself thought there was a place for
ancient as well as modern liberty.[48] But his essay had the effect of making adherents of liberal, Enlightenment politics recoil from earlier ideas
of freedom as they did from the ideas presented by their Romantic
antagonists. At least in the English tradition, they stood firmly by the
Hobbesian notion that freedom is the absence of interference and they
saw it as the only commonsense alternative to the high-flown and dangerous rhetoric of positive liberty.

I said that the Enlightenment perspective on republicanism, in particular the republican ideal of liberty, is still influential. One victim of
that perspective, I suggest, may be MacIntyre himself: unsurprisingly,
in view of the use to which he puts the perspective in generating his
own political alternatives. Concentrating as he does on purer Aristotelian
ideas of ethics and politics, he has little to say on the republican tradition, albeit that tradition was heavily influenced by certain Aristotelian
motifs. But what he does say suggests, quite clearly, that he sees the
tradition in the standard Romantic fashion. He takes republicanism as a
variation on the classical tradition which associates virtue with a concern
for the public good. And he casts the republican notion of freedom in
a characteristically positive light. '*Cui servire est regnare*, says the prayer
about God, or as the English version has it, "whom to serve is perfect
freedom," and what the Christian said about God the republican says of
the republic.'[49]

But enough of the Enlightenment misrepresentation of republican
liberty. What does such liberty, as I envisage it, involve? And how does
it serve to unify the republican themes mentioned above? I go on now
to sketch a hypothesis, leaving it to others to make a final historical
judgement on its plausibility. The historian whose work serves best to
bear out the hypothesis is Quentin Skinner. John Pocock, the other
great commentator on republicanism, continues to talk of republican liberty as a positive concept, although nothing in his work really requires
that reading.

The first thing to say about the republican notion of liberty is that,
like the liberal one, it focuses primarily on matters to do with interference and non-interference. That negative note is there already in the
originating, Roman conception. Hanna Pitkin sums up the refrain of
other writers. 'The Roman plebs struggled not for democracy but for
protection, not for public power but for private security. Of course they
sought public, institutionalised guarantees of that security. But *libertas*
... was "passive", "defensive", "predominantly negative".'[50] Skinner's
work on Machiavelli bears out the same theme. For Machiavelli, he
argues,

most men 'simply want not to be ruled'; they want to be able 'to live as free men' (*vivere liberi*), pursuing their own ends as far as possible without insecurity or unnecessary interference. They want, in particular, to be free (*liber*) to marry as they choose; to bring up their families without having to fear for their honour or their own welfare; and to be in a position 'freely (*liberamente*) to possess their own property'. This is what it means 'to enjoy personal liberty' (*la liberta*).[51]

We see the same emphasis, finally, in a late republican text like *Cato's Letters*.

> True and impartial Liberty is therefore the Right of every Man to pursue the natural, reasonable, and religious Dictates of his own Mind; to think what he will, and act as he thinks, provided he acts not to the Prejudice of another; to spend his own Money himself, and lay out the Produce of his Labour his own Way; and to labour for his own Pleasure and Profit.[52]

But if the republican ideal of liberty is negative in its focus on non-interference, what is the difference between this ideal and the liberal one? This is how my hypothesis goes.[53] On any negative conception of liberty individuals are free to the extent that they are free from the interference of others. But what is it to be free from interference? The liberal tradition says that it is simply to lack interference, to enjoy its absence. The republican tradition says that the absence of interference is not enough; what is also necessary is that the agent be protected against interference, that she be given guarantees which help to ensure against interference.

Of course the liberal, like the republican, will want to have laws and institutions that protect the liberty of people. But he will only want them to the extent that they maximize the expectation of non-interference overall. He will regard such laws and institutions as themselves invasions of liberty and he will only tolerate them so far as they reduce the aggregate expectation of invasion; they promise to cause less harm in the way of interference than they prevent. The republican's attitude will be quite different. He values secure non-interference as such and may put no value on the insecure enjoyment of non-interference. He sees the law and associated institutions as the instruments whereby secure non-interference is produced and he will look for just such measures as do best in promoting secure non-interference. He will deplore the resort to such measures beyond the point where they promote that good: say, at the point where they begin to be so oppressive that people's security is threatened. But up to that point he will not view the laws and institutions as themselves invasions of liberty, justified by the greater harm they prevent. He will view them, without ambivalence, as the very stuff of which republican liberty is made.

Perhaps the best way to mark the contrast between the liberal and republican conceptions of negative liberty is to look at their different antonyms. The liberal conception is a conception of liberty under which the antonym is any form of restraint or interference. If unfreedom consists in being restrained, then freedom involves not being restrained: it involves non-interference, pure and simple. The republican conception of liberty, on the other hand, is a conception under which the antonym is slavery or subjection or, more generally, any condition in which a person is vulnerable to the will of another. If unfreedom consists in being vulnerable in this way, then freedom involves not being vulnerable: it involves secure non-interference. In order to enjoy such freedom it is necessary not to be anyone's slave or subject and, more than that, it is necessary, as the Romans realized, to be the very opposite of a slave: to be a *liber* who is equally protected with the best, not just a *servus sine domino*, a slave without a master.[54]

It is understandable why, in the republican tradition, the antonym of liberty should have been slavery or subjection or vulnerability. There is a great deal of evidence now that the notion of liberty evolved in the classical and medieval worlds as a concept by means of which to mark off non-slaves and non-serfs.[55] The particular aim of republican theorists was to identify the characteristics of a society in virtue of which its citizens – its citizens as distinct from residents who do not enjoy citizenship – are distinguished from those who are the victims of despotic rule, corrupt officialdom, external control, and the like. They used the concept of liberty to serve this purpose of demarcation and so it is no surprise that they should have conceived of liberty as the opposite of slavery, in particular as the social status antithetical to slavery or subjection.

Skinner notes that according to Machiavelli the benefit of *liberta* is 'what enables people to recognise and rejoice in the fact "that they have been born as free men (*liberi*) and not as slaves" '.[56] And Jeffrey Isaac comments that in Harrington's work 'there operates a distinction between industry/liberty/commonwealth and luxury/servitude/monarchy'.[57] The contrast is clearly still in place in *Cato's Letters*. 'Liberty is, to live upon one's own Terms; Slavery is, to live at the mere Mercy of another; and a Life of Slavery is, to those who can bear it, a continual State of Uncertainty and Wretchedness, often an Apprehension of Violence, often the lingering Dread of a violent Death.'[58]

As it is intelligible why republican theorists should have taken vulnerability to be the antonym of liberty, so it is understandable why liberal thinkers in the late eighteenth and the nineteenth centuries should have begun to think of liberty as something primarily opposed, not to subjection, but to restraint. Liberal thinkers in that period, especially liberal thinkers in Britain, were concerned to argue that the interference of the state was undesirable: that it hampered commerce and trade and, ultimately, the well-being of all. Liberals were the prophets of the laissez-faire economics advocated in Adam Smith's *Wealth of Nations* and they were, in effect, the advocates of the rising commercial classes. The language of liberty offered them a rhetoric with which to combat the pretensions of the state – it was probably the only rhetoric that could have served their purposes adequately – and in adopting that language they reforged the existing conception of negative liberty. When they proclaimed the glories of liberty, they were not heaping scorn, as republicans did, on conditions of slavery or subjection or vulnerability. The other side of their devotion to liberty was an antipathy, not to such traditional ills, but to restraint, in particular to restraint imposed by the state: 'all restraint', qua restraint, is an evil,' as John Stuart Mill expressed the new orthodoxy.[59]

I have been arguing that the republican notion of liberty, far from instantiating the Romantic ideal of liberty as self-realization, is essentially focused on non-interference and, if it is to be cast in negative–positive terms, has to be seen as a variant on the negative concept of liberty rather than the positive. But if I am to make the claim plausible, then I have to show that with such an ideal of liberty in place, we can understand the continual emphasis of republicans on the rule of law, the need for checks and balances, and the requirement of civic virtue.

The emphasis on the rule of law, and the need for checks and balances, is immediately intelligible in the light of the concept of liberty that I have ascribed to republicans. They are the organizational instruments, as it were, whereby the enjoyment of non-interference is made secure or resilient; they are the institutional material out of which republican liberty is fashioned. If the rule of law gives way to the regime of the powerful ruler then, even assuming that the ruler is entirely beneficent, the security of people's non-interference is undermined. That ruler may not interfere with them and may do all that is possible to minimize their interfering with one another. But if he does not interfere with them, it remains the case that he could do so with impunity. They have no protection against any whim for interference that he might develop. They live, in the phrase from *Cato's Letters*, 'at the mere Mercy of another'.

If the rule of law contrasts with the rule of men, the regime of checks and balances contrasts with the arrangement under which those who serve the law, those in government and public office, are not constrained by pressures of scrutiny, debate and the like, to justify their actions to the public they serve. The republican tradition has always been fairly pessimistic about human nature, acknowledging a natural disposition in people to be selfish and sectarian, though the Romantic version of the tradition has often misrepresented it in this respect; the pessimism can scarcely escape the notice of anyone who reads Cicero or Machiavelli or Harrington. The assumption that people have natural, selfish tendencies means that if those in public office are unconstrained by checks and balances and the like, then it must be assumed that they will avail themselves of various opportunities to advance themselves or their own at the cost of others. But if this has to be assumed about a society where checks and balances are absent, then we must say that in such a society people do not enjoy security against the interference of public officials in their lives and affairs. And that is to say that they do not enjoy republican liberty. They do not have the secure or tenured grasp on non-interference, they do not enjoy the reliable protection against interference that is of the essence of such liberty.

We come, finally, to the republican emphasis on civic virtue. Virtue is three ways ambiguous.[60] It may mean just beneficence: that is, doing good. It may mean reliable beneficence: doing good reliably because of the incentives available. Or it may mean reliable, upright beneficence: doing good reliably because of an upright concern for the good. Even the enjoyment of liberty in the liberal sense requires the beneficence of others: at the least, it requires others not to interfere. So if the republican conception is to be distinctive it must be through requiring reliable beneficence or reliable, upright beneficence.

A little reflection reveals that it requires reliable beneficence, whether upright or not. It is not going to be enough for me to enjoy liberty in the sense of secure non-interference if other people just happen to do good by me, if they just happen not to interfere. I must be able to rely on them across a variety of contingencies, in particular contingencies of attitude shift, to refrain from interference themselves and, at least if this falls within their official brief, to deal appropriately with anyone who does interfere: to put a stop to continuing interference and to affirm my status as a citizen by pursuing and, if possible, convicting the offender. But if I can enjoy liberty only in the presence of reliably beneficent people, then there is a distinctive sense in which I can enjoy it only in the presence of virtuous compatriots.

It turns out that this is the sense in which many of those associated with the republican tradition connect virtue with liberty. Thus Machiavelli did not think that what was necessary for liberty was reliable, upright beneficence. He recognized that such uprightness was not generally available and that what we have seen in most republics is merely reliable beneficence, beneficence secured by the pressures of law and opinion. 'By the force of law', as Quentin Skinner writes in commentary, 'the people were liberated from the natural consequences of their own *corruzione* and transformed in effect into *virtuosi* citizens.'[61] Again, it is clear in someone like Montesquieu that what he cherished was reliable beneficence, however procured, not just reliable beneficence of the upright sort. Tocqueville writes of Montesquieu on virtue. 'We must not take Montesquieu's idea in a narrow sense ... When this triumph of man over temptation results from the weakness of the temptation or the consideration of personal interest, it does not constitute virtue in the eyes of the moralist, but it does enter into Montesquieu's conception, for he was speaking of the effect much more than the cause.'[62]

This is enough by way of characterizing the republican tradition that, so I allege, disappears in the Enlightenment/counter-Enlightenment perspective which dominates MacIntyre's work. Republicanism presents itself as a way of thinking about politics which is centred on a negative but distinctively social notion of freedom: a notion of freedom under which it becomes tantamount to citizenship in a suitably well-ordered society. It stresses civic order and civic virtue in its delineation of the good society but that is not because these are thought of as the prerequisites of Romantic self-realization. Rather, it is because civic order and civic virtue are the materials out of which security in non-interference is constituted. I enjoy status so far as others are disposed to think well of me and I enjoy power so far as they are disposed to answer to my will. I enjoy republican liberty, on the present account of the ideal, so far as my society is so well ordered, and my fellow citizens so virtuously disposed, that I am relatively secure against interference.

The Attractions of the Alternative

It is one thing to argue that MacIntyre overlooks the republican tradition of thought, assimilating it to a variety of the Romantic approach to politics. It is another to show that this oversight is a serious loss. After all, MacIntyre acknowledges that there were lots of premodern traditions besides Aristotelianism. His main argument is that no doctrine compares with it as a general philosophy of ethics and politics. 'Aristotelianism is *philosophically* the most powerful of the pre-modern modes of moral thought.'[63] I need to say something in conclusion, therefore, on why I think that the republican tradition I have sketched should appeal to those who are concerned with contemporary political theory.

The first thing I want to say is that the goal held out by republicanism for the state, and more generally the sociopolitical structure, to advance is an extremely attractive one. The liberal notion of liberty is concerned only with the quantity of non-interference enjoyed by someone, paying no attention to how the non-interference is won. For all that liberal theory requires, the non-interference that is won – say, by the slave without a master – through cunning and fawning and sheer good luck is just as desirable as the non-interference that is assured by the person's incorporation as the citizen of the society. The liberal concept of non-interference derives ultimately from Hobbes, as is often acknowledged, and it is striking that in *Leviathan* he is quite explicit that someone who has no social standing in a despotism like Constantinople may yet enjoy just as much liberty as the citizen of a republic like the Italian city of Lucca; he may be lucky or clever enough to enjoy the same measure of non-interference. 'Whether a Commonwealth be Monarchicall, or Popular, the Freedome is still the same.'[64]

The republican concept of liberty identifies a very different sort of condition from that to which the liberal and Hobbesian notion points us. It stresses, not the quantity of non-interference involved, but the quality: in particular, the protected or resilient quality of the non-interference. The consummation of the liberal ideal would be the condition enjoyed by the totally solitary individual, the individual on the heath. Not so with the republican. The ideal envisaged here is essentially social; it is the freedom of the city, not the freedom of the heath. It is freedom in the old sense of franchise: freedom in the sense in which it involves incorporation within a polity and protection before the law. Freedom in this sense is citizenship, or at least citizenship in a well-ordered, virtuous society: a society in which there is a rule of law and a regime of suitable checks and balances – for short, an appropriate civic order – and a good measure of civic virtue. The theme goes back to the earliest days of republican thought. 'At Rome and with regard to Romans,' one commentator notes, 'full *libertas* is coterminous with *civitas*.'[65] And, as another adds, 'the main feature of *civitas* is the rule of the law.'[66] The Roman connection was so salient to medieval adherents of civic humanism that one of them, Giovanni da Viterbo, speculated that the term *civitas*, citizenship, derived from *civium libertas*, the freedom of the citizens.[67]

Why do I think that the republican ideal of franchise is attractive? My basic reason is that it answers to what, by the testimony of long tradition, are deep human desires. To enjoy franchise is to have a resilient hold on the good of non-interference and the resilience thus provided makes for a sort of psychological satisfaction which it is hard to imagine anyone spurning. There are three aspects to the psychological satisfaction provided.

First, the fact that someone enjoys non-interference resiliently will give the person a security and a sense of security against the sorts of contingencies that would undermine the non-interference that she enjoys. What are those contingencies? They are the possible shifts in the perceived opportunities or the operative motives of others that would lead them to want to interfere. At the limit, they are the possible whims that might lead others to try to disrupt her life. If the agent enjoys her non-interference resiliently then she can relax – or at least relax to a greater extent than would otherwise be possible – about such contingencies: even if the shifts in question occurred, they would be unlikely to lead to interference or at least to lasting or uncompensated interference.

A second benefit that would flow from enjoying resilient – in particular, saliently resilient – non-interference is closely related to this first benefit but needs to be mentioned separately. The contingencies against which the resilience would give her security and a sense of security are contingencies that would inhibit her in the performance of certain activities: the exercise of the traditional liberties. The fact that she is consciously secure against such contingencies means that, at least in the ideal, she is given the scope for such activities and a sense of that scope. She has consciously available to her a province where she can make decisions autonomously, without having to consider whether this will annoy others and make them more likely to interfere. In the relevant area she can ignore others, or at least those others who represent a threat. In that area she is her own boss.

But apart from security and scope, having non-interference resiliently will also confer a third and different sort of benefit on an agent. Being salient, the fact of resilience ought to become a matter of awareness, not only for the person herself, but also for potential interferers. More than that, it ought to become a matter of common awareness, with each individual being aware that the person enjoys non-interference resiliently, each individual being aware that others are also aware of that resilience, and so on up the familiar hierarchy.[68] But if the resilience becomes a matter of common as well as personal awareness, then it will confer a certain status and sense of status: a sense of not being dependent on the grace of others and of not being in their debt for the non-interference bestowed.

With any benefit that a person receives at the hands of others, there is always the possibility of the experience being demeaning, with the recipient cast in the role of debtor and dependant. The only guarantee against this demeaning effect is a common recognition among the parties that if one of the donors of the good thought of reneging, then he would be prevented or deterred or, if he went ahead, still the recipient would not be so badly off: the offender would not be able to continue the offence and she, the victim, might even be compensated. The fact that the citizen of a republican regime enjoys non-interference as a legal entitlement, the fact that she enjoys it in a saliently resilient fashion, means that she retains a hold on it without suffering a demeaning effect. The recipient can stand eye to eye with those to whom she owes her non-interference, participating with them in the knowledge that she does not depend on their grace or fancy for its enjoyment. She can be frank with them, in the sense of frankness that is etymologically related to franchise. It is all very well for Hobbes to insist that the resident of Constantinople may enjoy the same extent of non-interference as the citizen of Lucca. But the fact that he enjoys it only because his luck or charm or cunning elicits the goodwill of the powerful – only, at the limit, because their whims are congenial – means that the non-interference comes tainted with the demeaning effect.

I have been arguing that the republican ideal of liberty is attractive. A second point I would urge in its defence is that it is a relevant ideal for a pluralist society of the kind that most of us nowadays inhabit. It is an ideal that ought to appeal to people across a range of different religious and other affiliations. It may not be entirely neutral but it comes as near as any ideal is likely ot come to the sort of neutrality that is appropriate in an ideal for a pluralist society. Consider any conception of the good life that can be pursued and realized, however partially, in a pluralist society. For almost any such conception, it appears that if a person is to be able to pursue it then she must have the independence from others, the relative lack of vulnerability to their wishes as to what she should do, that is provided by the enjoyment of franchise. In John Rawls's terms, franchise looks to be a primary good for members of a pluralist society: a good such that whatever else they desire, they must desire this as a prerequisite for the satisfaction of their other desires.[69]

But not only does its relative neutrality make the republican conception of liberty relevant in a pluralist society. It is also relevant because it holds out a number of intuitively attractive challenges on the matter of how such a society ought to organize its affairs. The ideal would lead us to support many traditional features of constitutional democracy, as most of us would want it to do, but it also offers a challenging perspective on matters that feature in current debates within our societies.[70] John Braithwaite and I have explored elsewhere the lessons of the republican ideal for our criminal justice system, arguing that the ideal suggests a radical reconceptualization of its nature and function.[71] If the point of a criminal justice system is to facilitate the enjoyment of franchise in a society, then many aspects of our current arrangements in the criminal justice area come under question. But the criminal justice system is but one example of where the republican ideal would have a direct policy-making relevance. It should be clear that equally the ideal impacts on how we think of the demands on the state in areas like education, medical provision and social security. If the state is to further the enjoyment of franchise in a society, then that has implications both for whether it provides services in these areas and for how it is to provide them.[72]

So much for the argument that the republican ideal is attractive and relevant. The last point I want to make in its defence is that it is an ideal that ought to appeal to MacIntyre, or at least an ideal that ought to appeal more than the liberal ideal does. Republican liberty may be a relatively neutral ideal but it has a number of features that should make it attractive to MacIntyre: it is, as I shall put it, a social good, an interactive good and a good internal to republican practice.

A non-social good is a property whose realization does not require that people are involved socially with one another. It is a striking feature of the liberal ideal of liberty that it is non-social in this sense. The point has been made already. In order for me to enjoy non-interference there need be no one else around or no one with whom I have social relationships. Indeed if there is no one else around, if I inhabit a solitary universe, then I will enjoy the maximum of non-interference. In order to enjoy resilient non-interference, however, at least where the resilience is provided by law and the like, then I must be part of a society. The ideal of franchise is an ideal of incorporation with a certain status in the company of others. It is an ideal that is realized only when the individual enjoys relationships with others that are governed by such a form of law, and in general shaped by such a protective culture, that she is more or less secure against their interference. There is no possibility of enjoying franchise out of society; out of society it is possible to enjoy only the freedom of the heath, not the freedom of the city. This feature of the franchise ideal ought to recommend it to MacIntyre, for it means that however negative and neutral the republican ideal of liberty, it is not an ideal that connects with the atomistic image of individuals in a way the liberal ideal does.

But not only is franchise a social good, it is also an interactive good in this distinctive sense: it is a good such that an individual's own possession of the good comes into question as soon as she sees others deprived of it; it is a good such that to pursue it for oneself is inevitably, at least in the real world, to pursue it for others; in short, it is a good which we do best to pursue collectively as a good that we can hold in common. The reason that another's deprivation will put my own possession of franchise in question is that since my position *vis-à-vis* potential interferers – my position so far as the enjoyment of franchise goes – is symmetrical with that of others, anything that happens to them teaches a lesson for what can happen to me. If I see another arrested without good cause, for example, then I know that the chances are I can be arrested without good cause. And to know this is to know that as things stand I do not enjoy franchise: I do not enjoy the protection necessary for a resilient hold on non-interference.[73] In this respect, as in the previous one, the ideal of franchise is far removed from the atomistic image of human beings associated by MacIntyre with liberalism.

We can link these first two points more closely to points made by MacIntyre. The social and interactive aspects of republican liberty mean that when it comes to the political sphere, there is no reason under the republican approach why people should be represented as deliberating *qua* individuals. If you think of individuals as existing, or as logically capable of existing, independently of society, then it is easy to represent them as each asking what society, what the state, provides for them: in particular, what it provides for them in terms of a non-social, non-interactive good, like that of mere non-interference, which can matter to them outside society. In that sense we may think of individuals as reasoning *qua* individuals about politics. But if the most basic political good we identify is itself social and interactive in nature, then we cannot think of them as reasoning in this sense *qua* individuals. Franchise is not something that individuals can enjoy outside society and the state and it does not offer a currency of evaluation that would make sense within such a deliberative economy. Thus to envisage this sort of good as what society and the state, at their best, can provide for individuals is to think of those who deliberate in terms of franchise, say as they assess different arrangements, as already reasoning *qua* members of the existing polity.

Franchise, finally, is an internal good as well as a social and interactive one. It is internal in roughly the sense MacIntyre has in mind when he says that practices have certain goods internal to them. Consider the relationship between civic order and civic virtue, on the one hand, and the franchise which they help to produce on the other. This relationship is not the sort of contingent, causal connection that would allow us to think of the order and virtue coming apart from the franchise to which they lead. On the contrary, the relationship is of a constitutive kind. If there is civic order and civic virtue, if the society is governed by appropriate laws and constraints, and if the members of the society are reliably beneficent, then there is no need to wait and see whether these measures produce franchise; it is not as if the measures put a causal factor in play such that we must look to see whether the influence is effective in generating franchise. Once there is civic order and virtue in place, then immediately there is franchise, for it is the provision of such a civic context that establishes people in the enjoyment of franchise. The upshot is that under the republican conception the institutions associated with the rule of law and the regime of checks and balances, and the dispositions associated with the presence of civic virtue, must all be seen, in MacIntyre's terms, as aspects of a social practice: the practice whereby we attain our individual and collective liberty.

I do not really expect the considerations I have been rehearsing to prove decisive with MacIntyre. But at least I hope that they may soften him up. They suggest that republican liberty – franchise – is a relatively neutral ideal around which we can organize the politics of a pluralist society, without embracing the atomism and instrumentalism that he finds at the heart of the liberal project. They should give someone of Aristotelian tastes more reason to be optimistic about contemporary society and politics. Republicanism is a premodern tradition of thinking and it bears the marks of its classical background. But it is a tradition with conceptual resources sufficient to mount a constructively critical perspective on modern society. It enables us to look at modern society and to find it wanting but it does not condemn us to longing for an irretrievable past. The critical perspective that it provides makes a variety of policy-making initiatives salient; it does not leave us in the paralysing grip of a wistful nostalgia.

NOTES

I am grateful for comments on an earlier draft of this chapter to Martin Krygier and the editors.

1 The word 'communitarian' is not prominent in MacIntyre's own work but it has such currency among commentators that it seemed the obvious choice.
2 See J. G .A. Pocock, *The Machiavellian Moment: Florentine Political Theory and the Atlantic Republican Tradition* (Princeton University Press, Princeton, 1975) and Quentin Skinner, 'Machiavelli on the maintenance of liberty', *Politics*, 18 (1983), pp. 3–15; 'The idea of negative liberty', in *Philosophy in History*, ed. R. Rorty, J. B. Schneewind and Q. Skinner (Cambridge University Press, Cambridge, 1984); 'The paradoxes of political liberty' in *The Tanner Lectures on Human Values*, vol. 7, ed. S. McMurrin (Cambridge University Press, Cambridge, 1986), pp. 225–50; and 'The republican ideal of political liberty', in *Machiavelli and Republicanism*, ed. G. Bock, Q. Skinner and M. Viroli (Cambridge University Press, Cambridge, 1990), pp. 293–309.
3 Skinner, 'The republican ideal of liberty', p. 308. It is particulary confusing that some contemporary communitarians identify themselves occasionally as civic republicans. See, for example, Michael Sandel, 'The political theory of the procedural republic', *Revue de Métaphysique et de Morale*, 93 (1988), pp. 57–68.
4 *After Virtue*, 2nd edn (Duckworth, London, 1985), p. 39.
5 Ibid., ch. 5. He might also have argued that it had to fail, on the grounds that there is no escaping tradition in the manner envisaged in the project; the inescapability of tradition is the main theme of *Whose Justice? Which Rationality?* (Duckworth, London, 1988).
6 *Whose Justice? Which Rationality?*, p. 335.

7 Ibid., p. 343. See too *After Virtue*, p. 295. This way of characterizing liberalism probably has its origins in Brian Barry's 1965 book on *Political Argument*. See the introduction to the 1990 reissue of the book (Harvester Press, Brighton), p. li.

8 *Whose Justice? Which Rationality?*, p. 338. There is a strange inconsistency in MacIntyre's thought, for the emotivist does not think that in decision-making agents generally reason from the ascription of desires to themselves; he thinks that they reason practically from judgements of desirability which, by his lights, only have the status of expressions of desire. The major premise of a practical syllogism is not, at least not in the general sort of case, 'I desire X' but 'X is desirable'. On related matters see Philip Pettit and Michael Smith, 'Backgrounding desire', *Philosophical Review*, 99 (1990), pp. 565–92. Perhaps MacIntyre has changed his mind between the books. Or perhaps he thinks that while we generally conform to emotivism, we conform to the other model – a subjectivist rather than an emotivist model, in the older jargon – in reasoning in liberal-political contexts.

9 *Whose Justice? Which Rationality?*, p. 339.

10 Ibid., p. 338.

11 Ibid., p. 344.

12 Ibid., p. 336.

13 Ibid., p. 345.

14 *After Virtue*, ch. 17.

15 *Whose Justice? Which Rationality?*, p. 345.

16 Ibid., pp. 346–8.

17 Ibid., p. 339.

18 On the Romantic tradition see Isaiah Berlin, *Vico and Herder* (Hogarth Press, London, 1976); Charles Taylor, *Hegel* (Cambridge University Press, Cambridge, 1975), ch. 1; and Charles Larmore, *Patterns of Moral Complexity* (Cambridge University Press, Cambridge, 1987), ch. 5. See also Stephen Holmes, 'The permanent structure of antiliberal thought', in *Liberalism and the Moral Life*, ed. Nancy Rosenblum (Harvard University Press, Cambridge, Mass., 1989).

19 For an argument in support of such a holistic picture, and an argument with Romantic connections, see my book *The Common Mind: An Essay on Psychology, Society and Politics* (Oxford University Press, New York, 1993).

20 For an early expression of this viewpoint see Thomas Hobbes, *Leviathan* (1651), ed. C. B. Macpherson (Penguin Books, Harmondsworth, 1968). For commentary see Jean Hampton, *Hobbes and the Social Contract Tradition* (Cambridge University Press, Cambridge, 1986), ch. 1.

21 One of the first to emphasize the theme was Rousseau. See his *The Social Contract and Discourses* (Dent, London, 1973), p. 63, and Robert Wokler, *Rousseau on Society, Politics, Music and Language* (Garland, New York, 1987). The theme was enthusiastically taken up by Herder, the father of German Romanticism.

22 *After Virtue*, p. 118.

23 Ibid., p. 187 and following.

24 Ibid., p. 188.

25 Ibid., pp. 193–4.

26 Ibid., p. 196.

27 Ibid., p. 191.

28 Ibid., p. 221.

29 Ibid., p. 255.

30 Larmove, *Patterns of Moral Complexity*, p. 93.

31 Berlin, *Vico and Herder*, p. 200. For more on this theme see Charles Taylor, *Hegel*.
32 *After Virtue*, p. 149.
33 Ibid., p. 227.
34 Ibid., pp. 76–7.
35 Ibid., p. 227.
36 Taylor, *Hegel*, p. 28.
37 See Pocock, *The Machiavellian Moment*.
38 John Trenchard and Thomas Gordon, *Cato's Letters*, 6th edn (1755) (2 vols, Da Capo, New York, 1971).
39 See Anthony Pagden (ed.), *The Languages of Political Theory in Early-Modern Europe* (Cambridge University Press, Cambridge, 1987).
40 See the references to Skinner's work in note 2 above.
41 Isaiah Berlin, *Two Concepts of Liberty* (Oxford University Press, Oxford, 1958).
42 For an articulation of this account of negative liberty see Philip Pettit, 'A definition of negative liberty', *Ratio*, NS, 2 (1989).
43 I avoid the problem of saying what it is to advance a value like negative liberty in this formulation. The notion may be understood in a consequentialist or non-consequentialist way, for example, so that the state is required either to honour the rights associated with negative liberty or to do what it can to promote the overall enjoyment of negative liberty: to do what it can, including perhaps the violation of some people's liberty. See my 'Consequentialism', in *A Companion to Ethics*, ed. Peter Singer (Blackwell, Oxford, 1991).
44 See Tom Baldwin, 'MacCallum and the two concepts of freedom', *Ratio*, 26 (1984).
45 Taylor, *Hegel*, p. 24.
46 See the discussion early in Skinner, 'The idea of negative liberty'.
47 Translated in *Constant: Political Writings*, ed. B. Fontana (Cambridge University Press, Cambridge, 1988).
48 See Stephen Holmes, *Benjamin Constant and the Making of Modern Liberalism* (Yale University Press, New Haven, 1984).
49 *After Virtue*, p. 237.
50 'Are freedom and liberty twins?', *Political Theory*, 16 (1988), pp. 534–5. The writer whom Pitkin is relying on here is Kurt Raaflaub. For similar themes, see Ch. Wirszubski, *Libertas as a Political Idea at Rome* (Oxford University Press, Oxford, 1968), p. 30.
51 Skinner, 'Machiavelli on the maintenance of liberty', as reprinted in *Contemporary Political Theory*, ed. Philip Pettit (Macmillan, New York, 1991), p. 38.
52 Trenchard and Gordon, *Cato's Letters*, vol. 2, p. 248.
53 I have defended this elsewhere and I summarize the idea here. See 'The freedom of the city', in *The Good Polity*, ed. Alan Hamlin and Philip Pettit (Blackwell, Oxford, 1989); John Braithwaite and Philip Pettit, *Not Just Deserts: A Republican Conception of Criminal Justice* (Oxford University Press, Oxford, 1990); and 'Negative liberty, liberal and republican', *European Journal of Philosophy*, vol. 1, 1993, pp. 15–38.
54 See Wirszubski, *Libertas as a Political at Rome*.
55 This is the theme of Orlando Patterson, *Freedom*, vol. 1: *Freedom in the Making of Western Culture* (Basic Books, New York, 1991). It is also a theme in Pitkin, 'Are freedom and liberty twins?'
56 Skinner, 'Machiavelli on the maintenance of liberty', p. 38.
57 J. Isaac, 'Republicanism vs liberalism? a reconsideration', *History of Political Thought*, 9 (1988), p. 367.

58 Trenchard and Gordon, *Cato's Letters*, vol 2, pp. 249–50. The theme also figures in Burke, as Chandran Kukathas has shown me. Burke denounces the idea that Dissenters might be left the liberty to practise their religion, without that liberty being protected in law, as 'a contradiction in terms. Liberty under a connivance! Connivance is a relaxation from slavery, not a definition of liberty.' *The Philosophy of Edmund Burke*, ed. L. I. Bredvold and R. G. Ross (University of Michigan Press. Ann Arbor, 1970), p. 77. The idea is reminiscent of the Roman distinction between the *liber* and the *servus sine domino*.

59 J. S. Hill, *On Liberty*, ed. H. B. Acton (Dent, London, 1972), ch. 5.

60 Here I benefited from a discussion with Michael Smith.

61 Skinner, 'Machiavelli on the maintenance of liberty', p. 11.

62 Quoted from the preparatory notes to vol. 2 of *Democracy in America* in Raymond Aron, *Main Currents in Sociological Thought*, vol 1 (Penguin Books, Harmondsworth, 1968), p. 201.

63 *After Virtue*, p. 118.

64 Hobbes, *Leviathan*, p. 266.

65 Wirszubski, *Libertas as a Political Idea at Rome*, p. 3.

66 Maurizio Viroli, 'Machiavelli and the republican idea of politics', in *Machiavelli and Republicanism*, ed. Bock, Skinner and Viroli, p. 149.

67 See Quentin Skinner, 'Pre-humanist origins of republican ideas', in *Machiavelli and Republicanism*, ed. Bock, Skinner and Viroli, p. 134.

68 See David Lewis, *Convention* (Harvard University Press, Cambridge, Mass., 1969), ch. 2, for why the resilience ought to become a matter of common awareness.

69 John Rawls, *A Theory of Justice* (Oxford University Press, Oxford, 1971).

70 Republicanism has begun to feature prominently in important efforts at re-thinking aspects of current legal and democratic practice. See, for example, Cass Sunstein, 'Beyond the republican revival', *Yale Law Journal*, 97 (1988). For an overview of this movement see Richard Fallon Jr, 'What is republicanism, and is it worth reviving?', *Harvard Law Review*, 102 (1989).

71 Braithwaite and Pettit, *Not Just Deserts*.

72 See my 'The freedom of the city' and also 'Liberty in the republic', in *Justice and Ethics in New Zealand Society*, ed. Graham Oddie and Roy Perrett (Oxford University Press, New Zealand, 1992).

73 Franchise may not be a public good in the technical sense of the economists; it can be produced for some without being produced for all, as in traditional republics that gave citizenship only to a restricted class of residents. But in modern societies differences of gender and colour and class have ceased to be relevant legitimating devices – though not, sadly, ceased to be operative marks of power distribution – and it is doubtful if the members of any group could know themselves to enjoy resilient non-interference while observing that others in their society do not.

11

Liberalism, Morality and Rationality: MacIntyre, Rawls and Cavell

Stephen Mulhall

In a series of books published during the 1980s, Alasdair MacIntyre proposed and developed a radical and wide-ranging critique of Western culture since the Enlightenment. That culture is of course fundamentally shaped by liberal individualism, and from the outset MacIntyre explicitly identified John Rawls's theory of justice as a central contemporary representative of that liberalism. In this paper I want to contribute to an evaluation of MacIntyre's general critique of modernity by assessing its accuracy and depth as a specific critique of Rawlsian liberalism. In so doing, I will argue for the following four claims:

1   that the focus of MacIntyre's attack upon Rawls has shifted over the years;
2   that this attack (in both its early and its later forms) rests on misinterpretations of Rawls' position;
3   that MacIntyre's practice-based account of rationality in morality and politics is in fact largely compatible with a recognizably liberal conception of these matters;
4   that his fundamental hostility to liberal emphases on autonomy and neutrality might none the less be maintained in a different form.

Rawls in *After Virtue*

MacIntyre's presentation of Rawls

In *After Virtue*,[1] MacIntyre argues that much of modern culture is founded on an emotivist conception of the self as something essentially distinct from any and all of its attributes, that such a conception is not so much unattractive as incoherent, and that (because it leaves no place for the interlinked notions of a practice, a tradition and the narrative unity of a human life) it cannot accommodate even the possibility of rational argument and objective progress in the domain of morality. John Rawls's theory of justice makes a relatively brief appearance in the course of this argument; but when it does, MacIntyre places it squarely within the radically individualistic tradition he has been criticizing.

> [F]or ... Rawls a society is composed of individuals, each with his or her own interest, who then have to come together and formulate common rules of life ... Individuals are thus ... primary and society secondary, and the identification of individual interests is prior to, and independent of, the construction of any moral or social bonds between them.... It is ... as though we had been shipwrecked on an uninhabited island with a group of other individuals, each of whom is a stranger to me and to all the others ... Rawls ... envisages entry into social life as – at least ideally – the voluntary act of at least potentially rational individuals with prior interests who have to ask the question 'What kind of social contract with others is it reasonable for me to enter into?' (*AV*, pp. 232–3)

Because of its foundation in such a picture of the individual's relation to the community, on MacIntyre's account Rawls's theory will be unable to accommodate the very concept on which it is predicated – the concept of social justice. For a Rawlsian political community would then be a private society, an association which is entered into solely for the purpose of achieving individual goals and protecting individual interests which are to be understood as specifiable without reference to, and existent prior to, the association itself; but on MacIntyre's view no individual good or end can be rendered intelligible independently of an account of the individual's membership of a community whose primary bond is a shared understanding of the good for human beings and the good of the community. Only against that shared understanding can the primary interests of any individual be identified; and only against such a communal background can the idea of just or unjust treatment of community members be specified by relating it to their contribution to the common tasks of that community in pursuing its shared goods. Since Rawls excludes any such understanding of the logical priority of community, his theory is doomed to failure.

As the earlier quotation implies, the main reason that MacIntyre offers in *After Virtue* for attributing this desert island picture of political community to Rawls is the latter's reliance on a contractarian approach to political theory. In *A Theory of Justice*,[2] this receives its expression in the centrality accorded to what Rawls calls 'the original position', the situation within which citizens are deemed to place themselves when determining what principles of justice are to govern their society. Crucial to the specification of this position is the veil of ignorance, which prevents the deliberators from knowing certain facts about themselves – the history and present form of their society, their own social class and role within it, their natural talents and endowments, even their conceptions of the good. This detachment of the individual from the facts of their social existence is taken by MacIntyre to imply that Rawls is committed to the emotivist assumption that those facts are irrelevant to the individual's real identity; and the exclusion of reference to conceptions of the good shows Rawls's failure to recognize that no rational progress can be made on any moral issue, and certainly not on any issue of social justice, except by reference to an essentially tradition-bound and practice-bound understanding of the good for human beings. In short, the original position seems to encapsulate from the outset the desert island conception of individuality as prior to community with which we began; the veil of ignorance seems to build the emotivist conception of the self into Rawls's ideal process of deliberation and so into the principles of justice which emerge from it.

And, of course, if Rawls is implicitly relying on an emotivist conception of the self, his theory will fall prey to the difficulties that MacIntyre has earlier specified in more general terms. It is important to emphasize that these difficulties render the theory not so much unattractive as incoherent or self-defeating; MacIntyre's attack on Rawlsian liberalism, in parallel with his more general attack on modernity, is thus methodological or conceptual rather than substantive. For the problem with this conception of the self is not (or not primarily) that it is an undesirable or objectionable ideal for individual moral agents to adopt, but that it lacks the logical resources to be able to make sense of human personhood and rational moral agency as real possibilities, and so is not in a position to underpin the articulation of political and moral ideals (whether attractive or unattractive) at all. Liberal political theory stands condemned because it is incapable of adequately comprehending the very notions of human agency and of rationality in morals without which its own project (of providing a rationally justifiable account of political values for the guidance of human social actors) makes no sense.

Re-presenting Rawls

The major difficulty with this critique of Rawls is the inaccuracy of its portrayal of the structure of Rawls's own theory. MacIntyre's attempt to categorize Rawls as an exponent in the realm of political theory of the manifold errors of post-Enlightenment culture in general depends almost entirely on his interpretation of the role of the original position and the veil of ignorance in Rawls's theorizing. In particular, it presupposes that Rawls's reason for advocating the use of the veil of ignorance is his commitment to an emotivist view of the person – one in which the

essence of personhood, and in particular the capacities which go to
make up moral agency, are held to be comprehensible independently of,
and detachable from, the natural and social endowments and the value
commitments of the particular individual.

But the original position is merely a device of representation in an
argument about politics: it simply dramatizes the claim that, when
thinking about social justice, we ought to refrain from basing our deliberations on our knowledge of what our natural and social endowments
and our value commitments really are.[3] If we allowed our knowledge
that we possessed a certain social status or talent to affect our choice, we
would be permitting an inequality that is arbitrary from a moral point
of view to distort our thinking about justice; we would not be treating
people as equal. And if we allowed our knowledge that we were committed to a given conception of the good to influence our deliberations,
we would be condemning those who had freely chosen or developed
different commitments to unfair treatment by the state; we would not
be treating people as free. Moreover, these epistemic limits are intended
to apply solely to matters of social justice. In the arena of private life,
people are free to invoke and depend on their value commitments as
much as they please; in those domains of their lives which do not involve
their interaction with one another through the state and the basic institutions of society, those domains in which it is not people understood
as citizens who are at issue, then the veil of ignorance has no role to
play.

In other words, the structure of the original position reflects Rawls's
substantive view that social justice demands that we regard our fellow
citizens as free and equal; it does not embody a general empirical claim
that persons can (phenomenologically) detach themselves from all their
roles, character traits and ends at any one time, or a general metaphysical claim that one's identity as a person is not bound up with such
matters. The veil of ignorance is a morally driven epistemic limit in
politics, not the manifestation of a phenomenological or ontological
hypothesis. There is accordingly plenty of scope for Rawls to accommodate MacIntyre's point that persons *qua* persons must understand their
lives as having a narrative unity which is lived out within a series of
overlapping practices and an overarching moral tradition; for the veil of
ignorance applies only to persons *qua* citizens. Moreover, even where
the veil of ignorance *does* apply, its imposition should not be seen as
reflecting a Rawlsian assumption that rationality can be exercised and
maintained in arguments about justice without making any reference to
conceptions of the good and traditions of moral thought; for the core of
Rawls's argument for the anti-perfectionist conception of politics which
the original position epitomizes is given by the process of reasoning by

means of which he gets his readers to *accept* the epistemic limit that the veil of ignorance represents. And as we have seen, that involves concrete arguments which clearly draw upon recognizably liberal conceptions of the requirements of fairness, and of what is involved in treating one's fellow citizens as free and equal. Such considerations may be inadequate or objectionable; but *they* are where Rawls stakes his claim to have generated a rationally superior conception of social justice, and any opposition to it must focus on those substantive matters. In short, the argumentative heart of the theory of justice as fairness is to be found in the considerations which lead us to pass through the veil of ignorance, not in the considerations to which we restrict ourselves on its further side.

And once we see that the original position is a device of representation *to* which a substantive moral theory drives us rather than *from* which moral theorizing is supposed to begin, then we can see that the conception of a political community which it embodies is not that of a mere association of individuals whose interests are given prior to their communal membership. For if the original position merely dramatizes certain morally driven epistemic limits, then its structure embodies no claim about the chronological or logical priority of the individual to society; it is perfectly open to Rawls to accept that individuals would be in no position to articulate values of the sort to which he is committed without being part of a liberal community and tradition. Moreover, if the anti-perfectionist political community Rawls advocates is indeed the concrete social embodiment of a substantive moral conception of the person as a free and equal citizen, then membership of that community allows people to achieve a common good (both for themselves as individuals and for the community as a whole) which could not possibly be achieved alone. In short, their interests as individual citizens are presented against the background of a community whose primary bond is to a particular shared conception of a political good – that of living under, and dispensing to one another, the rule of justice; and such a community is not simply an association of primarily self-interested individuals. So nothing in this theory gives us any reason to think that Rawls's moral individualism depends on a desert island conception of political community.

Morality and Rationality in *After Virtue*

None the less, it is clear that Rawls's political anti-perfectionism excludes the possibility of a certain type of political community – one whose members are bound together by a shared commitment to a conception

of what the good life for human beings really is, a shared commitment
to what Rawls in his more recent work calls a comprehensive moral or
religious doctrine. An anti-perfectionist liberal polity is an arena within
which a particular moral conception of the person as citizen holds sway
and certain political virtues and goods are to be developed and achieved;
but its anti-perfectionism precisely consists in preventing the state from
attempting to act according to the dictates of a conception of the good
life for human beings whose scope ranges far beyond the domain of
politics to encompass the many non-political aspects of human life and
well-being.

MacIntyre's critique of justice as fairness in *After Virtue* also focuses
on this aspect of the Rawlsian project: 'Rawls explicitly makes it a presupposition of his view that we must expect to disagree with others
about what the good life for man is and must therefore exclude any
understanding of it, that we may have from the formulation of our
principles of justice . . .' (*AV*, p. 233). MacIntyre does not suggest that
Rawls's sociological hypothesis about widespread disagreement over
comprehensive conceptions of the good is inaccurate. On the contrary,
he shares this perception, and takes it that the Rawlsian principle of
excluding reference to such conceptions which the veil of ignorance
embodies is an understandable response to the present state of Western
moral culture – a state in which the arena of public political debate
confronts individuals with a melange of incomplete and inconsistent
elements from many radically different moral frameworks, and so condemns arguments which draw upon such incommensurable resources
to irresolubility. Excluding reference to such resources will therefore
appear essential if political conclusions are to be reached and practical
decisions made. The problem is that, in the absence of some coherent
background conception of the good life for human beings, the project of
establishing rational agreement in political theory on matters of social
policy is no more likely to be successful than it is in political and moral
practice:

> we have all too many disparate and rival moral concepts, in this case rival
> and disparate concepts of justice, and the moral resources of the culture
> allow us no way of settling the issue between them rationally. Moral philo-
> sophy, as it is dominantly understood, reflects the debates and disagree-
> ments of the culture so faithfully that its controversies turn out to be
> unsettlable in just the way that the political and moral debates themselves
> are. (*AV*, p. 235)

In other words, the nature and fate of Rawls's anti-perfectionism is
presented as a specific political-theoretical manifestation of the general
absence of rationality in modern Western moral culture which MacIntyre

diagnoses at the beginning of *After Virtue*; the very same moral disorder to which Rawls's exclusion of conceptions of the good is a response ensures that the theory which embodies that exclusionary response will be incapable of triumphing over its rivals. Rawls's veil of ignorance is thus both an exemplary instance and an unwitting victim of the emotivism which MacIntyre argues has taken over contemporary moral culture.

If, however, Rawlsian political liberalism is to be criticized as a specific reflection or manifestation of the general emotivist disorder to which we have just referred, it is vital that there *be* such disorder; this diagnosis of the state of contemporary moral culture must be borne out. But there are good reasons for doubting its accuracy – reasons which we must now examine in detail.

The irresolubility of moral arguments

MacIntyre believes that political disputes (for instance, about the moral legitimacy of abortion or nuclear deterrence) are not just very unlikely to be resolved but irresoluble in principle. This, he claims, is because the moral views of the participants are fundamentally incommensurable: although a proponent of abortion rights can justify her view by invoking more general and basic beliefs which lead her to that view, those founding premises cannot themselves be justified against the founding premises of her opponent. Because they invoke concepts which cannot easily be translated into the concepts invoked by other interlocutors (for instance, rights compared with universalizability or the notion of a soul), there is no overarching framework within which the relative merits and worth of these concepts can be compared with one another and the rational superiority of one demonstrated: they are, in short, rationally incommensurable. And if we are unable to offer our opponents in public debate any good reason for adopting our views, we must lack any such reasons for holding them ourselves:

> if we possess no unassailable criteria, no set of compelling reasons by means of which we may convince our opponents, it follows that in the process of making up our own minds we can have made no appeal to such criteria or such reasons. If I lack any good reasons to invoke against you, it must seem that I lack any good reasons. Hence it seems that underlying my own position there must be some non-rational decision to adopt that position. (*AV*, p. 8)

In short, the interminability of argument that MacIntyre claims to identify in the public realm reflects an inherent arbitrariness in the private realm. Incommensurability and irrationality have infected the whole of our moral lives.

However, if he is to claim that we all lack any good reasons for cleaving to our various moral beliefs, MacIntyre must have some conception of what it is that we lack – some conception of what a 'good' reason might be; and in fact, the paradigm he has in mind is adumbrated in the passage we just quoted. According to its opening sentence, a good reason for holding a moral view is a compelling reason; a good criterion is an unassailable one. Presumably, a compelling reason is one which will be compelling for anyone *qua* competent moral agent, one the agent must acknowledge on pain of ceding any claim to competence in this domain; and an unassailable criterion will be one which cannot be assailed from any competing moral perspective – one which any competent moral agent must acknowledge to be beyond moral assault. So MacIntyre is in effect defining a rational moral judgement as one from which no competent moral agent could dissent; put otherwise, if universal agreement on that judgement were not *guaranteed*, if the procedures of moral reasoning did not compel convergence upon it, it could not count as a rationally correct or objective judgement. If one is measuring the domain of morality against such a standard of rationality, it is hardly surprising that it is going to fail the test; but is it the appropriate standard?

Its use is certainly one of the assumptions which leads many philosophers to reject the idea that moral argument could conceivably be objective or rational; but, as Stanley Cavell has remarked when discussing this assumption in *The Claim of Reason*,[4] the effect of so doing is to model rationality in morals on a paradigm which has its home in very different areas of human life – the domains of mathematics and science. In those domains, universal agreement on a given conclusion *is* guaranteed; logicians tend not to disagree over whether a given theorem has been proven, and scientists tend not to disagree over whether a given hypothesis has been established. But it may be hasty to regard their ability to reach such agreement in judgements as the criterion of the rationality of their practices; for this leaves unexplored the question of what permits or underpins that agreement.

How is it, for example, that the scientific community can compel agreement on the claim that there are mountains on the moon? Presumably by getting a dissenter to look through a telescope. But what if she refuses to accept the evidence of telescopes as pertinent to the question? Then she would be treated either as irrational or as incompetent in science; in other words, given the procedures and canons of science as that institution is now constituted, the woman would be deemed no scientist. So what permits agreement in scientific judgements is agreement about what constitutes science, scientific procedures and scientific evidence; being a scientist just is having a commitment to, and being competent at, the relevant modes of resolving disagreement.

What this perspective suggests is that the important locus of agreement here is not agreement on conclusions but agreement on the procedures of supporting and evaluating putative conclusions; for the possibility of agreeing on the former is a consequence of agreeing on the latter. But this relocates our sense of what makes science rational in a way which might radically alter our sense of the rationality of morals, as Cavell points out:

> If what makes science rational is not the fact of agreement about particular propositions itself, or about the acknowledged modes of arriving at it, but the fact of a *commitment* to certain modes of argument whose very nature is to lead to such agreement, then morality may be rational on exactly the same ground, namely that we commit ourselves to *certain* modes of argument, but now ones which do not lead, in the same ways, and sometimes not at all, to agreement (about a conclusion).[5]

In other words, despite the fact that our modes of moral argument do not guarantee agreement about conclusions, they do none the less impose objective constraints on how such arguments are to be conducted; for a commitment to those procedures involves a commitment to certain canons of relevance – a shared understanding of what is and what is not pertinent to the attempted resolution of a disagreement about any given conclusion. For example, one might not agree with Antigone's decision to disobey Creon because one did not agree with the weight she placed on her relationship with her brother; but one could only fail to acknowledge the relevance of that blood relationship to her decision on pain of revealing incompetence in the practice of moral argument.

Moreover, the fact that one *can* competently disagree with another competent moral reasoner's assignment of weight or significance to certain considerations does not mean that one *must* do so; the fact that these overarching procedures and canons of relevance do not guarantee agreement does not mean that they guarantee disagreement instead. Suppose that someone makes a promise, and then fails to keep it; in order to justify her failure to honour her commitment, she must point to considerations which are recognizably pertinent – she cannot, for example, simply say that it would have been a little too time-consuming to have fulfilled her promise. As we have just seen, the fact that a justification is competently entered does not *force* us to accept it – we can acknowledge its relevance without agreeing to the weight or significance that the promisor attaches to it in the present context. But by the same token, we are not *forced* to reject it either; we might agree with the weight she has attached to the competing considerations she confronted, and so agree with her conclusion (that is, accept her excuse). In short, we are not forced either to accept or reject her excuse on pain of incompetence in the practice of moral argument; within the parameters mentioned, both agreement and disagreement can be rational.

So, whereas MacIntyre takes the fact that, in a moral argument, agreement on a conclusion is not guaranteed to show that moral arguments lack rationality, Cavell takes it to show that rationality cannot be a matter of whether or not agreement on a conclusion is guaranteed. For Cavell, what makes the process of moral argument rational is that (just like the processes of scientific and mathematical argument) it is governed by procedures and canons of relevance that determine which considerations are pertinent to a given moral argument or disagreement, but which are not themselves open to argument or disagreement. In the case of morality, unlike that of science and mathematics, this impersonal framework does *not* also determine the weight to be attached to any given relevant consideration, and so it cannot guarantee agreement on conclusions. But since the contraints it does impose are objective, it at least creates a space within which rational agreement is *possible*; and it also ensures that, when agreement is not arrived at, those disagreeing might be able to respect one another despite their differences, since neither can deny either the pertinence of the considerations to which the other attaches weight or the other's right to determine the weight he or she attaches to them. In Cavell's eyes, contemporary moral argument is a domain which admits of many morally adequate positions being taken on any given topic; and as a result, the particular position a given individual takes up reveals as much about her as about the action or judgement under consideration. In this sense, moral argument is both objective (since its procedures are not determined by arbitrary, purely subjective preference) and personal (since those procedures can accommodate person-specific attributions of significance): it allows people to define and defend the position for which they are prepared to take responsibility to others, and it allows those others to determine whether that position is one they can respect.

Clearly, this account of rationality in morals is developed primarily as an account of private morality: its paradigm is an encounter between two people who wish to understand one another better and perhaps work towards an agreement, but whose relationship is clearly a fairly intimate one – perhaps one of friendship, perhaps one of love. It is therefore ill-suited to the domain of public political morality: the scale and form of the institutions and resources of the political arena are all wrong for it – political manifestos, party political broadcasts and parliamentary debates do not allow us the time or the flexibility required to engage with each and every citizen in such a way as to adapt our arguments to their particular views, to develop our arguments in the most appropriate ways, to attempt to understand the nuances of their position.

Moreover, they could not reasonably be expected to do so, given the imperatives which rightly tend to dominate there; the nuances and individuality of perspective which are the very stuff of personal moral argument will simply obstruct the development of swift and clear-cut action to ameliorate the position of those whose basic needs are not being met and whose basic rights are yet to be made real. This is not to say that there is no overlap between these perspectives or domains: issues such as abortion, nuclear deterrence and so on (precisely the issues on which MacIntyre concentrates) tend to cause severe problems in the political domain precisely because they bridge the gap between the two. However, from Cavell's perspective, the fact that a social consensus on such issues is very unlikely to be easily or quickly achieved will no longer appear to be an indication that we lack any good reasons for our own personal convictions on such matters; it will rather show that the modes of argument by means of which we can deploy and refine the reasoning which justifies them are such that the realm of politics is simply not able to embody them. It will show that it is simply unreasonable to expect *social* consensus on such matters; it will *not* show that the very idea of a rational judgement about them is chimerical.

It may seem that this Cavellian account of the nature of rationality in morals is open to an obvious riposte from MacIntyre; for the distinction between agreement on canons of relevance and agreement on conclusions leaves a gap of a sort to which MacIntyre has raised explicit objection in recent writings. In his Gifford lectures,[6] he makes the point with reference to his predecessors, and offers the following remark about one of the sources of their disagreements:

A set of relevant considerations are adduced which point towards rather than entail some conclusion which that particular lecturer wishes to establish. That those considerations are relevant, and that, if a particular weight is attached to them, they do indeed provide support for the conclusion in question is generally not in doubt. But as to why such weight or importance should be attached to this particular set of considerations but not to the members of certain other sets, the lecturers have generally been silent. And in this as in the range of their disagreements, they are typical of their culture. They speak as members of a culture in which the relevance of a wide range of disparate and often mutually incompatible considerations to conclusions concerning natural theology and the foundation of ethics is recognised, but in which there is no established agreement upon how these are to be ranked in importance or weight, such ranking being in practice largely a matter of individual preferences. (*TRV*, pp. 10–11)

In other words, how can Cavell's model of moral reasoning comprise a model of rationality, how can it permit us to think of a conclusion as objectively justified, if each individual must assign his or her own weight to whatever considerations are pertinent to the problem at hand; is this assignment not merely the expression of arbitrary personal preference, and thus the very opposite of a rational procedure?

Cavell might make three replies to this. First, although MacIntyre may be right to say that other Gifford lecturers were silent when asked to justify their claim that certain considerations should be given more weight than others, it is no part of Cavell's account of moral reasoning that a moral agent could or should preserve such a silence. On the contrary: once someone has offered a pertinent reason for the action she performed, the very canons of relevance which determine that it is pertinent also permit her interlocutor to introduce other considerations which pertinently counter the initial reason, to which it is then the responsibility of the actor to respond, again in ways determined by the framework – and so on. There may in the end be nothing which compels the two interlocutors to agree with one another's chains of reasoning; but such disagreement is the outcome of a potentially long and involved process of offering reasons, having them countered, and responding to the counters. To say that disagreement is possible is not to say that justifying one's stance is impossible or superfluous.

None the less, reasons may come to an end, and the interlocutors agree to disagree. But here Cavell could argue that regarding such a possibility as a proof of the irrationality of the preceding argument amounts to once again employing an inappropriate standard of rationality: for if a procedure is to be deemed irrational simply because it contains a stage at which an individual must make a decision whose outcome is not itself determined by the procedures themselves, then only the procedures of logic and (perhaps) science will pass the test – for only they provide impersonal criteria not only for determining the relevance of a given consideration but also for determining the precise weight to be attached to it. In short, MacIntyre's accusation seems to depend on a question-begging definition of what is to be counted as rational, and one which would entail that morality could not conceivably be deemed rational unless moral argument could take the form of proving or disproving theorems – a form in which *every* aspect of the reasoning process is impervious to the individual input of the participants. He would seem to require the mathematization of morality if moral argument is to be accounted rational.

And yet (here is Cavell's third riposte), such a mathematical model is precisely *not* what MacIntyre's own preferred paradigm of moral argument – his neo-Aristotelian practice-centred account – delivers. As an example of practice-bound reasoning, MacIntyre instances chess: his point is that acquiring competence in the practice is a matter of conforming to the conceptions of excellence, purpose and achievement that prevail in that practice, so that an ability to make judgements about chess excellence cannot be thought of as the expression of arbitrary subjective preference. However, it is no part of this account that acquiring such knowledge ensures that no two competent chess players will ever disagree over what constitutes excellence in chess; what makes an argument about whether Capablanca was a bettter player than Kasparov a rational one is not that any competent chess player must agree with every other one as to the correct conclusion, but rather that any such competent practitioner will be aware of which considerations are pertinent to the issue. They will know that these Grand Masters must be judged on the basis of such criteria as defensive solidity, strategic imagination, attacking flair, technical virtuosity and so on; but competence at the practice will not tell them which of these pertinent factors is to be assigned more weight than any other in this particular case. On the contrary, the tradition of chess-playing is constituted by a controlled but unending argument about precisely such matters. In short, a practice-based account of rationality does not provide us with compelling reasons or unassailable criteria; it does not provide a framework within which any competent reasoner is guaranteed to agree with all other reasoners upon the rectitude of a given judgement.

In fact, what is most striking about MacIntyre's account of practice-bound reasoning and Cavell's account of moral reasoning is their similarity. In particular, both seem to rely on drawing a distinction between agreement on procedures and canons of relevance and agreement on conclusions, and regard the former as that which makes the process of argumentation a rational one. The fundamental difference between them is therefore not over what constitutes rationality in morals, but over whether or not such rationality is available in contemporary moral culture; for MacIntyre, the frameworks within which moral debate can be a rational and objective project have been lost and must be reconstructed, but for Cavell, they have merely been lost from the sight of moral philosophers. In short, in what MacIntyre regards as his prescription for a barely imaginable future, Cavell would recognize a (partial) description of an often overlooked present.

Separating meaning and use

To this Cavellian claim, Macintyre would no doubt respond by falling back on the distinction between appearance and reality which is central to his diagnosis of the ills of contemporary culture. Cavell's analysis, he might say, is at best a depiction of certain aspects of the logic of our moral language – but these linguistic structures do not reflect the reality of contemporary moral practice, which is permeated with arbitrariness and subjectivity; those structures are rather all that remains of the historical periods in which that practice was genuinely and substantively rational, simply the trace of a past reality conferring the appearance of substance on the present. This distinction between the historically determined objective meanings and the practice-determined subjective uses of our moral vocabulary is, of course, something that MacIntyre relies upon in his general explanation of our failure to perceive the true nature of contemporary moral culture; distracted by an appearance of order, we overlook the disordered reality. But he can only make such a distinction if it makes sense to believe that moral discourse and the practices with which it is intertwined can become radically discrepant with one another; and this in turn only makes sense if it is possible for the meaning and the use of words to diverge so radically that the former can systematically contradict the latter. MacIntyre's proffered ground for thinking that meaning and use can be so easily separated from each other is, however, decidedly flimsy. In *After Virtue*, he cites an example from Gilbert Ryle: 'The angry schoolmaster . . . may vent his feelings by shouting at the small boy who has just made a mathematical mistake, "Seven times seven equals forty-nine!" but the use of this sentence to express feelings or attitudes has nothing whatsoever to do with its meaning' (p. 13).

But this is an instance of a local divergence between meaning and use – of a sentence with a given meaning being employed on a given occasion for an unusual purpose; all that it shows is that 'meaning' and 'use' are not synonyms. What MacIntyre requires in the case of morality, however, is a global and systematic divergence between meaning and use; we have to imagine that, despite the fact that a given word is uniformly employed to give expression to a feeling or attitude, its meaning continues to embody impersonal standards – that words employed in a practice in which their use is ultimately justified by the invocation of personal reasons might none the less possess a meaning which relates them to impersonal ones.

But if they cannot in fact be backed up by impersonal reasons, if they are employed to articulate personal preferences and justified in corresponding ways, how could the words themselves continue to retain their original impersonal meaning? MacIntyre seems to imagine that a past practice of employing signs in a given way might hover in a ghost-like manner around a later practice in which they are employed completely differently, so that their meaning might remain untouched by their new surroundings. But this would be akin to claiming that, if the words in the sentence 'Seven times seven is forty-nine!' were to become systematically and solely employed in expressions of anger (say, solely in sentences that are synonyms for 'damn and blast!' or substitutes for a growl), they might none the less retain a substantial mathematical meaning. Since, however, what gives these words mathematical meaning in the first place (what gives them such a mathematical sense and reference, in MacIntyre's Fregean terminology) is our employing them in a particular practice, then a radical and broadly uniform change in that practice would ensure that those words could no longer be said to have any mathematical sense at all.

It seems, then, that at the very least MacIntyre owes us an account of what fixes the meaning of a word in which no essential reference is made to prevailing practices of employing that word. In the absence of such an account, we must jettison one part of his description of contemporary moral culture: since meaning and use cannot be radically discrepant in the way his diagnosis presupposes, then he must either have misrepresented the meaning of our contemporary moral vocabulary, or he must have misrepresented its use. What Cavell's work on moral philosophy suggests is that it is the use which has been misdescribed: our moral culture retains a distinction between subjective and objective reasons, between expressions of preference and rationally justifiable judgements, not only in the logic of its language but also in the practices in which those linguistic terms are embedded. In short, the claim to rationality in morals which MacIntyre allowed to be part of the meaning of moral terms is one which the practice of making moral judgements does in fact meet.

Of course, if the account of the form of that rationality which Cavell offers is correct, then these practices of moral judgement are classically liberal ones. The procedures Cavell adumbrates are ones in which, within an agreed framework, individuals can agree to disagree; in such a framework, the possibility of discovering a moral community coexists with the possibility of taking a personal stand, making an assessment whose outcome is not dictated by that framework. In short, it is a practice in which the values of community and individuality are kept in balance without any sacrifice of rationality or objectivity. Moreover, given such an understanding of private moral discourse, a Rawlsian conception of political justice is likely to be the dominant mode of political organization; for if these interpersonal procedures simply could not be replicated on a society-wide level, if it would be unreasonable to expect them to function in a way which would generate universal agreement among citizens, then an anti-perfectionist state – one which refrains from forcing a particular moral position on those who are free to disagree with it – may seem the only possible and ethically justifiable option.

But, of course, if MacIntyre's basic historical hypothesis of the rise and dominance of liberal individualism is correct, this is precisely what we should expect – that the prevailing morality should be structured in an essentially liberal way. The difficulty with the position MacIntyre articulates in *After Virtue* is that he wishes simultaneously to argue that liberal individualism is dominant, that our culture is thoroughly emotivist, and that the conceptual resources of liberal individualism are incapable of accounting for the possibility of human agency and rational moral argument. Such a combination of claims is inherently unstable, for it amounts to arguing that the pervasive and dominant morality is logically incapable of functioning as a morality at all. Once again, since both parts of this claim cannot be correct, we are forced to choose between them; and the conclusions of this investigation suggest that we jettison the latter. MacIntyre's objection to liberalism ought not to be the methodological claim that it is conceptually incoherent, because that claim does not stand up to scrutiny; it should rather be that liberalism is a substantial and powerful moral tradition which we have substantive and powerful reasons for rejecting as undesirable or objectionable.

Rawls in *Whose Justice? Which Rationality?*

In fact, the treatment MacIntyre metes out to liberalism in general and to Rawls in particular when he returns to these issues in *Whose Justice? Which Rationality?*[7] conforms to (at least the negative part of) this prescription to such a degree that it seems rather as if MacIntyre had drawn these conclusions for himself. The crucial chapter for our purposes is, of course, 'Liberalism transformed into a tradition'; and, as its title makes clear, little of the methodological critique adumbrated in *After Virtue* seems to survive. MacIntyre locates liberal political theory as part of a historical project of founding a social order in which individuals could emancipate themselves from the contingency and particularity of traditions by appealing to genuinely universal, tradition-independent norms. Initially the liberal aim was to provide a political, legal and economic framework in which assent to one and the same rationally justifiable principles would enable those who espouse widely differing and incompatible conceptions of the good life to live peaceably together within the same society. According to MacIntyre, however, this goal necessarily entailed proscribing any attempts to reshape the life of the community in accord with any one particular conception of the good:

> And this qualification of course entails not only that liberal individualism does indeed have its own broad conception of the good, which it is engaged in imposing politically, legally, socially and culturally wherever it

has the power to do so, but also that in so doing its toleration of rival
conceptions of the good in the public arena is severely limited. (*WJWR*,
p. 336)

What MacIntyre includes under this broad liberal conception of the
good are such elements as a distinctive, primarily procedural conception
of a just social order, the treatment of moral beliefs within that order
simply as expressions of preference, and a conception of the good life
for human beings as one in which a variety of goods is pursued, appropriate to its own sphere, with no overall good supplying any overall
unity to life. And these elements are embodied, debated and carried
forward through the medium of a specific set of social, legal and cultural
institutions. In other words, what began as an attempt to found morality
upon tradition-independent principles which any human beings could
accept in so far as they were rational ended with the creation and per-
petuation of one more moral tradition: 'Liberal theory is best understood, not at all as an attempt to find a rationality independent of
tradition, but as itself the articulation of a historically developed and
developing set of social institutions and forms of activity, that is, as the
voice of a tradition' (*WJWR*, p. 345).

So MacIntyre is no longer claiming that liberalism lacks the conceptual resources to make sense of human agency and the rationality of
moral argument, and is accordingly incapable of generating a coherent
moral and political system; instead, he is acknowledging that liberalism
is a fully fledged tradition, and so possessed of just the resources he
originally suspected it of lacking. The main methodological problem he
sees now is rather that this acknowledgement is something that liberalism itself may be incapable of making, since it conflicts with its own
self-definition as somehow tradition-transcendent – as a moral and political blueprint which is neutral between competing conceptions of the
good. Whereas in *After Virtue*, the crucial methodological weakness of
liberalism was that it claimed to offer a distinctive account of human
agency and morality when it was in fact incapable of so doing, in *Whose
Justice? Which Rationality?* its crucial methodological weakness is that
it claims not to offer a distinctive account of human agency and morality
when it is in fact doing precisely that.

How does Rawlsian liberalism fit into this picture? From someone of
MacIntyre's persuasion, the general charge that a given political theorist
is functioning within the parameters of a given tradition cannot in itself
constitute a criticism, since it is impossible for any theorist to do otherwise. And given Rawls's more recent writings,[8] in which he claims that
the task of political theorizing in a democracy is to develop a more
systematic account of the intellectual resources prevalent in the public

political culture of the society, it is unlikely that he would regard the claim that his work constitutes a contemporary development of the post-Enlightenment tradition of liberalism as a criticism either. As MacIntyre admits:

> increasingly there have been liberal thinkers who, for one reason or an-
> other, have acknowledged that their theory and practice are after all that of
> one more contingently grounded and founded tradition, in conflict with
> other rival traditions as such and like several other traditions in claiming
> a right to universal allegiance, but unable to escape from the condition of
> a tradition. Even this, however, can be recognised without any inconsist-
> ency and had gradually been recognized by liberal writers such as Rawls,
> Rorty and Stout. (*WJWR*, p. 346)

But if Rawls can happily acknowledge in general terms that he is the representative of a tradition, he cannot equally happily plead guilty to MacIntyre's other charge that the liberal state – despite its protestations to the contrary – effectively imposes a specific and broad conception of the good upon those under its sway. Here, however, the charge itself needs more careful formulation than MacIntyre provides; for liberalism does not stake a claim to total neutrality. Indeed, according to any anti-perfectionist liberal, the state *must* discriminate against any broad conception of the good whose pursuit by individual citizens will interfere with the right of all citizens freely to pursue their own broad conception of the good; it would hardly be a *liberal* state if it did not, and the idea that any state could function without making *some* sort of distinction between permissible and impermissible broad conceptions of the good is nonsensical. So, to point this out – as MacIntyre does – as a contradiction is to attack a straw man; and Rawls could simply point out that his state is none the less significantly anti-perfectionist because it would refrain from utilizing state power to implement (or to encourage or discourage the implementation) of any broad conception of how human life in general should be lived, both within and outside the domain of politics. A state can hardly refrain from determining limits to legitimate action in the political sphere; but it might also attempt to govern the nature of citizens' beliefs and actions in other parts of their lives – and this is something against which the liberal state distinctively and coherently sets its face.

MacIntyre might reply to this that, even if such a liberal state refrained from acting on such broad conceptions of the good, the notion of such an anti-perfectionist state can only be defended by invoking a political theory which itself adds up to a broad conception of the good; in short, that any adequate defence of the idea of a neutral state cannot itself be neutral on a range of questions going far beyond the political domain. To this charge, however, Rawls has explicitly developed a further response. In effect, he distinguishes between a purely political liberalism and what he calls a comprehensive liberal doctrine – something that would be called a broad conception of the good in the terms MacIntyre employs; and Rawls claims that, although his theory of justice as fairness is indeed a substantive moral theory, it is a political rather than a comprehensive one. It applies only to the basic institutions of society; the intellectual resources from which it is developed are restricted only to those which are available in the public political culture and so might form the subject of an overlapping consensus between those committed to differing comprehensive doctrines; and the content of its conceptions is itself solely political in nature, for instance, its conception of the person as free and equal is a conception of the person as citizen, and is not intended to apply to other aspects of their lives.

To the best of my knowledge, MacIntyre has not addressed himself to this particular liberal response to charges such as his own; and in this sense, the argumentative ball remains in his court. However, it is worth pointing out in conclusion that the political/comprehensive distinction around which Rawls's recent thinking revolves is by no means invulnerable to criticism. For example, can the distinction itself be defended without violating it? In other words, can Rawls defend the need to draw a distinction between thinking of oneself as a citizen and thinking of oneself as a person without invoking elements of a comprehensive liberal doctrine? And his emphasis on restricting the political theorist to the resources available in the public political culture leaves obscure the importance of the content of those publicly available resources. If, for example, most or all citizens came to agree on the worthlessness of sado-masochism or the superiority of marriage over promiscuity, would it then be legitimate for their society to restrict its members' autonomy in accordance with such judgements, or would the fact that such actions would violate anti-perfectionist constraints trump their public justifiability?[9] In short, Rawls's distinction between political and comprehensive conceptions of the good may be neither as clear nor as stable as it looks; but this is something that MacIntyre has as yet given us no reason to believe.

Conclusion

MacIntyre's conception of liberalism and its weaknesses has shifted significantly over the last decade. In both *After Virtue* and *Whose Justice? Which Rationality?* he perceives internal methodological or conceptual incoherencies at its heart – but in the former book, these seem sufficent to disbar it from the status of a moral theory at all, whereas in the latter they seem to centre around the tenability of liberalism's claims to neutrality. In both, however, it seems that MacIntyre's criticisms miss their target: if they do not simply misrepresent the nature of contemporary liberal theory or contemporary moral practice, then they at least fail to acknowledge that a rival account of the phenomena about which MacIntyre is himself theorizing is available from within the liberal perspective. In other words, MacIntyre needs to acknowledge that liberalism is a genuine moral tradition, with its own conceptions of human life, rationality and morality; it is no more open to purely methodological or conceptual assault than is his own neo-Thomist tradition. Once this acknowledgement is made, MacIntyre can devote his energies to putting these two traditions into a meaningful, closely argued and entirely substantive debate; for only then, according to his own account of rationality in morals, can we judge which tradition can claim to be rationally superior to its rival. The position at which MacIntyre had arrived by the time of *Whose Justice? Which Rationality?* suggests that this advice is something which he has already begun to follow; but his Gifford lectures did not constitute the confrontation with contemporary liberal individualism for which we should be looking. Let us hope that this confrontation will not be long in coming.

NOTES

1 *After Virtue* (Duckworth, London, 1981), hereafter *AV* in the chapter text.
2 John Rawls, *A Theory of Justice* (Clarendon, Oxford, 1972).
3 If this was not sufficiently clear in *A Theory of Justice*, it was heavily underlined in Rawls's Dewey lectures, which were published (in the *Journal of Philosophy*, 77) under the title 'Kantian constructivism in moral theory' in 1980 – one year before the publication of *After Virtue*.
4 Stanley Cavell, *The Claim of Reason* (Oxford University Press, Oxford, 1979).
5 Ibid., pp. 261–2.
6 Published under the title *Three Rival Versions of Moral Enquiry* (Duckworth, London, 1990), hereafter *TRV* in the chapter text.
7 *Whose Justice? Which Rationality?* (Duckworth, London, 1988), hereafter *WJWR* in the chapter text.
8 For instance, John Rawls, 'Justice as fairness: political not metaphysical', *Philosophy and Public Affairs* (Summer 1985).
9 These worries are developed at greater length in S. Mulhall and A. Swift, *Liberals and Communitarians* (Blackwell, Oxford, 1992).

12

MacIntyre on Liberalism and its Critics: Tradition, Incommensurability and Disagreement

Andrew Mason

In *Whose Justice? Which Rationality?* Alasdair MacIntyre makes the interesting claim that liberalism has become a tradition with its own norms of rational inquiry and its own conceptions of justice and practical rationality, incommensurable with other traditions, such as Aristotelianism and Thomism, the development of which he thinks is guided by different norms of inquiry. Although liberals would be happy to see themselves as contributing to a body of thought and practice which has evolved historically, most would consider that the standards of assessment they use transcend that body of thought and apply equally to others; they would not regard themselves as representatives of what MacIntyre calls 'a tradition', if by that he means a body of thought which employs (and, as he would have it, must employ) only internal standards of justification. In this respect liberals are no different from many others, including Aristotelians and Thomists, whose thinking MacIntyre also regards as tradition-bound; if his account is correct, they are not (as they suppose) using methods of inquiry, or developing conceptions of practical rationality and justice, which are justifiable by independent standards. There need be nothing wrong with describing what these theorists are doing in terms which they would not accept, however, for they may misunderstand the status and nature of their own inquiries. My purpose is to explore whether MacIntyre's reconceptualization of liberalism as a tradition provides adequate resources to explain the intractability of disputes not only between liberals and their critics but also among liberals who advocate significantly different conceptions of justice.

In the first section I shall argue that MacIntyre's notion of incommensurability – the idea that people may fail to share standards of assessment – is more basic than his notion of a tradition in the explanation he gives for why current moral and political disputes are so persistent. He implicitly identifies a number of related ways in which conflicting positions may fail to share standards of assessment: they may start from different premises; they may have different conceptions of rational acceptability; they may be partially untranslatable. In the following sections I shall maintain that none of these ideas is well-suited to the role which MacIntyre accords them in explaining why moral and political disagreement, especially over which conception of justice we should adopt, resists resolution. In the final section I shall suggest that even though MacIntyre may be partially successful in distancing himself from what might be called (at the risk of oversimplification) 'the Enlightenment conception of rationality and rational resolvability', he implicitly accepts a key element of it by representing the confrontation between different traditions of thought and practice as a battle which can only be won (if it is to be won by rational means) by arguments which should satisfy anyone who meets his or her tradition's standards of reasonableness.

The Diversity within Liberalism

MacIntyre characterizes liberalism in terms of what he regards as its main aspiration, that is, to develop an account of justice-*as-such* and an account of practical rationality-*as-such* which can command *universal assent*, and in terms of what he thinks it actually achieves, namely, the construction of *particular conceptions* of justice and practical rationality the superiority of which *could not* be demonstrated by an appeal to shared norms of rational inquiry. My particular focus will be MacIntyre's remarks on the liberal view of justice, and the explanations he favours for why current disputes over the nature of justice which occur among liberals, and between liberals and others, resist resolution.

> According to MacIntyre, liberalism claims to provide a political, legal and economic framework in which assent to one and the same set of rationally justifiable principles would enable those who espouse widely different and incompatible conceptions of the good life for human beings to live together peaceably within the same society, enjoying the same political status and engaging in the same economic relationships.[1]

MacIntyre supposes that liberals aim to secure a justification for the political, legal and economic framework of society that is independent of any 'overall theory of the human good'[2] and believe that the state may not legitimately seek to impose one particular conception of the good on its citizens. He argues that liberalism does not fulfil its promise, however. Instead it delivers a particular understanding of what principles of justice should be designed to achieve,[3] and debate over the precise formulation of these principles has become partially constitutive of liberalism itself.[4] Far from providing a conception of justice and an argument for it that are independent of any comprehensive theory of the good, liberalism has come to embody such a theory, *viz.* 'the continued sustenance of the liberal social and political order'.[5]

But liberalism includes a broad and diverse body of thought, and some important forms of liberalism properly so-called do not have the content or aspirations that MacIntyre attributes to liberalism-in-general. Perhaps the most important divide within contemporary liberalism concerns the issue of state neutrality, an official commitment to which MacIntyre regards as partially constitutive of liberalism itself. Some of those whom we quite justifiably regard as liberals argue that the state should pursue perfectionist policies through subsidies that are designed to protect and promote valuable aspects of the culture. Here I am thinking especially of Joseph Raz's work.[6] Even those liberals who support neutrality would now (influenced by Raz) distinguish between neutrality of *effect* and neutrality of *justification* and would defend the latter but not the former: they would claim that the state should not include as part of the justification for its policies the idea that one conception of the good is better than another, but would not argue that policies which happen to favour one conception of the good more than another should be eschewed or that the state should intervene in order to compensate others for any benefits received, as a result of state policy, by those committed to one particular conception of the good.[7]

Even within what MacIntyre regards as the framework of liberalism, there is substantial disagreement about which specific conception of justice should govern basic institutions. For example, the conceptions defended by both Rawls and Nozick are compatible with the framework MacIntyre describes but the latter is a historical theory because it maintains that the justice of a set of holdings depends on how it arose, whereas the former is an end-state theory because according to it the justice of a distribution depends on its current shape rather than how it came about. As MacIntyre implicitly acknowledges elsewhere,[8] these disputes do not merely concern 'the precise formulation of the principles of justice'.[9] Moreover, liberalism as MacIntyre characterizes it has been given different underpinnings by different theorists: J. S. Mill, for example, attempted to ground his liberalism in utility, whereas other influential liberals, such as Rawls and Nozick, have supposed that the framework of liberalism is constituted by a set of rights which are wholly independent of utility.

My purpose in drawing attention to the diversity and difference within liberalism is not merely to suggest that it is more complex than MacIntyre acknowledges;[10] it is also to raise questions about how he regards disputes *among* liberals and how this relates to his account of why disputes between liberals and their critics are so intractable. MacIntyre seems to be faced with a dilemma if he is to hold on to the view that liberalism is a *single* tradition: either he has to acknowledge that one tradition may contain a plurality of incommensurable theories, each with its own conception of justice and governed by its own norms of rational inquiry; or he has to accept that the same tradition may include quite different conceptions of justice which, even though they are commensurable, give rise to disagreement which is sometimes as intractable as when it occurs between adherents to different traditions.

Although MacIntyre does not explicitly confront this dilemma, it is possible to reconstruct what at least appear to be inconsistent responses he has to it by focusing on what he says in different places.[11] In *After Virtue*, for example, he argues that Rawls's and Nozick's theories are incommensurable,[12] which suggests he would favour grasping the first horn of the dilemma and conceding that there may be different theories of justice within the same tradition which are nevertheless incommensurable. He also maintains that the notion of utility and the notion of natural or human rights are incommensurable,[13] which suggests that forms of liberalism constructed around these different ideas must also be incommensurable. But it is difficult to see how MacIntyre could accept the view that Rawls's and Nozick's theories (or forms of liberalism based upon utility and forms based upon rights that are conceived as independent of utility) are part of the same tradition but incommensurable without compromising the notion of a tradition, for in *Whose Justice? Which Rationality?* he seems to regard incommensurability as a central and distinguishing feature of the relation between *different* traditions. So would MacIntyre take the other option I have offered him and regard theories such as Rawls's and Nozick's (and utilitarian and deontological forms of liberalism) as commensurable even though disagreements between their advocates are intractable? If he did this, he would lose the explanation that he favours for why disputes between, say, Rawlsians and Nozickians are so intractable: for MacIntyre the intractability of a dispute is always a symptom of the presence of incommensurability.

One way in which MacIntyre might seek to avoid the dilemma I have tried to force on him is to deny that liberalism, as it is ordinarily understood, is a single tradition.[14] After all, he does suppose that when disagreements occur within a tradition 'we have a set of relatively unproblematic standards to which to appeal in making the comparison'[15] and does not regard this as true of the disputes between those such as Rawls and Nozick, which makes it difficult to see how he could regard their theories as part of the same tradition. Perhaps we should think of

Rawls and Nozick, perfectionist and neutralist liberals, and utilitarian and deontological liberals, as each part of different but overlapping traditions. (That idea might receive some support from political philosophers who describe Rawls as a liberal but Nozick as a libertarian while acknowledging the continuities between Nozick's theory and classical liberalism.) But I think MacIntyre would be reluctant to make this move for he seems to assume that there are relatively few traditions of thought and that there can be considerable diversity and development within each of them.[16] Furthermore, in a passage which I find difficult to make fully intelligible, he writes:

> the inconclusiveness of debates within liberalism as to the fundamental principles of liberal justice reinforces the view that liberal theory is best understood, not as an attempt to find a rationality independent of tradition, but as itself the articulation of an historically developed and developing set of social institutions and forms of activity, that is, as the voice of a tradition.[17]

In this passage MacIntyre seems to consider that the existence of intractable dispute over principles of justice between those such as Rawls and Nozick is *evidence* of the fact that they are representatives of a single tradition.[18]

I do not know how to make all of MacIntyre's claims consistent but the most plausible position I am able to construct out of them takes the following form: it holds that different theories or arguments may be commensurable in some respects but incommensurable in others; it allows that within a particular tradition standards of assessment may be only partially shared; it maintains that even across different traditions there must be some commensurability, for we must at least share an acceptance of the laws of logic;[19] it distinguishes traditions of inquiry (at least in part) in terms of what is and what is not shared by way of standards of assessment. This interpretation is supported to some extent by MacIntyre's claim that Rawls and Nozick share some of the same social presuppositions because neither gives any role to the notion of desert and because they both operate within an 'individualistic' framework.[20] Presumably this is part of what makes them adherents of the same tradition. On this reading, however, there is no reason to suppose that differences *within* a tradition will be superficial since even within a tradition there may be profound disagreements and significant incommensurabilities. From this perspective, the notion of incommensurability is more fundamental to MacIntyre's account of the intractability of contemporary political disagreement than the notion of a tradition: it is supposed to provide at least a partial explanation not only for why disputes between liberals and their critics resist resolution but also for why disputes among different liberals are so hard to settle.

If MacIntyre's account is to be illuminating he needs to supply us with relatively clear criteria for deciding where some degree of incommensurability exists and where it does not. To say that it is present whenever disputes resist rational resolution is unsatisfactory, for at best this is a symptom of incommensurability not a criterion of it. So what does MacIntyre mean by saying that some theories are incommensurable? At the most general level he believes that theories are partially incommensurable when they do not share all of the same standards of assessment by which they may be compared. At a more specific level he seems to think that there are a number of related ways in which different theories may fail to share all such standards: they may start from different premises; they may have different conceptions of rational acceptability; they may be partially untranslatable. Let me consider each of these possibilities in turn.

Incommensurability: Different Basic Premises

In *After Virtue* MacIntyre says the following when he discusses the relation between Rawls's and Nozick's conceptions of justice:

> Rawls makes primary what is in effect a principle of equality with respect to needs ... Nozick makes primary what is a principle of equality with respect to entitlement ... For Rawls ... justice is made into a matter of present patterns of distribution to which the past is irrelevant. For Nozick only evidence about what has been legitimately acquired in the past is relevant.[21]

In MacIntyre's view, the theories Rawls and Nozick defend are more articulate and more coherent versions of political arguments presented by 'ordinary non-philosophical citizens'. They inherit the general problem that although the conclusions each arrives at can be logically derived from the premises from which they start, there is no shared rational way of deciding between them.[22]

MacIntyre believes that disputes between Rawls and Nozick (and between the citizens whose views they represent in a more articulate form) are intractable at least partly because each starts from different basic premises.[23] The term 'basic premise' is not one that MacIntyre himself invokes and I employ it in a semi-technical sense: a premise is basic for a person if and only if she can have no further reasons for accepting it and no objections others bring to it count against it from her perspective, that is, given her set of beliefs, the norms of rational argument she accepts and those beliefs and norms she must accept on pain of unintelligibility. It seems to follow that if disputants do have different basic premises, then they will not share enough ground for disputes between them to be settled by rational means.

Do Rawls's and Nozick's theories of justice rest upon different basic premises? If so, what would these basic premises be? Consider some candidates that MacIntyre mentions. For Nozick:[24]

1   Each individual has inalienable rights;
2   A distribution is just provided that everyone is entitled to what they have;
3   A person is entitled to what he has provided that he acquired it by legitimate means.

For Rawls:[25]

4   The principles of justice for any social order are those principles that would be chosen by a rational agent from behind 'a veil of ignorance' such that he does not know what his place in society will be.

Are any of (1), (2), (3) and (4) basic premises in the sense described? As MacIntyre points out, Nozick does not offer much in the way of argument for (1), apart from some vague remarks about the separateness of persons; however, others have tried to offer considerations in support of it and those who accept is certainly do not regard it as foundational. This implies that it is not a basic premise. Construed in a suitably broad way, (2) and (3) are perhaps basic premises but only because they can then be understood as analytic truths: the substantive questions would have to do with what entitlements people have and what is to count as 'legitimate means'. (Arguably, however, not even analytic truths are basic premises, for it is possible to give reasons in favour of their acceptance, couched in terms of an explanation of the meanings of the expressions within them.) (4) is not a basic premise; others have given reasons against it which Rawlsians have acknowledged require a response and Rawls himself has defended it.

So (1) and (4) do not seem to be basic premises, and even if (2) and (3) are basic premises, when they are understood in this way they turn out to be mutually acceptable. It might be maintained that we merely have to go back further in order to demonstrate that debates between those such as Rawls and Nozick rest on different basic premises. But this is not self-evident and I do not know any way of reconstructing their theories in order to show that it is the case. It is not a logical requirement that there be basic premises. Our beliefs might fit together in such a way that no one belief was unsupported by others. Furthermore, it is unclear how a belief could ever be *justifiably* held if it rested on basic premises. A plausible epistemological principle is that *justifying beliefs must themselves be justifiable*. If this principle is correct, then were a belief to rest on basic premises it would lack justification unless these basic premises could themselves be justified. But how could a basic premise be justified if no reasons can be given in favour of it? In order to be justified in believing that p, it seems that one must *have reasons* for believing that p, therefore no basic premise can be justified. This line of argument, which I owe to David Brink, seems to provide support for a coherentist theory of justification, according to which a belief is justified provided that it coheres with others; the threat to the principle that justifying beliefs must be justifiable which is posed by the danger of an infinite regress of justifications is defused by recognizing the possibility of justificatory loops which are not *viciously* circular.[26]

This argument against the possibility of a justified basic premise is inconclusive, however, for one might plausibly ask why the requirement that justifying beliefs themselves be justified requires these beliefs to be justified by other *beliefs* rather than, say, by the fact that certain conditions obtain. I might be justified in believing that I am seeing a chair because I am perceiving the relevant object under conditions favourable for perception even if I had no second order *beliefs* about what kinds of conditions were favourable for perception. That is to say, one might defend an externalist theory of justification, just as some have defended an externalist theory of knowledge. An externalist theory of knowledge holds that a person may know that p even though he is unaware of satisfying one or all of the conditions which make it true that he knows that p: for example, Alvin Goldman supposes that A knows that p if and only if: (i) p is true; (ii) A believes that p; (iii) p is justified; (iv) the fact that p causes A's belief that p.[27] This theory of knowledge is externalist since the fact that p causes A's belief that p may be something of which A is unaware. Similarly one might defend an externalist theory of justification according to which A may be justified in believing that p by satisfying some condition that he or she was unaware of satisfying:[28] for instance, I might be justified in believing that Bill Clinton is President of the United States if my belief is acquired through reliable procedures, and my belief might be justified in this way even if I do not have any beliefs about what kind of methods are reliable for establishing its truth.

This problem with Brink's argument (or, at least, its inconclusiveness) does not seem to help MacIntyre, however. The most plausible externalist theory of moral justification would involve the idea that moral and political beliefs could be justified only if they were acquired as a result of employing reliable methods of inquiry, and it is unclear what a reliable method of inquiry could be, other than one which (in general) will lead to the truth. So if MacIntyre were to appeal to a theory of justification of this kind in order to show how moral beliefs which rested on basic premises could be justified by them, he would need to allow that two different but incompatible judgements which constituted basic premises for different people could be the deliverances of a reliable method of inquiry, and hence that we could be justified in accepting both as true. But as MacIntyre concedes elsewhere, it is part of the concept of truth that if two theses are incompatible they cannot both *be* true,[29] and since we know that they can't both be true, surely we can't be justified in believing either in the absence of reasons for accepting one rather than the other.

In *Whose Justice? Which Rationality?* MacIntyre seems to shift his position from the one that he maintained in *After Virtue*, for he acknowledges that even the 'first principles' of a tradition stand in need of justification:

> In systematizing and ordering the truths they take themselves to have discovered, the adherents of a tradition may well assign a primary place in the structures of their reasoning to certain truths and treat them as first metaphysical or practical principles . . . But such first principles themselves, and indeed the whole body of which they are a part, themselves will be understood to require justification.[30]

In MacIntyre's view, first principles are ultimately justified in terms of the success or failure of the *whole theory* in solving the problems it sets for itself, judged by its own standards. That concession allows first principles to meet the condition that justifying beliefs must themselves be justifiable; indeed, these principles would not be *basic* premises in my technical sense. But then it becomes unclear why the incorporation of different first principles should make two theories incommensurable, for it would not necessarily mean that they lacked shared standards of assessment; that would be a further claim, and would have to rest on a different basis.

Even if we allow the possibility of first principles which are subject to justification in terms of the success or failure of the whole theory in solving the problems it confronts, it does not follow that, for instance, Rawls's and Nozick's theories rest on different first principles. Indeed I have already cast doubt on that idea by arguing that the premises that MacIntyre supposes are the building blocks of each theory are not genuinely foundational because defenders of them do recognize, in the face of criticism, that they stand in need of some *local* justification; they are not judged solely in terms of the success or failure of the *whole* theory. It is far from clear that any of the moral and political positions currently available, or indeed any of the traditions MacIntyre narrates, embody what he calls 'first principles'. In explaining a theory we need to start somewhere, but it does not follow that what is taken for granted will amount to a set of first principles, for it may be given support by other parts of the theory which are described only later. Again there need be no first principles; a theory may be constituted by a network of beliefs none of which is primary in that sense.

Incommensurability: Different Conceptions of Rational Resolvability

The second way in which MacIntyre supposes that moral and political positions may be incommensurable is by employing different conceptions of rational acceptability. Although this is related to the idea that theories may rest on different basic premises or first principles, it is not reducible to that idea except when these premises or principles are norms of rational acceptability. (Since I have in effect already discussed that special case, I shall not consider it in this section.)

MacIntyre argues that there is more to rationality than the laws of logic:

> observance of the laws of logic is only a necessary and not a sufficient condition for rationality, whether theoretical or practical. It is on what has to be added to observance of the laws of logic to justify ascriptions of rationality – whether to oneself or to others, whether to modes of enquiry or to justifications of belief, or to courses of action and their justification – that disagreement arises.[31]

So MacIntyre might contend that whether a belief within a theory is rationally justified depends not only on the observance of the laws of logic but also on which particular principles of rational acceptability are employed in assessing it and what weighting is given to them. This kind of proposal has an analogue within the philosophy of science. Thomas Kuhn has argued that there is no neutral algorithm for theory choice within science and that scientists may disagree about the value to attach to considerations such as fruitfulness, scope and simplicity in comparing the merits of different theories: those who attribute great weight to fruitfulness may regard the acceptance of one theory as rationally justified that others who attribute great weight to simplicity would not.[32] But considerations such as simplicity, scope and fruitfulness do not seem to play a significant role in explaining the intractability of the kind of moral and political disputes that arise between Rawls and Nozick: the attaching of different importance to considerations such as fruitfulness, scope and simplicity does not seem to explain why these sorts of disagreement resist resolution.

The acceptability of a theory must depend, at least in part, on what it is aiming to achieve. Might it be the case that the *goals* of different theories of justice vary and thereby generate different conceptions of rational acceptability? It is tempting to reply that the goals of these theories cannot vary because each theory must aim to provide a correct or true account of the nature of justice. But that response ignores the way in which a conception of justice may be developed under different constraints. For example, Rawls currently understands the theory he has developed – 'justice as fairness' – as an attempt to secure agreement on a particular conception of justice in the face of conflicting comprehensive conceptions of the good. Rawls supposes that 'an overlapping consensus' of this kind is important because it would enable citizens to justify their major institutions to one another and thereby secure a morally acceptable basis for social unity.[33] He argues that in order to achieve it we should not presuppose any controversial ideas of the good, and should eschew controversial metaphysical assumptions in arguing for a conception of justice; indeed he would not say that 'justice as fairness' aims at the *truth*, for that would raise the contentious metaphysical question of whether theories of justice can be properly understood as attempts to describe some aspect of reality. It is not clear that Nozick's concerns are so different, however. Even if he would not share Rawls's reluctance to say that he aims to provide a true theory of justice, he, like Rawls, does aim to develop a theory that is rationally acceptable to all, and which delineates an area within which the state should not intervene but should allow individuals to pursue their own conceptions of the good, whatever they may be.

When we cast our net wider and consider liberal conceptions of justice which do not have the public justifiability of major institutions as one of their goals, or further still to include non-liberal conceptions such as an Aristotelian conception based on desert, it is unclear that differences in aim introduce any element of incommensurability. This is because it is possible to enter into debate about what constraints an adequate theory of justice *should* satisfy: each conception of justice is developed in the light of a set of beliefs about what makes it adequate and these beliefs are not, in general, regarded as immune to criticism. If the epistemological principle that justifying beliefs must themselves be justifiable is correct, the constraints imposed on an adequate theory of justice will stand in need of justification. So, for example, it can be argued against Rawls that reaching agreement should not be an overriding goal in developing a conception of justice, for that will lead to the exclusion of contentious considerations which are nevertheless morally relevant. Rawls needs to show that the considerations he excludes are not morally relevant for developing what (even by his own lights) is an adequate theory of justice.

Of course there may be profound differences in belief over what would constitute an adequate theory of justice: some will say that we should aim to develop a true theory; others, who doubt whether truth could be properly attributed to a theory of justice, may argue that we should construct a theory which matches our considered judgements, or a theory which allows for the possibility of an overlapping consensus, or a theory which furthers the interests of a particular class. These differences may also play a role in explaining the intractability of disputes over the acceptability of some theory of justice. But it does not follow that different theories of justice include different conceptions of *rational acceptability*, for defenders of these theories usually acknowledge that the goals which inform the development of them require justification. Futhermore if it is the case that no belief of this kind can be justified unless reasons can be given for accepting it, then these goals would stand in need of justification no matter how they were regarded by those who developed theories in the light of them. MacIntyre might argue that, nevertheless, the considerations one group of people regard as a rational justification for accepting some theory of justice will not be regarded in the same way by another group. But this would not show that it is impossible to give considerations which, properly understood, should have some force for all participants in the debate, given their existing methodological commitments, those they can be persuaded to accept on the basis of what they already believe, and those they must accept on pain of unintelligibility.

Incommensurability: Partial Untranslatability

The third source of incommensurability which MacIntyre acknowledges arises out of the difficulty there may be in *representing* the views expressed in one tradition or theory in another. MacIntyre argues that different claims made from within different theories or conceptual frameworks may be partially *untranslatable* from one to the other. Unlike the two previous sources of incommensurability, which allow that theories may be incommensurable *and* incompatible, where a failure of translatability exists it appears that there cannot be genuine incompatibility: if two claims cannot be adequately expressed in the same language they cannot be either compatible or incompatible.[34]

MacIntyre is, I think, successful in arguing for the *possibility* of partial failure of translatability:[35] the experience of coming to speak a second language as a native (that is, as 'a second first language') may give us good reason to suppose that a claim made in one of these languages cannot be fully and adequately expressed in the other. But what reasons do we have for thinking that the different moral and political stand-points confronting us today may be partially untranslatable from one to the other? A central theme of *After Virtue* is that our current moral discourse consists of bogus terms such as 'rights' and 'utility' which have no proper reference so are moral fictions,[36] and of fragments from older moral vocabularies, prised from the historical and social contexts which originally gave them their meaning:

> What we possess ... are the fragments of a conceptual scheme, parts of which now lack those contexts from which their significance derived. We possess indeed simulacra of morality, we continue to use many of the key expressions. But we have – very largely, if not entirely – lost our comprehension, both theoretical and practical, of morality.[37]

One example MacIntyre gives to illustrate this general thesis is the use of the concept of desert in discussions of matters of distributive justice. Appeals to desert exhibit 'an adherence to an older, more traditional, more Aristotelian and Christian view of justice. ... In the conceptual melange of moral thought and practice today fragments from the tradition – virtue concepts for the most part – are still found alongside modern individualist concepts such as those of rights or utility.'[38] So perhaps MacIntyre is supposing that when moral claims are framed in terms of desert they are not fully translatable into any claim of equivalent meaning that is expressible in a liberal-individualist framework, even after an attempt has been made to speak each 'language' as a first language. He contends that the 'notion of desert is at home *only* in the context of a community whose primary bond is a shared understanding both of the good for man and of the good of that community and where individuals identify their primary interests with reference to those goods.'[39] But it is far from obvious that MacIntyre is correct if he does mean to suggest that claims about distributive justice based on desert cannot be *expressed* in a liberal-individualist framework. All his argument entitles him to conclude is that claims which relate distributive justice to desert are *incompatible* with a liberal-individualist framework and if they are genuinely incompatible with it that would show that it is possible for them to be adequately *represented* within it; incompatibility implies translatability.

This point applies quite generally. Suppose that there are difficulties in translating from, say, ancient Greek to contemporary English. If (as MacIntyre accepts) 'the languages of modernity' do, to some extent at least, genuinely draw on ancient thought and practice, what reason do we have for believing that this process will create untranslatabilities within these languages rather than provide the resources for constructing incompatible (and hence intertranslatable) theories, for instance, theories of justice based on utility and theories of justice based on desert?

Tradition-Dependent Rationality and Conceptions of Rational Resolvability

The arguments considered so far have not been sufficient to justify MacIntyre's belief in the existence of significant incommensurabilities between the different moral and political positions that confront us today and compete for our allegiances. We have not been given sufficient reason to think that different moral and political positions rest on different basic premises or first principles, or that they embody different norms of rational acceptability, and have not been given sufficient reason to believe that the claims made from any one of the moral and political positions which are available to us cannot be adequately represented in the others. Consequently MacIntyre has not provided us with a justification for accepting the explanation he proposes for why contemporary disagreements among liberals, and between liberals and their critics, are so intractable.

MacIntyre's discussion of these issues is nevertheless illuminating in other respects. What I find attractive in it is his rejection of the idea that rationality is something which is independent of any social practice: in his view rationality, or rationalities, are *immanent* in human practice, in traditions of thought and activity; they do not *transcend* that practice. The idea that rationality is immanent in social practice is largely what distances MacIntyre from what we might call (at the risk of some over-simplification) 'the Enlightenment conception of rationality'. In this respect MacIntyre's writings are congruent with the work of several of those who have been influenced by the later Wittgenstein, such as Susan Hurley, Jonathan Lear, Sabina Lovibond and John McDowell.[40] According to the line of thought they have developed, what a person means by some term or expression, and what it is for her to apply it in the same way in future situations, is not (and could not be) determined by some inner mental act or entity, but rather is determined by the practice of which the use of that term or expression is a part. Consequently whether a consideration is a reason for a person to draw some conclusion cannot be assessed from some standpoint independent of the practice, but must be judged from within the practice itself. This brief description glosses over several issues which divide the authors whom I have mentioned, and the moves I have attributed to them stand in need of defence; my purpose was merely to draw attention to the affinity of their ideas to MacIntyre's account.

According to Lear's variant of the position described, not even the laws of logic transcend human practice: our ability to grasp these laws and to employ them depends on our being 'minded' in one way rather than another as a result of an ultimately coercive process of socialization. We share 'the perceptions of salience, routes of interest, feelings of naturalness in following a rule, etc. that constitute being part of a certain form of life'[41] because we have been inducted into it. But if we accept the view that rationality is immanent in human practice, can we avoid MacIntyre's conclusion that rationality and justification vary from one tradition of thought to another? If what counts as justification is determined by social practice, why can't there be a variety of moral and political practices within a single society, each embodying different conceptions of justice and different norms of justification?

We cannot make sense of the idea that, for example, the laws of deductive logic might vary from one social practice to another: we could never have a reason to say of others that they followed different rules of logic as opposed to made meaningless noises. If we are to be justified in attributing *thought* to others, we must regard them as following the laws of logic.[42] But beyond the laws of logic, there is no *guarantee* that norms of justification will be shared by all those we number as thinking beings. In principle at least, it would be possible for there to be a number of equally coherent but mutually exclusive sets of beliefs for interpreting and reconstructing the social world. In that case what counted as a reason for one group of people to draw a conclusion might not count as a reason for others to do so. Nothing I have said in the last three sections denies the *possibility* of this kind of incommensurability between different outlooks: different positions might start from conflicting basic premises; they might embody different conceptions of rational acceptability; the claims of one might be untranslatable into the other. My argument has merely been that MacIntyre is unsuccessful in showing that any of these possibilities is actualized within present-day moral and political debate. So why has it seemed so natural to many, such as MacIntyre, to conclude that one or more of these possibilities has been actualized and that this is why contemporary moral and political disagreement is so intractable?

I think the conviction that there are important incommensurabilities between the moral and political positions which confront us – that partly explain why, for example, disagreements among liberals and between liberals and their critics are so intractable – is often motivated by the implicit acceptance of a feature of the Enlightenment conception of rational resolvability. This feature is the idea that if an argument is a good one it must be persuasive for any reasonable person who accepts its premises, and hence its conclusion is a potential object of a rational consensus among all reasonable persons who accept its premises.[43] It seems unlikely that the premises we share could ever enable us to construct rationally coercive arguments of this kind in order to resolve moral and political disputes, and so we are tempted to conclude that different positions apply different standards of assessment.

But if a person may reasonably but mistakenly refuse to accept the conclusion of a good argument despite accepting its premises, it becomes more plausible to suppose that many disagreements may in principle be rationally resolvable by appeal to shared standards of assessment, even though they are intractable in practice. The intractability of a dispute would not then be a reliable sign of the presence of incommensurability of one sort or another; the achievement of consensus would not be something we should expect, and, indeed, continued disagreement would be predictable.[44] I suggest that in morality and politics there is considerable scope for what we might call 'reasonable disagreement': it is often possible for two people (A and B) to disagree about the truth of some moral and political judgement, when even though A is mistaken, and B can be justified in regarding A as mistaken, it would not be unreasonable or absurd (by anyone's lights) for A to continue to hold on to her belief in its truth, even when confronted by B's good reasons for rejecting it.

MacIntyre comes close to identifying the idea that if an argument is a good one it must be persuasive for any reasonable person who accepts its premises as an element of the Enlightenment conception of rational resolvability. For example, he says it is a tenet of Enlightenment cultures that 'rational debate could always, if adequately conducted, have a conclusive outcome. The point and purpose of rational debate was to establish truths and only those methods were acceptable which led to the conclusive refutation of error and vindication of truth.'[45] He also expresses scepticism about the possibility of demonstrative argument in philosophy and maintains that issues may be settled rationally in the absence of proof:

> Arguments in philosophy rarely take the form of proofs; and the most successful arguments on topics central to philosophy never do. (The ideal of *proof* is a relatively barren one in philosophy.) Consequently those who wish to resist some particular conclusion are equally rarely without any resort. Let me hasten to add immediately that I do not mean to suggest by this that no central issues in philosophy are settlable; on the contrary. We can often establish the truth in areas where no proofs are available.[46]

But, I shall argue, MacIntyre does not give ideas such as these the role and significance he ought.

MacIntyre notes the possibility of moral arguments which 'point towards rather than entail some conclusion', in which the considerations cited 'provide support for the conclusion if a particular kind of weight is attached to them'.[47] However, he contends that there is no established agreement on *why* one set of considerations is relevant but not another and 'no established agreement upon how these [considerations] are to be ranked in importance or weight, such ranking being in practice largely a matter of individual preferences'.[48] But why rule out the possibility of there being considerations which on balance count in favour of a conclusion, but which nevertheless do not ensure its truth, and where it is impossible to give a *principled* account of the relative importance of these considerations? Of course there will generally be disputes over the ranking of the different considerations which on balance provide support for a conclusion but this does not show that these judgements must be subjective or merely reflect personal preferences: I suggest that the temptation to believe this is the case arises from MacIntyre's implicit belief that if an argument is a good one (within a tradition, of course!), it must be persuasive for a person who accepts its premises and is reasonable by the standards of *any* tradition.[49]

MacIntyre may be right that *in practice* the ranking of different considerations tends to be merely a matter of personal preferences but this does not rule out the possibility that the weightings people give as a consequence of their personal preferences are mistaken. Of course it would be naive to expect consensus even when people's rankings are not motivated by their personal preferences: reasonable people may continue to disagree. However, that does not imply there is no correct ranking to be given to the various considerations. Acknowledging the possibility that there may be a correct ranking of considerations even though the correctness of this ranking cannot be demonstrated to the satisfaction of every reasonable person who accepts that they each have *some* force also has the advantage of being faithful to the phenomenology of moral experience: we do not generally believe that it is merely a matter of personal preference how we balance out competing considerations and we do struggle to find what what we think is a correct weighting.

MacIntyre does allow that disputes between traditions with their own norms of rational inquiry may be rationally resolvable in some cases.[50] A particular tradition T1 may face an epistemological crisis in which it confronts and fails to deal with what is for it an important incoherence and in which another tradition T2 can provide a cogent and illuminating explanation, by the standards of T1, for why this incoherence has arisen within T1. Nevertheless the picture that MacIntyre seems to work with is one according to which epistemological crises are (as a matter of fact) resolved by rationally compelling and irresistible arguments offered by adherents of one tradition to those of another: epistemological crises occur when 'trusted methods of inquiry have become sterile';[51] the solution to them requires the development of new types of theory which meet 'three highly exacting requirements';[52] when other traditions develop these theories, those who adhere to the tradition in crisis are 'compelled' to give up their allegiance to it since it has been 'defeated'.[53] MacIntyre ignores what seems to me to be the norm, *viz.*, the circumstance in which a person gradually shifts her position as a result of arguments which are neither individually nor jointly compelling, since a reasonable person might reject them even if they accept their premises, but which are nevertheless rationally persuasive.

Of course, a failure to be persuaded by a good argument (within a tradition) may be explicable by factors other than the reasons a person has for making the judgements they do. No doubt in many cases (most, I expect), non-rational factors will be relevant in explaining a person's allegiances, and the most powerful explanations will integrate rational and non-rational considerations in explaining why a consideration is salient or overriding for one person but not for another.

NOTES

I would like to thank Roger Crisp, John Horton, John Kenyon, Sabina Lovibond, Susan Mendus and Andrew Moore for their helpful comments on this piece. Most of the work for it was completed while I was a British Academy Postdoctoral Fellow and I would like to thank the Academy for their support.

1   *Whose Justice? Which Rationality?* (Duckworth, London, 1988), pp. 335–6.
2   Ibid., p. 343.
3   See ibid., p. 344.
4   See ibid., pp. 335, 344.
5   Ibid., p. 345.
6   See J. Raz, *The Morality of Freedom* (Oxford University Press, Oxford, 1986).
7   See W. Kymlicka, 'Liberal individualism and liberal neutrality', *Ethics*, 99 (1989); J. Rawls, 'The priority of right and ideas of the good', *Philosophy and Public Affairs*, 17 (1988).
8   *After Virtue* (University of Notre Dame Press, Notre Dame, 1981), ch. 17.
9   *Whose Justice? Which Rationality?*, p. 344.
10 Cf. B. Barry, 'The light that failed?', *Ethics*, 100 (1989), p. 166; R. P. George, 'Moral particularism, Thomism, and traditions', *Review of Metaphysics*, 42 (1989), pp. 604–5.
11 There is some reason to think that MacIntyre has changed his attitude towards liberalism and has moved from regarding it in *After Virtue* as the absence of tradition to regarding it in *Whose Justice? Which Rationality?* as the expression of one. (On this point, see S. Mulhall, 'Liberalism, morality and rationality: MacIntyre, Rawls and Cavell', ch. 11 above.) Unless MacIntyre has also changed his position on the relation between Rawls's and Nozick's theories of justice, and on the notions of rights and utility, I see no harm in drawing on his earlier views on these matters in order to illuminate his present understanding of liberalism.

12 See *After Virtue*, pp. 229–32.

13 See ibid., p. 70.

14 Cf. Barry, 'The light that failed?', p. 165.

15 *Whose Justice? Which Rationality?*, p. 328.

16 In *Whose Justice?* MacIntyre considers four traditions: Aristotelianism, Aquinas's synthesis of Aristotelianism and Augustinian Christianity, the seventeenth- and eighteenth-century Scottish tradition and liberalism. He also mentions the possibility of giving accounts of Judaism, the Prussian Tradition, and the traditions 'engendered in India and China'. Ibid., pp. 10–11.

17 Ibid., p. 345; cf. p. 349.

18 Admittedly that is not the main point MacIntyre is making in the passage quoted: he is emphasizing that liberalism is best understood as presenting a conception of justice dependent on a tradition rather than a conception of justice-as-such.

19 See, e.g., *Whose Justice? Which Rationality?*, p. 351.

20 See *After Virtue*, pp. 231–4. MacIntyre writes: 'Individuals are thus in both accounts primary and society secondary, and the identification of individual interests is prior to, and independent of, the construction of any moral or social bonds between them' (ibid.).

21 Ibid., p. 231.

22 See ibid., pp. 8, 231.

23 See ibid., ch. 2.

24 See ibid., p. 230–1.

25 See ibid., pp. 229–31.

26 See D. Brink, *Moral Realism and the Foundations of Ethics* (Cambridge University Press, Cambridge, 1989), ch. 5.

27 See A. Goldman, 'A causal theory of knowledge', *Journal of Philosophy*, 64 (1967), pp. 357–72. See also R. Nozick, *Philosophical Explanations* (Oxford University Press, Oxford, 1981), ch. 3, for a defence of an alternative externalist theory.

28 See J. Dancy, *Introduction to Contemporary Epistemology* (Blackwell, Oxford, 1986), 9.2–4.

29 See *Whose Justice? Which Rationality?*, pp. 352ff. MacIntyre does not want to identify 'truth' with 'warranted assertability' for that might have the consequence that two mutually incompatible beliefs were true. Cf. *Three Rival Versions of Moral Enquiry* (Duckworth, London, 1990), pp. 121–2.

30 *Whose Justice? Which Rationality?*, p. 360.

31 Ibid., p. 4.

32 See T. Kuhn, *The Structure of Scientific Revolutions*, 2nd edn (University of Chicago Press, Chicago, 1970), esp. section 5 of the Postscript; 'Objectivity, value judgement, and theory choice', in *The Essential Tension* (University of Chicago Press, Chicago, 1977).

33 See J. Rawls, 'The idea of an overlapping consensus', *Oxford Journal of Legal Studies*, 7 (1987).

34 Cf. D. McNaughton, *Moral Vision: An Introduction to Ethics* (Blackwell, Oxford, 1988), 10.2.

35 See *Whose Justice? Which Rationality?*, ch. 19.

36 See *After Virtue*, ch. 6.

37 Ibid., p. 8. Cf. *Three Rival Versions*, p. 29.

38 *After Virtue*, p. 234.

39 Ibid., p. 233, emphasis added.

40 See S. Hurley, *Natural Reasons: Persons and Polity* (Oxford University Press,

Oxford, 1989); S. Lovibond, *Realism and Imagination in Ethics* (Blackwell, Oxford, 1983), sections 10, 36; J. Lear, 'Leaving the world alone', *Journal of Philosophy*, 79 (1982); J. McDowell, 'Virtue and reason', *The Monist*, 62 (1979), and 'Values and secondary qualities', in *Morality and Objectivity: A Tribute to J. L. Mackie*, ed. T. Honderich (Routledge and Kegan Paul, London, 1985).

41 Lear, 'Leaving the world alone', p. 385.

42 Cf. D. Davidson, 'On the very idea of a conceptual scheme' in his *Inquiries into Truth and Interpretation* (Oxford University Press, Oxford, 1984). Davidson would go further and would say that a person couldn't *have* thoughts unless they followed the laws of logic.

43 The assumption that if an argument is a good one it must be persuasive for any reasonable person who accepts its premises has led many philosophers to celebrate deductive reasoning and to attempt to force their arguments into this form, for deductive arguments are such that any reasonable person who accepts the premises must (on pain of absurdity) accept the conclusion when they become aware of the deductive relation between them. Inductive arguments, by contrast, have frequently been regarded as problematic and in need of justification in a way that deductive arguments are not because it is not so clearly absurd to accept the premises yet deny the conclusion of a good inductive argument.

44 In my *Explaining Political Disagreement* (Cambridge University Press, Cambridge, 1993), ch. 2, I argue that the best understanding of the notion of an essentially contested concept incorporates this idea.

45 *Three Rival Versions*, p. 172; cf. pp. 170, 225.

46 *After Virtue*, p. 241.

47 *Three Rival Versions*, p. 10.

48 Ibid., p. 11.

49 Mulhall makes a related claim about MacIntyre's conception of what constitutes a good moral reason: see p. 212 above.

50 See *Whose Justice? Which Rationality?*, pp. 364–6. This seems to mark a shift from MacIntyre's position in *After Virtue* where he writes that 'the facts of incommensurability *ensure* that protestors [against the invasion of someone's rights in the name of someone else's utility] can never win an *argument*' (p. 69, first emphasis added).

51 *Whose Justice? Which Rationality?*, p. 362.

52 Ibid.

53 See ibid., pp. 364–5.

13

Virtues, Practices and Justice

David Miller

Alasdair MacIntyre has proposed to us, in his books *After Virtue* and *Whose Justice? Which Rationality?*, an account of the moral virtues, and in particular the virtue of justice, which contrasts radically with the accounts that are standardly given in contemporary moral and political philosophy. According to MacIntyre, morality itself must primarily be understood in terms of the virtues exhibited by moral agents (rather than, say, in terms of rules or obligations); and these virtues themselves must first of all be understood in terms of those forms of human activity that he calls 'practices'. Among the virtues, justice occupies a central place, and so to provide a satisfactory answer to the question 'What is justice?' we must begin by examining the practices which give justice both its content and its rationale: by looking at these practices we can discover what justice is, concretely, and also why it should be counted a virtue. Although the specific requirements of justice will differ from practice to practice, a common thread running through these various manifestations is the idea of *desert*. 'Justice is a disposition to give to each person, including oneself, what that person deserves and to treat no one in a way incompatible with their deserts.'[1]

In giving this account, MacIntyre sets himself in diametric opposition to modern liberalism and the moral and political philosophy that corresponds to it. According to MacIntyre, the general defect of that philosophy, when it is not merely emotivist or subjectivist, is that it tries to derive moral rules and injunctions from an abstract principle of reason. But such an enterprise is bound to fail, for none of the principles that have been proposed can actually be made to yield concrete conclusions, as the history of both utilitarianism and Kantianism shows. In the case of justice, we find a proliferation of principles and theories of justice each claiming to embody demonstrable truth, but there is no reason to think that the contest between them will ever be resolved. Liberalism, MacIntyre claims, has become a tradition within which enquiries into the nature of justice are ceaselessly pursued, but it is tacitly taken for granted that the search will never, in fact, come to an end.

In giving this brief sketch of those claims of MacIntyre's that I wish to discuss, I have drawn on both *After Virtue* and *Whose Justice? Which Rationality?*, but before beginning the substantive enquiry I need to say a little about the relationship between the two books.[2] MacIntyre's own view is that the second is a continuation of the first and was written primarily in order to fill a major lacuna in *After Virtue*, namely the omission of any account of practical rationality which would enable us to say in what sense moral disputes could be rationally resolved within a tradition of thought, as well as to adjudicate between competing traditions.[3] This methodological shift is, however, also accompanied by a change of substance which is more germane to my enquiry here. It can be summed up by saying that whereas Aristotle is the hero of *After Virtue*, Aquinas is at least nominally the hero of *Whose Justice? Which Rationality?*. In the first book, the preferred alternative to liberalism is a morality of the virtues, which explicates the latter primarily in terms of their role in sustaining practices, and the account given of justice exemplifies that pattern. Aristotle is presented as the main protagonist of this position. In the second book, however, the Aristotelian account of justice is presented as being incorporated in, and superseded by, the Thomist account. But in this account practices no longer occupy a central place (if indeed any place at all), and justice is understood first and foremost in terms of legality – to be just is to do what the law, natural or positive, requires of you. MacIntyre signals this shift of approach in the postscript to the second edition of *After Virtue* and in the preface to *Whose Justice? Which Rationality?*. But he fails to explore its implications for the contrast between premodern and modern conceptions of morality and justice which provides both books with their main organizing idea. For it seems that we have here two very different premodern understandings of justice, and also that the Thomist account to which MacIntyre eventually gives his blessing is in several respects closer than the Aristotelian account to the liberal view of justice that he rejects, especially in its Lockean and Kantian incarnations.

So we face an expository and critical difficulty. Which of the two texts should we use in a critical assessment of MacIntyre on justice? I think that we need to be guided not by temporal sequence but by the interest and cogency of the ideas expressed. And here *After Virtue* scores inasmuch as we are given a clear exposition and defence of the Aristotelian position, whereas in *Whose Justice? Which Rationality?* that account is repeated in its essentials, but then juxtaposed to a second view which, as I have just argued, is inconsistent with the first; moreover MacIntyre gives only the most cursory of indications as to why he prefers the

Thomist view to the Aristotelian. I shall therefore identify as MacIntyre's main doctrine the practice-based account of the virtues developed in *After Virtue* and reiterated in the case of justice in the early chapters of *Whose Justice? Which Rationality?*. Most of the paper will be devoted to the analysis and critical appraisal of that doctrine, and only towards the end will I turn to consider, briefly, whether the Thomist position might provide a more promising account of justice.

So let us now turn to examine MacIntyre's argument that the virtues must first of all be explained in terms of those forms of human activity that he calls 'practices'. To show that a quality is a virtue is to show that its possession is essential to sustain one or more practices and to achieve those goods which the practices serve to foster. As the argument proceeds, this initial claim is qualified in certain respects. The concrete virtues that are displayed as one engages in a series of practices must knit together in such a way that a life of virtue can be seen overall as a coherent good life for a particular person. Moreover a society's range of practices must harmonize with one another so that it forms a community with an overarching conception of the good life within which specific virtues have a well-defined place. In this way MacIntyre imposes coherence conditions – individual and communal – on his original account. None the less, the original account remains central to his claim that modern society can no longer sustain a morality of virtue, for the basis of that claim is precisely that modern society lacks the practices which might give the virtues a determinate content.

What, then, does MacIntyre mean by a practice? It is, he says,

> any coherent and complex form of socially established co-operative human activity through which goods internal to that form of activity are realised in the course of trying to achieve those standards of excellence which are appropriate to, and partially definitive of, that form of activity, with the result that human powers to achieve excellence, and human conceptions of the ends and goods involved, are systematically extended.[4]

Among the examples he gives are games (chess and football), productive activities (farming and architecture), intellectual activities (science and history), artistic pursuits (painting and music) and politics (creating a political community). Other activities are firmly ruled out: tic-tac-toe, bricklaying and planting turnips. To make sense of the inclusions and the exclusions, we need to pay attention to two elements in the lengthy definition cited above: the idea of internal goods and the idea of standards of excellence. Goods internal to a practice are distinguished from those external to it by the fact that those in the former class can *only* be achieved by participating in the practice in question. To borrow MacIntyre's example, the good that consists in playing chess well is an internal good, whereas the money one may earn through being a champion chess player is an external good: it is merely contingent that playing chess should be the means whereby somebody enriches himself, whereas the good of playing well can for obvious reasons only be achieved by the actual playing of chess. Moreover the good in question has to be achieved by attempting to excel, that is by endeavouring to rival or outdo those previous practitioners whose activities make up the history of the practice. Thus (presumably) the ground for excluding tic-tac-toe, bricklaying and turnip-planting from the list of 'practices' is that, although there may be specific kinds of pleasure to be had from engaging in them, there are no historically developed standards of excellence to apply, and hence no internal goods of the right kind to be enjoyed.

To understand the virtues, primary examples of which include truth-telling, courage and justice, we must examine the ways in which these qualities are essential to achieve the goods that are internal to a range of such practices. Without, say, honesty or courage, we may succeed in obtaining some of the external goods that a society's institutions attach to practices (for instance we may win prizes by means of deception), but we cannot attain the internal goods. For to attain such goods, we must be guided in our actions by the relevant rules, and we must also sustain the appropriate relationships with our fellow practitioners, which is only possible if we possess qualities of character of the kind just identified.

To see what justice means when understood in this light, we need to focus our attention on *Whose Justice? Which Rationality?*, where MacIntyre adopts a slightly different vocabulary to present what is nevertheless essentially the same position.[5] Instead of 'practices' he speaks of 'types of systematic activity', and the distinction between internal and external goods is replaced by a distinction between 'the goods of excellence' and 'the goods of effectiveness'. The former are the intrinsic goods that consist in excelling in practices such as games, the arts and sciences, or politics; the latter are the various material rewards – wealth, social status, power – which one may contingently acquire by performing successfully in one of these fields. Now the fundamental requirement of justice is that one should be guided in one's participation in any practice by a quest for the goods of excellence, and this issues in two secondary requirements: first that one's actions should be governed by the rules and conventions that do indeed foster excellence (rather than attempting to win or succeed by any means or at any cost), and second that when rewards are to be distributed, they should be allocated on the basis of desert as defined by the standards of excellence internal to the practice. Thus there are, one might say, two kinds of justice, the justice of the participant and the justice of the spectator-cum-assessor, but both are to be guided by the basic principle that the rewards of performance – both internal and external – should go to the genuinely deserving, those who manifest to the highest degree the qualities that the practice in question seeks to foster.

MacIntyre is thus claiming that an understanding of practices is essential to our understanding of the virtues in two related respects. On the one hand, we cannot know what it means in concrete terms to possess a virtue unless we are familiar with the range of practices within which that virtue is displayed. To know what justice is, we must know what the criteria of desert are in practices like games, scientific research and so forth. On the other hand, we cannot understand why justice, say, *is* a virtue unless we grasp its role in sustaining such practices. If we cared only about the goods of effectiveness, we would value only such qualities as were maximally useful in achieving such goods, either for the individual or for society as a whole. This, MacIntyre asserts, is what lies behind those lists of pseudo-virtues found in modern moral philosophy – for instance Benjamin Franklin's catalogue of the qualities useful for achieving earthly prosperity and heavenly rewards.[6]

I noted above that, in MacIntyre's view, a complete account of the virtues, and *a fortiori* the virtue of justice, would also have to examine the way in which specific practices could be brought into harmony with one another, both from the perspective of the unity of a person's life and from the point of view of the community as a whole. How would this alter the account just given? First of all a quality that served a person well in achieving excellence of a particular kind would not count as a virtue if it simultaneously prevented him or her from achieving the goods that are internal to other practices. The example MacIntyre gives here is that of relentlessness in the sense of the ability to drive oneself single-mindedly in the pursuit of a specific goal.[7] This quality is valuable in games or in exploration, say, but it is likely to prevent one from successfully sustaining a family life, for example, and this disqualifies it from being a virtue. Second, if a society's practices are going to knit together in the required way then participants have to have a sense of the relative demands that each makes on them, and so a full account of justice (especially) will need to refer to the proper ordering of goods *between* practices as well as within them.[8] Finally there are forms of behaviour which are universally destructive of any form of community – MacIntyre cites the taking of innocent life, theft, perjury and betrayal – and these will give rise to moral injunctions (and precepts of justice) which are not tied to any specific practice. Thus MacIntyre claims that such a communitarian perspective allows us to undertand those aspects of justice which concern the upholding of basic moral laws.[9]

Having spelt out the way in which MacIntyre ties his account of the
virtues to an account of practices, I now want to look at his position
more critically. Here we must begin by looking closely at the related
notions of a practice and of an internal good. It is immediately apparent
that the list of practices that MacIntyre supplies to illustrate his position
is somewhat heterogeneous, and this complicates our undertanding of
the latter notion. There is an important distinction to be drawn between
practices whose *raison d'être* consists entirely in the internal goods
achieved by participants and the contemplation of those achievements
by others (I shall refer to such practices as 'self-contained') and practices
which exist to serve social ends beyond themselves (I shall refer to these
as 'purposive'). Games, from which much of MacIntyre's thinking
about practices seems to be drawn, are the main exemplars of the first
category. Here the contrast between internal and external goods has its
clearest and most straightforward application. The good which consists
in playing a fine innings at cricket is obviously incomprehensible in
the absence of the game itself, and moreover the standard of excellence
involved – what it is that makes the innings a fine one – can only be
identified by reference to the history of the game, to the canons of
judgement that have been developed by practitioners and spectators.[10]
This is obviously distinct from the money or prestige which a successful player may additionally acquire. On the other hand, in the case of a
productive activity like architecture or farming, or in the case of an
intellectual activity like physics, there is an external purpose which gives
the practice its point and in terms of which it may be judged – in the
cases in question we might say, respectively, the creation of attractive
and comfortable buildings, the production of food for the community,
and the discovery of scientific truth. Now this introduces a certain complexity into the argument. There is still a distinction to be drawn between the good of being an excellent architect, farmer or physicist and
the various extrinsic goods which may be achieved by being successful
in these fields. But the former good is not simply constituted internally
to each practice. Indeed one might say that in so far as it *is* so constituted,
the practice is to that extent a deformed one.

Take the example of medicine, a practice not included in MacIntyre's
initial list, but mentioned in the course of his discussion (and surely
properly so in view of its Aristotelian associations). In contrast to the
external goods of money, etc., the internal good provided by this practice is the good of being an excellent doctor. But this in turn may mean,
simply, 'an excellent healer of the sick' or 'an exemplar of those standards of excellence which have evolved in the medical community'. To
the extent to which these two meanings diverge – say if the medical
community has come to attach special weight to the capacity to perform

certain spectacular operations whose long-term efficacy is doubtful – the practice has fallen victim to professional deformation. A good practice here is one whose standards of excellence are related directly to its wider purpose.

The distinction between self-contained and purposive practices seems clear enough in itself, but it may in certain cases be disputed whether a particular practice has an external purpose or not. The visual arts, for instance, may be seen as practices whose development is governed entirely by internal canons of excellence, or alternatively they may be seen as serving social needs for the embellishment of public and private space. The view taken will determine who should be counted as a good artist. There is a somewhat similar dispute in the case of the practice of politics (compare the views, say, of Oakeshott and Lenin).

But let us continue with the cases where the distinction can be applied without controversy. A major difference between the two kinds of practice is that, in the case of self-contained practices, critical assessment can only be carried out from within the practice itself, whereas in the case of purposive practices, the whole practice may be reviewed in the light of the end it is meant to serve. The rules of cricket may be changed to encourage the batsmen to play more ambitious strokes, or to discourage the bowlers from bowling merely defensively. Here the point of the change is to foster those excellences already recognized in the practice. On the other hand it makes perfect sense to compare entire forms of medicine (say Western medicine and Chinese medicine) in respect of their effectiveness in curing the sick. (I do not mean to imply that the result of such a comparison will necessarily be a straightforward preference for one form over the other regardless of context.) Or one might wish to compare the results of a private system of medicine with the results of a state-funded system. If the upshots of these comparisons gain widespread acceptance, standards of excellence may be changed: a good acupuncturist is not the same as a good surgeon. This follows immediately from the fact that, in these cases, the standards in question ought to be related directly to the ends of the practice.

MacIntyre does not make the distinction I have been making between self-contained and purposive practices. It is nevertheless clear that, for the purpose of developing his account of the virtues, he regards all practices as if they belonged to the self-contained category, even in cases (such as farming) where there is clearly an external purpose that the practice serves.[11] This is indicated both by his choice of examples and by the way in which he treats standards of excellence as developing through internal debate within each practice, rather than in response to wider needs. It is this assumption that practices are self-sustaining that allows him to present the ethics of virtue as categorically distinct from both teleological and deontological ethical theories, as these are usually understood. To interpret virtues as qualities needed to achieve some goal such as the general welfare, or as qualities that allow their possessor to conform to certain rules, is to fall victim to the error of liberal individualism. Instead, as we have seen, a virtue properly understood is a quality that is necessary to achieve the goods internal to one or more practices. These goods may change over time as practices develop, so the virtues themselves are not immutable, but at any moment the list must be taken as given.[12] It cannot be revised by invoking some social goal or purpose in the light of which different personal qualities would take on the character of virtues.

But suppose instead that the virtues were to be understood primarily in terms of purposive practices. It would then be impossible to defend any particular list of virtues without making reference to the social purposes which the practices that require them are meant to serve. To the extent that there is controversy about the proper form of any practice – of the kind that I tried to bring out through the example of medicine – such controversy is almost certain to spill over on to the associated virtues. Thus the virtues will no longer be self-sufficient; although it may still be impossible to *reduce* them to other kinds of moral considerations (considerations of goodness or rightness), they will nevertheless have a dependent status. It will be impossible to understand them except by reference to the needs and purposes that predominate in a particular society.

The issue we must therefore face is whether the practices with which the virtues are centrally connected are (in the terms I have been using) self-contained or purposive. Here I want to make two observations about the self-contained practices. The first is that they can only exist on the proviso that more basic social functions have been discharged. They are in that sense luxury items: they can flourish to the extent that a society's resources and human capacity are not required to meet the demands of material production, the maintenance of social order and so forth. No doubt it is an important feature of human beings that they engage in play (understood here in a broad sense to mean rule-governed activities that have no immediate instrumental purpose). Yet it seems reasonable to suppose that originally forms of play were linked more closely to wider social needs (for instance that games were developed in order to encourage those skills and abilities required in hunting or battle). From this point of view, it is by no means clear whether the transition from premodern to modern society should be seen as beneficial or harmful to the self-contained practices. On the one hand, MacIntyre might argue (as it seems likely he would) that the acquisitive culture that modern market societies foster diverts people away from the pursuit of goods internal to practices towards the pursuit of money, status and the other goods of effectiveness. On the other hand, the astonishing material productivity of these societies also creates the resources and the leisure time which allow self-contained practices – sports, the arts and so forth – to flourish if people choose to engage in them. This ambivalence has worrying consequences for MacIntyre's general thesis. For if the virtues are to be understood in terms of self-contained practices, and if there is no reason to think that modern social conditions are less hospitable to these practices than, say, the Athens of Aristotle's time, then it is surely paradoxical that the contemporary world should have witnessed the almost complete erosion of the virtues, as that thesis maintains.

But my second observation is that it is in any case doubtful whether the virtues should primarily be understood in terms of their role in sustaining self-contained practices. Certainly it is possible to use such practices as a kind of training ground for the virtues, as Victorian public schools tried to do with their practices of sport. But are they the main arena in which the virtues are manifested? I shall look at the virtue of justice in greater detail in a moment, but consider first the case of courage. When would we think of people as displaying courage? First of all, and most obviously, on the battlefield; next when carrying out some humane act in circumstances of danger – say manning a lifeboat in high seas; third, when facing intense pain with equanimity or deciding to carry out some arduous task such as raising a severely handicapped child. These are some central cases. We might also speak of courage as being displayed in certain sporting activities such as parachuting or hang-gliding, but interestingly enough we might here prefer some alternative term such as 'daring'. Why is this? The very fact that these activities are optional, in the sense that participants are not required to engage in them, either by physical necessity or by a sense of moral obligation, counts against the application of an essentially moral term like 'courage'. Unlike courage displayed in the service of a valued end such as the saving of life or the defence of one's homeland, courage displayed merely for its own sake is hardly the genuine thing.[13]

Much the same may be said about the virtue of justice. We think primarily of justice (or fairness) as being displayed by legislators, administrators, judges, educators, employers and so forth – people whose decisions bear crucially on the interests of others, and the quality of whose conduct therefore vitally affects the general character of a society. There *is* a justice-like quality which manifests itself in games and other such self-contained practices, namely a willingness to abide by the rules and apply them impartially to oneself and others. But we would normally refer to this by some term such as 'good sportsmanship' rather than 'fairness' (and certainly not 'justice') – in order, I suggest, to indicate the relatively trivial nature of the interests that are served in exercising this quality. (*Children* may talk a lot about fairness and unfairness in games, but children of course tend to think that much more is at stake in games than adults.)[14]

So a plausible practice-based account of justice is going to have to concern itself centrally with purposive rather than self-contained practices. Purposive practices, to recall, are those forms of human activity which, although having internal standards of excellence, serve broader social ends and are therefore open to critical review in the light of those ends. What role does justice play in purposive practices? Here we need crucially to distinguish between two forms of justice, which I shall label procedural and substantive justice. Procedural justice is a matter of applying established procedures to the case in hand in an impartial manner. It involves rule-following, but it should not be reduced to the mechanical application of rules, since in some cases the established procedure requires the exercise of judgement, as I shall shortly illustrate. Substantive justice, by contrast, is a matter of bringing about outcomes in which each person receives what is due to them by virtue of relevant personal characteristics (for instance those qualities that serve as a basis of personal desert). It is not a quality of procedures, but a condition which well-designed procedures may help to achieve.

I want to claim that practices typically require those who engage in them to exhibit both forms of justice, but the role of justice is very different in the two cases. Procedural justice is required at the moment of engagement, because the practice cannot be sustained unless its procedures are followed in a fair way. In order for excellence to be manifest, and the wider ends of the practice promoted, all those who participate in it must do so under the same conditions, and this requires, for instance, that those who are charged with applying the rules that govern the practice must do so impartially. Substantive justice, on the other hand, is invoked at the point at which the practice is being brought under critical review. I don't mean that the main end of a practice will normally be to promote substantive justice, although this may be the case in some instances. Rather the main aim must be pursued in a way that is consistent with substantive justice. Thus if we take a practice such as medicine, its main aim is not justice but the healing of the sick; nevertheless it is also important that this end be pursued in a fair way, so that for instance two equally sick people should as far as possible have the same chance of being cured.

It is possible, of course, for a practice to have as one of its procedural requirements that a person (or a committee) should at some point make a judgement of substantive justice. Consider, for instance, a literary competition. This will typically have all sorts of rules and qualifying conditions ('Only books published in 1990 are eligible to be considered') which require its administrators to exercise merely the most straightforward kind of procedural justice. But there will be a moment when the jury has to make a judgement of literary merit and decide which book deserves first prize. At this point the procedures require the participants to be guided by considerations of substantive justice. Notice, however, that the basis of the judgement is whatever is specified in the rules of the competition and the jury's job is to identify merit so defined, and to go no further. Thus the rules or conventions may require that only works published in the English language should be considered, that only works of fiction are 'literature' from the point of view of this competition, and so on. A different kind of substantive justice would be invoked if we were to ask whether the competition as it is now run is 'fair' from the point of view of the whole world of literature it is meant to serve. So we can acknowledge that practices may require practitioners, on occasion, to make judgements of substantive justice, while still continuing to distinguish between procedural justice, which helps to sustain the practice in its present form, and substantive justice, a criterion in terms of which the practice may be assessed from the outside.

The relevance of this point to MacIntyre's argument will now become clear. MacIntyre, as we have seen, defines justice in terms of desert, but at the same time he regards justice as something constituted internally to practices.[15] How can this be? 'Desert' must here be taken to refer to the specific forms of desert that a particular practice at any moment takes to correspond to its notions of excellence. That is, the practice establishes standards of achievement, and justice is done when everyone behaves in such a way that the highest achievers receive the highest rewards, and so forth. Let us call this a practice-defined notion of desert.

How adequate is such a notion? Observe first of all that what practices require of people by way of procedural justice has very often nothing directly to do with desert. In competitions, for example, the proper role of officials is likely to be that of applying the same rules and criteria to each participant so that desert may manifest itself spontaneously, so to speak, whereas an official attempting to implement desert criteria directly will very likely distort the result.[16] So although norms of procedural justice may be guided by the general aim of ensuring that people are treated according to their deserts, it is by no means clear that this is the best way to capture the quality of justice that practitioners must exhibit. Second, we have seen that the criterion of desert employed in any practice at any moment may be challenged by reference to wider social purposes. An example I gave earlier was that of medicine, where, because of professional deformation, the most 'deserving' practitioners come to be seen as those who are most accomplished at performing organ transplants and other such spectacular operations. Here one wants to appeal to an alternative criterion of desert, deriving from the social purposes of medicine, such that a highly competent and hard-working family practitioner who cares for his patients in an all-round way can be seen as more deserving (of both the internal and the external goods of medicine) than the transplant specialist.

I am suggesting here that the practice-defined notion of desert favoured by MacIntyre misconceives the primary role that desert plays in relation to practices. That role is above all a critical one. We appeal to desert in order to show that a practice is not working as it should, either because its rules and procedures are badly calculated to ensure that participants get goods in proportion to their deserts, or (more radically) because the criterion of desert that underlies present practice is misjudged.

Since this claim about the critical role of desert criteria is crucial to my argument here, it may be worth citing a well-known example of an appeal to desert of precisely this kind. Stripped of its utilitarian trappings (in this case relatively superficial), John Stuart Mill's *The Subjection of Women* is an extended and eloquent plea for current practices – family life, professional employment, public office – to be reformed in such a way that women's deserts are given due recognition. Mill's argument is partly that women share relevant qualities with men, partly that they have complementary qualities, but in general that there is no basis in desert for an enforced division of labour in the family, for the exclusion of women from political life, and so forth. If desert (and justice) were indeed ideas defined internally to practices, it is difficult to see how an argument such as Mill's could coherently be made, for it would be open to a defender of existing arrangements to make the conclusive retort that politics (say) is a practice the qualifying criteria for which simply include that of being male. It is precisely because we are able to reflect on the ends that politics should serve, and therefore on what it means genuinely to excel in this field, that arguments such as Mill's are able to get a grip.

To this claim about the critical role of desert MacIntyre has an implicit reply, namely that outside of practices notions of desert lose their determinacy, so that what we would expect to find is an interminable debate in which no one is able to establish to the satisfaction of the other parties that he has come up with the correct criterion of desert for assessing a particular practice. He believes, for instance, that contemporary disputes about the justice of positive discrimination are irresolvable in this way. In a society from which genuine practices have almost disappeared, 'we have all too many disparate and rival moral concepts, in this case rival and disparate concepts of justice, and . . . the moral resources of the culture allow us no way of settling the issue between them rationally.' Thus 'modern politics is civil war carried on by other means, and *Bakke* was an engagement whose antecedents were at Gettysburg and Shiloh.'[17]

What are we to make of this? I have already expressed some scepticism about the claim that the modern world has been denuded of the practices that used to flourish in the ancient, and I now want to be equally sceptical about the idea that general notions of justice (and desert) are more contestable among ourselves than among our predecessors. And here it may be useful to begin with an observation of Aristotle's that MacIntyre cites, but whose deeper significance seems to escape him. This is his report of the dispute between democrats and oligarchs over the proper basis for holding political office. Both sides agree that those who are equally meritorious should be equally eligible to hold office, but they disagree about what the relevant test of merit consists in: 'The oligarchs think that superiority on one point – in their case wealth – means superiority on all: the democrats believe that equality in one respect – for instance, that of free birth – means equality all round.'[18] Now in reporting this dispute Aristotle was recording the views of two opposing and irreconcilable factions in Greek politics, and he was equally clear that the dispute stemmed to some degree from the conflicting interests of the two parties, who, he said, 'are judging in their own case; and most men, as a rule, are bad judges where their own interests are involved.'[19] So here we find a cardinal dispute about the conception of desert that is relevant when public office is to be allocated; and although Aristotle has his own proposal to make, he is under no illusion that he is likely in practice to persuade the conflicting parties to agree. If we were to apply the same standards of political realism to fourth-century Athens as MacIntyre applies to contemporary America, we might conclude that Athenian politics was civil war carried on by other means, and that Aristotle's *Politics* was an engagement whose antecedents were Cleisthenes' revolution of 508 and the oligarchs' coup of 411.[20]

In general, in any complex society which contains a variety of practices, each having its own internal standards of excellence, we should expect to find some agreement about criteria of desert and some disagreement; and the disagreement will be attributable in part to the conflicting interests of different groups in the society who stand to gain or lose from having their favoured criterion generally adopted, as blacks and whites do from having different criteria of merit used in university admissions today, and oligarchs and democrats did from having different criteria of merit used for political office in fourth-century Athens. To this commonplace observation I want, however, to add a qualification. Contrary to MacIntyre's belief, the modern age has not witnessed the decline of the notion of desert, but if anything its apotheosis. The reasons for this lie in the comparatively open and fluid social structure of contemporary market societies, by virtue of which it is easier to draw a line between someone's personal qualities and accomplishments and their ascribed social position. We no longer have any inclination to think that people can deserve goods by virtue of their rank or station, whereas Greek thinkers had to work within an ethical vocabulary that tended to conflate the claims of personal merit and social standing: it was for instance an open and disputed question whether key terms of appraisal such as *agathos* should apply to those who were well-born and wealthy or to those who displayed moral virtues.[21] In contemporary discourse we use the term 'merit' to refer broadly to a person's admirable qualities, while tending to reserve 'desert' more specifically for cases in which someone is responsible for the results he or she brings about. There is no Greek equivalent for 'desert' in this specific sense. The Greek term *axia* which corresponds to 'merit' has broad connotations: to Aristotle there is nothing unintelligible about judging merit by wealth or noble birth, even though his own recommendation is that it should be gauged by moral virtue.[22] (It is therefore potentially misleading when translators use 'desert' and 'merit' interchangeably when rendering Aristotle into English.)

MacIntyre might concede that the notion of desert retains a strong hold on popular moral consciousness.[23] In his discussion of the competing liberal theories of justice advanced by Rawls and Nozick, he points out that these theories are separated from the more popular views of justice to which they would otherwise correspond precisely by their overt repudiation of that notion. But he presents this as a case of the liberal philosophers being clear-sighted about what justice has to mean under modern conditions (essentially a set of rules whereby everyone may successfully pursue the goods of effectiveness), whereas the common man is simply inconsistent in wanting to hang on to a notion of desert that belongs within a traditional conception of justice alongside modern ideas of rights and utility. This, however, depends on establishing that desert criteria cannot be applied successfully to the institutions and practices of contemporary societies. Such a view would be hard to sustain. Think for instance of higher education and public employment as two kinds of goods access to which is continually being reshaped by criteria of desert. Or think of job evaluation schemes as involving a systematic attempt to bring the rewards and perquisites of job-holding in line with the comparative merits of the occupants.

This last example, however, challenges one of MacIntyre's principal reasons for seeing modern society as the graveyard of desert. He believes that in a market economy there can be no genuine apportionment of reward to desert.

> There is no relationship of desert or merit connecting work and its products on the one hand and endeavour and skill on the other. Of course in a market economy endeavour and skill will receive their rewards insofar as they have been embodied in successful attempts to give what they want to those who have money in their pockets. But even so the reward is not for success in whatever form of activity of doing or making is in question, but for having done or made that for which there is economic demand.[24]

What is being claimed here is that work or more generally economic activity in contemporary societies does not take place within practices in the MacIntyrean sense: there are no internal goods to achieve or standards of excellence to comply with. Granting this – and at best it is a partial truth, for many work communities do embody just such standards of excellence and offer their members the internal goods of recognition and esteem – why is it inconceivable that people should deserve rewards simply for their success in providing others with that they want as shown by their willingness to pay?[25] A valuable activity is being undertaken voluntarily; economic demand gives a measure, albeit an imperfect one, of that value. Even if we believe that in existing markets the rewards people receive are often disproportionate to the contributions they make, we may still go on to claim that by reshaping the property rights and other institutions surrounding the market, a closer fit can be achieved. Here the notion of desert is employed in its critical capacity, as a criterion against which existing arrangements, and the distribution of goods which flows from them, can be judged.

In putting this case, I do not mean to imply that economic desert of the kind just identified is the only kind of desert available to the denizens of modern societies. On the contrary: I have been at pains to stress that MacIntyre's decline-and-fall-of-the-practices thesis is at best a gross exaggeration, and it follows that there are many contemporary forms of human activity within which different criteria of justice apply. The deserts of doctors, teachers and public administrators are not assessed in the same way as the deserts of businessmen or manual workers. But I do want to claim that the arrival of societies in which the market economy has a central role also ushers in desert as a key criterion for assessing the distribution of goods. For the first time, perhaps, almost everyone can aspire to a state of affairs in which their merits are recognized and duly rewarded. In earlier societies, including the Greek city-states, the majority of men and women were excluded from the practices – politics, the arts and sciences, the professions and so forth – within which notions of desert or merit had a place. Desert was publicly recognized and re-warded only among those who inhabited a social plateau, access to which depended almost entirely on birth, sex and other ascriptive qualities.

With this in mind, we can turn finally to look at MacIntyre's endorse-ment of a Thomist view of justice in the later parts of *Whose Justice? Which Rationality?*. Although in passing from Aristotle to Aquinas we are moving forward in time, we should not assume too readily that the social and political context provided by thirteenth-century AD Paris is closer to our own than that of fourth-century BC Athens. In some respects it seems more distant: the scope of the market economy was more narrowly circumscribed, there was greater fixity in social ranking (though of course slavery had disappeared) and there was a lesser degree of popular participation in the government of the polity. So it may turn out that Aquinas's understanding of the virtues and of justice rests on assumptions that make it less relevant to our contemporary predicament than that of Aristotle.

Two points emerge clearly from even the most cursory reading of Aquinas's account of justice. The first is that justice, along with the other virtues, is not defined primarily in terms of its role in sustaining practices (in MacIntyre's sense of 'practice'). The second is that desert only features peripherally in that account. Justice is defined, in accord-ance with a longstanding tradition, as 'a habit whereby a man renders to each one his due by a constant and perpetual will'.[26] This is then sub-divided into general justice, which Aquinas identifies with legal justice, adherence to the precepts of natural and positive law; and particular justice, which again has two subdivisions, commutative and distributive. Commutative justice is not our concern here, though it is worth under-lining how much of Aquinas's discussion is taken up with matters of legal procedure – with the principles of compensation, with the conduct of trials, and so forth. One could sum this up by saying that for Aquinas justice has centrally to do with the law: its primary requirement is that we should abide by the law in our dealings with our fellows, and its main secondary requirement is that where the law is broken, just procedures should be used to compensate the victim and punish the offender. In most cases the law in question will be the positive law of a particular polity, though if positive law should conflict with the rational precepts of natural law, then justice requires us to obey the latter.

This already indicates the distance that separates Aquinas's account from any practice-based understanding of justice. But now let us look at what he has to say about distributive justice, where we might expect to find that distance lessened. Distributive justice concerns the sharing out of the common resources of a community among its members, and the principle is that each person's share should be proportional to his 'due'. How is the latter established? Aquinas tells us to look towards the common good of the community to see what a person's 'due' is in a particular case. If people are destitute and the community's resources can help them, then need becomes the criterion.[27] If the question is who should be promoted to a professorship, then the relevant quality is the extent of a person's knowledge.[28] In other cases social standing is the criterion: 'The rich ought to be honoured by reason of their occupying a higher position in the community' (though not merely for being rich).[29] We should say that desert was being recognized in the second case but not the third, but interestingly Aquinas draws no such sharp line. For instance in considering the issue whether the doctrine of the mean applies in the same way to commutative as to distributive justice, he poses the following objection: 'In order to observe the mean in distributive justice, we have to consider the various deserts of persons. Now a person's deserts are considered also in commutative justice, for instance, in punishments; thus a man who strikes a prince is punished more than one who strikes a private individual.'[30] To which Aquinas replies as follows: 'In actions and passions a person's station affects the quantity of a thing: for it is a greater injury to strike a prince than a private person. Hence in distributive justice a person's station is considered in itself, whereas in commutative justice it is considered in so far as it causes a diversity of things.'[31]

It is surely remarkable (from our point of view) that Aquinas should reply to an argument couched in terms of desert – and this is one of the few places in his discussion of justice where the term is explicitly used – by talking about the different ways in which a person's *station* is relevant to the two kinds of justice. It suggests very strongly that we have here once again a world-view in which the claims of personal merit and of social standing have not been disentangled, so that to Aquinas it would not seem incongruous to speak of someone as 'deserving' something merely by virtue of their rank within the community. Now this is hardly surprising given the hierarchical nature of the society to which Aquinas belonged; but it confirms our earlier speculation that his social experience is, if anything, more remote from our own than that of the Greek philosophers of democratic Athens, and his account of justice to that degree less relevant to us.

MacIntyre might want to see this remoteness as a virtue rather than a vice. He points out that Aquinas's conception of justice, particularly his views on usury, would condemn 'the standard commercial and financial practices of capitalism'.[32] But my claim is not merely that a Thomist theory of justice would be critical of present-day market societies, but that it would be critical in a way that renders it unavailable to us. For the Thomist view presupposes an ordered community within which people occupy well-defined positions whose respective contributions to the common good can be meaningfully compared. We do not have such a community, nor can we aspire to have one. Many of MacIntyre's critics have pointed out that his general account of the decline of morality tells us virtually nothing about how we might hope to revive it under modern conditions. In the case of justice, we can be more specific: to the extent that MacIntyre now wishes to defend a Thomistic account of justice in place of an Aristotelian account, he is committing himself to the revival of a form of life which is categorically, and not merely contingently, excluded by the social structures of the modern world.[33]

Let me now summarize the critical points I have been trying to establish in the course of my argument:

1   In so far as we are to understand the virtues, and especially the virtue of justice, in terms of their role in sustaining practices, we must look towards purposive, not self-contained, practices;
2   Such practices are, however, not to be evaluated wholly in terms of criteria internal to them, but are open to critical assessment in the light of the ends they are meant to serve;
3   Justice in its procedural form is a quality that sustains practices, but in its substantive form it serves as a criterion by which practices may be assessed;
4   Desert is a principle of substantive justice, and so it is not properly defined internally to practices;
5   Desert has flourished rather than atrophied in modern market societies; and its meaning is no more contestable now than it ever was;
6   In older theories of justice – such as Aristotle's and especially Aquinas's – desert proper tends to be displaced by a looser notion of merit which amalgamates personal qualities with social status.

The upshot is that, while it may be possible to develop a theory of justice as a practice-sustaining virtue, one cannot at the same time define it in terms of desert. Nor is there much warrant for attributing such a theory to the two main protagonists of MacIntyre's books, both of whom endorse the notion of distributive justice as a set of criteria to govern the allocation of a society's common resources. So both conceptually and historically MacIntyre's thesis is suspect; and we have seen already that it cannot help us in our search for a conception of justice to guide the development of modern societies.

NOTES

This paper incorporates some material from an earlier article of mine, 'Virtues and practices', *Analyse und Kritik*, 6 (1984), pp. 49–60, and I am grateful to the editors of that journal for permission to reproduce it. Rather more than half of the present paper is newly written. I should like to thank Anton Leist and Joseph Raz for their very helpful comments on the original paper, and Jerry Cohen, Janet Coleman, John Horton, and the members of the Nuffield Political Theory Workship for their equally helpful criticisms of the new draft.

1   *Whose Justice? Which Rationality?* (Duckworth, London, 1988), p. 39.
2   I have not considered MacIntyre's most recent book, *Three Rival Versions of Moral Enquiry*, which has much less to say on the topics which are my concern here.
3   See *Whose Justice? Which Rationality?*, Preface.
4   *After Virtue* (Duckworth, London, 1981), p. 175.
5   See *Whose Justice? Which Rationality?*, esp. chs 3 and 7.
6   *After Virtue*, pp. 170–3.
7   *After Virtue*, 2nd edn (Duckworth, London, 1985), p. 275.
8   MacIntyre's discussion of this point is fairly cryptic (see *After Virtue*, p. 188) but presumably what he has in mind is that someone who entirely subordinates his pursuit of the goods internal to politics to his pursuit of the goods internal to sport, say, fails to manifest fully the virtue of justice; so equally does a society which esteems and rewards sportsmen more highly than politicians, even though within each category it treats individuals fairly.
9   *After Virtue*, pp. 141–3.
10 Although *on the whole* the best player is the one who wins most often or who contributes most to his team's victory, this equation is not a precise one. Devotees will judge a player by his skill, his inventiveness and so forth, as well as by his brute effectiveness.
11 This is confirmed in his response to my earlier critical appraisal ('Virtues and practices') where he is perfectly ready to describe as 'self-contained' the practices which he relies upon to underpin his account of the virtues. See A. MacIntyre, 'Rights, practices and Marxism: reply to six critics', *Analyse und Kritik*, 7 (1985), pp. 234–48.
12 MacIntyre does not consider the problem posed by someone who simply refuses to recognize an internal good *as* a good – i.e. as a valuable human end – and who therefore rejects any virtue that is uniquely connected with the practice in question. Apparently he presupposes that there is a (shifting) consensus about which practices are worth sustaining, so the only problem that may arise is how different practices are to be threaded together in the life of a particular person or of a community.
13 To avoid misunderstanding here, I should emphasize that my claim is a claim about the primary arenas in which virtues such as courage and justice are displayed. It is not a claim about what may motivate particular virtuous acts. A person may act courageously without looking beyond what his or her immediate circumstances seem to require, without considering the wider ends which acts of that kind serve to promote. When I dismiss 'courage displayed merely for its own sake', I mean that someone who deliberately seeks out dangerous predicaments in order to show how plucky he is does not exhibit the moral quality of courage.
14 'Il faut noter que les jeux des enfants ne sont pas jeux, et les faut juger en eux comme leurs plus sérieuses actions' ('It must be noted that children's games are not games to them, and should be judged as their most serious actions'): Montaigne, *Essais*, ed. P. Villey (Presses Universitaires de France, Paris, 1965), p. 110.
15 At least initially. We have observed that a complete account of justice (according to MacIntyre) will also need to enquire into the ordering of practices within a person's life and within a community.

16　I am thinking, for instance, of a race official who tries to bring it about that the person who in his judgement is the fastest runner wins the race by advantaging her in some way.

17　*After Virtue*, pp. 235–6.

18　Aristotle, *The Politics*, ed. E. Barker (Oxford University Press, Oxford, 1978), p. 118.

19　Ibid., p. 117.

20　For a view of Aristotle's *Politics* as an inevitably unsuccessful attempt to reconcile oligarchic and democratic principles, see J. Ober, *Mass and Elite in Democratic Athens* (Princeton University Press, Princeton, 1989), esp. pp. 293–5.

21　See A. W. H. Adkins, *Merit and Responsibility: a Study in Greek Values* (Oxford University Press, Oxford, 1960).

22　See Aristotle, *Nicomachean Ethics*, ed. J. A. K. Thomson (Penguin, Harmondsworth, 1953), Book V, ch. 3 (p. 146).

23　For evidence that this is indeed so, see my paper 'Distributive justice: what the people think', *Ethics*, 102 (1992), pp. 555–93.

24　MacIntyre, 'Rights, practices and Marxism', p. 245.

25　There are various possible reasons why one might think it was indeed inconceivable, some of which are obliquely hinted at in the way that MacIntyre puts his case in the quotation above. These need to be brought out into the open and discussed. For a defence of the view that market allocations may in principle reward participants in proportion to their deserts see my *Market, State and Community: Theoretical Foundations of Market Socialism* (Clarendon, Oxford, 1989), ch. 6.

26　Aquinas, *Summa Theologica* (Burns, Oates and Washbourne, London, 1918), II-II, Qu. 58 (vol. 10, p. 115).

27　Ibid. II-II, Qus. 58, art. 11, 66 art. 7 (vol. 10, pp. 133, 232–3).

28　Ibid. II-II, Qu. 63, art. 1 (vol. 10, p. 187).

29　Ibid. II-II, Qu. 63, art. 4 (vol. 10, p. 193).

30　Ibid. II-II, Qu. 61, art. 2 (vol. 10, p. 160).

31　Ibid. II-II, Qu. 61, art. 2 (vol. 10, p. 162).

32　*Whose Justice? Which Rationality?*, p. 200. Although I agree with the general claim, the particular argument he offers in support appears to be based on a misreading of Aquinas. MacIntyre (ibid.) asserts that Aquinas would have counted as usury the profits one might receive from investing in a partnership. But in Qu. 78, art. 2, reply to obj. 5, Aquinas distinguishes receiving interest on a simple loan from entrusting money to a merchant or craftsman 'so as to form a kind of society', where, because one does not transfer ownership of the capital, one is entitled to receive a share of the profits. (For a general discussion of Aquinas's attitude to profit-making which confirms this point, see J. Coleman, 'Property and poverty', in *The Cambridge History of Medieval Political Thought c.350–c.1450*, ed. J. H. Burns (Cambridge University Press, Cambridge, 1988), pp. 621–5.)

33　It would be possible to modify this conclusion somewhat by playing down Aquinas's account of distributive justice, and placing the emphasis instead on his general conception of justice as legality, which as we have seen belongs firmly within the tradition of natural law. This would bring him closer to early liberal thinkers such as Locke. I do not think MacIntyre would be at all sympathetic to such a reading.

14

MacIntyre, Feminism and the Concept of Practice

Elizabeth Frazer and Nicola Lacey

Introduction

Significant aspects of the enterprise of academic feminism have striking affinities with MacIntyre's work, as well as that of other communitarian theorists with whom he is frequently grouped. These affinities are the starting point for our paper.

We are here taking for granted the feminist critique of how the categories 'feminine', 'female' and 'woman' have been conceptualized and deployed in empirical, theoretical and literary discourses in 'Western thought', and how these discourses mesh with material gender and sexual relations and social actors' experience of these.[1] One way of characterizing the force of all this work is that feminists level a methodological complaint against much political philosophy and theory: that it is sociologically inadequate, that is, methods and conceptions fail to identify and explain significant aspects of social reality. Feminist critics have excoriated the social sciences and humanities for ignoring the sexual division of labour, male violence against women and the experience of the social and material worlds which is typical for women and not for men or so-called ideal subjects.

At the level of practical politics, feminist campaigns about sexual inequality have focused on rape, battering, childcare, medical practices, sexual harassment, unequal access to food and so on. All of these social phenomena are centred on the body, which both as a reality and as an object of analysis cannot be ignored. At the level of theory and philosophy, feminists have focused on the central motif of the ideally rational subject who is effectively disembodied and 'transcendent'. They have criticized the concomitant dominant tendency in social science and philosophy to ignore or neglect the fact of embodiment.[2]

The empiricist and positivist traditions in social science and philosophy are particularly attacked in this connection. Their emphasis on measurement and statistical analysis, which renders social reality as variables, by definition abstracts away from the material reality of the body. The emphasis on 'objective' facts has been said to conceal both the partial and specific standpoints from which the facts are observed and described and the social construction of the facts themselves. It is asked, for example, from whose perspective boys are more rational than girls in ethical reasoning. If there is a difference in degree or modes of rationality, then this begs an examination not only of the concept of rationality in use, but also of the social forces and structures which underlie and generate the 'facts'. But empiricist scientific method has a very uneasy attitude to 'unobservable' entities or forces.[3] Empiricism is linked, historically and philosophically, with liberalism: and especially with the metaphysical and moral individualism central to the liberal tradition. Feminist and other critics of empiricism are wary, however, of the structuralist solution, which is to take an extremely sceptical attitude towards the apparent facticity of the world and to identify the deep and logical structures which generate the appearances. Structuralism came to bury empiricism and liberalism, and buried our experience of the world we inhabit, our agency and subjectivity, with it.[4] We shall return to these issues later in the paper.

For now we want to point out that the communitarian critics of liberalism voice a similar set of concerns. Their main focus is on liberalism's individualism, and the disembodied and asocial conception of the individual deployed. The adequacy of rational choice theory as a methodology and research programme for social science, and as it is employed normatively in, for example, John Rawls's *A Theory of Justice*, is at issue. So too are the inadequacies of structuralist explanations of human action which downgrade agency.[5] MacIntyre makes this criticism explicit in *After Virtue* when he says that '[no] adequate philosophical analysis ... could escape being also a sociological hypothesis, and *vice versa*' (p. 72). He argues that

> it would generally be a decisive refutation of a moral philosophy to show that moral agency on its own account of the matter could never be socially embodied; and it also follows that we have not yet fully understood the claims of any moral philosophy until we have spelled out what its social embodiment would be. (p. 23)

He complains that twentieth-century philosophers in the dominant tradition, with its narrow conception of the philosophical enterprise, have been able, seemingly without embarrasment or discomfort, to ignore this task.

The critical, poststructuralist, post-empiricist emphasis on the object of the social sciences and philosophy as an embodied and social being (not an abstract, ideally rational subject, or a cluster of objective and measurable variables) has been bound up with attention to *practices*. We find this concept more or less explicitly developed in the communitarian work too – in MacIntyre's it is explicitly invoked and plays a central role.

The concept of practice has been an essential element in the project of collapsing a series of dichotomies: structure/agency, society/individual, objectivism/subjectivism, descriptivism/prescriptivism, reality/concept. Structure is reconceptualized as instantiated only in social actions, while action must be socially enabled and constrained (structured). The individual does not, therefore, stand in opposition to the social; but neither is the individual a mere epiphenomenon of structures or forces. And the dilemma that if we lose universally applicable or objectively valid principles and values, we are forced to retreat to a subjectivism where what is right or good is merely a matter of opinion or whatever anyone says it is, is also addressed, with an emphasis on intersubjectivity and the social grounding of value. From the point of view of the analyst or philosopher, social reality is not to be examined and described objectively, but must be interpreted from a particular standpoint – for the philosopher is a social being too. Philosophy and analysis themselves are social practices, bound up with discourses and understandings.

For MacIntyre, this attack on the traditional antinomies of Western philosophy is important. The concept of practice is important, further, in his construction of a core concept of 'virtue'. In this paper we examine MacIntyre's use of the concept, and compare it with that developed in contemporary feminist and other critical social theory as briefly outlined above. We find that MacIntyre's conception poses him with the particular problem of how to cope with the existence of evil practices. This problem, we shall argue, is at the core of feminists' eventual dissatisfaction with MacIntyre's work – rape, battering, the pathologization and medicalization of women's discontent with the sexual division of labour, the unequal and unfair distribution of food and work have all been identified as socially rooted and normative practices, which it is feminism's project to overturn and transform. MacIntyre addresses the problem, but briefly and unsatisfactorily.

In the latter sections of *After Virtue*, and in *Whose Justice? Which Rationality?* and *Three Rival Versions of Moral Enquiry*, the concept of practice tends to be eclipsed by MacIntyre's elaboration of the concept of tradition. His major preoccupation shifts from the defence of a core concept of virtue and its place in philosophical and practical morality to a defence of the rationality of traditions in an attempt to deconstruct the subjectivism/objectivism antinomy which dogs liberal moral philosophy. In this part of the enterprise the metaphor of craft becomes central, with the craftsman as a model for the exerciser of virtue, and the argument that philosophy is a craft.

Practices are elements in traditions: it is through traditions that practices develop.[6] MacIntyre's central examples of 'practice' are chess, football, architecture and (although this is not elaborated) the building and maintenance of human communities.[7] Crafts, too, are traditional, and the craftsman must be initiated into the tradition.[8] Examples of 'craft' are furniture-making, fishing and farming (and philosophy, of course).[9] Although MacIntyre himself does not elaborate the exact relationship between practice, craft and tradition in sociological theoretical terms, then, it seems reasonable to understand both practice and craft as fundamental categories of moral and social theory.

It therefore also seems reasonable to look at MacIntyre's use of the concept of practice in the context of other anti-liberal, anti-empiricist and critical social theory. In the next section we compare his conception with a constructed conception based on our reading and understanding of a rather wide range of contemporary theory.[10] This reading is likely to be somewhat contentious, as the concept of 'practice' is in many contexts bound up with the concept of 'discourse', leading readers into the treacherous terrain of literary theory. Furthermore, Althusser and Foucault, whose work is of significance here, can both be located in the *structuralist* tradition, although their work has been significant in the development of poststructuralism.

The Concept of 'Practice'

Contemporary social theory

In this work, practice refers to human action which is socially based and organized, underpinned by formal or informal institutions – usually a combination of these. In the cases of medicine, chess, social work, carpentry or plumbing, for example, there are governing bodies and lines of authority with written rules, procedures, standards and regulations. In other cases – motherhood, sexuality, social interactions and events like dinner parties or demonstrations – rules, procedures and standards are still articulable (usually with most clarity in the face of a breach, as the rules of etiquette become clearest when we encounter a drunk at a party). Indeed, 'authorities' might enforce these. Practices are bound up with discourse (speech, writing and other productions of meaning), which both is produced by and produces the practice – like law, scholarship, fashion journalism or barrack-room, bar-room or changing-room talk. Practices and discourses pre-exist individual social subjects – chess grand masters, seven-year-old chess learners, homosexuals, psychiatrists, mental patients, students and academics exist as such by virtue of the prior existence of practices, discourses and their institutions.

The materiality of social reality in this conceptualization is important. Social states of affairs are not the mere summation of individual drives, attitudes, opinions, preferences or even desires. Social identity and social structure are bound up together. The social subject is not a theoretical cluster of variables (age, race, sex, class, educational attainment), or an irreducible and unified ego of the Cartesian type, or an epiphememon of structures or forces. So the theoretical power of the approach is also important – it promises to explain social stability and the reproduction of social reality, while showing how social reality differs from physical reality. This is not the place to consider whether a specific concept of cause must be developed to deal with human practice-based social action, or whether we should eschew the notion of cause in explanation here altogether. Suffice it to say that this analysis makes of human social beings actors or doers, not behavers. If the existence of practices is a significant element in the causal antecedents of our actions, then the upshot of our actions is not determined as the position of a billiard ball is determined in Humean causation. The analysis is also non-atomistic – actors are connected with each other, and are not atoms either of the autonomous and self-driven, or of the billiard ball variety (at the mercy of external forces).

MacIntyre

MacIntyre says that he uses the concept of practice in a specific way which departs from ordinary uses, as

> any coherent and complex form of socially established co-operative human activity through which goods internal to that form of activity are realised in the course of trying to achieve those standards of excellence which are appropriate to, and partially definitive of, that form of activity, with the result that human powers to achieve excellence, and human conceptions of the ends and goods involved, are systematically extended.[11]

There is much here that is common with the concept we identified in the previous section: social establishment, objective standards of excellence – external to the individual participant, internal to the practice itself – the open-endedness and possibility of extending and altering conceptions or ends of practices. MacIntyre later mentions formal and informal institutional underpinning. What is specific in MacIntyre's characterization is not the conception itself, but the explicitly evaluative teleology which is part of it, and, of course, its place in a theory of *virtue*. This contrast must not be overdrawn, however, and certainly not glossed as a descriptive/prescriptive distinction. MacIntyre, as we have seen, is committed to a sociologically adequate basis for moral and political philosophy. And poststructuralist social theorists inevitably use the concept normatively, as we shall go on to discuss.

The concept of 'practice', as we have remarked, is important in enabling MacIntyre to conceptualize an objective (or at least, not subjective) good, right and virtue, without making claims to universality or neutrality. Liberalism can only either make the good, the right, the virtuous, a matter of subjective opinion, or falsely universalize the judgement of an ideal rational individual. MacIntyre and other critics trace this dilemma to liberalism's individualism. MacIntyre elaborates his criticism of liberal individualism into a positive thesis of social identity and social structure (which are two aspects or moments of the same thing – by contrast to dualistic liberal analysis which separates the individual from and confronts him with the social whole). Social identity and social structure are set in time – in traditions which have narrative unity (as does the good human life which is informed by the quest for narrative coherence). This critique of liberalism connects with MacIntyre's criticism of the broad tendencies of Enlightenment and post-Enlightenment philosophy, which sever the individual from his social basis. But also of first importance in this analysis is the disavowal of conservative understandings of tradition as irrational or non-rational, and of the equation of the ethical with an attitude of unquestioning acceptance of tradition and authority. To be guided by, and indeed to be constructed by, tradition is not to be divested of rationality.

So, for MacIntyre, man's moral nature and moral practice are tied up with his sociality, his membership of a tradition and his participation in practices: not with his individuality and autonomy. To do the right and to pursue the good is not to act on or pursue individual preference; it is to live that good life which is given in a tradition. To exercise virtue is to do what is necessary to attain enjoyment of goods which are internal to practices. Practices are socially established and will usually be sustained by social institutions, like bodies of authority, codes, rules and regulations. Standards of excellence and criteria for judging whether one is doing the practice right are therefore objective, or at least intersubjective. But there is room for individual creativity, for pushing the boundaries forward, for doing better than any other practitioner has dreamed of.

Comparison

MacIntyre's central examples of practices, as we have seen, are architecture, chess and football. He deploys these examples to illustrate the public nature of standards and norms, the formal and institutionalized nature of these standards and norms and an authority which can and will enforce them, to emphasize participants' situatedness in an ongoing enterprise whose parameters are accepted although not unchangeable, and therefore to emphasize how our judgements and actions are determined, although with space for our own developments, innovations and challenges to authority. No one can really predict the progress and outcome of a chess game. Over time accepted standards of excellence in architecture alter, and the rules of football change. These indeterminacies and changes occur through participants' conscious efforts and arguments about what the practice, and the tradition, *is* – that is, by what we might call a process of interpretive criticism or critique.[12] Our social identities are structured by the prior existence of practices, and the practices are constituted by social actors.

When we look at the examples other social theorists use in their theoretical work, and in empirical research, we find a very different picture. Althusser puts at the centre of his social theory practices institutionalized in the ideological and repressive state apparatuses: social control and punishment by the police and courts, the maintenance of the capitalist division of labour.[13] Foucault concentrates on practices institutionalized in the disciplines: psychiatry, medicine, criminology and other new sciences underpin the treatment of the ill and the mad, state punishment of the criminal and deviant, norms and standards of health and sexuality.[14] Feminist theory understands male power as exercised and maintained in and through practices. And feminism adds a reflexive twist to the analysis of practice – as it is, itself, rooted in the practice of consciousness raising. In each of these cases the concept of practice is understood as irreducibly *political* – that is, as involving the exercise of power which calls for justification or critical scrutiny.

For example, liberal feminism of the current wave introduced a new concept into language: 'sexism' was defined as a particular set of attitudes and a particular and discriminatory way of treating women and men. The liberal feminist project was one of changing attitudes; feminists and their critics were pessimistic or optimistic about this project as they tended to believe in genes (the pessimists) or reason (the liberals and the optimists). The optimists of course lived constantly with the shadow of pessimism, as there was vagueness about precisely how the force of reason was to prevail, and how change was to come about. It was not long before the feminist critics of liberalism were pointing out that the whole analysis tended to individualism – individuals have attitudes, and individuals 'treat' other people one way or another – and was therefore flawed.

By contrast, in anti-individualist or 'postliberal' feminism the concept of practice is brought to bear both theoretically and practically, both critically and positively.[15] To begin with, the way things are done in groups, meetings and campaigns is problematized and their constructive and normative functions explicitly discussed. Campaigns and committees have been organized non-hierarchically. Consciousness raising (the practice in which women's and men's understanding of women's social position and how it works has often been developed) involves sharing and comparing experience (and, as it happens, finding much in common with each other) in groups, and thereby changing the meaning of the experiences in question, changing the experiences themselves. The group process is governed by rules which are more or less tacit or articulated: 'honesty' is valued, as is acceptance of other people's experience; equality of participation, of access to the floor is a rule; listening has to be supportive. There has been argument (among sociolinguists and other social theorists) as to whether this form of communication is a naturally feminine, women's way of doing things.[16] Whatever the answer to this question, participants often find the set-up strange at first – many articulate women find it hard not to interrupt or to jump in to fill silence. Thus new identities are constructed.

The development of this practice transforms the liberal understanding of 'sexism' too. Women's own practical experience of the power of rules, structures, processes brings a new understanding of rape, sexual harassment, parenting and childrearing, the sexual division of labour. These are now seen not as matters of individual attitude or individual treatment of individuals, but as more deeply and systematically rooted. Sexual harassment, for example, is understood as norm and rule governed (although these norms and rules are, of course, contested). It is underpinned by social institutions of masculinity and normal sexuality – whether one is doing masculinity right is not merely up to one to decide; there is a public, objective fact of the matter about standards. The practice itself is an item in a matrix of sexual practices that are constitutive of a particular and concrete masculine sexuality. The practice and the institutions have their counterpart in discourse: pornography, men's talk, women's talk and other discourse of gender from women's magazines and romantic fiction to psychoanalysis and sociobiology.

The theoretical work of feminists, Althusser and Foucault has spawned an enormous amount of empirical research into practices – feminist campaigns on sexual harassment, rape, domestic violence; academic research into women's economic relations with each other and how these interact with kinship and friendship,[17] into teenage subcultures and their place in the wider social formation,[18] into education and psychology,[19] into sexuality.[20] Some of this work emphasizes discourse, ideology and culture – the level of speech, writing and sign – more than practice.

Some is explicitly indebted to other major theorists – Gramsci, for example, whom we do not discuss in this paper.[21] But all can be seen as investigations into how social actors are bound up in practices, in already institutionalized and normative ways of doing things, and how these ways of doing things actually construct social identities.

What marks all this work off from MacIntyre's is that it is over-whelmingly *critical* of the practices in question (critical of practices like feminist discussion groups as much as practices like rape). In many cases the emphasis is on unequal power situations and on one group's interests being pursued and satisfied at the expense of another's. Teenage girls' sexuality is subordinated to the masculine interest in penetration, norms of masculinity and shopfloor culture serve the interests of capital, male sexuality disadvantages women in the public realm and the workplace, the mentally ill have been displayed in cages, the body is disciplined and the interests of individuals subordinated to bourgeois imperatives. In other practices, like feminism itself, there is an attempt to distribute power equally, but power is not then absent – it is still material in the situation. Further, we must be aware of the materiality of power in constituting practices themselves – women have exercised power and in some cases managed to impose equality and informality in committees and the like. All of this work deploys, albeit in different senses, a *theory of power*; and it is the lack of this in MacIntyre which is the source of the problem of evil practices.[22]

The Problem of Evil Practices

MacIntyre, as we have seen, defines virtue as the exercise of what is necessary to attain goods internal to practices. Truth, courage and justice are necessary if we are genuinely to enter into a relationship with past and present practitioners.[23] The integrity of a practice requires the exercise of the virtues.[24] Conversely, the exercise of virtue is bound up with the existence and moral value of practices. This analysis obviously makes practices, as such, by definition good. MacIntyre argues that the human institutions which underpin practices may be vulnerable to corruption, so that practices themselves might in turn be corrupted. Presumably, chess might become commercialized and professionalized, so that the practice of chess could degenerate, and seven-year-olds might be deprived of learning the peculiar good of pursuing excellence in chess for the sake of excellence in chess. This, however, does not threaten the goodness of practices as such.

Turning to some more difficult examples, MacIntyre addresses the possibility that torture, or sado-masochistic sexual practices, are practices in his sense, with the upshot that wholehearted participation in them is virtuous notwithstanding that they are evil.[25] He repeats that he intends that practices *qua* practices are bound up with virtue (not merely *good* practices). And he accepts that there *may* be evil practices, but records his scepticism that any candidate (like torture) which may be marshalled actually *is* a practice.[26]

We think that in MacIntyre's own terms torture as it is practised now, and has been in the past, in contexts like that so graphically described by Foucault in the opening passages of *Discipline and Punish*, must certainly count as a practice. It is coherent, complex and socially established. It relies on cooperation and a division of labour. As in any skill, craft or profession, goods internal to the practice are realized. (It is common in debates about capital punishment in Britain for the fact that the executioner is a craftsman (and that the craft has almost died out) to be referred to.) Rape and other forms of sexual violence, too, realize goods which are internal to them. Feminist analysis, the testimony of rapists themselves and readings of cultural discourses of sexuality reveal how masculine dominance and the symbolic and material subjugation of femininity can be uniquely realized through the penetration of a woman, with the phallus, against her will.[27] And these are certainly coherent, complex, socially established and cooperative activities. An apparently individual act of sexual violence on the part of a lone man actually, of course, partakes of social meanings which construct the experience of the act for the perpetrator, victim and audience. Formally, what makes a rape a rape has the same structure as what makes the child kicking a ball on a deserted bombsite a footballer. As we have remarked, MacIntyre's response to this analysis is brief. If we were to press him to respond in more detail, what could he say?

There seem to be two possibilities. The first is substantive – he could appeal to some independent and substantial criteria so as to exclude rape and torture, but not football, from the list of genuine practices. It is worth noting at this point that other contemporary moral theorists who share many of MacIntyre's tendencies and commitments do take a substantive route here. Finnis, for example, expounds a theory of basic goods (which include such items as life, knowledge and practical reasonableness) which the practically reasonable man will come to appreciate as basically valuable, and self-evidently so. These constitute ends in a teleological scheme.[28] But MacIntyre has ruled this strategy out by defining goods purely in the framework of practices, crafts and traditions.

The second possible strategy is a procedural one. This seems to be the route that MacIntyre would be inclined to pursue, given his scepticism about whether apparently evil practices really are practices. He might claim that evil practices would inevitably be incoherent, or contradictory, or self-defeating, or would 'lack integrity'. Some legal theorists have developed this kind of argument and claim that if procedural 'moral' canons are obeyed then substantive goodness will be promoted or produced.[29] Needless to say, other theorists have been quick to point to regimes which respect procedural fairness, but still score high on substantive evil.[30] The procedural line of argument is therefore far from promising.

In summary of our argument so far, then, in the context of social theory generally, MacIntyre's emphasis on practice is methodologically very promising. However, we are struck by the neglect of a theory of power and the analysis of power relations in social life – of the political relevance of practices. This lack, and MacIntyre's definition of practices as prior to the good, gives rise to the insuperable difficulty of evil practices.

Practice and Politics

In this final section we are going to elaborate on some of these points. We shall develop them into a discussion of membership and practices of inclusion and exclusion, and of how consideration of these issues impacts on MacIntyre's own understanding of how traditions, practices and crafts might be changed from within. To begin with, we want to suggest that focusing on the case of torture (and sado-masochism – although the practice of sado-masochism has more committed and articulate defenders in the contemporary world than torture would probably muster[31]) actually makes life rather too easy for MacIntyre. Because it is commonly agreed to be exceptional this example makes it easy for him to skate over the issue of evil or oppressive practices in the way he does, ignoring the relevance of the issue to a much wider range of cases. Instead we intend to go back to the kind of examples we mentioned earlier and focus on heterosexuality, which is commonly considered to be normal, in both the statistical and moral senses.

Heterosexuality is quite clearly a *practice*. It has been treated as such in feminist discourses, and must be, we believe, by MacIntyre. Heterosexual identity is taken up in and through a complex set of practices – social, romantic and erotic relations with the opposite sex, which are done in standard ways and which are sustained and regulated by society and culture, and articulated in discourses such as advertising, fiction, advice columns and science. Certainly, becoming *properly* heterosexual realizes goods that are internal to the practice (well, for boys at least, but that is to pre-empt our argument). As soon as we begin to try to characterize these practices in more detail, however, it becomes clear that in 'our culture' there are many competing interpretations and descriptions.

Feminist analyses of heterosexuality in the last twenty years have noted that in Western culture the dominant discourses of sexuality invoke conceptions of health (both psychic and physical), pleasure, reproduction, and crucially, and especially for girls, trouble. The trouble takes a variety of forms – the possibility of unwanted pregnancy or of disease, and more fundamentally, the problem of managing male sexuality. Boys get carried away and can't control themselves, and girls have to be careful about this, because they will get the blame. More sinister, boys and men might deliberately and malevolently attack and rape, or even kill. Girls are explicitly or implicitly taught all these facts at the onset of their development into sexual beings. Psychological, sociological and cultural research and theory connects the dominant model and practice of male sexuality with girls' and women's difficulty with the pleasure of sexuality, or to put it more bluntly with vast numbers of women's dissatisfaction. The discursive and practical connection of sexuality and reproduction, together with cherished understandings of male dominance, make conventional intercourse the dominant sexual practice. This goes together with a common and routine denigration of feminine sexuality, and a common and routine aggressive, sometimes violent, masculine sexuality. This is problematic for women's pleasure; and women who do not find pleasure in normal sexuality are in a difficult position given our culture's connection of sexual activity and health (unlike our Victorian grandmothers, who coped with conceptions of duty that our feminist generation decreasingly faces).[32]

Therefore, central to feminist politics, which takes a variety of institutional forms and adopts a variety of strategies, is the project of *changing* the practice of heterosexuality and fundamentally altering the nature of the good internal to it. Briefly, feminists and other critics of the dominant model and practice are not satisfied with a sexuality whose central good is the affirmation of male superiority and activity, and of female passivity.

Our explication of this feminist understanding of the practice of heterosexuality and its place in a culture or tradition raises several significant issues: first, the terms on which social actors do or do not participate in a practice; second, their differential power to alter a practice; third, the existence and status of competing interpretations of the nature of the good internal to a practice; fourth, the status and grounding of such critical understandings and struggles over practices as the feminist campaigns about heterosexuality.

Two problems arise under the heading of the terms of participation.

In the present case, of heterosexuality, the issue is that of inclusion. From this perspective girls' apprenticeship and participation in the practice of heterosexuality is the upshot of an asymmetric power structure (with sex as the line of cleavage) and is the material realization of men's (men of a particular sort) not women's interests or good. Women's interests will be served when girls don't have to fear or negotiate with the labels 'slag' and 'tight', when they are introduced to sexual practices which put their pleasure first or at least equal first, and where domination as such is not so central to 'normal' male sexual pleasure and practice as sociological research and cultural studies reveal it to be.[33] Here, then, is a practice in which antagonism is deeply seated and implicated in the very nature of the enterprise. It is hence an example of a very different kind from *either* chess *or* torture. The existence of many such practices raises important questions about MacIntyre's choice of examples. Girls are certainly *participants* in the practice of normal heterosexuality – a crucial aspect of critical work on sexuality has been to dispense with the idea that they are brainwashed, or duped, or passive victims.[34] But their active taking up of a particular role does not alter the validity of this critical analysis of power and interest.

Many practices, on the other hand, exclude particular social actors. To take one of MacIntyre's examples, it might be that the children playing football change the rules of their game so that a child in a wheelchair can join in. But if they are playing seriously, this is more or less inconceivable. Given football as a practice, on what grounds should any children alter the way they do it? (Given, that is, that practices are indeed prior to the good, as such.) The issue of exclusion has been central in sexual politics, of course. Women have been excluded from sports clubs, the legislature, the judiciary, the university. And the conceptions of good generated in these institutions' practices have had the exclusion of women, or the feminine, at their very heart. Materially, the identity of a late nineteenth-century don in an Oxford college presupposed the existence of college servants and/or wives; morally, scholarship and teaching required the cultivation of mind (and body) in a way that would transcend the mess connected symbolically, and materially, with the feminine body. Arguably, the heroic ethic MacIntyre discusses, while undoubtedly grounded in shared values, depended on a conception of masculinity in which femininity meant the eternal paradox of Siren and Penelope (Eve and Mary, whore and wife . . .).[35]

But, here we are – *we* are Oxford 'dons' now. And the practice is changing. Doing the job in the traditional way still presupposes the existence of a wife who attends to one's bodily and material needs (or the pursuit of a monastic lifestyle in college); but more and more of us don't have wives – so the traditional ways must change. Once groups previously excluded are inside the institution and participating in the practice, then, does change come about in the way MacIntyre theorizes?

His main accounts of change centre on two sorts of example. First there is the football case – over time, it is understood that the game goes better if the offside rule is changed; this change will be the outcome of suggestions, argument, counterargument, players unofficially altering the way they play, and so on. Second, there is the case of representatives and bearers of rival traditions engaging in enquiry and argument in some cultural and institutional setting (the university, for example). In each case the protagonists are arguing about the tradition and practice and what it really *is* – football is more true to itself (according to the reformists in this example) when the offside rule is changed. Thus MacIntyre emphasizes dispute, argument and conversation. He also acknowledges the complexity of social identity – he says, for example, that the citizen will also be someone's son, that the craftsperson will be a 'member of this or that local community'.[36] But we argue that neither of these models of change is a good model of feminist politics and its achievements.

First, both the feminist criticism of heterosexuality and the liberal and feminist demands that women be admitted to the university (for instance) involve the pursuit of goods which would be positively damaging to the tradition being criticized. Goods internal to the practice (male dominance and transcendence, for example) could not be realized at all if the feminist challenge were successful. The change in power relations and the distribution of goods between men and women changes the family, the nature of work, the nature of public life, the idea and practice of private life, and so on.

Second, the feminist critique is only partly an 'immanent critique'. It is immanent in two senses. First, it is from within the practice and within the tradition – although as we have made clear we would depart from MacIntyre's characterization of this as the process of asking what the good of the practice *is*. Instead it is the process of identifying the ways in which what is said in the dominant discourse to be the good for women (motherhood, feminine virtue, the maintenance of the private sphere, passivity and so on) is good *only from a particular standpoint*. Second, it is immanent critique in the sense that feminists find already written in the 'logic' and theory of the tradition and the practice something very like the feminist understanding of heterosexuality we have outlined.[37] Our culture is not short of commentators who also understand sex as being centrally about male dominance, the subjection of women, the subjugation and even annihilation of the feminine, and so on.[38] But they put a different *value* on these projects, and celebrate them; and their critics can reveal incoherence, contradiction and just plain evil in their work.

But feminism is also an external critique. First and most simply, feminists are in conversation with women engaged in feminist struggle over sexual relations in quite different traditions where the practices are quite different. Second, feminism is itself a tradition consisting of a range of practices which, as we have seen, constitutes identities and values of its own. Now this means that it is a commonplace for women to experience split and fragmentary identity. MacIntyre's example of son and citizen invokes a picture of *nested* elements adding up to a whole but complex identity. By contrast, feminist and Oxford 'don', mother and university lecturer are *clashing* elements. This is not to say that we don't 'manage' these fragmentary and difficult identities – rather that the subject, even if engaged in a quest for narrative unity, must survive a degree of conflict and tension without allowing its sense of identity to be undermined. Despite MacIntyre's gestures towards the recognition of fragmentation (both of identity and of traditional and practical context) his theory seems to presuppose a world as homogeneous as the elite Greek world he invokes (or constructs). This is an unsatisfactory state of theoretical affairs for any theory which sees itself as engaged in a political process.

Third, this picture demands an account of the political process by which the excluded find a voice and make it heard, and by which the included (but dominated) come to a critical understanding. To find such an account is not a difficult problem – fragmented experience generates contradictory experience which can, in turn, generate critical ideas when subjects try to make sense of their lives. Teenage girls live in a culture in which they are blamed for being 'slags', and blamed for being 'tight'; and a basic feminist analysis of gender relations comes easily to them.[39] Even in the case of practices such as football – in which the good is relatively unproblematic and internally coherent – the participants do have to negotiate with their own experience of the excluded, who may well be in the audience, even if they haven't yet found a voice to argue that ball games should be less competitive, should allow wider participation, or whatever. But MacIntyre offers no gesture towards such an account, and, if our analysis is right, his own conceptual framework prevents him from going further.

The validity of these remarks and criticisms rests on an attendance to social reality, the way things are in the world we inhabit – which is the world in which moral and political philosophy are to work, and to be assessed. We return to our first thought: that philosophy and theory must be sociologically adequate. The concept of practice is a great advance on the decontextualized conceptions of free will and agency that have been invoked in liberalism, and on the determinism or abstraction of empiricism. But we need to study the political conditions under which practices emerge, the workings of power in structuring agency, participation, membership and access to institutions. Without this study, MacIntyre's work does not make up the deficiencies he identifies in classical liberalism.

NOTES

1 See, for example, Diana Coole, *Women in Political Theory: From Ancient Misogyny to Contemporary Feminism* (Harvester Wheatsheaf, Hemel Hempstead, 1988); Alison Jaggar, *Feminist Politics and Human Nature* (Harvester, Brighton, 1983); Ellen Kennedy and Susan Mendus (eds), *Women in Western Political Philosophy* (Wheatsheaf, Brighton, 1987); Eva Kittay and Diana Meyers (eds), *Women and Moral Philosophy* (Rowman and Littlefield, Totowa, NJ, 1986); Genevieve Lloyd, *The Man of Reason: 'Male' and 'Female' in Western Philosophy* (Methuen, London, 1984); Susan Moller Okin, *Women in Western Political Thought* (Virago, London, 1980) and *Justice, Gender and the Family* (Basic Books, New York, 1989); Carole Pateman, *The Disorder of Women* (Polity, Cambridge, 1989); Mary Lyndon Shanley and Carole Pateman (eds), *Feminist Interpretations and Political Theory* (Polity, Cambridge, 1991).

2 See Lloyd, *The Man of Reason*. Dorothy Smith, *The Everyday World as Problematic* (Open University Press, Milton Keynes, 1988) is an argument in sociological method that women's bodily life is the foundation of social reality and should therefore be the prime focus of sociological research. For an overview of the feminist criticism of sociology, see Mary Maynard, 'The re-shaping of sociology: trends in the study of gender', *Sociology*, 24 (2) (May 1990). Another writer who takes issue with social science and theory's neglect of the body is R. W. Connell *Gender and Power* (Polity, Cambridge, 1987). And the work of Michel Foucault is, of course, very significant here.

3 See Carole Gilligan, *In a Different Voice: Psychological Theory and Women's Development* (Harvard University Press, Cambridge, Mass., 1982). For a more general discussion of the critique of empiricism, see Sandra Harding, *The Science Question in Feminism* (Open University Press, Milton Keynes, 1986); *Feminism and Methodology* (Open University Press, Milton Keynes, 1987).

4 Despite its professed liberalism, much the same can be said of the 'pragmatist' philosophy represented by Rorty, see Richard Rorty, *Contingency Irony and Solidarity* (Cambridge University Press, Cambridge, 1989); *Objectivity, Realism and Truth* (Cambridge University Press, Cambridge, 1991). See also Martin Hollis, 'The poetics of personhood', in *Reading Rorty*, ed. Alan Malachowski (Blackwell, Oxford, 1990).

5 See Michael Sandel, *Liberalism and the Limits of Justice* (Cambridge University Press, Cambridge, 1982); Charles Taylor, *Philosophy and the Human Sciences* and *Human Agency and Language* (both Cambridge University Press, Cambridge, 1985) – Taylor especially addresses himself to problems of structuralism. See also Michael Walzer, *Spheres of Justice* (Princeton University Press, Princeton, 1983).

6 *After Virtue* (Duckworth, London, 1981), p. 221.

7 Ibid., pp. 187–8.

8 *Three Rival Versions of Moral Enquiry* (Duckworth, London, 1990), p. 128.

9 Ibid., p. 68.

10 References we have in mind include Louis Althusser, 'Ideology and ideological state apparatuses', in *Lenin and Philosophy, and Other Essays* (New Left Books, London, 1971); Seyla Benhabib and Drucilla Cornell (eds), *Feminism as Critique* (Polity, Cambridge, 1987); Deborah Cameron, 'De-mythologising sociolinguistics: why language does not reflect society', in *Ideologies of Language*, ed. John E. Joseph and Talbot J. Taylor (Routledge, London, 1990); Connell, *Gender and Power*; Michel Foucault, *Madness and Civilisation* (Tavistock, London, 1967), *The Birth of the Clinic* (Tavistock, London, 1973), *Discipline and Punish* (Allen Lane, London, 1977), *The History of Sexuality*, vol. 1 (Penguin, Harmondsworth, 1979), *Power/Knowledge: Selected Writings and Interviews* (Harvester, Brighton, 1980); Anthony Giddens, *Central Problems in Social Theory* (Macmillan, London, 1979), *Social Theory and Modern Sociology* (Polity, Cambridge, 1987); Diane Macdonnell, *Theories of Discourse* (Blackwell, Oxford, 1986); Taylor *Philosophy and the Human Sciences* and *Human Agency and Language*; John B. Thompson, *Studies in the Theory of Ideology* (Polity, Cambridge, 1984).

11 *After Virtue*, p. 187.

12 Ibid., p. 222.

13 Althusser 'Ideology and ideological state apparatuses'.

14 Foucault, *Madness and Civilisation*; *The Birth of the Clinic*; *Discipline and Punish*; *The History of Sexuality*, vols 1, 2, 3.

15 This is not to imply that liberal feminism has been defeated as such: the debate continues. See Susan Moller Okin, 'Humanist liberalism', in *Liberalism and the Moral Life*, ed. Nancy L. Rosenblum (Harvard University Press, Cambridge, Mass., 1991), for a recent contribution. (But all would agree that a feminist liberalism is a transformed liberalism.)

16 Deborah Cameron, *Feminism and Linguistic Theory* (Macmillan, London, 1985), pp. 34–44.

17 For example, Henrietta Moore, *Feminism and Anthropology* (Polity, Cambridge, 1988).

18 For example Stuart Hall and Tony Jefferson (eds), *Resistance through Ritual* (Hutchinson, London, 1976); Paul Willis, *Learning to Labour* (Saxon House, London, 1977).

19 For example, Julian Henriques et al., *Changing the Subject: Psychology, Social Regulation and Subjectivity* (Methuen, London, 1984).

20 For example, Angela MacRobbie, 'Teenage girls and the culture of femininity', in CCCS Women's Group, *Women Take Issue* (Hutchinson, London, 1978); Julian Woods, 'Groping towards sexism', in *Gender and Generation*, ed. Angela MacRobbie and Mica Nava (Macmillan, London, 1984).

21 Especially the work from the Centre for Contemporary Cultural Studies at Birmingham University during the 1970s and 1980s: Stuart Hall (ed.), *On Ideology* (Hutchinson, London, 1978), and Stuart Hall and Tony Jefferson (eds), *Resistance through Ritual* (Hutchinson, London, 1976).

22 Clearly, our argument here and in what follows presupposes rather than states an adequate theory of power. The scope of such a theory is a complex and controversial issue which cannot be addressed in this chapter (although we develop it in *The Politics of Community* (Harvester Press, Hemel Hempstead, 1993). Briefly, we want to follow Foucault a little way into his structuring conception of power, but want to maintain elements of the older notion of power exercised, of agency being more than an epiphenomenon of power. See Foucault, *Power/Knowledge*; Stephen Lukes (ed), *Power* (Blackwell, Oxford, 1986).

23 *After Virtue*, p. 194.
24 Ibid., p. 195.
25 Ibid., pp. 199–200.
26 Ibid., p. 200.
27 See Susan Brownmiller, *Against Our Will: Men, Women and Rape* (Penguin, Harmondsworth, 1976); Elizabeth Stanko, *Intimate Intrusions: Women's Experience of Male Violence* (Unwin Hyman, London, 1985); Liz Kelly, *Surviving Sexual Violence* (Polity, Cambridge, 1988).
28 John Finnis, *Natural Law and Natural Rights* (Clarendon, Oxford, 1980).
29 Lon Fuller, *The Morality of Law* (Yale University Press, New Haven, 1964).
30 J. Raz, 'The rule of law and its virtue', in *The Authority of Law* (Clarendon, Oxford, 1979); Finnis, *Natural Law and Natural Rights*, pp. 270–6.
31 See for example papers in Carole Vance (ed.), *Pleasure and Danger: Exploring Female Sexuality* (Routledge and Kegan Paul, London, 1984), and discussion in Jeffrey Weeks, *Sexuality and its Discontents: Meanings, Myths and Modern Sexualities* (Routledge and Kegan Paul, London, 1985).
32 For more detailed discussions and constructions of a feminist theory of heterosexuality, and for empirical research, see Deborah Cameron and Elizabeth Frazer, *The Lust to Kill: A Feminist Investigation of Sexual Murder* (Polity, Cambridge, 1987); Feminist Review, *Sexuality: A Reader* (Virago, London, 1987); Jalna Hanmer and Sheila Saunders, *Well Founded Fear: A Community Study of Violence to Women* (Hutchinson, London, 1984); Kelly, *Surviving Sexual Violence*; Sue Lees, *Losing Out: Sexuality and Adolescent Girls* (Hutchinson, London, 1986); MacRobbie, 'Teenage girls'; Stanko, *Intimate Intrusions*; Woods, 'Groping towards sexism'.
33 Empirical studies of sexual practices include Lees, *Losing Out*; Woods, 'Groping towards sexism'. Relevant cultural studies include Tania Modleski, *Loving with a Vengeance: Mass Produced Fantasies for Women* (Methuen, New York, 1984); Kate Millett, *Sexual Politics* (Virago, London, 1977).
34 See especially MacRobbie, 'Teenage girls', and the other work from the Centre for Contemporary Cultural Studies at Birmingham University for the empirical and theoretical emphasis on actors' willing participation in practices.
35 Lloyd, *The Man of Reason* for the argument that femininity is the 'other' by which masculinity is defined. See also Moller Okin, *Justice, Gender and the Family*, ch. 3 for a criticism of MacIntyre's neglect of the gender implications of the traditions he discusses.
36 *After Virtue*, p. 220; *Three Rival Versions*, p. 128.
37 For this second sense of 'immanent critique' see Roberto Mangabeira Unger, *The Critical Legal Studies Movement* (Harvard University Press, Cambridge, Mass., 1986).
38 'High art' and 'popular culture' alike, D. H. Lawrence, Norman Mailer, women's romantic fiction, film, pornography, philosophy are read in this way in Andrea Dworkin, *Pornography: Men Possessing Women* (Women's Press, London, 1981); Barbara Ehrenreich, *The Hearts of Men: American Dreams and the Flight from Commitment* (Pluto, London, 1983); Millett, *Sexual Politics*; Modleski, *Loving with a Vengeance*. These critics uncover (they don't have to dig very deep) the explicit misogyny in a significant part of contemporary and past Western culture, and connect these discourses to social reality. The feminist reading of political theory and philosophy employs the same methodology.
39 Elizabeth Frazer, 'Teenage girls talking about class', *Sociology*, 22.3 (1988); 'Feminist talk and talking about feminism: teenage girls' discourses of gender', *Oxford Review of Education*, 15.3 (1989); Lees, *Losing Out*; MacRobbie, 'Teenage girls'.

15

A Partial Response to my Critics

Alasdair MacIntyre

It has been a rewarding experience for me to read and to think about the essays in this book. Because their authors have raised many more issues than I am able to respond to – I have after all one essay in which to respond to thirteen – I must regretfully concentrate on some at the expense of others. To no objection will I be able to reply at anything like sufficient length, and some I have had to put altogether on one side for later, separate consideration. At best what I am offering here is a promissory note, redeemable, I hope, at some time in the next fifteen years. I shall begin by providing what I hope is a clearer, if still too brief account of two notions central to the theses about the virtues that I have defended: that of a practice and that of a rational tradition. On the first I shall be concerned with questions raised by David Miller, by Elizabeth Frazer and Nicola Lacey, and by Charles Taylor, on the second initially with issues raised in the essays by Stephen Mulhall, Andrew Mason, Paul Kelly and Robert Stern, and then with matters concerning truth and relativism which derive from my conception of a tradition. Here it will be John Haldane and Gordon Graham to whom I am responding.

I shall then consider first Robert Wokler's charge that I have misunderstood the Enlightenment and next Janet Coleman's accusation that I have misunderstood both Aristotle and Aquinas. Finally I will turn to the discussions of Aristotelian and non-Aristotelian politics by Peter Johnson and Philip Pettit. I do not expect my critics always to be convinced by my replies. Often of course they will be unpersuaded simply because of the inadequacy of those replies. But it is also worth noting that, if the central theses in favour of which I have been arguing for nearly twenty years are true, then we should expect them to be rejected by the most articulate and able representatives of the dominant culture of modernity. If my views are true, they are going to appear highly questionable to many, something that makes it more and not less necessary to treat even my most outraged critics with great seriousness.

I

At the core of David Miller's criticism of my account of the relationship of practices to virtues are three closely related theses: that there is a crucial distinction between practices which serve some socially valuable purpose external to the practice itself and those which do not; that in cases where there is such an external purpose, a practice may be evaluated by how well it serves that purpose; and that standards of justice external to practices are required, if we are to be able to criticize adequately the activities of those engaged in a particular practice at a particular time and place (pp. 250–5). Miller notices in a note that on my view what he calls 'a complete account of justice' will have to refer to the place of justice 'in a person's life and within a community' (see pp. 255 and 263, note 15). He fails to notice that, on my view, no quality is to be accounted a virtue except in respect of its being such as to enable the achievement of three distinct kinds of good: those internal to practices, those which are the goods of an individual life and those which are the goods of community. It is not that an account of justice in terms only of practices is incomplete; it is that such an account is not yet an account of justice or indeed of any other virtue.

Secondly Miller altogether ignores a second crucial distinction, that between a practice and the way in which it is institutionalized. The importance of these two points for understanding not only how, on my view, the different kinds of good are related to each other, but also how virtues are related to goods may have been obscured by my lack of attention to productive practices, those productive crafts such as farming and fishing, architecture and construction, of just the kind upon which Miller focuses attention. The aim internal to such productive crafts, when they are in good order, is never only to catch fish, or to produce beef or milk, or to build houses. It is to do so in a manner consonant with the excellences of the craft, so that not only is there a good product, but the craftsperson is perfected through and in her or his activity. This is what apprentices in a craft have to learn. It is from this that the sense of a craft's dignity derives. And it is in terms of this that the virtues receive their initial, if partial, definition. Consider in this light the difference between two kinds of fishing crew. My descriptions of these will be of ideal types, defining the extremes of a spectrum on which there are many points. But that there are in fact fishing crews whose lives embody one extreme or the other is beyond doubt.

A fishing crew may be organized and understood as a purely technical and economic means to a productive end, whose aim is only or overridingly to satisfy as profitably as possible some market's demand for fish. Just as those managing its organization aim at a high level of profits, so also the individual crew members aim at a high level of reward. Not only the skills, but also the qualities of character valued by those who manage the organization, will be those well designed to achieve a high level of profitability. And each individual at work as a member of such a fishing crew will value those qualities of character in her or himself or in others which are apt to produce a high level of reward for her or himself. When however the level of reward is insufficiently high, then the individual whose motivations and values are of this kind will have from her or his own point of view the best of reasons for leaving this particular crew or even taking to another trade. And when the level of profitability is insufficiently high, relative to comparative return on investment elsewhere, management will from its point of view have no good reason not to fire crew members, and owners will have no good reason not to invest their money elsewhere.

Consider by contrast a crew whose members may well have initially joined for the sake of their wage or other share of the catch, but who have acquired from the rest of the crew an understanding of and devotion to excellence in fishing and to excellence in playing one's part as a member of such a crew. Excellence of the requisite kind is a matter of skills and qualities of character required both for the fishing and for achievement of the goods of the common life of such a crew. The dependence of each member on the qualities of character and skills of others will be accompanied by a recognition that from time to time one's own life will be in danger and that whether one drowns or not may depend upon someone else's courage. And the consequent concern of each member of the crew for the others, if it is to have the stamp of genuine concern, will characteristically have to extend to those for whom those others care: the members of their immediate families. So the interdependence of the members of a fishing crew in respect of skills, the achievement of goods and the acquisition of virtues will extend to an interdependence of the families of crew members and perhaps beyond them to the whole society of a fishing village. When someone dies at sea, fellow crew members, their families and the rest of the fishing community will share a common affliction and common responsibilities.

For the members of such a crew and the inhabitants of such a village, the goods to be achieved in attaining excellence in the activities of fishing and in one's role within the crew will, for as long as possible, outweigh the economic hardships of low wages and periods of bad catches or low prices for fish. Of course no fishing crew can ever completely ignore the economic dimensions of their enterprise. But we have enough experience of members of crews preferring to endure the hardships of economic bad times in their trade, when they could have earned far higher wages elsewhere, for us to know that the subordination of economic goods to goods of practice can be a rewarding reality. For members of such crews, continuing allegiance to one's fellow crew members and to the way of life of a fishing community will therefore not be conditional upon the economic rewards being such as to enable one to satisfy one's individual antecedent desires, those that one brought with one when first initiated into the life of a fishing crew.

The activities and relationships of such a crew provide a prime example of what I have meant to identify in speaking of practices. It will now be clear, I hope, why therefore Miller's classification of what he calls practices is from my standpoint misconceived and why I have to reject his claim that practices are to be valued for their external products. When they are so valued, we are always dealing with a type of activity at once alien and antagonistic to practices and very much at home in modern economic orders. And much modern industrial productive and service work is organized so as to exclude the features distinctive of a practice. Of course by using the word 'practice' in this way, a word variously employed by recent philosophers, I must take responsibility for risking just this kind of misunderstanding, one that in Miller's case extends beyond his theses about why practices are to be valued to his criticism of what I say about justice. For the standard of justice relevant to practices is one formulable and intelligible only in the light *both* of the goods internal to practices, such as those of such a fishing crew – and the contrast by means of which I characterized the relevant kind of crew has of course equal application to the activities of string quartets, of those engaged in building houses or cathedrals, and of chess players – *and* also of the goods of an individual life and of those of a community. How those goods are together related to the virtues and more particularly to justice is a question arising not only from Miller's criticisms, but also from those advanced by Charles Taylor.

Taylor makes his own distinction between goods internal to practices and goods which 'transcend all our practices' (p. 35). Among the latter Taylor includes 'the modern idea of disengaged reason' (p. 36), an idea which, although it can on occasion mislead, is part of 'a vision of the good, that of disengaged, free, rational agency, one of the most important, formative transcendent goods of our civilization' (p. 36). If I understand Taylor aright, he takes this to be a genuine good, misleading only those who exalt it so as to deny other genuine goods with which it is, on occasion, in conflict (see his *Sources of the Self*, Cambridge, Massachusetts, 1989, especially chapters 8 and 25). The ideal of disengaged reason, on Taylor's view, involves a conception of freedom as rational autonomy which is closely linked to a modern conception of human dignity, and we ought not abandon the moral vision which inspires it.

So there emerges the first of a number of major differences between Taylor and myself.

For Taylor asserts that we need to recognize both the goods acknowledged within a practice-based and generally Aristotelian view of the world and goods such as those involved in the ideal of disengaged reason. He correctly ascribes to me the belief that recognition of the former set of goods excludes recognition of the latter. Secondly Taylor argues in parallel fashion about the virtue of justice (pp. 37–42). A recognition of justice as a practice-based virtue, to which the notion of desert is central, not only does not exclude, but should be accompanied by a recognition of justice as conceived by John Rawls. So the acceptance of a multiplicity of not always compatible goods is accompanied by the endorsement of a multiplicity of understandings of justice.

Thirdly Taylor asserts that this acceptance and endorsement is consistent with an Aristotelian standpoint: 'the Aristotelian theory can make sense of a conflict of goods from independent sources, like one between a transcendent good and one internal to some practice' (p. 39). At one stage I might have agreed with this, but I am now convinced that this is a mistaken reading of Aristotle. Taylor moreover believes not only that one can accord recognition both to the ideal of disengaged reason and to the practice-based goods of Aristotelianism, but also that the modern world has been unable wholly to escape from a practice-based and Aristotelian understanding of itself. And he rightly takes it to be part of my critique of modernity to hold that the distinctive culture of modernity is successfully non-Aristotelian in its stances. So here there is a fourth apparent disagreement. But is it really one?

Practices, as I understand them, are a universal feature of human cultures, although in some they may be radically marginalized and their significance deeply obscured. What this may prevent and does prevent in the cultures distinctive of modernity is the development of an Aristotelian understanding of the significance of practices in terms of the whole life of an individual and the lives of communities. Because only in an Aristotelian perspective can that significance be rightly understood, the potentiality that all plain persons have for developing out of their experience of practices an Aristotelian understanding of themselves can be frustrated. And the dominant cultures of modernity are apt so to frustrate it, except among those who live on their margins. They are therefore cultures inhabited by many more or less frustrated and usually unrecognized Aristotelians. But Aristotelian revivals are locally recurrent. So do Taylor and I in fact disagree over this? Perhaps we do not.

There is no doubt that we do disagree first about those types of good which, on Taylor's formulation, transcend practices, goods such as that of the autonomy associated with the modern ideal of disengaged reason,

and secondly, and correspondingly, about how the need for both practice-based and practice-transcending conceptions of justice is to be conceived. (I put on one side for the moment the issue of how Aristotle is
to be understood on these matters.) Why are we at odds on these two
issues?

It is not of course because I assert that all goods are goods internal to
such particular practices as those of fishing crews and string quartets.
For this of course I deny. Not only are there goods externally and
contingently related to practices such as those of money, status and
power, but, more importantly, my account of the virtues characterizes
them not only as qualities enabling their possessors to achieve the goods
internal to practices, but also as qualities enabling their possessors to
achieve both the goods of a whole human life and the goods of those
types of communities in and through which the goods of individual lives
are characteristically achieved. Where Taylor and I differ is that I understand these latter types of goods as integrative of and partly structured
in terms of the goods internal to particular practices, and never to be
understood as wholly independent of them – indeed the work of inte-
grating those goods into individual and communal lives itself has the
structure of a practice – while the goods which Taylor identifies as
transcending 'all our practices' (p. 35) are taken by him to be not only
wholly independent of practices, but sometimes in conflict with the
goods internal to practices.

Individuals characteristically find themselves participating in a number
of types of activity, each with its own set of goods. When therefore they
seriously ask themselves the question 'What is *my* good?' one of their
concerns in answering it must be to become able to put in order the
various goods which they acknowledge, finding for each its due place in
relation both to other such goods and to their own overall good. And
this they can only succeed in doing in company with those others who
participate with them and with each other in various practices, and who
also participate with them in the common life of their whole community. So the ordering of goods within the activities of individual lives, so
that the good of each such life may be achieved, is found to be inseparable
from the ordering of those goods in achieving the common good. And
the shared making and sustaining of the types of community within
which the common good can be achieved – families, farming house-
holds, fishing crews, local forms of political community – are activities
which themselves have the structure of practices, within which the same
virtues are needed for the achievement of the goods internal to those
practices as are needed elsewhere. All goods are thus partially defined by
their relationship to practices and to the common good.

How then can one respond to Taylor's claim that there are goods and

virtues which are independent of practices? It can only be by considering each good and virtue alleged to be thus independent and showing
that, in so far as it is a good or a virtue, it is not wholly independent of
practices and, in so far as it is wholly independent of practices, it is not
a good or a virtue. Consider in this light, as just one example, the ideal
of disengaged reason. Reflective enquiries, either within some practice
upon its own activities or themselves organized as some type of philosophical, scientific or literary practice, always have to be able to disengage
from any commitment or perspective which either is, or is with reason
suspected to be, a contingent source of distortion or illusion. And
rationality, whether theoretical or practical, requires this capacity for
disengagement, lacking which the relevant practice would, by its own
standards internal to it, always be in danger of being injured or deformed,
for unscrutinized considerations independent of and possibly at odds
with the practices' goods and the virtues required would have become
influential in the activities and relationships of its participants. Nothing
can claim exemption from reflective critique, but well-founded reflective
critique can never be disengaged from those contexts of practice from
within which it acquires its point and purpose.

Yet from the fact that an indefinite range of occasions may arise on
which a capacity for such disengagement needs to be exercised, it does
not follow that there is some standpoint which is that of reason disengaged as such, independent of all practice-based standpoints. Belief in
reason disengaged as such is a philosophical illusion, one that has both
Cartesian and empiricist versions. Just because it is an illusion, to tie
important beliefs about human dignity to it would be to cast needless
doubt on those beliefs.

The distortions and illusions within practices of which we need to be
cured are of course both real and recurrent. Practices are often distorted
by their modes of institutionalization, when irrelevant considerations
relating to money, power and status are allowed to invade the practice.
The relationships of those within the practice to each other or to those
in the wider community may be informed not by that justice which
assigns to each what is her or his due, in virtue of her or his contribution
and place in the practice and in the community, but by externally based
judgements deriving from unrecognized prejudice. One class of persons
often excluded, often demeaned, and often exploited by such deformed
judgements has been women.

Elizabeth Frazer and Nicola Lacey, although intentionally using the
word 'practice' of a much wider range of phenomena than I do, are
therefore completely in the right in underlining the feminist emphasis
on the evils this have historically been bound up with practices. Whether
Frazer and Lacey and I would agree about the nature and extent of those

evils in the history of particular practice-embodying institutions, such as
the family, is another matter. But that even the best of such institutions
is always corruptible and often corrupted is certain and it would be
difficult to exaggerate the harm resulting from such corruption. Frazer
and Lacey could indeed have remarked on the amount of harm done
thereby not only to women, but also to practices. They justly remark
that, compared to Foucault and others, I have said very little by way of
critique of these evils. And they argue that, were I to conduct such a
critique, I should *either* have to invoke some substantive conception and
standard of justice quite independent of and external to practices *or* else
fall back upon merely procedural considerations (pp. 274–5). But this
dilemma does not arise if a conception of justice and of other virtues,
which is adequate both to the relationships internal to practices and to
those between participants in particular practices and the wider local
community, can be invoked against deformation and prejudice. The
conception of justice as a virtue which is required if the goods internal
to practices are to be achieved, let alone the goods of individual lives and
of communities, is itself sufficient to provide a standard for identifying
and condemning the deformations and distortions to which practices
may be subjected, and the consequent injustices to women and others.
To attempt needlessly to supplement this conception and this standard
by adding to them, as Taylor proposes to do, Rawlsian principles of
justice inconsistent with them would merely introduce incoherence into
our judgements and thereby make it more difficult to achieve justice.

II

In the course of their resourceful defences of liberalism both Andrew
Mason and Stephen Mulhall pose important questions about my conception of a tradition. Mason understands that one, even if only one, of
my reasons for appealing to the notion of a tradition is that I take it to
be the case that disputes within a single tradition are characteristically
disputes in which one and the same set of standards of truth and rational
justification are appealed to, and correspondingly that the discovery of
fundamental incommensurability in some debate is equally characteristically the mark of a confrontation between the representatives of different and rival traditions. But he also notes that I take disputes in
modern liberal societies between those who advance claims grounded on
appeals to rational rights and those who dispute those claims in the
name of utility not to be settlable by appeal to any common standard,
while at the same time I treat the liberalism within which both sets of
claims are advanced as a single tradition (pp. 227–8). Mason's accusation
here is not merely that, unless I revise my views in some respect, I shall

be guilty of inconsistency. It is also that in so far as my reasons for appealing to the notion of tradition are first that disagreements within traditions are very different from disagreements between traditions, and secondly that this difference is a matter of the incommensurability involved in the latter, my treatment of liberalism raises serious doubt about the soundness of those reasons.

Mulhall, observing correctly that my account of liberalism in *After Virtue* as hostile to any grounding in tradition was followed by an account in *Whose Justice? Which Rationality?* of how liberalism had developed into a tradition, ascribes to me in consequence an abandonment of my earlier claim 'that liberalism lacks the conceptual resources to make sense of human agency and the rationality of political argument, and is accordingly incapable of generating a coherent moral and political system; instead, he is acknowledging that liberalism is a fully fledged tradition, and so possessed of just the resources he originally suspected it of lacking' (p. 221), although he adds that I believe that liberalism may be in some difficulties over acknowledging its status as a tradition (p. 221). To respond to Mulhall's misunderstanding of my views about liberalism, I need first, as in the case of Mason, to say more about agreements and disagreements within traditions.

Let me begin by distinguishing the significance which inconsistency in belief, attitude and action possesses within what I have called a tradition of enquiry from the significance which it possesses within larger social and cultural traditions. The identification, and in the longer run the elimination of inconsistency is bound to be a major preoccupation in any tradition of enquiry. Often enough it is the uncovering of inconsistency in the established beliefs of some group that originally generates enquiry. What inconsistency always presents to those engaged in enquiry is a *problem*, that of how to reconcile whatever truth two inconsistent sets of beliefs may each possess in such a way as to arrive at a consistent view.

It is however because enquiry tends to put established beliefs in question, by treating inconsistencies as problematic, that enquiry is sometimes viewed with suspicion by the authoritative representatives of established belief in social and cultural traditions. For the survival of this or that particular tradition may on occasion depend upon sustaining some system of inconsistent beliefs and attitudes, and the protection of those values to which the participants in that tradition have given their allegiance may depend upon those inconsistencies not being made explicit. But this is of course not the only way in which incoherence may be socially and politically protected. Where some particular social tradition involves incompatible commitment those incompatible commitments may be expressed in the form of a set of continuing and unresolvable conflicts and debates, so that the basic agreements which constitute that order are expressed as agreements about which disagreements are crucial and why. Consider in this light the political and moral culture of those advanced societies whose dominant mode is liberalism.

Liberalism is a set of agreements to disagree. The interminable disagreements between utilitarians and natural rights theorists, between both and contractarians, between all three and Kantians, give expression to a set of conflicting principles presupposed in the institutionalized life of individualist societies, according to which each individual is understood both as someone engaged in the pursuit of her or his own interests, whatever they are, and as someone correspondingly requiring protection from others similarly engaged. Each of the major moral theories current in liberal society proposes a principled resolution of the conflicting claims which result from this double understanding. But the rationally unresolvable character of those conflicts reappears in ineliminable disagreements at the level of theory. What such theorists agree in rejecting is any standpoint according to which the basic understanding of the individual, presupposed by all the conflicting theories, is itself misconceived. Hence derives the shared rejection of all accounts of human beings as by their natures participants in forms of community aimed at a single, if a complex good, most notably of Platonic or Aristotelian or Thomistic accounts.

Liberalism, then, as a form of social life, is partly constituted by its continuing internal debates between rival incommensurable points of view. In this it resembles many other social and cultural traditions. Each one of those points of view has itself been elaborated within a tradition of enquiry constituted by agreements upon shared standards. So that characteristically, at least up to a certain point, within each tradition there has been by its own standards progress in problem-solving, while in the conflicts between traditions there has been no rational progress at all. Incommensurability has precluded it. And in understanding this we can understand why both Mason's and Mulhall's criticisms are misdirected.

Mason failed to take account of the different characteristics ascribed on the one hand to traditions of enquiry, within which, so long as they are in good order, there are shared standards, and on the other hand to those larger social and cultural traditions within which traditions of enquiry are embedded and to which they stand in varying relationships. Mulhall supposed that in taking note of the fact that liberalism, originally the critic of all appeals to tradition, has itself become a tradition and that some liberal theorists have become aware of this, I was now ascribing to liberalism the kind of coherence and developed mode of understanding characteristic of a flourishing tradition of enquiry, whereas what I was recognizing was that liberalism has become the kind of social and cultural tradition in which incoherence may be and, in the case of liberalism, is at home. In *Whose Justice? Which Rationality?* I was adding to and not withdrawing from the critique of liberalism advanced in *After Virtue*.

Of that earlier critique Mulhall wrote that I wished 'simultaneously to argue that liberal individualism is dominant, that our culture is thoroughly emotivist, and that the conceptual resources of liberal individualism are incapable of accounting for the possibility of human agency and rational moral argument. Such a combination of claims is inherently unstable, for it amounts to arguing that the pervasive and dominant morality is logically incapable of functioning as a morality at all' (p. 220). This is almost, but not quite right. It is not that the pervasive and dominant morality cannot function as a morality , but that it cannot function as a *coherent* morality. And that incoherence is perhaps exhibited most clearly in the moral dimension of the politics of the nation-states of the West. But the particular and various traditions of enquiry which partially constitute liberalism do not of course necessarily suffer from the same kind of incoherence.

Utilitarianism is characteristic of the traditions of enquiry which have developed within and contributed to the transformation of the liberal culture of modernity. P. J. Kelly recognizes that the question about it is not whether particular versions of utilitarianism fail but whether the whole enterprise fails (pp. 131–2). The contemporary utilitarians whom he cites in his notes 3, 17 and 19 (the majority of whom published their work after *After Virtue* was published) are indeed the heirs of a tradition initiated by Bentham and Mill and continued by Sidgwick, in which each generation inherits from its predecessors not only theses and arguments, but also problems. One recurrent problem for utilitarians, already evident in Mill, is that of how to understand the principle of utility in a way that allows for the variety of ends which are in fact pursued, and the variety of considerations which in fact motivate, without rendering it vacuous, a problem identified by Richard Wollheim, when he describes how in Mill's writings 'Not merely do secondary principles appear alongside the primary principle, but now they are not subordinate to it' ('John Stuart Mill and Isaiah Berlin: the ends of life and the preliminaries of morality,' in *The Idea of Freedom*, ed. A. Ryan, Oxford, 1979, p. 262) and by me in 'Utilitarianism and the presuppositions of cost–benefit analysis' (in *Values in the Electric Power Industry*, ed. K. Sayre, Notre Dame, 1977).

It is just this problem which Kelly confronts in his remarks about the resources which utilitarianism has for responding to problems of commensurability. About what he says two very different questions arise. One is only for utilitarians themselves: are they able to agree on a resolution of this problem in a way which provides them with an effective standard both for judging progress or lack of it within their own tradition and for solving the problems which they now confront? Failure to agree might after all be a sign of the kind of failure in respect of commensurability within a tradition of enquiry which is characteristically a sign of its impending dissolution. But commentary by an external critic on this would be premature.

A second question concerns the relationship of utilitarianism to its rivals, especially to Humean, Kantian and contractarian theorists, and the continuing inability of each of these contending parties to defeat its rivals. Why should this matter? Each of those rival views was originally formulated as claiming the allegiance of all rational persons whatsoever by appeal to what were taken to be the standards of their shared rationality. Each has in the course of its history learned from its rivals, including something of their principles in its own. But in fundamentals they remain at odds and the resources invoked by Kelly hold out no promise of altering this situation. So that nothing has occurred or seems likely to occur to overthrow the verdict on their debates proposed in *After Virtue*, that no party to these debates has provided compelling reasons for accepting its conclusions as those of any adequately rational and informed person. And this itself provides initial grounds for the further verdict proposed in *Whose Justice? Which Rationality?* that what we are presented with are not merely rival views of what morality requires, but rival conceptions of rationality.

Each party in these debates then succeeds by the standards internal to its own tradition of moral enquiry, but fails by the standards internal to the traditions of its opponents. Incommensurability does after all seem to be present. But how then, it may be asked, could it have been otherwise? And if the argument takes us to this point, will we not have to go further, so that we will be unable to avoid commitment to some version of relativism? From the standpoint of each particular tradition, of course, relativism fails, just as do the contentions of its rivals. None the less, anyone who has accepted the thesis that all enquiry is carried on from the standpoint of some particular tradition must, as John Haldane says, understand 'the situation of competing traditions' as one 'which invites a relativist description' (p. 97). One does not have to be outside any tradition, as I wrongly supposed in *Whose Justice? Which Rationality?* – and I am grateful to John Haldane for making my mistake clear to me – but only to be able to place oneself in imagination in the situation of those inhabiting rival traditions, in order to understand how this is so.

Moreover the case for relativism must appear to be strengthened by considerations on which I have to rely in order to reply to Gordon Graham's central thesis and to John Haldane's remarks about the difficulties which he takes to arise from my disagreements with Davidson. Graham argues that my use of the concept of a tradition and of that history of development recounted within each tradition as a constitutive element of it requires an independent philosophical grasp of that concept and of the criteria for its use and application. Without such a grasp we would be unable to individuate traditions adequately or to identify their continuities and discontinuities: 'normative stories of the past require us to have an independent conceptual grasp of the relevant, identifying norms' (p. 174). And Graham adds that, if I were to acknowledge this, I would be more at one with Hegel than I am. About this last he is certainly right. But I am irremediably anti-Hegelian in rejecting the notion of an absolute standpoint, independent of the particularity of all traditions. I therefore have to assert that the concept of a tradition, together with the criteria for its use and application, is itself one developed from within one particular tradition-based standpoint. This does not preclude its application to the very tradition within which it was developed. Nor does it preclude its being used to frame universal claims about all traditions. More generally there is nothing paradoxical at all in asserting that from within particular traditions assertions of universal import may be and are made, assertions formulated within the limits set by the conceptual, linguistic and argumentative possibilities of that tradition, but assertions which involve the explicit rejection of any incompatible claim, advanced in any terms whatsoever from any rival standpoint. So within every major cultural and social tradition we find some distinctive view of human nature and some distinctive conception of the human good presented as – *true*. And although these claims to truth are supported within different traditions by appeal to rival and often de facto incommensurable standards of rational justification, no such tradition is or can be relativistic either about the truth of its own assertions or about truth. (This is of course compatible with differences in the way in which truth is thought about. For a brief account of how one and the same concern with truth can be discerned in traditions in which truth is theorized about in different ways, see *Whose Justice? Which Rationality?*, pp. 356–9.) But how then can this anti-relativistic commitment to truth coexist with an awareness of those facts about different and rival standards of rational justification internal to different traditions which seem, as Haldane puts it, to invite a relativist description?

I am strongly inclined to think that any contemporary philosophy which does not find this question inescapable and central must be gravely defective. How should we attempt to answer it? We need first to note that it is one significant mark of its being *truth* to which a given tradition is committed that its adherents find it difficult, when seriously confronted with claims to intellectual or moral allegiance advanced from within some rival tradition, to avoid raising the question of what the grounds are on which they themselves allege the falsity of those rival claims. Even if they condemn the rival view by appeal to their own tradition's standards, as they must initially, they have to find some means, out of the resources afforded by the concepts, idioms and arguments of their own tradition, of providing an adequate representation of the contentions of their rivals, if they are to be able to achieve the required invidious comparison. (For a more extended, even if still too brief discussion of some of the problems involved see my 'Incommensurability, truth and the conversation between Confucians and Aristotelians about the virtues', in *Culture and Modernity*, ed. E. Deutsch, Honolulu, 1991, pp. 104–22.) It is here that problems of translatability and untranslatability arise. Haldane on Davidsonian grounds takes the notion of untranslatability to be puzzling. If having become thoroughly at home in more than one language, I discover that some things that can be said in one language cannot be said in and are not translatable into some other language, then 'how does one know what one is saying, or indeed that one is saying anything coherent at all?' (p. 95).

The answer is: very easily. For in each natural language the standards of coherence and meaningfulness are internal to that language (which is not to say that they are specific to that language). But what one may learn on occasion is that, in trying to say what these particular sentences of language L_1 have been used by oneself and other speakers of L_1 to say, in *any* set of sentences at present available in language L_2, the result has been and has to be a failure to say anything coherent in L_2. And this is the same discovery that is made when, attempting to articulate claims made within one tradition of enquiry in the only language presently available to the adherents of some rival tradition, one discovers that that language lacks concepts, idioms or modes of argument necessary for the statement of those claims. Perhaps indeed and additionally the beliefs presupposed in the everyday linguistic uses of those who inhabit that rival tradition are just too much at odds with one's own to make any plausible statement of one's own position possible in their language, something that one could only have learned by becoming at home in the language of that rival tradition. But now consider what kind of problem this poses for the adherents of that rival tradition, if and in so far as theirs is a tradition of enquiry.

They can only vindicate the rational superiority of their theses and arguments, if and in so far as they can provide within their own language in use an adequate representation of the claims which they reject. But in order to achieve this, their language in use will have to be enriched, perhaps in a variety of ways, as, for example, Latin had to be enriched by Cicero and others, so that those who gave their allegiance to inherited Roman beliefs could be provided in Latin with an adequate representation of Greek philosophical theories, some of which constituted a challenge to those beliefs. Certain things sayable in Greek thus became for the first time sayable in Latin.

To have achieved this of course is not necessarily as yet to have achieved commensurability of standards. But it may have made possible a dialectical interchange between the two rival standpoints, out of which there may emerge a discovery of common standards, standards hitherto presupposed, but never before made articulate. And, if this does not happen, the question becomes inescapable for each contending party of how their fundamental and continuing disagreement is to be accounted for. Only a theoretical standpoint which is able to provide an explanation of why, if it is true, just this kind of disagreement with it by the adherents of rival points of view is to be expected will be in a position to vindicate its claim to truth. The adherents of a theoretical standpoint without the resources to achieve such an explanation can never therefore avoid the question of whether there may not be some standpoint more comprehensive than their own in principles and conceptually richer, still to be discovered, in the light of which the inability of both contending parties to resolve their disagreements will become explicable.

Notice that what generates this type of progress, in which the frustration of all attempts to resolve disputed key issues in the debates between rival traditions of enquiry always remains a possibility, but through which such frustrations are from time to time overcome or circumvented, is the shared presupposition of the contending enquires in respect of *truth*. It is this shared presupposition that makes relativism a position tenable only by spectators of such enquiry, viewing it, whether in imagination or in actuality, from some external vantage point, but not at all by participants. It is the continuing possibility of such frustration that makes relativism a permanent temptation for such spectators.

Sufficient has now been said to identify my central disagreement with Robert Stern. Given the generous and constructive defence of my work by Stern, any disagreement must seem ungrateful. But in one respect his understanding of my work and my understanding of it are at odds, and it may be more difficult to mount his kind of defence of it than he supposes. Stern compares my position to that of Larry Laudan in the philosophy of science (pp. 151–3) and also draws parallels between my view of progress in enquiry and how progress occurs in artistic development (pp. 154–7). But what Laudan and I are most in disagreement over is the place of truth in enquiry, and progress in artistic development is often understood – perhaps misunderstood – without reference to truth. I had hoped that what I had said about truth in enquiry in chapter 18 of *Whose Justice? Which Rationality?* would have made it adequately clear that I regard any attempt to eliminate the notion of truth from that of enquiry as bound to fail. It is in part for this reason that I regard the Nietzschean tradition as always in danger of lapsing into fatal incoherence.

III

The accounts which I have given in various places of the moral philosophies of Socrates, Plato, Aristotle and Aquinas have all stressed the extent to which the latter three responded to questions arising from the assertions and arguments of his predecessors and in so doing transcended what those predecessors by their own standards would have had to recognize as their own limitations. Thereby a tradition of enquiry was constituted, one revived in the later Middle Ages and the Renaissance, and again in the nineteenth century. In the course of my writing those accounts two major changes occurred. In *After Virtue* I did not as yet recognize how Aquinas had enriched and reconstituted the tradition and given it its definitive form. And I also had to learn how, if Aquinas's key philosophical positions were to be rationally vindicated, they had to provide the resources not only for refuting the major rival alternatives in his own Aristotelian terms, but also for explaining how, if his central conclusions were true, the failures of those alternatives could be identified and explained more compellingly than they could be in the terms of those alternative positions themselves. More particularly the history of the fragmentation and the interminable disagreements of Enlightenment and post-Enlightenment moral philosophy would have to be so explained. Thomist Aristotelianism would have to meet the standards by which alone one tradition of enquiry can vindicate the conclusions which have emerged within it, not only against the rival claims made within that same tradition, but also against the claims advanced from within rival traditions of enquiry. This is the point which I had reached in chapter 6 of *Three Rival Versions of Moral Enquiry* (see especially p. 140), where I briefly described the work yet to be done, if Thomist Aristotelianism is to be vindicated in this way.

The task therefore now confronts me of writing the kind of history of moral and political philosophy in which these goals can be achieved. I have made so far in unpublished writing a significant beginning in carrying through the preliminary work required for this task, but I do recognize that until I am able to publish a suitably large-scale history of this kind, I will not have provided a sufficient answer to my critics, either to those who have contributed to this book or to those who have written elsewhere. What such critics have done for me is to identify not

only my earlier mistakes and inadequacies, but also those obstacles that
I now have to overcome, if this task is to be successfully completed. I
am indebted to Robert Wokler and to Janet Coleman for what they have
contributed on both counts.

What I have to learn from Wokler is that if I am to propose an
explanation of Enlightenment moral philosophy, I must first give an
account of that moral philosophy which embeds it in the overall culture
of the Enlightenment, in a way which does justice to the complexity of
both philosophy and culture. About the need to say much more than I
have hitherto said he is completely in the right. But he unfortunately
misconstrues my limited intentions in a number of ways. I have been
chiefly concerned up till now only with three aspects of the Enlightenment: first with the failure of its major moral philosophers to secure
agreement among themselves or more generally on either the status of
moral principles or their content, something that each of them clearly
attempted to secure; secondly with some later consequences of that failure;
and thirdly in the Scottish Enlightenment with the fact and the implications of the fact that Hume emerged as victor from its debates. When
therefore, concerning the first of these, Wokler suggests that the whole
notion of an Enlightenment project to secure moral agreement is
'wonderfully confused' (p. 115), I can only ask why he might think that
the project of securing rational agreement was not a major concern of
Enlightenment thinkers. On this he is silent. And, like some others, he
misunderstands my view of Hume, supposing mistakenly that my dis-
like of his moral views involves blindness to the power of his philosophy.
What is important about Hume is that his arguments and insights were
such as to defeat his philosophical opponents. Hume's account of justice, for example, is on the view that I was taking of it in *Whose Justice?
Which Rationality? the* view which needs to be answered. One of the
problems for any later philosopher is that of how it is possible not to
be a Humean. The beginning of an answer is to be found, I have suggested, in situating Hume within the Scottish tradition from which he
emerged, so as to be in a better position to identify and evaluate his
underlying assumptions.

A more impressive set of obstacles to my project are presented by
Coleman, who argues that I have fatally misunderstood both Aristotle
and Aquinas. Coleman says that the standards by which practices are to
be judged from an Aristotelian or Thomist standpoint 'have no history,
they are universals absolutely, they are the natures or essences grasped
by the definition of their goal. Hence MacIntyre, in asserting that standards are not immune from criticism, misunderstands how Aristotle and
Aquinas define practices in terms of what they aim to achieve, their
ends. A definition is not culture bound nor is it temporal' (p. 81). And

she concludes that I am not a Thomist, when I assert that 'we cannot be initiated into a practice without accepting the authority of the best standards realized so far' (*After Virtue*, p. 190). 'This places definition in the hands of cultures with conventional codes of self-expression,' whereas, for Aristotle and Aquinas definitions 'grasp the nature of something thought of which is, as a thought, not conventional but species specific, universal and timeless' (pp. 81–2).

What Coleman fails to distinguish are three distinct sets of questions. The first set concerns apprenticeship to any tradition-constituted practice, including practices of enquiry: by what standards are apprentices to be guided and from whom are they to learn what those standards are and why? The second set of questions concerns the nature of rational justification and of that attainment of truth which constitutes the telos of rational enquiry: what is it to have achieved finality of understanding concerning this or that subject-matter and in what terms must this understanding be given expression? The third set of questions is about how answers given to the second set of questions are to be rationally defended against rival answers proposed from within the standpoint of some fundamentally different tradition.

Most of what I have written concerns the answers to be given to members of the first and third sets. Coleman supplies answers, with most of which I am wholly in agreement, to members of the second set. And, at least in so far as I agree with her answers to the second set, what she asserts and what I have asserted are, contrary to what she takes to be the case, wholly consistent. Both Aristotle and Aquinas recognize a distinction between those timeless truths about natural kinds, essential properties and the teleological ordering of things and persons in terms of which all true and justified explanation and understanding has to be framed and the varyingly adequate attempts to formulate those truths which marked the history of enquiry, first from Thales to Aristotle and then onwards, through Aristotle's Islamic and Jewish interpreters, to Aquinas.

It is this contingent history of successive and successively more adequate formulations which needs to be understood as the history of a practice of enquiry conducted within a tradition. And it, like all those other contingent histories of other rival projects of enquiry which at various points went astray and failed to reach their goal of understanding, itself needs to be understood in terms of natural kinds, essential properties and teleological ordering. It is indeed precisely because and in so far as Thomist Aristotelianism enables us to achieve an adequate understanding both of our own history and of that of others in this way that it vindicates its claim to have identified the standards by appeal to which all practices and traditions are to be evaluated. Both Aristotle and

Aquinas themselves recognize this in what they say about the history of enquiry. It is, so they teach us, from the dialectial interrogation of our disputing predecessors, from the identification of what truth it was that each of them had discerned and into what errors each had been led by the limitations of their different standpoints, that enquiry begins to move towards the telos of understanding, characterized much as it is characterized by Coleman. She acknowledges the telos, but she ignores the history which leads towards it. It is perhaps because she ignores this that she sees more disagreement between us than is actually there.

I have had to put on one side a number of minor, but not unimportant disagreements about Aristotle, not only with Coleman, but also with others. I must not, however, omit to notice that the truths of Thomistic Aristotelianism, as I have defended them, have to be detached from, and happily are detachable from, not only Aristotle's false assertions about women, but also his false assertions about the capacities of those engaged in productive labour. It is my own experience, and not only mine, that some members of certain types of fishing crews and some small farmers are much better at recognizing the Aristotelian features of their lives and practices, even although they may not frame that understanding in Aristotelian terms, than are, for exmple, characteristic members of the contemporary legal, financial and academic professions. Aristotelian theory articulates the presuppositions of a range of practices a good deal wider than Aristotle himself was able to recognize.

IV

One disagreement about the interpretation of Aristotle does however need to be taken up. I admire much of Peter Johnson's reconstruction of the Aristotelian ruler in contemporary terms. But Johnson takes Aristotle to be in agreement with those modern theorists who suppose that political responsibility requires a readiness to do what is otherwise believed to be morally wrong. So he can speak of 'Aristotle's acknowledgement that there may be circumstances in which it is right to do what is wrong' (p. 50), citing Michael Stocker's discussion in *Plural and Conflicting Values* (Oxford, 1990, pp. 51–85). But Aristotle in his discussion at the beginning of Book III of the *Nicomachean Ethics* does not say what Stocker and Johnson take him to say. What he does assert is that under certain circumstances those who perform disgraceful acts are not to be blamed and those who *undergo* what is disgraceful and painful in return for the achievement of what is great and fine are praised. The latter are sufferers, not doers, and the former are not said to act rightly, but to act excusably. Aristotle nowhere asserts that it can ever be right to perform actions of types which are blamed as bad in themselves, but only that in blaming the action we need not be blaming the agent. (For the importance of this see my 'Moral dilemmas', *Philosophy and Phenomenological Research*, so supplement, Fall, 1990, pp. 367–82.)

Those who rule in modern states of all kinds are of course on occasion required by their role and function to do what is wrong. This means that any credible modern version of an Aristotelian ruler would have to exercise her or his role and function, whatever that might be, other than as an official of such a state. The differences between political community conceived in Aristotelian terms and any modern nation-state is just too great. But it is this difference to which quite insufficient attention has been paid in recent debates between liberals and communitarians. And it is once again ignored by Philip Pettit in his presentation of republicanism as a third alternative to communitarianism and liberalism.

Contemporary communitarians, from whom I have strongly dissociated myself whenever I have had an opportunity to do so, advance their proposals as a contribution to the politics of the nation-state. Where liberals have characteristically insisted that government within a nation-state should remain neutral between rival conceptions of the human good, contemporary communitarians have urged that such government should give expression to some shared vision of the human good, a vision defining some type of community. Where liberals have characteristically urged that it is in the activities of subordinate voluntary associations, such as those constituted by religious groups, that shared visions of the good should be articulated, communitarians have insisted that the nation itself through the institutions of the nation-state ought to be constituted to some significant degree as a community. In the United States this has become a debate within the Democratic Party, a debate in which from my own point of view communitarians have attacked liberals on one issue on which liberals have been consistently in the right.

It was indeed, as Pettit points out, a distinctively Romantic vision of nations which conceived of them as actual or potential communities, whose unity could be expressed through the institutions of the state. But that Romantic vision – even although it ofen involved an idealization of ancient Greek life – had little in common with genuinely Aristotelian conceptions of the polis, which for a variety of reasons has to be a relatively small-scale and local form of political association. And when practice-based forms of Aristotelian community are generated in the modern world, they are always, and could not but be, small-scale and local. (There is of course a contemporary version of Romantic politics which glorifies the small-scale and local as such. But from an Aristotelian standpoint small communities as such have no particular merit.) The confusion of the Romantic vision with the Aristotelian conception did indeed lead some German thinkers to frame just that view of the nation-state as all-embracing community which liberals have rightly resisted, understandng how it generates totalitarian and other evils.

Liberals however mistakenly suppose that those evils arise from any form of political community which embodies substantive practical agreement upon some strong conception of the human good. I by contrast take them to arise from the specific character of the modern nation-state, thus agreeing with liberals in this at least, that modern nation-states which masquerade as embodiments of community are always to be resisted. The modern nation-state, in whatever guise, is a dangerous and unmanageable institution, presenting itself on the one hand as a bureaucratic supplier of goods and services, which is always about to, but never actually does, give its clients value for money, and on the other as a repository of sacred values, which from time to time invites one to lay down one's life on its behalf. As I have remarked elsewhere ('Poetry as political philosophy: notes on Burke and Yeats', in *On Modern Poetry: Essays Presented to Donald Davie*, ed. V. Bell and L. Lerner, Nashville, 1988, p. 149), it is like being asked to die for the telephone company.

Sometimes of course there are evils only to be resisted by *ad hoc* participation in some particular enterprises of some nation-state: in resisting Hitler and Stalin, most notably. And it is prudent to pay one's taxes and always just to accept obligations which one has incurred to the state and to its agencies. But to empower even the liberal state as a bearer of values always imperils those values, something that liberals could have learned from John Anderson. In any case the liberal critique of those nation-states which pretend to embody the values of community has little to say to those Aristotelians, such as myself, for whom the nation-state is not and cannot be the locus of community.

Like those German thinkers of whom I spoke, Pettit has assimilated the Aristotelian rejection of the Enlightenment to the Romantic rejection (p. 182 and pp. 184–6). This not only leads him to misunderstand my views. It also perhaps prevents him from raising certain types of issue about his own republicianism. Pettit argues that 'if the most basic political good we identify is itself social and interactive in nature, then we cannot think' of individuals in republican forms of political association as reasoning only *qua* individuals. They will deliberate together *qua* republican citizens (p. 200). But is such a form of shared deliberation open to those whose politics is the politics of the nation-state? If the answer is 'No', as I think that it should be, then the question for Pettit is: in what kinds of institution can the republicanism which he advocates be embodied?

V

This reply to my critics is one contribution to what I hope will be a series of continuing conversations. To all those who have helped me to understand my own point of view better and to correct or supplement it where it badly needed to be corrected or supplemented I am most grateful. In the case of those who are most antagonistic – some of whom are also among those who have helped me most – I can only hope that, by defining their own positions over against mine, they have clarified their own theses and arguments in ways useful to them. Whether I have learned as much as I should from all my critics is a matter not so much of this essay, as of their impact upon my future writing.

Selected Bibliography of the Publications of Alasdair MacIntyre

Reprintings of articles and extracts from the books, and some book reviews, are not included.

'Analogy in metaphysics', *Downside Review*, vol. 69, 1950–1, pp. 45–61.

Marxism: An Interpretation, SCM Press, London, 1953, 126 pp. Revised as *Marxism and Christianity*, Schocken Books, New York; Duckworth, London, 1968, ix + 143 pp. Notre Dame University Press, Notre Dame, 1984.

Edited with Antony G. N. Flew, *New Essays in Philosophical Theology*, SCM Press, London, 1955, x + 274 pp.; Macmillan, New York, 1964. 'Preface', pp. vii–x; 'Visions', pp. 254–60.

'Cause and cure in psychotherapy', *Aristotelian Society*, suppl. vol. 29, 1955, pp. 43–58.

'A note on immortality', *Mind*, vol. 64, 1955, pp. 396–9.

'Manchester: the modern universities and the English tradition', *Twentieth Century*, vol. 159, Feb. 1956, p. 948.

'Marxist tracts', *Philosophical Quarterly*, vol. 6, 1956, pp. 366–70.

'A society without a metaphysics', *The Listener*, 13 Sept. 1956, pp. 375–6.

'The logical status of religious beliefs', in Stephen Toulmin, Ronald W. Hepburn and Alasdair MacIntyre, *Metaphysical Beliefs: Three Essays*, SCM Press, London, 1957, pp. 157–201. Second edition, SCM Press, London; Schocken Books, New York, 1970; with new Preface, pp. vii–xii.

'Determinism', *Mind*, vol. 66, 1957, pp. 28–41.

'What morality is not', *Philosophy*, vol. 32, 1957, pp. 325–35. Reprinted in *Against the Self-Images of the Age* (below, 1971), pp. 96–108.

The Unconscious: A Conceptual Analysis, Routledge and Kegan Paul, London; Humanities Press, New York, 1958, ix + 100 pp. Translated into German by Gudrun Sauter, Suhrkamp, Frankfurt am Main, 1968. Translated into French by Gabrielle Nagler, Presses Universitaires de France, Paris, 1984.

'Notes from the moral wilderness I', *New Reasoner*, vol. 7, Winter 1958–9, pp. 90–100.

Difficulties in Christian Belief, SCM Press, London; Philosophical Library, New York, 1959, 126 pp.

'Notes from the moral wilderness II', *New Reasoner*, vol. 8, Spring 1959, pp. 89–98.

'Hume on "Is" and "Ought"', *Philosophical Review*, vol. 68, 1959, pp. 451–68. Reprinted in *Against the Self-Images of the Age* (below, 1971), pp. 109–24.

'Straw men of the age [review of Hugh Thomas (ed.), *The Establishment*]', *New Statesman*, vol. 58, 3 Oct. 1959, p. 433.

'Breaking the chains of reason', in *Out of Apathy*, introduced by E. P. Thompson, Stevens and Sons, London, 1960, pp. 195–240.

'Positivism in perspective [on A. J. Ayer's *Language, Truth and Logic*]', *New Statesman*, vol. 59, 2 Apr. 1960, pp. 490–1.

'Purpose and intelligent action', *Aristotelian Society*, suppl. vol. 34, 1960, pp. 79–96.

'Comment upon "commitment and objectivity"', in *Moral Issues in the Training of Teachers and Social Workers*, ed. Paul Halmos, Sociological Review Monograph 3, 1960, pp. 89–92.

'Marxists and Christians', *The Twentieth Century*, vol. 170, Autumn 1961, pp. 28–37.

'A mistake about causality in social science', in *Philosophy, Politics and Society (Second Series)*, ed. Peter Laslett and W. G. Runciman, Blackwell, Oxford, 1962, pp. 48–70.

'God and the theologians [review of John Robinson, *Honest to God*]', *Encounter*, Sept. 1963, pp. 3–10. Reprinted in *Against the Self-Images of the Age* (below, 1971), pp. 12–26.

'Trotsky in exile [review of Isaac Deutscher, *The Prophet Outcast*]', *Encounter*, Dec. 1963, pp. 73–8. Reprinted in *Against the Self-Images of the Age* (below, 1971), pp. 52–9.

'Freudian and Christian dogmas as equally unverifiable', in *Faith and the Philosophers*, ed. John Hick, Macmillan, London, 1964, pp. 110–11.

'Is understanding religion compatible with believing?', in *Faith and the Philosophers*, ed. John Hick, Macmillan, London, 1964, pp. 115–33.

'Against utilitarianism', in *Aims in Education: The Philosophic Approach*, ed. T. H. B. Hollins, Manchester University Press, Manchester, 1964, pp. 1–23.

'Existentialism', in *A Critical History of Western Philosophy*, ed. D. J. O'Connor, Free Press, New York; Collier-Macmillan, London, 1964, pp. 509–29.

'Marx', in *Western Political Philosophers*, ed. M. Cranston, Bodley Head, London, 1964, pp. 99–108.

'Freud as moralist [review of Heinrich Meng and Ernst L. Freud (eds), *The Letters of Sigmund Freud and Oskar Pfister*]', *New York Review of Books*, 20 Feb. 1964, p. 7.

'The socialism of R. H. Tawney [review of R. H. Tawney, *The Radical Tradition*]', *New York Review of Books*, 30 July 1964, pp. 21–7. Reprinted in *Against the Self-Images of the Age* (below, 1971), pp. 38–42.

'After Hegel [review of Karl Löwith, *From Hegel to Nietzsche: The Revolution in Nineteenth Century Thought*]', *New York Review of Books*, 24 Sept. 1964, pp. 15–16.

'Pascal and Marx: on Lucian Goldman's "Hidden God" ', *Encounter*, Oct. 1964, pp. 69–76. Reprinted in *Against the Self-Images of the Age* (below, 1971), pp. 76–87.

Edited, *Hume's Ethical Writings: Selections from David Hume edited, with an Introduction*, Collier Books, New York; Collier-Macmillan, London, 1965, 339 pp. 'Editor's introduction', pp. 9–17. University of Notre Dame Press, Notre Dame, 1979.

'Pleasure as a reason for action', *The Monist*, vol. 49, 1965, pp. 215–33. Reprinted in *Against the Self-Images of the Age* (below, 1971), pp. 173–90.

'The psychoanalysts: the future of an illusion', *Encounter*, May 1965, pp. 38–43. Reprinted in *Against the Self-Images of the Age* (below, 1971), pp. 27–37.

'Imperatives, reasons for action, and morals', *Journal of Philosophy*, vol. 62, 1965, pp. 513–24. Reprinted in *Against the Self-Images of the Age* (below, 1971), pp. 125–35.

'Irrational man [review of C. G. Jung (ed.), *Man and His Symbols* and Morris Philipson, *Outline of a Jungian Aesthetics*]', *New York Review of Books*, 25 Feb. 1965, pp. 5–6.

'Marxist mask and romantic face: Lukács on Thomas Mann [review of Georg Lukács, *Essays on Thomas Mann*]', *Encounter*, Apr. 1965, pp. 64–72. Reprinted in *Against the Self-Images of the Age* (below, 1971), pp. 60–9.

A Short History of Ethics, Macmillan, New York, 1966, viii + 280 pp. Routledge and Kegan Paul, London, 1967, viii + 280 pp. Translated into Dutch by J. A. Aldington, Boom Meppel, Amsterdam, 1974. Translated into German by Hans-Jürgen Miller, Athenaum, Konigstein, 1984.

'Recent political thought', in *Political Ideas*, ed. David Thomson, Watts, London, 1966, pp. 189–200.

'The antecedents of action', in *British Analytic Philosophy*, ed. Bernard Williams and Alan Montefiore, Routledge and Kegan Paul, London; Humanities Press, New York, 1966, pp. 205–25. Reprinted in *Against the Self-Images of the Age* (below, 1971), pp. 191–210.

'Modern times [review of Geoffrey Barraclough, *An Introduction to Contemporary History* and Herbert Rosinski, *Power and Human Destiny*]', *New York Review of Books*, 17 Mar. 1966, pp. 24–6.

Secularisation and Moral Change: The Riddell Memorial Lectures ... 1964, Oxford University Press (for University of Newcastle upon Tyne Publications), London, 1967, 76 pp.

'The idea of a social science', *Aristotelian Society*, suppl. vol. 41, 1967, pp. 95–114. Reprinted (omitting second paragraph) in *Against the Self-Images of the Age* (below, 1971), pp. 211–29.

'Sociology and the novel', *Times Literary Supplement*, 27 July 1967, pp. 657–8.

Entries in *Encyclopaedia of Philosophy*, ed. Paul Edwards, Macmillan, New York, 1967: 'Being', vol. 1, pp. 273–7; 'Brunner, Emil', vol. 1, pp. 403–5; 'Egoism and altruism', vol. 2, pp. 462–6; 'Essence and existence', vol. 3, pp. 59–61; 'Existentialism', vol. 3, pp. 147–54; 'Freud, Sigmund', vol. 3, pp. 249–53; 'Jung, Carl Gustav', vol. 4, pp. 294–6; 'Kierkegaard, Soren Aabye', vol. 4, pp. 336–40; 'Myth', vol. 5, pp. 434–7; 'Ontology', vol. 5, pp. 542–3; 'Pantheism', vol. 6, pp. 31–5; and 'Spinoza, Benedict (Baruch)', vol. 7, pp. 530–41.

'The well-dressed theologian [review of Ved Mehta, *The New Theologian*]', *Encounter*, vol. 28, Mar. 1967, pp. 76–8.

'Emasculating history: on Mazlish's "riddle" [review of Bruce Mazlish, *The Riddle of History*]', *Encounter*, vol. 29, Aug. 1967, pp. 78–80.

'[Book review] *Twenty Letters to a Friend* by Svetlana Alliluyeva', *Yale Law Journal*, vol. 77, 1967–8, pp. 1032–6. Reprinted in *Against the Self-Images of the Age* (below, 1971), pp. 48–51.

'Secularisation', *The Listener*, 15 Feb. 1968, pp. 193–5.

'Noam Chomsky's view of language', *The Listener*, 30 May 1968, pp. 685–6.

'Death and the English', *The Listener*, 6 June 1968, pp. 719–20.

'The strange death of social democratic England', *The Listener*, 4 July 1968, pp. 7–8.

'Who gets killed – Alasdair MacIntyre discusses the death of Senator Kennedy', *The Listener*, 18 July 1968, pp. 80–1.

'How to write about Lenin – and how not to [review of Leonard Schapiro and Peter Reddaway (eds), *Lenin: The Man, the Theorist, the Leader*]', *Encounter*, May 1968, pp. 71–4. Reprinted in *Against the Self-Images of the Age* (below, 1971), pp. 43–7.

'Son of ideology [review of George Lichtheim, *The Concept of Ideology and Other Essays*]', *New York Review of Books*, 9 May 1968, pp. 26–8.

'Doubts about Koestler [review of Arthur Koestler, *Drinkers of Infinity: Essays 1955–67*]', *The Listener*, 12 Sept. 1968, p. 342.

'In place of Harold Wilson? [review of Paul Foot, *The Politics of Harold Wilson* and Tyrrell Burgess (ed.), *Matters of Principle: Labour's Last Chance*]', *The Listener*, 10 Oct. 1968, p. 476.

'Technocratic Smokescreen [review of Jean Meynaud, *Technocracy*]', *The Listener*, 28 Nov. 1968, pp. 723–4.

'The debate about God: Victorian relevance and contemporary irrelevance', in Alasdair MacIntyre and Paul Ricoeur, *The Religious Significance of Atheism* [Bampton Lectures in America delivered at Columbia University, 1966], Columbia University Press, New York and London, 1969, pp. 1–55.

'On Marcuse', *New York Review of Books*, 23 Oct. 1969, pp. 37–8. Reprinted in *Marcuse* (below, 1970), as ch. 8.

'Made in the USA [review of David Sills (ed.), *International Encyclopaedia of the Social Sciences*]', *New York Review of Books*, 27 Feb. 1969, pp. 14–16.

'Philosophy and sanity: Nietzsche's titanism [review of F. Nietzsche, *The Will to Power*, trans. W. Kaufmann and R. J. Holingdale]', *Encounter*, vol. 32, Apr. 1969, pp. 79–82.

'Marxism of the will [review of John Gerassi (ed.), *Venceremos! The Speeches and Writings of Che Guevara*; Che Guevara, *Reminiscences of the Cuban Revolutionary War*; Daniel James (ed.), *The Complete Bolivian Diaries of Che Guevara*; Ricardo Rojo, *My Friend Che*; Regis Debray, *Revolution in the Revolution*; and Jean-Paul Sartre, *The Communists and the Peace*]', *Partisan Review*, vol. 36, 1969, pp. 128–33. Reprinted in *Against the Self-Images of the Age* (below, 1971), pp. 70–5.

Marcuse, Collins, London; Viking Press, New York, 1970, 95 pp. Also issued with type reset and index added, *Herbert Marcuse: An Exposition and a Polemic*, Viking, New York, 1970, 114 pp. Translated into Chinese by Zhang Xiaoming and Zhao Yidan, Chinese State Publishing House, Beijing, 1990.

Edited with Dorothy Emmet, *Sociological Theory and Philosophical Analysis: A Collection Edited with an Introduction*, Macmillan, London and New York, 1970, xxiv + 232 pp. 'Introduction', pp. ix–xxiv.

'Gods and sociologists', *Encounter*, vol. 34, Mar. 1970, pp. 68–74.

Against the Self-Images of the Age: Essays on Ideology and Philosophy, Duckworth, London; Schocken Books, New York, 1971, x + 284 pp. University of Notre Dame Press, Notre Dame, 1978. Reprints 15 papers (see above), with 8 new ones.

'Conversations with philosophers – Alasdair MacIntyre talks to Bryan Magee about political philosophy and its emergence from the doldrums', *The Listener*, 25 Feb. 1971, pp. 235–8.

'A perspective on philosophy', *Social Research*, vol. 38, 1971, pp. 655–68.

'Mr Wilson's pragmatism [review of Harold Wilson, *The Labour Government 1966–70: A Personal Record*]', *The Listener*, 29 July 1971, pp. 150–1.

'Tell me where you stand on Kronstadt [review of Paul Avrich, *Kronstadt 1921*]', *New York Review of Books*, 12 Aug. 1971, pp. 24–5.

'Praxis and action [critical study of Richard Bernstein, *Praxis and Action*]', *Review of Metaphysics*, vol. 25, 1971–2, pp. 737–44.

Edited, *Hegel: A Collection of Critical Essays*, Doubleday, Garden City, New York, 1972, ix + 350 pp. 'Introduction', pp. vii–viii; 'Hegel on faces and skulls', pp. 219–36. University of Notre Dame Press, Notre Dame, 1976.

'Predictability and explanation in the social sciences', *Philosophic Exchange*, vol. 1, no. 3, 1972, pp. 5–13.

'Justice: a new theory and some old questions [review of John Rawls, *A Theory of Justice*]', *Boston University Law Review*, vol. 52, 1972, pp. 330–4.

'Rational science [review of Karl Popper, *Objective Knowledge: An Evolutionary Approach*]', *The Listener*, 14 Dec. 1972, pp. 835–6.

'Ideology, social science, and revolution', *Comparative Politics*, vol. 5, 1972–3, pp. 321–42.

'Mr Wilson's pragmatism, in *A Second Listener Anthology*, ed. K. Miller, BBC, London, 1973.

'The essential contestability of some social concepts', *Ethics*, vol. 84, 1973–4, pp. 1–9.

'Ancient politics and modern issues [review essay on David Daube, *Civil Disobedience in Antiquity* and Ramsay MacMullen, *Enemies of the Roman Order*]', *Arion*, NS, vol. 1, 1973–4, pp. 425–30.

'Sunningdale: a "colonial" solution', *Irish Press,* 5 June 1974.

'Irish conflicts and British illusions', *New Statesman*, vol. 88, 19 July 1974, pp. 75–6.

'Durkheim's call to order [review of Steven Lukes, *Émile Durkheim: His Life and Work*]', *New York Review of Books*, 7 Mar. 1974, pp. 25–6.

'How virtues become vices: medicine and society', *Encounter*, vol. 45, July 1975, pp. 11–17; also in *Evaluation and Explanation in the Biomedical Sciences*, ed. H. T. Engelhardt and S. F. Spicker, Reidel, Dordrecht, 1975, pp. 97–111.

'Has science any future?', in *Science and Society: Past, Present, and Future*, ed. Nicholas Hans Stenech, University of Michigan Press, Ann Arbor, 1975, pp. 356–62.

With Samuel Gorovitz, 'Toward a theory of medical fallibility', *Hastings Center Report*, vol. 5, 1975, pp. 13–23.

'Interpretation of the Bible [review of Hans W. Frei, *The Eclipse of Biblical Narrative*]', *Yale Review*, vol. 65, 1975–6, pp. 251–5.

'On democratic theory: *Essays in Retrieval* by C. B. MacPherson', *Canadian Journal of Philosophy*, vol. 6, 1976, pp. 177–81.

'Causality and history', in *Essays on Explanation and Understanding: Studies in the Foundations of Humanities and Social Sciences*, ed. J. Manninen and R. Tuomela, Reidel, Dordrecht and Boston, 1976, pp. 137–58.

'Power and virtue in the American republic', in *The Case For and Against Power for the Federal Government*, Ripon College Press, Ripon, 1976, pp. 16–20.

'Who judges whom? [review of Isaiah Berlin, *Vico and Herder: Two Studies in the History of Ideas*]', *The Listener*, 26 Feb. 1976, p. 251.

'Patients as agents', in *Philosophical Medical Ethics: Its Nature and Significance*, ed. Stuart F. Spicker and H. Tristram Engelhardt, Reidel, Dordrecht and Boston, 1977, pp. 197–212.

'Epistemological crises, dramatic narrative, and the philosophy of science', *The Monist*, vol. 60, 1977, pp. 453–72.

'Can medicine dispense with a theological perspective on human nature?' and 'A rejoinder to a rejoinder', in *Knowledge, Value and Belief*, ed. H. Tristram Engelhardt, Jr, and Daniel Callahan, Hastings Center, Hastings-on-Hudson, 1977, pp. 25–43 and 75–8.

'Utilitarianism and the presuppositions of cost–benefit analysis', in *Values in the Electric Power Industry*, ed. Kenneth Sayre, University of Notre Dame Press, Notre Dame and London, 1977, pp. 217–37.

'How to identify ethical principles', in *The Belmont Report: Ethical Principles and Guidelines for the Protection of Human Subjects of Research* I, DHEW pub. no. (OS) 78–0013, Washington, 1978.

'Behaviorism: philosophical analysis', in *Encyclopaedia of Bioethics*, ed. Warren T. Reich et al., Macmillan, New York, 1978, pp. 110–15.

'Kissinger–Brinkley horror comic', *New York Times*, 3 Feb. 1978.

'The right to die garrulously', in *Death and Decision*, ed. Ernan McMullin, American Association for the Advancement of Science Selected Symposium 18, Westview Press, Boulder, 1978, pp. 75–84.

'What has ethics to learn from medical ethics?', *Philosophic Exchange*, vol. 2, no. 4, Summer 1978, pp. 37–47.

'Objectivity in morality and objectivity in science', in *Morals, Science and Sociality*, ed. H. T. Engelhardt and D. Callahan, Hastings Center, Hastings-on-Hudson, 1978, pp. 21–39.

'[Book reviews] *Lying* by Sisela Bok; *Right and Wrong* by Charles Fried; and *Ethics at the Edges of Life* by Paul Ramsay', *New Republic*, 6 May 1978, pp. 28–30.

'[Book review] *The Legitimation of Belief* by E. Gellner', *British Journal for the Philosophy of Science*, vol. 29, 1978, pp. 105–10.

'[Book review] *A History of Philosophy in America* by E. Flower and M. G. Murphy', *New England Quarterly*, vol. 51, 1978, pp. 439–32.

'Ethical issues in attending physician–resident relations: a philosopher's view', *Bulletin of the New York Academy of Medicine*, vol. 55, no. 1, Jan. 1979, pp. 57–61.

'Seven traits for the future', *Hastings Center Report*, vol. 9, Feb. 1979, pp. 5–7.

'Why is the search for the foundations of ethics so frustrating?', *Hastings Center Report*, vol. 9, Aug. 1979, pp. 16–22.

'Corporate modernity and moral judgment: are they mutually exclusive?', in *Ethics and Problems of the 21st Century*, ed. Kenneth M. Sayre and Kenneth E. Goodpaster, Notre Dame University Press, Notre Dame and London, 1979, pp. 122–35.

'Power industry morality', in *Symposium*, Edison Electric Institute, Washington, 1979, pp. 94–108.

'Social science methodology as the ideology of bureaucratic authority', in *Through the Looking Glass: Epistemology and the Conduct of Enquiry: An Anthology*, ed. Maria J. Falco, University Press of America, Washington, 1979, pp. 42–58.

'Theology, ethics, and the ethics of medicine and health care: comments on papers by Novak, Mouw, Roach, Cahill, and Hartt', *Journal of Medicine and Philosophy*, vol. 4, 1979, pp. 435–43.

'[Book review] *The Social and Political Thought of Leon Trotsky* by B. Knei-Paz', *American Historical Review*, vol. 84, 1979, pp. 113–14.

'[Book review] *Rationality and the Social Sciences*, ed. S. I. Benn and G. W. Mortimer', *American Journal of Sociology*, vol. 85, 1979, pp. 217–19.

'[Book review] *Concepts and Categories* by Isaiah Berlin', *New Republic*, 9 June 1979, pp. 34–5.

'The poverty of political theory [review of John Dunn, *Western Political Theory in the Face of the Future*]', *London Review of Books*, 20 Dec. 1979, pp. 4, 6.

'Regulation: a substitute for morality', *Hastings Center Report*, vol. 10, Feb. 1980, pp. 31–3.

'A crisis in moral philosophy', in *Knowing and Valuing the Search for Common Roots*, ed. H. Tristram Engelhardt, Hastings Center, Hastings-on-Hudson, 1980, pp. 18–35.

'Contexts of interpretation: reflections on Hans George Gadamer's *Truth and Method*', *Boston University Journal*, vol. 26, 1980, pp. 173–6.

'The American idea', in *America and Ireland, 1776–1976: The American Identity and the Irish Connection*, ed. David Noel Doyle and Owen Dudley Edwards, Greenwood Press, Westport, 1980, pp. 57–68.

'Rumpelstilskin's rules', *Wellesley Wragtime*, Dec. 1980, p. 6.

'Ayer, Anscombe and empiricism [review of G. E. MacDonald (ed.), *Perception and Identity: Essays Presented to A. J. Ayer with his Replies to Them* and Cora Diamond and Jenny Teichman (eds), *Intention and Intentionality: Essays in Honour of G. E. M. Anscombe*]', *London Review of Books*, 17 Apr. 1980, pp. 9–10.

'The claims of philosophy [review of Richard Rorty, *Philosophy and the Mirror of Nature*; Stanley Cavell, *The Claim of Reason: Wittgenstein, Skepticism, Morality and Tragedy*; and Ted Honderich and Myles Burnyeat (eds), *Philosophy As It Is*]', *London Review of Books*, 5 June 1980, pp. 15–16.

'John Stuart Mill's forgotten victory [review of J. M. Robson (ed.), *An Examination of Sir William Hamilton's Philosophy* by J. S. Mill]', *London Review of Books*, 16 Oct. 1980, pp. 13–14.

'The idea of America [review of Garry Wills, *Inventing America: Jefferson's Declaration of Independence*]', *London Review of Books*, 6 Nov. 1980, pp. 14–15.

'[Book review] *The Greek Concept of Justice* by Eric Havelock', *American Historical Review*, vol. 85, 1980, p. 605.

'[Book review] *Truth, Love and Immortality: An Introduction to McTaggart's Philosophy* by Peter T. Geach', *Ethics*, vol. 91, 1980–1, pp. 667–8.

After Virtue: A Study in Moral Theory, Duckworth, London; University of Notre Dame Press, Notre Dame, 1981, ix + 252 pp. Second (corrected) edition, with Postscript, University of Notre Dame Press, Notre Dame, 1984; Duckworth, London, 1985, xi + 286 pp. Translated into German by Wolfgang Riehl, Campus Verlag, Frankfurt, 1987. Translated into Spanish by Amelia Valcarcel, Editorial Critica, Barcelona, 1987.

Co-authored with 12 others, *Experimentation in the Law: Report of the Federal Judicial Center Advisory Committee on Experimentation to Chief Justice Warren Burger*, Federal Judicial Center, Washington, 1981, viii + 134 pp.

'The nature of the virtues: from Homer to Benjamin Franklin', *Hastings Center Report*, vol. 11, Apr. 1981, pp. 27–34.

'Dr. Küng's Fiasco [review of Hans Küng, *Does God Exist?*]', *London Review of Books*, 5 Feb. 1981, pp. 7–8.

'Strangers [review of Vincent Descombes, *Modern French Philosophy*]', *London Review of Books*, 16 Apr. 1981, pp. 15–16.

'Pluralistic philosophy [review of *Philosophical Explanations* by Robert Nozick]', *New York Times Book Review*, 20 Sept. 1981, pp. 7, 34.

'[Book review] *The Teaching of Ethics in the Social Sciences* by Donald P. Warwick', *Teaching Philosophy*, vol. 4, 1981, pp. 170–1.

'Philosophy, "other" disciplines and their histories: a rejoinder to Richard Rorty', *Soundings*, vol. 65, 1982, pp. 127–45.

'Risk, harm, and benefit assessment', in *Ethical Issues in Social Science Research*, ed. Tom L. Beauchamp, R. R. Faden, R. J. Wallace, Jr, and L. Walters, Johns Hopkins Press, Baltimore, 1982, pp. 175–92.

'Comments on Frankfurt's "The importance of what we care about"', *Synthèse*, vol. 53, 1982, pp. 291–4.

'How moral agents became ghosts: or why the history of ethics diverged from that of the philosophy of mind', *Synthèse*, vol. 53, 1982, pp. 295–312.

'Philosophy and its history', *Analyse und Kritik*, vol. 1, 1982, pp. 101–15.

'Contemporary moral culture', *Catholic Commission on Intellectual and Cultural Affairs Annual 1982*, Catholic Commission on Intellectual and Cultural Affairs, Notre Dame, 1982, pp. 26–34.

'Intelligibility, goods, and rules [Abstract]', *Journal of Philosophy*, vol. 79, 1982, pp. 663–5.

'Public virtue [review of Gary Wills, *Explaining America* and David Hoeveler, *James McCosh and the Scottish Intellectual Tradition*]', *London Review of Books*, 18 Feb. 1982, p. 14.

'Good for nothing [review essay on Elizabeth Dipple, *Iris Murdoch: Work for the Spirit*]', *London Review of Books*, 3 June 1982, pp. 15–16.

'Hannah Arendt as thinker [review of Elisabeth Young-Bruehl, *Hannah Arendt: For Love of the World*]', *Commonweal*, 10 Sept. 1982, pp. 471–2.

'After Bertrand Russell [review of A. J. Ayer, *Philosophy in the Twentieth Century*]', *New York Times Book Review*, 28 Nov. 1982, pp. 3, 26.

'[Book review] *Religion and Public Doctrine in England* by Maurice Cowling', *Political Theory*, vol. 10, 1982, pp. 129–32.

'[Book review] *Moral Philosophy at Seventeenth Century Harvard* by Norman Fiering', *William and Mary Quarterly*, vol. 39, 1982, pp. 687–9.

Edited with Stanley Hauerwas, *Revisions: Changing Perspectives in Moral Philosophy*, University of Notre Dame Press, Notre Dame and London, 1983, x + 286 pp. 'Preface', p. vii; 'Moral philosophy: what next?', pp. 1–15.

'The indispensability of political theory', in *The Nature of Political Theory*, ed. David Miller and Larry Siedentop, Clarendon Press, Oxford, 1983, pp. 17–33.

'To whom is the nurse responsible?', in *Ethical Problems in the Nurse–Patient Relationship*, ed. Catherine P. Murphy and Howard Hunter, Allyn and Bacon, Boston, 1983, pp. 73–83.

'Moral rationality, tradition, and Aristotle: a reply to Onora O'Neill, Raimond Gaita, and Stephen R. L. Clark', *Inquiry*, vol. 26, 1983, pp. 447–66.

'Moral arguments and social contexts [Abstract]', *Journal of Philosophy*, vol. 80, 1983, pp. 590–1.

'[Book review] *Beyond Marxism* by Vrajendra Raj Mehta', *Political Theory*, vol. 11, 1983, pp. 623–6.

'[Book review] *Sartre* by Peter Caws', *Journal of Philosophy*, vol. 80, 1983, pp. 813–17.

'The magic in the pronoun "my" [review of Bernard Williams, *Moral Luck*]', *Ethics*, vol. 94, 1983–4, pp. 113–25.

Is Patriotism a Virtue? [The Lindley Lecture, 1984], Department of Philosophy, University of Kansas, Lawrence, 1984, 20 pp.

'The claims of *After Virtue*', *Analyse und Kritik*, vol. 6, 1984, pp. 3–7.

'Bernstein's distorting mirrors', *Soundings*, vol. 67, 1984, pp. 30–41.

'*After Virtue* and Marxism: a response to Wartofsky', *Inquiry*, vol. 27, 1984, pp. 251–4.

'Does applied ethics rest on a mistake?', *The Monist*, vol. 67, 1984, pp. 498–513.

'Philosophy and politics', in *Philosophy and Human Enterprise*, USMA Class of 1951 Lecture Series 1982–83, West Point, 1984, pp. 131–61.

'The relationship of philosophy to its past', in *Philosophy in History: Essays in the Historiography of Philosophy*, ed. Richard Rorty, J. B. Schneewind and Quentin Skinner, Cambridge University Press, Cambridge and New York, 1984, pp. 31–48.

'[Book review] *Ethica Thomistica* by Ralph McInerny', *Teaching Philosophy*, vol. 7, 1984, pp. 168–70.

'[Book review] *David Hume: Common-sense Moralist, Sceptical Metaphysician* by David Fate Norton', *Nous*, vol. 18, 1984, pp. 379–82.

'Medicine aimed at the care of persons rather than what?', in *Changing Values in Medicine*, ed. Eric J. Cassell and Mark Siegler, University Publications of America, Frederick, Md, 1985, pp. 83–96.

'Rights, practices and Marxism: reply to six critics', *Analyse und Kritik*, vol. 7, 1985, pp. 234–48.

'How psychology makes itself true – or false', in *A Century of Psychology As Science*, ed. Sigmund Koch and Daniel E. Leary, McGraw Hill, New York, 1985, pp. 897–903.

'[Book review] *Goods and Virtues* by Michael Slote', *Faith and Philosophy*, vol. 2, 1985, pp. 204–7.

'[Book review] *The Moral Psychology of the Virtues* by N. J. H. Dent', *Review of Politics*, vol. 47, 1985, pp. 436–8.

'[Book review] *The Legitimacy of the Modern Age* by Hans Blumenberg', *American Journal of Sociology*, vol. 90, 1985, pp. 924–6.

'[Book review] *Slavery and Human Progress* by D. B. Davis and *Bribes* by J. T. Noonan, Jr', *Ethics*, vol. 96, 1985–6, pp. 429–31.

'Positivism, sociology, and practical reasoning: notes on Durkheim's *Suicide*', in *Human Nature and Natural Knowledge*, ed. Alan Donagan, A. N. Perovich, Jr, and M. V. Wedin, Reidel, Dordrecht, 1986, pp. 87–104.

'The intelligibility of action', in *Rationality, Relativism and the Human Sciences*, ed. J. Margolis, M. Krausz and R. M. Burian, Martinus Nijhoff, Dordrecht, 1986, pp. 63–80.

'Which God ought we to obey and why?', *Faith and Philosophy*, vol. 3, 1986, pp. 359–71.

'The humanities and the conflicts of and with traditions', in *Interpreting the Humanities 1986*, Princeton, 1986, pp. 17–33.

'[Book review] *The Theory of the Will in Classical Antiquity* by A. Dihle', *Ancient Philosophy*, vol. 6, 1986, pp. 242–5.

How to Be a North American, Federation of State Humanities Councils, Washington, 1987, 20 pp.

'Practical rationalities as forms of social structure', *Irish Philosophical Journal*, vol. 4, 1987, pp. 3–19.

'The idea of an educated public', in *Education and Values*, ed. Graham Haydon, Institute of Education, London, 1987, pp. 15–36.

'Can one be unintelligible to oneself?', in *Philosophy in its Variety: Essays in Memory of François Bordet*, ed. Christopher McKnight and Marcel Stchedroff, Queen's University of Belfast, Belfast, 1987, pp. 23–37.

'Post-Skinner and Post-Freud: philosophical causes of scientific disagreements', in *Scientific Controversies: Case Studies in the Resolution and Closure of Disputes in Science and Technology*, ed. H. Tristram Engelhardt, Jr, and Arthur L. Caplan, Cambridge University Press, Cambridge, 1987, pp. 295–311.

'Philosophy: past conflict and future direction', *Proceedings and Addresses of the American Philosophical Association*, suppl. vol. 61, no. 1, Sept. 1987, pp. 81–7.

'Relativism, power, and philosophy', in *After Philosophy: End or Transformation?*, ed. Kenneth Baynes, James Bohman and Thomas McCarthy, MIT Press, Cambridge, Mass. and London, 1987, pp. 385–411.

'J. N. Findlay 1903–87', *Bulletin of the Hegel Society of Great Britain*, no. 16, Autumn/Winter 1987, pp. 4–7.

'[Book review] *Visions of Virtue in Tokugawa Japan* by Tetsuo Najita', *Ethics*, vol. 98, 1987–8, pp. 587–8.

Whose Justice? Which Rationality?, Duckworth, London; University of Notre Dame Press, Notre Dame, 1988, xi + 410 pp.

'Rival justices, competing rationalities', *This World*, no. 21, Spring 1988, pp. 78–87.

'Poetry as political philosophy: notes on Burke and Yeats', in *On Modern Poetry: Essays Presented to Donald Davie*, ed. Verene Bell and Laurence Lerner, Vanderbilt University Press, Nashville, 1988, pp. 145–58.

'Sōphrosunē: how a virtue can become socially disruptive', *Midwest Studies in Philosophy*, vol. 13, 1988, pp. 1–11.

'Imaginative universals and historical falsification: a rejoinder to Professor Verene', *New Vico Studies*, vol. 6, 1988, pp. 21–30.

With Eduardo Nolla Blance, 'Qué puede aprender la Nueva Europa de la vieja América?', *Veintiuno*, vol. 1, 1989, pp. 74–85.

'[Book review] *Human Character and Morality* by Stephen D. Hudson', *Nous*, vol. 23, 1989, pp. 389–90.

Three Rival Versions of Moral Enquiry: Encyclopaedia, Genealogy, Tradition, Duckworth, London; University of Notre Dame Press, Notre Dame, 1990, x + 241 pp.

First Principles, Final Ends and Contemporary Philosophical Issues: The Aquinas Lecture 1990, Marquette University Press, Milwaukee, 1990, 69 pp.

'The Gifford lectures: some modest proposals', *Scots Philosophical Newsletter*, vol. 3, 1990, pp. 4–6.

'The form of the good, tradition and enquiry', in *Value and Understanding: Essays for Peter Winch*, ed. Raimond Gaita, Routledge, London and New York, 1990, pp. 242–62.

'La Idea de un público educado', *Rivista de Educacion*, no. 292, May/August 1990, pp. 119–36.

'Individual and social morality in Japan and the United States: rival conceptions of the self', *Philosophy East and West*, vol. 40, 1990, 489–97.

'The privatization of Good. An inaugural lecture', *Review of Politics*, vol. 52, 1990, pp. 344–61. [And see next item.]

'Rejoinder to my critics, especially Solomon', *Review of Politics*, vol. 52, 1990, pp. 375–7.

'Moral dilemmas', *Philosophy and Phenomenological Research*, suppl. to vol. 50, 1990, pp. 367–82.

'Después de Tras la Virtud', *Atlántida*, vol. 1, no. 4, 1990, pp. 87–95.

'The return to virtue ethics', in *The Twenty-Fifth Anniversary of Vatican II*, ed. Russell E. Smith, The Pope John Centre, Braintree, 1990, pp. 239–49.

'[Book review] *The Abuse of Casuistry: A History of Moral Reasoning* by A. R. Jonsen and S. Toulmin', *Journal of the History of Philosophy*, vol. 28, 1990, pp. 634–5.

'[Book review] *Contingency, Irony and Solidarity* by Richard Rorty', *Journal of Philosophy*, vol. 87, 1990, pp. 708–11.

'[Book review] *The Idea of Political Theory: Reflections on the Self in Political Time and Place* by Tracy B. Strong', *Ethics*, vol. 101, 1990–1, pp. 878–9.

'Nietzsche O Aristotele?', in *Conversazioni americane*, ed. G. Borradori, Editori Laterza, Roma-Bari, 1991, pp. 169–87.

'Community, law, and the idiom and rhetoric of rights', *Listening*, vol. 26, 1991, pp. 96–110.

'I'm not a communitarian, but ...', *The Responsive Community*, vol. 1, no. 3, Summer 1991, pp. 91–2.

How to seem virtuous without actually being so, Occasional Paper Series no. 1 of the Centre for the Study of Cultural Values, Lancaster University, Lancaster, 1991, 20 pp.

'An interview with Alasdair MacIntyre', *Cogito*, vol. 5, no. 2, 1991, pp. 67–73.

'How is intellectual excellence in philosophy to be understood by a Catholic philosopher?', *Current Issues in Catholic Higher Education*, vol. 12, no. 1, Summer 1991, pp. 47–50.

'Incommensurability, truth, and the conversation between Confucians and Aristotelians about the virtues', in *Culture and Modernity: East–West philosophic perspectives*, ed. Eliot Deutsch, University of Hawaii Press, Honolulu, 1991, pp. 104–22.

'La idea de una comunida ilustrada', *Diálogo Filosófico*, no. 21, Sept./Dec. 1991, pp. 324–42.

'[Book review] *The Persistence of Faith* by Jonathan Sacks', *The Tablet*, 23 Feb. 1991, pp. 240–2.

'[Book review] *The Tradition of Scottish Philosophy* by Alexander Broadie', *Philosophical Quarterly*, vol. 41, 1991, pp. 258–60.

'[Book review] *Newman After a Hundred Years*, ed. I. Ker and A. G. Hill', *Philosophical Books*, vol. 32, 1991, pp. 154–6.

'[Book review] *An Introduction to the Metaphysics of Knowledge* by Yves Simon', *American Catholic Philosophical Quarterly*, vol. 65, 1991, pp. 112–14.

'[Book review] *Persons and Human Beings*, ed. Christopher Gill', *Arion*, 3rd series, vol. 1, no. 3, Fall 1991, pp. 188–94.

'[Book review] *The Fabric of Character: Aristotle's Theory of Virtue* by Nancy Sherman', *Mind*, vol. 100, 1991, pp. 415–16.

'Précis of *Whose Justice? Which Rationality?*', *Philosophy and Phenomenological Research*, vol. 51, 1991–2, pp. 149–52.

'[Reply to Dahl, Baier and Schneewind', *Philosophy and Phenomenological Research*, vol. 51, 1991–2, pp. 169–78.

'Reply to Roque', *Philosophy and Phenomenological Research*, vol. 51, 1991–2, pp. 619–20.

'Plain persons and moral philosophy: rules, virtues and goods', *American Catholic Philosophical Quarterly*, vol. 66, 1992, pp. 3–20.

'What has *not* happened in moral philosophy', *Yale Journal of Criticism*, vol. 5, 1992, pp. 193–9.

'Die Idee einer gebildeten Öffentlichkeit', *Zeitschrift für Pädagogik*, vol. 28, 1992, pp. 25–44.

'[Book review] *Mind in Action* by Amelie O. Rorty', *Nous*, vol. 26, 1992, pp. 101–2.

'[Book review] *The Ennobling of Democracy: The Challenge of the Postmodern Age* by Thomas L. Pangle', *Review of Politics*, vol. 54, 1992, pp. 311–13.

'[Book review] *The Moral Virtues and Theological Ethics* by Romanus Cessario', *The Thomist*, vol. 56, 1992, pp. 339–44.

'[Book review] *Cultural Otherness: Correspondence with Richard Rorty* by Anindita Niyogi Balslev', *Philosophy East and West*, vol. 42, 1992, pp. 682–4.

'Are philosophical problems insoluble?: the relevance of system and history', in *Philosophical Imagination and Cultural Memory: Appropriating Historical Traditions*, ed. Patricia Cook, Duke University Press, Durham, NC, 1993, pp. 65–82.

Index

Alasdair MacIntyre's books are referred to throughout so only the more major references to his works are included in the index.